THE URBAN WILDERNESS

CLASSICS IN URBAN HISTORY

Michael H. Ebner, Editor

The
Urban
Wilderness

A HISTORY OF THE AMERICAN CITY

Sam Bass Warner, Jr.

Foreword by Charles Tilly

UNIVERSITY OF CALIFORNIA PRESS
Berkeley · Los Angeles · London

University of California Press
Berkeley and Los Angeles, California

University of California Press, Ltd.
London, England

First California Paperback Printing 1995

Library of Congress Cataloging-in-Publication Data

Warner, Sam Bass, 1928–
    The urban wilderness : a history of the American city / Sam Bass
  Warner, Jr. ; foreword by Charles Tilly.
      p.   cm. — (Classics in urban history ; 5)
  Originally published: New York: Harper & Row, [1972]
  ISBN 0-520-20224-4
  1. Cities and towns—United States.   I. Tilly, Charles.
 II. Title.   III. Series.
 HT123.W235   1995
 307.76'0973—dc20   95-3437
                                        CIP

Printed in the United States of America
9 8 7 6 5 4 3 2 1

The paper used in this publication meets the minimum requirements
of American National Standard for Information Sciences—Permanence
of Paper for Printed Library Materials, ANSI Z39.48 – 1984. ⊗

To my student and faculty colleagues
in the University of Michigan's Program
in Education for Social Change

Contents

Illustrations

The Automobile Metropolis *(following page 134)*

Elements of Growth

Centers

Foreword

Charles Tilly

Sam Bass Warner, Jr. has been enlightening Americans about their urban heritage for thirty-five years. In 1962, *Streetcar Suburbs* told us about Boston's rail-led expansion beyond the two-mile–radius pedestrian city of the 1850s, illustrating the story with one chart, eleven maps, and sixty-six photographs. In 1968 *The Private City* arrived, a richly illustrated and more quantitative study of Philadelphia from the eighteenth to the twentieth century. The year 1977 brought *The Way We Really Live*, a set of lectures on Boston's history that combined slides, statistics, and sage reflections—a sort of backdrop for *Province of Reason* (1984), which presented biographies of nineteenth- and twentieth-century Bostonians. *To Dwell Is to Garden* (1987) traced Boston's community gardens in an effort to show how citydwellers interact with their environment. In the midst of publishing these volumes, in 1972 Warner wrote his most general urban history, which covered the whole country but concentrated on New York, Chicago, and Los Angeles; he called it *The Urban Wilderness*.[1]

For a generation Sam Warner has written about American urban history by sketching the development of particular cities. A 1994 poll of urban

1. Sam Bass Warner, Jr., *Streetcar Suburbs: The Process of Growth in Boston, 1870–1900* (Cambridge: Harvard University Press, 1962); *The Private City: Philadelphia in Three Periods of Its Growth* (Philadelphia: University of Pennsylvania Press, 1968); *The Urban Wilderness: A History of the American City* (New York: Harper & Row, 1972; Berkeley and Los Angeles: University of California Press, 1995); *The Way We Really*

history scholars identified him as the country's most influential urban historian, named his first book, *Streetcar Suburbs*, the most influential book in the field and ranked another of his books fourth in the same category, and designated *Urban Wilderness* as one of the books they would recommend most strongly as an introduction to North American urban history.[2] The same *Journal of Urban History* issue that reported the poll included an article concerning the intellectual's place in the formulation of public policy. The article offered reflections on Charles E. Merriam's career as a professor at the University of Chicago, an unsuccessful candidate for mayor of Chicago, and an adviser to political leaders, among them Franklin D. Roosevelt. It ended with a plea for scholarship that would promote the improvement of human life. The article's author: Sam Bass Warner, Jr.[3]

Many urban historians write about cities as collective works of art, while others treat them as museums displaying famous structures, as political organizations, as economic engines, or as sites of population change. Warner gives due attention to all these aspects of urban history, but he examines cities especially as settings for human life, reflecting incessantly on how human life could improve through wise, historically informed public action. Warner's essay on public-policy pundit Charles Merriam exudes a certain nostalgia for the decisive reformism of the New Deal, a measure of sadness at American unreadiness to take advantage of wisdom already available, and a hint of anger at the blindness of today's public figures concerning the stakes of urban policy. In those regards, Warner recalls Merriam less than he does the great urban historian and critic Lewis Mumford.

Like Mumford, Warner has always insisted on the interdependence of historical development, city planning, and quality of life. The preface to Warner's first book, *Streetcar Suburbs* (1962), invoked Mumford as a model. "Rare," wrote Warner, "are works like Lewis Mumford's which combine a sense of the totality of the city with an understanding of how it grew."[4] No doubt he was thinking of Mumford's *Culture of Cities*, which had been published twenty-four years before *Streetcar Suburbs*, as well as Mum-

---

Live: Social Change in Metropolitan Boston Since 1920 (Boston: Boston Public Library, 1977); *Province of Reason* (Cambridge: Harvard University Press, 1984); *To Dwell Is To Garden: A History of Boston's Community Gardens* (Boston: Northeastern University Press, 1987).

2. Carl Abbott, "Reading Urban History: Influential Books and Historians," *Journal of Urban History* 21 (1994): 31–43.

3. Sam Bass Warner, Jr., "What To Do When No One Is Listening," *Journal of Urban History* 21 (1994): 44–54.

4. Warner, *Streetcar Suburbs*, viii.

ford's *City in History*, which had just appeared in 1961.[5] Warner then took ten years to work his way from his close study of Boston through his broader book on Philadelphia to his sweeping analysis of American urbanization, *Urban Wilderness*. Another twenty-four years beyond *Wilderness*, we can see reflections of Mumford's vision in Warner's work. But we can also see the effects of vast changes in urban America.

Mumford's prophetic *Culture of Cities* appeared in 1938; Warner's prophetic *Urban Wilderness* in 1972. Between those years the world went through great upheavals: the most destructive war in history, expansion of state-directed genocide to a scale never previously seen, dismantling of the world's major fascist regimes, disintegration of wartime alliances into a standoff between the Soviet Union and the United States, establishment of the U.S. as the world's leading economic and military power, a series of wars between the U.S. and its allies and communist and leftist regimes, and major rebuilding of ravaged economies in Eastern and Western Europe and Japan. Within the U.S., mobilization for war lifted the economy out of its long depression: industrial concentration proceeded apace, veterans' benefits stimulated both housing construction and the expansion of higher education, women entered paid employment in record numbers despite a dramatic postwar baby boom, blacks mobilized effectively against discrimination in education and other public facilities, and on campuses students not only joined civil rights actions but also mounted sharp opposition to American involvement in fighting the leftist regimes of Southeast Asia.

The changes of those thirty-four years marked American cities deeply. The application of wartime mass construction techniques and government-sponsored mortgages by a new breed of well-capitalized housing merchandizers converted vast tracts of farmland around major cities into suburban developments. A grand network of federally sponsored superhighways linked major cities to each other as well as to their burgeoning suburbs. Automobile transportation became ever more dominant over mass transit and pedestrian movement. Segregation sharpened between centrally located, minority-occupied, often decaying dwelling areas and the newer, more prosperous, predominantly white zones of the metropolitan periphery as urban renewal became the controversial but far-reaching government-promoted program that tore down whole blocks of old dwellings and replaced them with new structures and open spaces, many dedicated to civic

5. Lewis Mumford, *The Culture of Cities* (New York: Harcourt, Brace, 1938); *The City In History: Its Origins, Its Transformations, and Its Prospects* (New York: Harcourt, Brace, 1961).

centers, parks, roads, and commercial enterprises rather than to housing for the poor and black people they most often displaced.

When Lewis Mumford guided the Museum of Modern Art's production of the still-gripping film *The City* (musical score by Aaron Copland) in 1939, he stamped onto film the image he had written into *The Culture of Cities*: once people lived on a small scale in harmony with nature and each other; the capitalist-industrial city expanded technology and accumulation to an inhumane scale, to the detriment of almost everyone; new technologies of production, housing, and urban planning made possible a new humane decentralization. The film vivified its contrasts by representing a harmonious mill village, juxtaposed against scenes of smoke-choked Pittsburgh, traffic-strangled New York, and chaos on the highways, only to close with bucolic views of planned towns in the style of Radburn, New Jersey, and Greenbelt, Maryland. Mumford confronted viewers with an inescapable choice—and left no doubt of his recommendation.

Mumford's *Culture of Cities* offered a similar analysis of western experience from medieval times onward, just as his *City in History* extended his analysis to most of history and some of prehistory, beginning with Neolithic villages. In each version Mumford argued for a principle of limits: concentrations of political power and productive capacity make urban life possible, but that life only remains healthy at a certain modest scale and in the presence of a well-regulated balance between these two city-building forces. Push political power too far, you get the showy corruption of Rome or baroque capitals; push production too far, you get the lethal wage-slavery of Coketown; push both too far, you get the unlivable excesses of our time. Lewis Mumford wrote sweeping history to serve his own vision of the future.

In *The Urban Wilderness*, Sam Bass Warner did the same. Although he concentrated on the urban history of the United States, he offered Mumford's *Culture of Cities* as a benchmark, adapting a chronological scheme Mumford himself had extended from Patrick Geddes—eotechnic, neotechnic, and biotechnic—to a division of modern American history into technologically distinct periods: 1820–1870, 1870–1920, and 1920 onward. Like Mumford's, Warner's book teemed with eye-catching illustrations, mordantly labeled. More important, he deliberately built a present-minded book, devoted to drawing lessons concerning what is possible today from critical scrutiny of past accomplishments and failures. Like Mumford's great book, Warner's *Urban Wilderness* displays clear-eyed vision, vigorous language, faith in planning, confidence that technology can serve humane ends, and taciturnity about the political moves that would realize its program.

Warner does not, however, mimic Mumford. His bibliographic commentary on Mumford mentions his "own more limited structural approach," and indeed, he attributes far more importance to specific public programs than Mumford did. Note the influence Warner assigns to hub-and-wheel metropolitan freeway designs, as well as to grid-form interstate highways, and his enthusiasm for Los Angeles as a freewheeling city, enhancing people's choices. As compared to the ultimately aristocratic Mumford, Warner comes across as an optimistic populist, a democrat who cares a great deal about individual liberties. Warner stated his creed in public lectures given five years after publication of *Wilderness*: "It is my belief that many of the destructive, indeed self-destructive, aspects of our human settlement come not from iron necessities, but from our unwillingness to confront what we as a society know about ourselves. The computer technician does not set his machine to the urgent tasks revealed by the novelist or the politician, and these gentlemen do not take time even to read the social portraits the computer draws. The rationality and universality of business and government are kept separate from the wisdom of home and community, while the fellowship and emotional richness of these domestic worlds are not regarded as acceptable measures of business and public life."[6]

Whereas Mumford intimates that it will take acts of creative genius and benevolent despotism to bring about the better world of which he dreams, Warner claims we have the essential knowledge for improvement and need democratic discussion to recognize our common needs. Nor are Mumford's and Warner's likely agents of change the same. Despite Mumford's commitment to the tradition of town planning that sprang from nineteenth century utopians (Mumford's first book was *The Story of Utopias*), he claimed that, properly communalized, such architects as Frank Lloyd Wright could serve the future decentralized city. Warner remains suspicious of architects on their own, but he expresses hope for enlightened, populist city planning.

That enlightened populism marked the Sam Warner of 1972 as it marked the era. Warner wrote his book at the University of Michigan, Ann Arbor, then a major center of student political mobilization, the initial base of Students for a Democratic Society, and the site of the first teach-ins. In fact, Warner played a significant part in Ann Arbor's left politics, both on

6. Warner, *The Way We Really Live*, 27.

campus and off. That background helps explain his initial self-description in *Urban Wilderness*, not as a prize-winning professional urbanist and professor but as a responsible citizen: "And my ordinary citizen's life contributed to this point of view. A brief term as an editor of a weekly newspaper in an industrial and residential satellite town and my dabbling in municipal reform politics carried me into the midst of the conflicts of a giant state university. Here, in seeking to aid blacks gain admission and staff positions, helping in antiwar campaigns and drives to end secret military research, and finally in confronting the ultimate contradictions of a closed and self-serving public university seeking to resist open-enrollment demands, my citizen's life and my urban research converged."[7]

Although 1972 brought the Watergate burglary, the reelection of Richard Nixon, and the acceleration of American intervention in Vietnam, it also brought some hope to American populists. The relative success of the civil rights movement, occasionally effective action against urban renewal, swelling campus organization against the war, and, more uncertainly, intermittent rebellions of black urbanites against city police all sustained hope that popular collective action would blunt or even redirect the forces of evil.

Another influential populist book that emerged from the same Michigan milieu in the early 1970s, William Gamson's *Strategy of Social Protest*, illustrates the political commitments of the time.[8] As Gamson explored the historical conditions under which "challenging groups" had gained advantages in American politics between 1810 and 1950, with an eye to present and future challenges, Warner explored the history of implicit and explicit choices concerning the futures of American cities. If we can read *Urban Wilderness* as an enduring commentary on American cities, we can also read it as a product of the wave of radical and populist political mobilization that welled up in the United States during the 1960s.

---

7. *Urban Wilderness*, 4. Lest my own voice sound too distant and timeless, let me explain my interest. Sam Warner and I were college classmates and then received our doctorates from the same graduate school within a year of each other. In the early 1960s, when we were both recent Ph.D.'s, I took up appointments at Harvard and the MIT-Harvard Joint Center for Urban Studies as he was leaving both of them for Washington University, St. Louis. While he was writing *The Urban Wilderness*, we were both teaching at Michigan and participating in some of the same on-campus political actions. When Warner left Michigan for Boston University, he bequeathed to me his magnificent collection of lantern slides, including some illustrations from *Urban Wilderness*; 35-millimeter copies of those slides brightened my own lectures in urban history for many years. Although we have met only rarely during the last two decades, I write not as a dispassionate urban historian but as an old friend and admirer.

8. William A. Gamson, *The Strategy of Social Protest* (Homewood, Ill.: Dorsey, 1975; second edition, Belmont, Calif.: Wadsworth, 1990).

Between the 1960 and 1970 censuses, the U.S. population passed 200 million—and grew to 249 million by 1990. By relaxed census standards, 73.5 percent of the 1970 population lived in urban areas, with the majority in great webs of cities and suburbs down the East Coast, in the Midwest, around the Gulf of Mexico, and along the West Coast. Median education for persons 25 or older was 12.1 years—roughly high school graduation—while median family income was $9,586. A mere 10.8 percent of families were headed by a woman. The American labor force then consisted of about 50 million men and 30 million women; of the women, 57 percent were married with their husband present.[9] Since 1970, the U.S. population has shifted toward the South and the West, education and income have risen while becoming more unequally distributed, women's labor force participation has risen substantially, the proportion of working women who are married and living with their husbands has continued to decline, one-parent families have become much more common, as have cohabiting unmarried couples, and the clustering of Americans in a few intermetropolitan regions has only increased. In all these regards, 1972 was merely a stopping point in the course of long-established population trends.

Warner never said otherwise. His recognition that the present he confronted offered no more than a moment in processes of continuous change gave him two large advantages. First, it reduced the danger of the sort of present-oriented history he undertook to write; instead of treating all the past as a preparation for today's or tomorrow's culmination, he could reasonably search for the origins of continuing American conditions. Second, it allowed him to show that the past had more than one outcome; in some sense, New York, Chicago, and Los Angeles (his three main case studies) all resulted from similar processes under changing conditions. Thus the book's three-part logic:

1. Initial conditions and continuously acting causes
   a) Seventeenth-century settlement
   b) Land law and provisions for planning

2. Stages in the urbanization process
   a) New York 1820–1870
   b) Chicago 1870–1920
   c) Los Angeles 1920–1970

9. U.S. Department of Commerce, *County and City Data Book 1972* (Washington, D.C.: U.S. Government Printing Office, 1972), Table 1.

3. How those pasts produced today's problems and choices
   a) Diverse cultures and neighborhoods
   b) Attempts to define and settle urban problems
   c) Housing and health care as public failures
   d) What we can do now

Ultimately Warner insists that the past was open, subject to collective choices that Americans made without always foreseeing the consequences. He also insists that the future is still open, subject to collective choices with consequences reasoned history helps us anticipate. Urban history can guide public policy. Thus, Warner argues late in the book, consumers and employees improperly lack representation in the decisions of large enterprises, but the New Deal and Great Society experiments demonstrate how both can gain voice—if only Americans summon up the collective will to give them voice.

In pursuing this ambitious plan Warner provides only the sketchiest economic analysis. Except for occasional references to immigration and international flows of capital, the world economy plays little part in his story. He relies on Alfred Chandler for the history of economic organizations and ends up implicitly optimistic about the capacity of American enterprise to hold its own, sustain growth, and solve its problems. As critics of the original edition noted, *Urban Wilderness* provides even less information about the political processes that have generated decisions affecting cities in the past and that might implement better decisions in the future. Although Warner's analysis of the defeat of national health insurance in 1917–19 resonates with failed recent attempts to reform American health care, in general he does not tell us how the structure of American politics would have to change if his representation of popular interests were to come about or what might produce such changes.

Warner's analysis of shifting urban population, geography, and activity patterns goes much further, especially in tracing the effects of transportation changes, housing technology, and industrial organization. Seen from the 1990s, however, his urban newsreel has a number of blank frames. His four main social categories—white Catholic, white Jewish, white Protestant, and black Protestant—do not exhaust an urban scene in which Cubans, Central Americans, Koreans, Chinese, South Asians, and other streams of recent immigrants now figure prominently. Homosexual communities play no part in Warner's cities. Women's distinctive urban experiences as mothers, wives, lovers, workers, consumers, housekeepers, and victims of violence receive no particular attention. We can understand the absence of AIDS, not yet identified in 1972, from his account, but hard drugs, home-lessness, and homicide loom much larger in retrospect than they did when Warner was writing. Costs of welfare and medical care, declining indus-trial bases, resulting fiscal crises, and the federal government's attempts to shift the burden for public services to states and municipalities constitute a much larger part of American urban politics than Warner's account would lead us to expect.

Rewriting *The Urban Wilderness* in 1995, Warner would surely have to say more about political relations among cities, states, and the federal gov-ernment. He might well moderate his enthusiasm for the Los Angeles solu-tion to American urban ills, which has proved vulnerable to pollution, tangled traffic, aging industrial plant, racial-ethnic division, and segrega-tion just as radical as the ghettoization of older East Coast cities.[10] Nor did the Warner of 1972 see the extent to which American cities would continue the pattern he had actually documented in *Streetcar Suburbs*: incessant ex-pansion at their outer edges into enormous, sprawling, many-centered metropolises with multiple interstitial areas simply left to decay. Which is to say, merely, that in the realm of urban problems none of us, not even Warner, owns an unclouded crystal ball. The wonder is that the book's prophetic portions stand up to scrutiny so well more than two decades after it was written.

The wonder, or the despair. Warner's analyses show us how fecklessly we have faced the challenge of our cities. Things have gotten worse, for in the 1990s Americans are prepared to accept politicians' declarations that cities have become too unmanageable, too expensive, too dangerous, too packed with undeserving freeloaders for effective intervention—except for the protected high-income neighborhoods, office buildings, and entertain-ment districts they often frequent. Today's urban policy prescribes cost-cutting, containment, control, and construction of prisons, plus cooptation for the few who can prove themselves worthy. Inequalities of wealth and living conditions within cities have only sharpened since 1972, and show no signs of abating. We can still read Sam Warner with illumination concern-ing the sources of our urban malaise, if with dwindling hope of combatting that malaise by means of concerted public action.

10. For a recent report from the Los Angeles front, see Mike Davis, *City of Quartz: Excavating the Future in Los Angeles* (London: Verso, 1990).

Preface

Any author must fear the rereading of something written twenty-odd years ago. You anticipate that the past two decades of history will mock the passages you once fancied your wisest. After all, who but a historian knows better that the commonplace assumptions of an era are likely to be the awkward postures of a moment?

I don't feel that embarrassment for this book, although it is very much a creation of 1972. Hope for the possibility for change and the ability to relieve long-endured suffering and injustice suffuse the text. There is an optimism that was buoyed by the successes of the civil rights movement and the energy of the anti-Vietnam War movement. Such a tone may be anomalous in 1995, but I maintain it nevertheless. Our nation is, and always has been, one that brims with possibilities, including knowing and improving our largest collective undertaking—the building of cities.

In this book there is also a reach for inclusiveness, an attempt to include all Americans, that would be difficult to sustain amidst the political narrowness of today's scholarly discourse. The progressive spirit of the 1960s encouraged such outreach, which was reinforced by my personal experience. I had been teaching in St. Louis and Detroit and also studying Philadelphia's history. It was the attempt to understand these giant regional metropolises that encouraged me to survey the history of urban America.

Since 1972 I have been living and working in an uncommon American place, the nineteenth-century center of an old American city, Boston. This has not been a good vantage point for observing the rapid diffusion of the modern American metropolis, the malling of America, or the rise of Sun Belt cities. Urban renewal and styles of corporate investment, however, have brought a big mall to my neighborhood, and my friends have been showing me the growth of their cities. Thus, despite my peculiar situation, I have seen what is out there. To me it seems only an extension of the highways, subdivisions, strip malls, and office centers that were already in place in 1972. Because of the magnitude of the suburban growth in jobs, housing, and malls, however, today's metropolis is no longer merely an extension of a historical center city; it has become a new entity of its own.

The Urban Wilderness was written at the end of the 1924–1968 era of restricted immigration. The metropolises of 1972 were thus the creations of small-town Americans, and the children and grandchildren of immigrants. The text, therefore, concentrates on the institutions and processes of urban absorption and consensus, not on the first stages of immigrant adjustment. Today Los Angeles is an immigrant city as New York was in 1910, and the prediction is that New York will resemble its old immigrant self by 2010. To a historian the current fears of native workers that they will lose their jobs to cheap immigrant labor, the stereotyping of Hispanics and Asians, the resumption of night-school English teaching, and the rise of nativism are all familiar responses. Our 1995 fears resemble those of the 1850s and the 1900s. Yet, because this book was written during a decade of relatively few newcomers (see Table 3 on page 168), the reader will have to incorporate the effects of recent migrations into their way of thinking about the American metropolis.

The movement for women's liberation was also new in 1972. Although Betty Friedan had published her landmark book, *The Feminine Mystique*, in 1963, and although I recall women's consciousness-raising groups all around the University of Michigan in those years, the sexual specifics of metropolitan life had not yet become clear to me when I wrote this book. Those issues came into focus later, when I read Dolores Hayden's *Redesigning the American Dream* in 1984. Again, the reader will have to extrapolate from the wage-earning husband and stay-at-home wife of my book to the current forms of two-wage-earning couples, single-headed households, and single mothers with children that, added together, are more common than the old form of the family unit.

The term "Negro" may strike a contemporary reader as odd, but in the 1970s the popular term for an African American was in transition from Negro to black to Afro-American. The book's failure to deal with the environmental goals of metropolitan design may also surprise today's reader.

To be sure, Earth Day 1970 proved to be an important awakening of public consciousness, and 1972 was the year of President Nixon's environmental initiatives, but few of us had yet seen how the demands for clean air and clean water would express themselves in urban design. In fact, Anne Whiston Spirn did not write her guide to environmental urban design, *The Granite Garden*, until 1985.

My suggestions for the physical rebuilding of the metropolis now seem rigid and old-fashioned. There is an excessive emphasis on "neighborhood unit plans" and "new towns," as if these were the most efficacious routes to creating lively small communities within large urban agglomerations. Over the past two decades I have visited a variety of American communities that seem to function very well: parts of continuous street grids where a shopping corner at an intersection serves as an effective community center; neighborhoods of poor people's housing where the interstate highway or the railroad establishes a useful boundary; dense seaside towns composed of a jumble of modest cottages; and old apartment clusters and local shopping streets that provide comfortable environments for their residents. Were I to rewrite Chapters 7 and 8 today, I would stress the possibilities of these precedents. I would also call for the active management of the air, water, and forest resources of the metropolis, and I would emphasize the necessity of promoting low-rise, high-density settlement and the efficacy of a variety of public transportation systems.

Medical institutions have grown to be major determinants of the well being of city dwellers, but recent trends toward making health care a business seem self-defeating. I have always thought of medicine as a profession, and physicians and nurses as professionals whose jobs, like that of teachers, include a large measure of public service as well as private skill and profit. Indeed, what distinguishes a profession from other forms of employment is the element of public service, which can be one of the most important personal rewards of such work. Therefore, the rapid growth of private, profit-making medical corporations, large and small, has come as an unwelcome surprise to me. Since 1972 profit-making hospitals, insurance company health maintenance organizations, nursing homes, and health service companies of all kinds have multiplied lustily while community-based, voluntary organizations and municipal hospitals have languished. To me this expansion seems to be feeding on the inevitable frailties and misfortunes of our fellow citizens. The American health-care system now seems to care primarily for insurance carriers and hospital corporations.

The opportunity for this moneymaking was provided by the large corporate health-insurance and Blue Cross–Blue Shield policies of the 1960s that offered substantial profit to organizations that limited their coverage to the young and healthy, cut back on staffing and services, and found ways to push the chronically ill, the old, and the poor onto federal, state, municipal, and charitable budgets. As a consequence, in 1995 our medical system serves us both as well and as badly as the suburban shopping mall.

Finally, the call for democratic planning echoes throughout this book. It is a call to make public what is now customarily private, and to subject decisions that affect us all to open democratic process. Neither planning nor the special problems of the democratic management of planning are at the forefront of contemporary public discussion. Indeed, conservative political voices in America continue to link planning with socialism, and socialism with tyranny, despite the fact that socialism, planning, and democracy all prevail in both the United States and Europe.

Whenever large numbers of people live and work together, or whenever large sums of money are managed, planning comes to the fore. The questions of how to weigh costly alternatives, how to provide expensive capital investments, and how to balance conflicting goals all demand planning for the future. In a democratic society like ours planning takes on special urgency. If the essential decisions lie in the hands of those with large accumulations of capital or political power, then the citizens of a democracy live at the mercy of decisions that are beyond their control; public politics will become more and more peripheral to daily life, and private politics will take over. The decline in voter participation in the United States is an ominous telltale of such a process.

Since 1972 private corporate tendencies have continued to grow. Planning decisions, of course, are made every day: decisions to extend electric power lines, decisions to develop open land, decisions to build a new factory or business, or to close an old one, decisions to launch new communications systems, decisions to manage farmland and farm products, decisions to make loans, decisions to import products or services from overseas, and so forth. All of these decisions affect the jobs, wages, environment, race relations, and living conditions of a city and its suburbs. Some of these decisions are currently regulated by public utility, business practice, and environmental laws, but few are subject to public scrutiny and debate over their likely consequences in a metropolitan region or for their effects upon the national network of cities.

During the 1960s and early 1970s the public demanded more participation in local land-use, highway, public-facility, and environmental decisions.

In cities and towns, and even in some states, there have been considerable advances in public participation, openness of hearings, and public consultation, especially in comparison to the former urban renewal and highway practices of the 1950s. Moreover, thanks to the Model Cities and Great Society era federal and state programs, there has been a multiplication of local nonprofit, membership organizations at every scale, from community gardens to large community development corporations. These groups represent important extensions of democratic communities in the United States (see Robert Fisher, *Let the People Decide*, 1994). Yet these organizations depend on the federal government and the states to protect the local economies that enable the nonprofits to exist. When corporations decide to close down the businesses of Trenton or Youngstown, there is no way for the local citizens to defend themselves. Similarly, if people are to find jobs outside the ghettos or beyond the depressed metropolitan areas, national economic planning will be required to maintain full employment and ensure a living wage. Or, if all the children of a metropolis are to be given access to a decent education, then the state must see that there are schools for the children to attend.

It is not easy to make national economic planning a democratic institution, but it can be done. The Federal Reserve Board is now a national planning institution, though not a democratic one. Its limited functions, however, are exemplary. In a nation the size of the United States the federal government can plan successfully in only a few areas; the rest must be undertaken by the states, the counties, the cities, and the towns.

All of America's metropolitan and municipal institutions are created by state governments. The variety of alternatives that these present make up an ample resource for any governor or legislature to study and adopt. What remains absent today, even more so than in 1972, is a sense among Americans that as dwellers in a highly integrated metropolitan economy of networks of cities and suburbs we depend on one another. We do not realize this interdependence, so we lack a sense of the possibilities of our shared life and consensus goals. Our lives, our cities, and our suburbs need not be subject to the private decisions of finance capitalists, corporate managers, and their special-interest lobbyists if we citizens are willing to assume responsibility for our own well-being.

S. B. W.
Boston
January 1995

Acknowledgments

Any broad canvass of American urban history necessarily cuts across the lines of established disciplines and demands that the author seek help and criticism from many sources. I have been particularly fortunate in receiving assistance from many experts whose suggestions and comments have enabled me to deal with a range of topics far beyond the reach of conventional history.

John W. Shy and Kenneth A. Lockridge of the University of Michigan offered useful criticism of my views of the New England town. O. K. Christenson and his staff at the County of Los Angeles Regional Planning Commission ran a seminar for my benefit and assisted with advance reports and materials from their files; Milton C. Stark of the California Division of Highways, District #7, lent me office space and passed me along through the transportation research projects then in progress in Los Angeles; and Robert J. S. Ross of the Institute for Social Research of the University of Michigan brought his city planning research to bear on a criticism of the planning sections of the manuscript.

Several scholars have helped with the history of the economy and the national network of cities as it passed through successive revisions. I would like to acknowledge the readings and comments of Robert L. Heilbroner of the New School for Social Research, Peter G. Goheen and Jack Meltzer of the University of Chicago, Rich Rothstein of Northeastern Illinois State College, Franklin G. Moore of the School of Business Administration here at Michigan, and four members of my department, William G. Rosenberg, John B. Sharpless II, and Phyllis V. and Lewis A. Erenberg.

Edward O. Laumann of the Michigan Sociology Department has borne patiently with my many attempts to write a comprehensive essay on migration and American urban culture, and several of these drafts have been improved by the comments and suggestions of Clyde Griffen of Vassar College, Stephan Thernstrom of the University of California, Los Angeles, and James Hennesey, S.J., of the Graduate Theological Union, Berkeley. I was introduced to the literature of medical economics by Solomon J. Axelrod of the Michigan School of Public Health and his associates Eugenia S. Carpenter and Jack H. Tobias.

Two former colleagues from Washington University, Joseph Passonneau and Roger Montgomery, have continued to teach me about the American city. This time Joe has been instructing me about the logic of urban transportation and Roger has encouraged me to seek the widest definition for the rationale of the physical development of the city.

The photographic evidence, which for me is an essential source for the understanding of our urban past, has been made available through the gift of time and knowledge by many archivists and historians. The pictures published in this book are but a small fraction of the data which these collections opened up to me. I would like to acknowledge the help of John M. Cahoun of the history division of the Los Angeles County Museum of Natural History, Victor R. Plukas, historian of the Security Pacific National Bank, Los Angeles, Mason Dooley of the planning department of the City of Los Angeles, Harriett Blitzer of the Photographic Service of the Metropolitan Museum of Art, New York, Philip S. Benjamin, director of the Urban Archives Center, Temple University, Brenda Adams of the printing and visual arts division of the Department of Housing and Urban Development, Nancy Stutzman of the J. C. Nichols Company, Kansas City, and the staff of the National Archives and Records Service, the New York Regional Plan Association, and the prints division of the New York Public Library. I am particularly indebted to Charlotte LaRue of the photo library of the Museum of the City of New York and Leroy Bellamy of the prints and visual arts division of the Library of Congress, who have helped me on many occasions; Mary Frances Rhymer of the Chicago Historical Society, who offered both research and archival skills to aid me with my Chicago development problems; and the staff of the New-York Historical Society, who have become outstanding urban historians in their own right. The professionals of the University of Michigan's photographic services have assisted me countless times, and the clarity of the maps derives from the skill of Garland Green of the Geography Department.

The writing of the book itself was enormously benefited by my colleagues here at the University of Michigan History Department, who made possible a semester's research leave during the winter of 1971 through the award of the department's Richard Hudson Professorship. Joan Blos gave up her own work to help with a rush deadline. I owe many thanks to editor Alice Gibson, who put in patient and energetic hours of queries, comments, and suggestions over the past three years as the book has progressed through successive preliminary forms and drafts. It owes much of its present clarity to her efforts.

Finally, I would like to thank my wife, Lyle, who lifted the heavy end of the family log during the past year when the demands of writing absorbed most of my time and energy.

S.B.W.

Ann Arbor
April, 1972

ONE

▲ TAKING UP THE LAND

1

Tradition as Determinant

—

New England folk planning,

the weight of English custom,

resistance to change

THE GIANT CITIES of our country have always seemed to me, as they have to most Americans, vast incomprehensible places in which I could at most know a few people, my own block or suburb, my shopping center, and my commuting paths. I have lived with a pervasive sense of existing as a dweller in small clearings in the midst of an urban wilderness. Only the rich and powerful escape this sensation because their well-protected institutions and cosmopolitan style enable them to pretend that they are not part of the same world the rest of America lives in. All my professional career has been spent trying to understand these giant urban wildernesses by seeking the historical background to their problems—problems which flooded in toward me from newspapers and television and from just walking and riding around the cities I had settled in.

Over the years of this study I have become more and more convinced that a long tradition has accounted for the endless failures of Americans to build and maintain humane cities. Unlike many, I don't believe there ever was a good old days, a flowering of New York or Boston. Rather, like neurotic middle-aged patients, our cities are case histories of the repercussions of basic flaws and conflicts. This conviction came from many sources: from the study of patterns of suburban growth in Boston, from examining the conditions of working-class life at the turn of the century, from a survey of the long history of Philadelphia, the nation's first big industrial city, and from a review of current planning problems. And my ordinary citizen's life contributed to this point of view. A brief term as an editor of a weekly newspaper in an industrial and residential satellite town and my dabbling in municipal reform politics carried me into the midst of the conflicts of a giant state university. Here, in seeking to aid blacks gain admission and staff positions, helping in antiwar campaigns and drives to end secret military research, and finally in confronting the ultimate contradictions of a closed and self-serving public university seeking to resist open-enrollment demands, my citizen's life and my urban research converged.

From this experience I have made the discovery that Americans have no urban history. They live in one of the world's most urbanized countries as if it were a wilderness in both time and space. Beyond some civic and ethnic myths and a few family and neighborhood memories, Americans are not conscious that they have a past and that by their actions they participate in making their future. As they tackle today's problems, either with good will or anger, they have no sense of where cities came from, how they grew, or even what direction the large forces of history are taking them. Whether one speaks to an official in Washington or to a neighborhood action group, the same blindness prevails. Without a sense of history, they hammer against today's crises without any means to choose their targets to fit the trends which they must confront, work with, or avoid.

Thus, the basic purpose of this book is to gather together what is now known about cities and to cast that knowledge in the form of a series of present-oriented historical essays which will give the reader a framework for understanding the giant and confusing urban world he must cope with. A great deal has been learned since Lewis Mumford published his excellent *The Culture of Cities* in 1938, and it is time once again to portray the logic of our urban past.

Put another way, the goal of this book is to attempt to use history to replace the diffuse fears and sporadic panics which now characterize the popular perceptions of our cities with a systematic way of looking at our present urban condition. The hope is that by presenting people with their history, panic can give way to understanding, and that by bringing out what is now known about how our huge urban system performs, people can choose for themselves intelligently what needs to be done and what can be done to build humane cities in America.

There are many ways to judge cities, but for anyone who is trying to bring the lessons of the historical past upon present problems the most useful way is to hold the city up to the measure of three traditional goals: open competition, community, and innovation. These standards are not arbitrary; they constitute the cherished ideals of our society. The goal of open competition is that in a successful city every resident should have a fair chance to compete for society's wealth and prizes. It is a goal compounded in the early years of the Republic from popular enthusiasm for egalitarian politics and laissez-faire capitalism. The second goal, community, holds that a successful city should encompass a safe, healthy, decent environment in which every man participates as a citizen, regardless of personal wealth or poverty, success or failure. This goal is again a blend in which political egalitarianism and nineteenth-century humanitarianism merged. The third goal, innovation, is directed to the principle that a city should be a place of wide personal freedom; that the variety and individuality of citizens should find expression in new ideas, new art, new tools and products, new manners and morals. This goal is a restatement of the cherished American ideal of progress. Today, after half a century of almost continuous war and unabated human suffering, the reality of progress is deeply compromised, but as a society we have passed so far beyond the modes of living by tradition that our cities will henceforth be forced to maintain their existence through innovation.

These three goals are by no means a harmonious triad; they conflict at many points. In the past as in the present, our cities have favored innovation and competition at the expense of community. New products and methods of production, new transportation, new ways of doing business have been introduced without regard for the dislocation and suffering they create. Skills have been wiped out, whole industries rendered obsolete, millions driven off the land or harried from one city to another. Competition for jobs, wealth, and power has been severe and even lethal, never completely open and fair. Blacks, women, immigrants, children, and old people have always been at a disadvantage. The inherent nature of our capitalistic system has bestowed differential and cumulative rewards so that the successful exercise a disproportionate control over the city and the lives of its residents. Consequently the strong prey on the weak, and to him that has shall be given. Today's state, serving the white middle class, is only the most recent manifestation of social and economic competition.

Although the mainstream of our history has favored certain aspects of innovation and open competition, the goal of community has always

been an important and not always benign force. Political bosses, armed
with the language of equality and the techniques of particularism, men
like James Michael Curley in Boston or Richard Daley in Chicago, have
closed competition and blocked the modernization of their cities for
years at a time; unions of skilled workers and professionals have frequently refused to meet the needs of the public and have closed their
doors against newcomers. Grassroots citizen groups have used their
solidarity to exclude the blacks and the poor from their jurisdictions—
both by law and by violence—or have fought off, delayed, or distorted
the logical location of rail lines and highways, as well as civic improvements of all kinds.

Innovation uproots people. The sheer volume of the constant movement of Americans levies a terrible toll on the stability of our families,
neighborhoods, and cities. Competition has never been fair and open;
throughout our history businessmen, workers, and communities have
sought to restrict it in their sector of interest or to manipulate it for their
particular advantage. Community is often the enemy of innovation and
equitable competition. These conflicts, the inevitable tensions engendered by such goals, can never be avoided.

Nevertheless we can choose how and where these conflicts will
occur. Through democratic planning we can prescribe the self-conscious
social choice of where and how the conflicts of the city are to be expressed, how the costs will be borne, how the profits reaped. Shall we
stress competition or community or innovation in our schools, factories,
and offices? What should the neighborhood demand of the highway
engineer? Should the bohemian areas of our cities be enlarged? Should
not projects for racial equality override all other claims for political
power? If General Motors were to be nationalized, would its factory
communities be more or less protected against corporate exploitation?
Should doctors, professors, and army officers continue to be paid more
than nurses, schoolteachers, and carpenters? Should new housing continue to be segregated by income level, or should the classes be mixed
residentially?

Such questions are the questions of planning. A decision consciously
arrived at can point out the policy to be adopted. Alternatively, questions can be sidestepped and common practice left to the workings of
the marketplace and the outcome of the political power structure in the
city. Whether by planning or inertia, at any given moment each city will
be favoring certain aspects of our three goals over others. The success of

our cities may of course be judged subjectively by the degree to which urban patterns conform to one's personal evaluation of the goals. There is no final answer, no ultimate master plan, but there are and have been very different cities from those in which we now live. The size of our cities, the weight of the physical plant, the drag of law and custom, the obstructive interests of bureaucracies seem to restrict us to the narrowest of choices. Yet if history shows anything, it shows that American cities have been changing at a rate so rapid that in the course of one or two decades we do have enough choices to be able to plan for a balance among the three goals and to plan for balances quite different from those we now confront.

This book, then, hopes to survey the basic historical sequences that have shaped today's cities: the destruction of folk planning (Chapter 1); our tradition of land management (Chapter 2); our unfolding national economy with its accompanying internal structure of cities (Chapters 3, 4, and 5); our immigration and migration that formed a national urban culture and defined the class, racial, and religious subcultures upon which local politics play (Chapter 6). After this view of the controlling hand of the past, we will turn to a review of early efforts to rationalize the American city (Chapters 7 and 8). This study of past programs will focus particularly on the goal of community and on projects undertaken to make the community a safe and decent environment. It will also examine the historical concerns of health and housing to demonstrate how our tradition defines the present city. The history will conclude (Chapter 9) with an assessment of the choices and constraints surrounding today's urban problems.

Concern for the basic needs of human society, a concern often lost in the private opportunities and shifting complexities of our developing cities, may be illustrated by a brief introductory look at the New England town of the seventeenth century, the most completely planned of any American settlement. The Puritans dealt with the same basic issues and components, but they handled them in a way unique to folk planning. Puritan folk planning flourished along the Atlantic coast from Maine to Long Island a century before what is now the United States had a town large enough to be defined as a city. For a generation or two, medieval English village traditions fused with religious ideology to create a consensus concerning the religious, social, economic, and political framework for a good life. Each of the several hundred villages repeated a basic pattern. No royal statute, no master plan, no strong legislative controls, no central administrative officers, no sheriffs or justices of the peace, no synods of prelates, none of the apparatus typical of government then or now was required to draft or execute these plans. The country folk of New England did not need guidance, subsidies, or constraints upon the management of their property, grants-in-aid for public works or unemployment relief, or assistance for the injured or old. Rather they carried in their heads the specifications for a good life and a decent community, and for a time they were able to realize them.

But after two or three generations, the consensus crumbled and with it the replication of the towns. The culture proved inherently unstable, and the neglect of the time element in town planning and social ideals wrecked the township system. Only one feature of the seventeenth-century experience has descended to us. The Puritan form of private landholding survives as the dominant land tenure in our real-property law. In contrast to our modern planning goals, the Puritans sought a community where order and stability would enable all men to live according to a Biblical morality of love and virtue. The Puritans saw themselves as establishing a timeless system. The relationships among men, the laws and customs of the village, the pursuit of agriculture and the trades, the reading of the Bible and the gathering of the congregation to hear the preaching of the ministry—all these, they thought, would permanently maintain their earthly segment of a divine universe.[1]

The planning problem of the Puritans was to harness the land hunger of seventeenth-century Englishmen to the task of establishing a stable community where frontiersmen might live and worship. The planning solution was to identify the family as the basic unit of labor and production and the core element in social organization, and the town as the unit of settlement. The town was to be nearly self-sufficient economically, to exist by corporate self-government and corporate allocation of land, and to nourish a congregational church. The two hundred–odd Puritan towns had at their inception a group of families, with or without a minister, who had applied to the colonial legislature for township grants. In Connecticut, Rhode Island, and Maine, towns were initially founded by squatting on land purchased from the Indians, but later these settlements sought and received confirmation of their township and individual land titles. In the typical Massachusetts case the

1. Kenneth A. Lockridge, *A New England Town, the First Hundred Years, Dedham, Massachusetts, 1636–1736*, New York, 1970, pp. 50–56.

legislature offered previously surveyed wilderness tracts or granted a license to survey and locate a township. The conditions of such grants were two: the town planters had to occupy the sites, erect houses, and create a going community within two or three years; and they had to be numerous and prosperous enough to support a minister and a church. In some cases the founders failed and the legislature intervened, revoked the grant, and took a direct hand in supervising the development of the struggling village.[2] Such conditions were unlike those in most of the colonies and unlike those during most of the subsequent history of the United States, in that land grants were contingent upon an intent to settle and to build a community. The more usual American style was to seek out land for future speculation, to settle as individual families instead of in village groups, and to allow villages and towns to rise or not, depending upon the natural course of commerce and real-estate promotion.

Following the grant of a Puritan township—free except for surveying costs and sometimes a purchase payment to the Indians—the founding families declared themselves a permanent community by signing a covenant.[3] The covenant essentially said that each signatory (and his family and heirs) agreed to be bound by the laws and to accept the taxes, duties, and obligations of the town. At this beginning moment the covenanted corporation held title to all the land of the township, many square miles of wilderness. The church, although supported by township taxes, was a separate entity, governed by the more limited membership of those Puritans who had undergone conversion, but attendance and possibility of membership was open to all the men, women, and children of the town.[4]

The mode of allocating town land assured the early achievement of the community and religious goals. The land resources were immense by English standards, thirty to a hundred square miles of raw land, but the founding families were not allowed to scatter or to homestead isolated family farms. Neither was a Bible communism to arise from community

2. William Haller, Jr., *The Puritan Frontier, Town-Planting in New England Colonial Development 1630–1660*, New York, 1951, pp. 17–28, 31–42, 104–105.

3. Page Smith in *As a City Upon a Hill, The Town in American History*, New York, 1966, pp. 3–16, has tried to make the seventeenth-century Puritan settlers covenant a cultural precedent for all American towns, but the Puritan town is not the parent of the commonplace nineteenth-century small town. It descends instead from the settlement habits of New York, Pennsylvania, and Virginia.

4. Lockridge, *New England Town*, pp. 23–36.

property and community labor. Legally the town moved to set up individually owned and worked family parcels, but by manipulating the placement of these parcels it sought to bind independent families into the social unity of an English village.[5]

Upon completion of the survey of the future village, each family was immediately granted a home lot. On this lot the husbandman was to erect his house and barns, set his fruit trees and garden, and tend his family stock of milch cows, oxen, sheep, and poultry. These home lots, which varied from as little as half an acre for a poor bachelor to as much as twenty acres for a wealthy family, were laid out against one or two streets that adjoined a strip of fenced common land where cattle could be penned and the future church erected. The first church was a modest affair, but in the late eighteenth and early nineteenth centuries the townsmen built the large white Christopher Wren churches which established the modern standard "colonial" church for American Protestantism. Also, these later generations drove the cattle off the commons, refencing and landscaping the rough village space and thereby transforming it into the town greens which have been the envy of most suburban subdivisions ever since.[6] Home-lot grants varied according to a number of factors. The size of a man's family counted; men with many children received larger than normal allocations, bachelors small lots. The community's need for a man's services counted; millers, blacksmiths, and ministers were attracted by offering double and triple allocations. Finally, because as seventeenth-century Englishmen and Puritans the settlers recognized hierarchy to be the natural and desirable order of society, men of means or status were given larger allocations or subsequent land bonuses.

Despite such differentials, most families in fact received very similar parcels, and with few exceptions the largest grants were not more than eight times the smallest. In Boston the wealthy grasped much more of the town's wealth in their hands. By all later American standards these first townships were the most equitable allocations of resources the

5. Philip J. Greven, Jr., *Four Generations: Population, Land, and Family in Colonial Andover, Massachusetts,* Ithaca, 1970, pp. 50–55; Lockridge, *New England Town,* pp. 10–13; Sumner C. Powell, *Puritan Village, the Formation of a New England Town,* New York, 1965, pp. 107–108, plates 9, 10.

6. John W. Reps, *The Making of Urban America, A History of City Planning in the United States,* Princeton, 1965, pp. 124–28; Paul Zucker, *Town and Square, From the Agora to the Village Green,* New York, 1959, pp. 242–44.

country ever knew. A rough commonalty of property prevailed, and no one was left out. Never again was popular consensus able to forge so inclusive and equitable an economic program.[7]

Beyond the village home lots lay the farm parcels, intentionally scattered so that no family should locate on a single tract. In these years a family normally received about a hundred and twenty acres, of which only about twenty-five acres could be actively cultivated. The remainder was to be used for grazing cattle, mowing wild grasses, and cutting firewood. Wheat and rye, the major grain crops that lay at the core of this subsistence agriculture, were grown in one or two common fields in which each family was given a strip proportionate in size to its home lot, and here each farmer was to work his own allotment. In the first years, when many settlers arrived without tools or cattle, the plowing of the strips in the common field must often have been a community project. But at the core of New England farming—as of New England religion—lay individual effort and responsibility.[8]

The early towns were intended only to support a primitive economy of self-sufficient families and autonomous villages. Farming was crude and laborious, and the output of each farmer varied with his energy and that of his family. Instead of searching for specialties that might bring a higher cash return, as their eighteenth-century descendants were to do, the first generation seemed content to clear the land slowly and to strive for a stable agricultural routine. Since most of the towns were located along the coast or on a river, they relied on water transport for their infrequent dealings with the outside world. Indian footpaths, trails that wound through the forests, were the only long-distance roads in the colonies, and many towns did not build roads even to connect the villages of one township to its next neighbors. Some towns were too self-centered even to meet their obligation to send representatives to each assembly of the legislature. There were, to be sure, occasional promoters and merchants, and each town had a storekeeper who took in grain and cattle and arranged for the purchase in Boston and elsewhere of salt, cloth, iron, and other goods. The market was not, however, a primary orientation for these farmers.[9] For them, worldly wealth consisted of an

7. Greven, *Four Generations*, pp. 44–48.
8. Darrett B. Rutman, *Husbandmen of Plymouth, Farms and Villages in the Old Colony 1620–1692*, Boston, 1967, pp. 59–61.
9. Anthony N. B. Garvan, *Architecture and Town Planning in Colonial Connecticut*, New Haven, 1951, p. 54; Rutman, *Husbandmen of Plymouth*, pp. 20–21.

estate in land, and this goal the township could and did guarantee to the first generations of its members.[10]

Clearly population growth, economic change, or cultural modification spelled conflict and disruption for the order and stability of the cluster of closed villages. For about two generations the ease of founding new townships when old ones were filled or split by controversy made New England a stable system of multiplying cells. The founding families welcomed newcomers to a full share of the town's land divisions until the resident community sensed that it was complete; thereafter no more home lots were granted. Such a moment sometimes came with the crowding of the wild meadow by the townsmen's cattle. More often the land-distribution rolls closed when, typically after ten to fifteen years, the first families felt that their town had enough settlers to become a viable village. Latecomers continued to arrive in the more prosperous towns, and they could and did purchase land from the founding families, but folk planning did not anticipate and made no allowance for continuous expansion.[11]

The genius of the township system, distinct from later planning ideals and achievements, lay in its crude organization of freedom and opportunity in group, not individual, terms. More strongly than in the tightest urban ethnic or racial ghetto or in the closed union or in the inbred family corporation, the unity of land control combined with a common village and religious experience to force men of the time to seek change only in group terms. The young and dissident could not break away as individuals from village constraints, since to have done so would have cost them their culture. Only to the extent that the disaffected could form themselves into new town-building groups could they gain direction over their own futures.[12]

Town division, however, could not alone cope with long-term changes. Steady, undramatic demographic and economic pressures eroded the established culture. Perhaps most surprising to the founding families was the fact that the religious consensus was the first element in

---

10. J. B. Jackson has written a beautiful summary of the orientation of the first generations, "The Westward-moving House," in *Landscapes, Selected Writings of J. B. Jackson,* Ervin H. Zube, ed., Amherst, 1970, pp. 10–19.

11. English custom, continued for a time here, sought to maintain a permanent village of a more or less fixed number of families. The method of control was the father's holding title to the property upon which his sons settled. Greven, *Four Generations,* pp. 75–84, 98–99.

12. Powell, *Puritan Village,* pp. 167–77.

the township culture to give way. Most of the children of the first settlers did not live the intense religious life of their parents, and the experience of conversion which informed adult life of the older generation did not so often repeat itself in the children and grandchildren. Protestantism was itself becoming an ever-shifting, ever-dividing mass of religions, and soon after the migrations of the 1630s Quakers and Baptists and lesser heretics began to appear in the towns. The loss of deep orthodox faith created in each village a dangerous ideological potential. Religious indifference or dissent lay in wait, ready to reinforce any demographic or economic change that might press in upon the old unities.[13]

Even within the oldest townships the single-nucleus village could not be maintained against demographic pressures. New villages were started within the large townships and inevitably brought with them demands for multiple congregations, conflicts over town management, religious schism, and political divisions. If, as was often the case, the old township kept its political boundaries but sheltered within it many villages and many churches, the unified cultural, religious, and social life of the Puritan village was lost there forever.

A new farm pattern also emerged as the generations went on. To preserve intact the home lots along the common, sons and grandsons were often given outer parcels of land. By such inheritance practices the old New England towns came to resemble the speculator-managed eighteenth-century farm settlements, and thus New England fell in with common American ways.[14] As the countryside advanced across the wilderness by single-family farms and crossroad store clusters, the political units—townships and counties—were woven into a fabric of low-density settlement and multiple villages. The eighteenth-century social geography matched its economy, oriented to the markets and to specialized agriculture.

The moral of the story depends, as in all historical tales, upon the eye of the beholder. For the seventeenth-century pioneers the story foretold the "ruin of New England."[15] For the eighteenth century it repre-

---

13. Richard L. Bushman, *From Puritan to Yankee*, Cambridge, 1967, pp. 54–82, 107–21; J. M. Bumsted, "Revivalism and Separatism in New England: The First Society of Norwich, Connecticut as a Case Study," *William and Mary Quarterly*, 24 (October 1967), 588–612.

14. Garvan, *Architecture and Town Planning*, pp. 61–77; Glenn T. Trewartha, "Types of Rural Settlement in Colonial America," *Geographical Review*, 36 (October 1946), 569–80.

15. William Bradford, *Of Plymouth Plantation 1620–1647*, Samuel E. Morison, ed., New York, 1952, pp. 252–54.

sented a happy escape into prosperity and personal freedom. For the nineteenth century and today's boosters of modernization the story reveals the benign hand of progress. The history of the New England township system carries multiple meanings, but as a base for the examination of the American city surely its most pervasive theme carries the most important message: to plan without regard for the processes of change is inevitably to fail.

2

Saving Yesterday's Property

—

*Management of land,
zoning, city planning,
and interstate highways*

LAND LAW IS THE ONE ELEMENT from America's seventeenth-century heritage that has survived and flourished. This law, as brought to our shores by settlers in both Virginia and New England, has persisted ever since as the framework for a basic concern of our cities—the management of land. The pioneers can scarcely be blamed for such an anomaly, for in their time they envisioned no cities at all. The responsibility rests rather with successive generations of Americans who, by their unwillingness to move beyond the confines of private landownership, have produced today's disordered, inhumane, and restricted city. The story of the adventures that seventeenth-century law encountered in our lightly settled continent is worth telling because it documents the inevitable failures awaiting any nation that honors the vested powers of the past over the human needs of the present. In addition, the attempts of nineteenth- and twentieth-century reformers to stay within the confines of the old law, despite its obvious inability to cope with ever more severe problems, reveal the special irony of our tradition: our almost universal faith in private property as the anchor of personal freedom, and our recurrent recognition of private property's social, economic, and political tyrannies.

The genius of seventeenth-century land law and the wellspring of its subsequent support lay in its identification of land as a civil liberty instead of as a social resource. A philosopher in any age might state

15

without fear of contradiction that property owes its very being to the society that protects it, and that land law is nothing except the social rules whereby rights in land are transferred from the group to the individual. Yet such a statement was and still is essentially meaningless to New World landowners and land seekers. The first settlers came as land-hungry Europeans, greedy for the freedom and independence that land-ownership necessarily confers in an agricultural society. Even in the New England exception, where old village ways persisted for a time, private ownership of land became the avenue of escape from village and church restraints.

There can be no doubt about the vision of the firstcomers. The proprietors of the earliest settlement corporations sought the least feudal of available English modes of landholding, the Kentish tenure, and later colonists expanded the freedom of that tenure until the energy and enthusiasm of the Revolution swept away all barriers and established our modern fee-simple ownership as the common form in America. Under the Kentish rule no farmer or landowner owed feudal duties of military or other service to a king or lord in return for a right to occupy land. By the same token the ownership of land gave no man govern-mental powers over others; no king, lord, or gentleman had the right to hold special manorial courts, or carry on any other judicial or govern-mental function merely because he owned land or controlled a village of tenants.[1] In America a man owned land and paid taxes, or rented land and paid cash or goods to the landlord, but neither as owner or tenant did anyone have the right to dictate to whom he might or might not sell his land, who might inherit his property, or whom his son or daughter might marry. Such considerations nourished the first settlers' vision of land as a civil right, a right against the long-standing obligations of a crumbling feudal society. The sheer abundance of land here and the almost unlimited possibilities for its ownership fed the fires of enthusi-asm for an individualistic land law. In this popular form the faith of farmers and townsmen in land as a civil liberty meant not only freedom from the meddling of feudal lords or town officials, at least as important, it meant freedom for even the poorest farm family to win autonomy, freedom to profit from rising values in a country teeming with new settlers, and freedom to achieve the dignities and prerogatives that went with the possession of even the smallest holding. In colonial times the

1. Marshall D. Harris, *Origin of the Land Tenure System in the United States,* Ames, Iowa, 1953, pp. 37–38, 99, 191–92.

ownership of land conferred the right to vote and to be a member of the political community; today it means security, credit, and the social standing that is a protection against the harassments of police, welfare, and health officials.

A few ancient customs did endure through colonial times only to be swept away during the American Revolution. The large holdings of the Penn family in Pennsylvania, the Pepperells in Maine, the De Lanceys in New York, and other proprietors of vast royal grants were seized by the states and sold. Primogeniture was abolished. The tradition of the descent of property to the eldest son had never been popular in the colonies, where most people bequeathed their property in equal shares or followed the Biblical custom of a double share for the eldest son and equal shares to all the others. Likewise the right of the landowner to entail his property in his will—that is, to forbid its sale by his descendants—was made illegal. In all the states, constitutions and court decisions confirmed these reforms. Finally the Northwest Ordinances of 1784–87 and the new federal Constitution codified colonial custom and Revolutionary modifications so that thereafter all land west of the Alleghenies would be held and descend according to fee-simple tenure.[2]

This codification meant that most American land has ever since been free to reflect the economic market and to respond to the social and political barometer of contemporary events. No hindrance has been imposed by the existence of giant tracts of land tied up in enduring legal restrictions, except that much of it has customarily remained subject to the traditional prejudice against black ownership of land.[3] Briefly, land could be leased, bought, sold, and bequeathed with great simplicity. Three witnesses and a written document were all that was required for a binding land transaction. As for inheritance, wills again needed only a written document and three witnesses. Resident and nonresident landholders were to be taxed equally, and no tax was to be levied on federal government land. Finally, no private property was to be seized by any governmental agency except under due process of law. A man's property represented his free status, and it was not to be disturbed except for important public purposes, and only then after a full hearing and just compensation.

2. J. Franklin Jameson, *The American Revolution Considered as a Social Movement,* Princeton, 1940; Frank E. Horack, Jr., and Val Noland, Jr., *Land Use Controls, Supplementary Materials on Real Property,* St. Paul, 1955.
3. Leon F. Litwack, *North of Slavery,* Chicago, 1961, pp. 93, 168–70.

Thus the nation emerged from the Revolution and the formation of the Union with the freest land system anywhere in the world. As the first modern republic it quite appropriately basked in its enthusiasm for the rights and liberties of a society of small proprietors. But ugly surprises were in store: the unlooked-for consequences of the play of social and economic forces upon the ultimate scarcity of land itself.

The inability of the traditions of land law and land management to deal with land as a social resource was productive of many disorders, but a few major cases will suffice to demonstrate the seriousness of the error of viewing land only in terms of a civil liberty. In the cities of the nineteenth century the prevailing habits of mind blocked municipal building projects and doomed to short fall even modest efforts to make the environment safe. In the late nineteenth century, when the growing size of the city and the rising values of its downtown land upset all balance between local government and landowner, the law broke down. The builders of skyscrapers pushed their gigantic social and economic costs off upon the municipalities and their fellow citizens. In the suburbs thousands of small proprietors destroyed civil liberties by racial covenants and class and racial zoning. Finally city planning, that most ambitious of all attempts to adapt land tradition to modern urban needs, collapsed under the pressures of the mammoth highway projects of our own day. Despite the best efforts of generations of reformers who have attempted to work without disturbing the basic relationships of private property within our tradition of land law and land management, the American city is the inhumane place it is because we cling to the formulations of the seventeenth century and the myths of a society of small proprietors.

The failure of the public to consider land as a social resource first brought defeat to the concept of a nation of independent landowners in the agricultural areas. The relentless pressure for easy access to public lands led the federal government to adopt a system of automatic disposal of the public domain to private owners. For the first seventy years the government's land-disposal acts (and it has been estimated that one-quarter of all Congressional activity in the nineteenth century was concerned with land legislation) moved in regular progression toward cheaper prices for land and easier methods of acquisition. Until 1800 the smallest unit that could be purchased was a section of 640 acres, the price $1,280. By 1841, under the widely utilized Pre-Emption Act, 160 acres or less could be obtained merely by occupying it and paying the

government $1.25 an acre for it. By 1862, with the passage of the
Homestead Act, a settler could receive 160 acres of surveyed land after
five years' residence upon payment of a registration fee of $26 to $34.[4]

The consequence of this federal policy of easy, unsupervised land
disposal was to deliver up the development of the West—farms, plantations, villages, towns, and cities—to private speculator control. Speculators determined much of the subsequent history of the West because
they had money or had access to capital with which to cover the development costs of the new land, and to the initial investment were added
the costs of clearing, sod-busting, the building of barns and houses,
fences, machinery, drains, livestock, and seed. Given the unequal distribution of capital in the nation, abundant land meant, first and foremost,
abundance for those with capital.

By and large, the federal government sold land at a uniform minimum price; anyone could purchase as much as he wanted. But all land
was not equally valuable. Those who had private capital, or were
bankers or agents for Eastern money, had an enormous advantage. Such
men could purchase a whole valley, a promising townsite, whatever they
wished. They could then sell part of it cheaply to settlers and retain
large tracts and await the substantial price rise that would follow in the
wake of the development of adjacent land. Through large-scale purchases the speculator became a central figure in the allocation of physical resources, and this role was reinforced by his further activity as
local moneylender. The pioneers, whether homesteaders, squatters, or
farmers who could pay cash for land, needed capital for improvements,
and few of them had resources outside their farms. It was inevitable that
the lending of money should give speculators a strong local control over
the development of land owned by others.

The influence of these remote speculators on modern America has
been substantial. In the first place, farm tenancy was introduced and
extended by their hold on land disposal. Squatters customarily had to
borrow money at usurious frontier interest rates to meet the purchase
price of land that had been surveyed and put up for government auction,
and many of them failed or slipped into tenancy at this point. Even
those able to pay for the initial purchase often could not meet the
additional cost of improvements and thus fell into tenancy. In short, the

4. Paul W. Gates, *History of Public Land Law Development,* Washington,
1968, pp. 33–48; Roy M. Robbins, *Our Landed Heritage, The Public Domain,
1776–1936,* Princeton, 1942.

abundance of vacant land did not obviate the need for capital to develop it, and the price of much of this capital was farm tenancy.

Speculators also determined in specific ways the locations of heavy public and private capital expenditures. The history of the placing of a canal, railroad, county seat, college, or hospital is more often than not the history of competition among interested investors who hoped to acquire the overflow benefits for their own properties. For instance, promoters from Cairo, Illinois, long distorted the plans for the route of the Illinois Central Railroad in the hope of making themselves rich in land grants and town locations. Because of their perseverance it took fourteen years of pulling and hauling among local, state, and national interests before the final more rational route could be mapped out. Kansas was torn apart by groups warring for different railroad locations as much as by the issue of slavery, and Atchison is still served by three railroads as a result of the corrupt activities of a speculator named Samuel C. Pomeroy. To such wasteful practices in the field of transportation must also be attributed the impaired functioning of innumerable poorly located colleges, hospitals, and other state and federal institutions. Such are the unfortunate legacies of the large speculator and his hold on legislative chambers.[5]

Finally there was a political result from the federal land policy and its control by local speculators. This control, by concentrating landownership and allocation powers in a few hands in the small towns and cities, settled a vast class of conservative interest across the nation: it installed men who saw the duty of government to be the defense of private property in every town in North America. These men and their successors opposed the introduction of a ten-hour day in their mills, opposed Granger laws, and continue today to work against any legislation that threatens their local economic power. These rural capitalists have been partially bought off in the twentieth century with agricultural subsidies. Their urban counterparts, formerly owners and dealers in municipal government, like the small-town capitalists, are also beginning to be harnessed to the federal government. The big-city real-estate owners, insurance dealers, retail merchants, and contractors are more and more seeking and receiving aid for private business from Washington.

5. Paul W. Gates, "The Role of the Land Speculator in Western Development," and Allan G. Bogue and Margaret B. Bogue, "Profits and the Frontier Land Speculator," in Vernon Carstensen, ed., *The Public Lands*, Madison, 1963, pp. 349–94.

Another heritage from the federal land system of the early nine-teenth century is the federal survey system that underlies the mapping of most neighborhoods west of the Alleghenies. The survey's basic element was the township, a square six miles on a side subdivided into thirty-six square sections of 640 acres each. These townships and their subdividing lines have contributed permanent features to our urban landscape.[6] Today in most parts of the nation the pedestrian or motorist moves along straight streets bordered by rows of shade trees. Ahead is a distant horizon, not a wall of buildings that gives him a sense of urban en-closure. Flanking him are rows of small buildings, usually wooden, freestanding, and set back from the street by lawns. This standard visual environment, compounded of the commonplace tradition of wooden house construction and the constraints of the rectangular survey, is our visual heritage. It is the townscape we repeat over and over on a slightly expanded scale, and with surprisingly few modifications, in the suburbs of megalopolis.

What the grid failed to do was to produce centered and bounded neighborhoods. Without parks or plazas it lacked a center; the natural center of the federal land survey became the main street, the highway strip. Although such commercial concentrations were expedient, they failed to mark town centers or subcenters, as plazas do or as the old New England town green with its meetinghouse did. In addition the open grid pattern provided no fixed boundaries for neighborhoods, no point from which city dwellers could define their own vicinity visually and socially against the endless metropolitan complex.

Within large cities the concept of land as a civil liberty brought repeated failures with highly serious and enduring consequences. The Northwest Ordinance of 1787 and the Constitution of the United States in its Fifth and Fourteenth Amendments both specified that no private property should be seized by any agency of the government or any corporation granted the government's rights except by proper hearing, proper compensation, and for a legitimate public purpose. The Fifth Amendment states: ". . . nor shall private property be taken for public use without just compensation." And the words of the Fourteenth Amendment are: "No State shall . . . deprive any person of life, liberty, or property, without due process of law; nor deny to any person within its jurisdiction the equal protection of the laws." American courts

6. Norman J. W. Thrower, *Original Survey and Land Subdivision,* Chicago, 1966.

have interpreted these statements to mean that, above and beyond the private landowner's right to compensation for his property, there stands some residual right against the government, perhaps best described as a right not to be disturbed unless some public purpose requires the seizure of his property. Neither the state nor the federal government may interpose its power to seize property merely for the purpose of transferring land from one private owner to another.

In the early nineteenth century these provisions of the Fifth Amendment and the Northwest Ordinances, and similar provisions in state constitutions, caused no difficulties. Courts interpreted as "public purpose" whatever public bodies ordered. Private companies formed for the purpose of constructing turnpikes and bridges were given the state powers of eminent domain in order to assemble their rights of way. Milldams, canals, telegraph lines, projects for waterworks or gasworks, and municipal markets all went forward by virtue of the use of state or federal powers of eminent domain.

During the Jacksonian era, as public projects became larger and private corporations (especially those formed for canal and railroad projects) gained strength, the courts began to narrow the definition of public purpose, hoping thereby to limit governmental action. Railroads appeared as dangerous monopolies and showed themselves powerful enough to purchase entire legislatures. Farmers and city dwellers feared that they would lose their farms and homes to railroad rights-of-way, as people today fear the incursions of highway projects. Cities and towns and even states went into bankruptcy in the 1840s and 1850s because they had pledged public funds to private canal and railroad corporations. Large-scale municipal corruption began to be revealed, and a general bias against governmental undertakings of all sorts set in. For the next half century the powers of eminent domain were increasingly narrowed by a succession of court decisions.[7]

Thus at the very moment when municipal projects needed to be enlarged to accommodate themselves to the ever-growing American city, the courts began to restrict municipal powers over land. Boston, even after a disastrous fire in 1872, was forbidden to use city funds to aid owners of private property in an ambitious redevelopment scheme for the downtown area.

In Boston also the common law had allowed the city to seize surplus

7. Philip Nichols, Jr., "The Meaning of Public Use in the Law of Eminent Domain," *Boston University Law Review,* 20 (November 1940), 615–41.

land surrounding a public building and sell it back to private owners, on condition that they develop their private parcels in a manner harmonious with the new public one. In 1910 a conservative court forbade such condemnations, although the city had followed this identical procedure when it built its handsome Quincy Market in 1825.[8] A Pennsylvania court forbade similar practice in that state.

The municipal and state reforms of the Progressive era of the early twentieth century, however, did slowly widen judicial narrowness in this field. Between 1911 and 1933, fifteen states either amended their constitutions or enacted specific legislation to allow more generous condemnation rights so that land near public highways and buildings could be controlled as part of the projects themselves. At the same time state and federal courts relaxed the rules laid down in the previous century, but they failed to return to the full freedom of action of the earliest years of the nation.[9] The continued sway of the conservative judicial heritage has proved a grave misfortune for the American city.

During the New Deal the Federal Emergency Administrator of Public Works, in response to unemployment, instituted a number of public housing projects to make work for the building trades and to create cheap, sanitary, low-cost shelter. These were the first peacetime public housing projects ever undertaken by the federal government, indeed among the first by any American governmental agency. Many saw them as a radical departure, a long step toward European socialist methods.

At that moment a United States Circuit Court, reviving the waning doctrine of public purpose, ruled in the *Louisville Lands* case that the federal government could not condemn private land for low-cost housing: such undertakings exceeded the powers of the Constitution and were therefore not legitimately to be defined as public purpose.[10] One circuit judge dissented and the decision was later overruled, but the political damage had been done. Just when Congress was debating the

---

8. Walter H. Kilham, *Boston After Bulfinch,* Cambridge, 1964, p. 22.

9. For examples of judicial confusion, such as an interpretation that the Fourteenth Amendment forbade excess condemnation even though a state's constitution specifically authorized such a practice, see *Cincinnati* v. *Vester,* 33 Federal 2d 242 (1929), 281 U.S. 439 (1929); for the newer liberality, holding that a government may seize property for the benefit of a private person if the transaction is related to an important public purpose, see *International Paper Co.* v. *United States,* 282 U.S. 399 (1931).

10. *United States* v. *Certain Lands in the City of Louisville,* 78 Federal 2d 684 (1935).

issue of public housing and popular opinion was clearly divided, this ruling made the supporters of federal participation in the field decide to abandon direct action and to institute in its place an indirect grants-in-aid program. This modification, originally designed to soften the opposition of conservatives between 1935 and 1937, has created the structure under which all federal housing and urban renewal has gone forward ever since. As a consequence, housing and renewal efforts have been tied to the boundaries of each municipal corporation, and our national administrative powers in respect to housing have depended upon the capabilities of municipal civil servants. In the context of today's concerns, this structure has meant that until after World War II public housing was racially segregated according to each city's traditions; it means at present that public housing cannot be located in a metropolis on the basis of free choice but only in accordance with the class and racial prejudices of each municipal subdivision.[11]

Finally, the narrow interpretation of the public-purpose doctrine has contributed to an unforeseen pejorative attitude toward contemporary housing projects. The doctrine, first meant to cast judicial suspicion on all projects, persists in the superheated language concerning poverty, disease, and moral decay used to justify public land appropriations. The dissenting judge in the *Louisville Lands* case, trying to uphold the project under the doctrine of police and welfare powers, said, "The slum is the breeding place of disease and crime. . . . If disease and crime are to be rooted out of slum neighborhoods, the residents must be placed in houses which they can rent or buy. The wrecking of the rookeries must be followed by new and inexpensive housing." The famous New York case, *New York City Housing Authority* v. *Muller,* supporting public housing followed, and it confirmed the principle of public action on the ground of the "menace" of the slum.[12] So lawyers have been arguing ever since. To fight off the conservative attack on public projects and to guard against a return to a set of dubious nineteenth-century precedents, our courts and newspapers still reiterate "menace" and "blight." Instead of testifying to the positive need of our fellow citizens for decent homes, we feel a compulsion to frighten ourselves with the specter of cancerous social ills.

11. Some Southern cities have even used their municipal independence under urban-renewal and public housing grants to move blacks about in order to create single ghettos where Negro settlements were scattered through the city. Theodore J. Lowi, *The End of Liberalism*, New York, 1969, pp. 251–66.

12. *New York City Housing Authority* v. *Muller,* 270 New York 333 (1936).

The unreasonable warping of municipal and public housing programs was by no means the only legacy of the legal escalation of the dimensions of private landownership. In hundreds of ways this narrow focus prevented our cities from responding successfully to the conditions of their own growth. To put it most simply, while the American tradition of land management was concentrating on the rights of the owners of each bit of land, the city was growing into a giant system whose interactions and intercommunications spread over many miles. Despite immense public works, the stretching of old common-law concepts, the invention of zoning, and the institution of the practice of city planning, the tradition has proved unable either to meet the new need to treat land as a social resource or to defend the old reliance on land as the basis of personal freedom.

Cities attempted to resolve the conflicts between the integrity of each small plot and the growing interdependencies of the city in two ways: by establishing networks of public services in the streets to bind together individual parcels, and by expanding the regulations of private behavior outward from the old common-law base. As early as the epidemic of 1793, Philadelphia discovered that each section of personal property could not safely support a private well. That year, yellow fever killed four thousand residents, a twelfth of the population. Such plagues returned to Philadelphia and other cities for the next seventy years. Slowly, first in Philadelphia and then in Baltimore, Boston, and New York, the booming cities invested millions upon millions of dollars to construct public waterworks.[13] In their finished form these systems carried pure water through the streets parallel to the boundaries of each private lot, and the cities spent more millions to build sewers to carry off the wastes.[14] Toward the same objective—a safe and sanitary city— municipal authorities hired street-cleaning crews and instituted trash and garbage collection. In addition to this publicly financed effort, the concentrated population of the large cities made it possible for many new services to be offered for profit by municipal or private monopolies: coal gas for cooking and lighting, electricity, street railways, and elevated

13. Nelson M. Blake, *Water for the Cities,* Syracuse, 1956.
14. The magnitude of this sanitary effort is not commonly appreciated by historians. It can be grasped immediately by a survey of the annual reports of any city or of summaries like Charles P. Huse's *The Financial History of Boston,* Cambridge, 1916. Twentieth-century municipalities, however, have failed to carry on this effort with the same energy as in the past, thereby contributing to today's ecological crisis. See Solomon Fabricant, *The Trend in Government Activity in the United States Since 1900,* New York, 1952, pp. 72–83.

and subway systems. The regulation of these monopolies in the interest of the mass of small consumers proved exceedingly difficult and occupied a major place in the nineteenth- and early twentieth-century politics. All in all, the multiplication of public and private utilities was a major accomplishment of the nineteenth-century city and one in which contemporaries took justifiable pride.[15]

Yet the entire century, for all its accomplishments, was in fact the backdrop for a seesaw battle waged by municipal services and timid regulations against the behavior of landlords and the excessive individualism of the land law. As booming growth offered chances for profit in slum housing and sweatshops, private owners increasingly ignored or attacked the health and safety of their fellow men by intolerable crowding of streets and structures and by deliberately cutting off light and air from tenants and neighbors. Only very slowly and cautiously were the old public duties of landowners redefined to combat some of these urban conditions. The ancient prohibitions of nuisance law, such as those against noxious trades, dangerous construction, and disorderly houses, were slowly expanded to support fire, health, and building codes. These codes specified the materials and methods of construction that would make buildings slow-burning or fireproof and that walls and floors must be structurally sound. Ultimately health codes for tenements and multiple dwellings set forth the number of persons who might legally occupy a single room, the size of windows, provision of water and toilets, and so on. But enforcement of such regulations has never been popular, and there has always been much evasion of them in declining neighborhoods.[16]

The weaknesses of the nineteenth-century achievements lay in the legal moat surrounding private land. Affirmative municipal action had to stop at the margin of the street. If toilets, lights, fire barriers, windows, stairs, and central heating were to be installed, the landowner had to do it, and execution therefore was dependent upon his financial capabilities and his personal willingness to modernize. Philadelphia, as the pioneer in waterworks, was the first to discover that to bring a water pipe to the

15. The complementary public and private amenities of the century are discussed in James Marston Fitch, *American Building,* v. 1, 2nd ed., Boston, 1966, p. 108.

16. Joseph D. McGoldrick, Seymour Graubard, and Raymond J. Horowitz, *Building Regulation in New York City,* New York, 1944, pp. 38–145; Edith Abbott and Sophonisba Breckinridge, *The Tenements of Chicago, 1908–1935,* Chicago, 1936.

sidewalk was still a long step from installing taps, toilets, or tubs inside the houses. For the urban poor, a generation and even longer elapsed before owners of slum properties installed plumbing.[17] Within the boundaries of the private lot itself the city could only admonish, harass, and fine; it could not install or repair on its own initiative. Such was the tenderness of the law toward landlords that the tenant (and many more than half of America's city dwellers were tenants until after World War II) could neither withhold his rent nor sue for damages for his land-lord's failure to comply with regulations. Nor could landowners compel the owners of nearby property to conform to the codes of the day, even though neglected, mismanaged property lowered the value of the entire block. So stubbornly has our law rejected the social dimensions of property ownership that even today tenants' unions, rent strikes, private rights of action for code violations, and municipally executed repairs stand in the vanguard of our urban politics and property law.[18] Mean-while, everywhere in the vast aging tracts of our cities the private owner's personal profit, the tenant's poverty, the neighborhood's obso-lescence, and the law's timidity conspire to maintain dangerous structures, and millions of houses, stores, and blocks stand well below current standards for a decent living environment.

   In Europe, especially after World War I, when the limitations of regulation had become clear, cities undertook massive public housing programs. In Germany and Sweden substantial fractions of the building costs were offset by municipal participation in the land market. Cities, like private speculators, purchased outlying farms in anticipation of future growth, and in later years when these sites were developed for housing the municipality itself reaped the profit from its investment.[19] In America most cities were and are forbidden by statute and state constitution to enter the private land market freely, and neither city, state, nor federal government receives much popular support for major public housing programs. Compared to the rest of the modern world, we have started late and done little. As city dwellers, we have remained what we were as farmers: a nation of small proprietors, jealously pro-

   17. Sam Bass Warner, Jr., *The Private City: Philadelphia in Three Periods of Its Growth,* Philadelphia, 1968, pp. 109–11.
   18. National Commission on Urban Problems, *Legal Remedies for Housing Code Violations, Research Report No. 14,* Frank P. Grad, ed., Washington, 1968, pp. 109–48.
   19. Shirley S. Passow, "Land Resources and Teamwork in Planning Stockholm," *Journal of the American Institute of Planners,* 36 (May 1970), 179–88.

tecting our individual property rights as if they were the cornerstone of
our civil liberties. Public housing here has been a mean and narrow
philanthropy. We have steadfastly protected the privileges of millions of
small owners and have refused to provide decent protection against rats,
cold, disease, overcrowding, and fire for millions more.

The inability of such a tradition to cope with the positive issues of
city building is nicely illustrated by the history of zoning. In this case the
problem was to deal with urban growth, a new kind of downtown, and a
new kind of residential area, instead of with residential obsolescence and
lingering poverty. The response of the law, given its traditional mold,
could be only regulatory, as it had always been. It attempted to order
growth under the guise of preserving established values, allowing titanic
costs to be pushed on those at the center of the metropolis, and it
permitted the wholesale denial of civil liberties to be imposed at the
growing residential periphery.

The standard zoning ordinance of American cities was originally
conceived from a union of two fears—fear of the Chinese and fear of
skyscrapers. In California a wave of racial prejudice had swept over the
state after Chinese settlers were imported to build the railroads and
work in the mines. Ingenious lawyers in San Francisco found that the
old common law of nuisance could be applied for indirect discrimination
against the Chinese in situations where the constitution of the state
forbade direct discrimination. Chinese laundries of the 1880s had
become social centers for Chinese servants who lived outside the China-
town ghetto. To whites they represented only clusters of "undesirables"
in the residential areas where Chinese were living singly among them as
house servants. By declaring the laundries nuisances and fire hazards,
San Francisco hoped to exclude Chinese from most sections of the city
and to break the Oriental monopoly of the operation of laundries.
Indeed the first statute, imperfect as it was, threatened to put 310 laundries out of business. The San Francisco ordinance failed to pass in the
federal courts because it gave arbitrary powers of racial discrimination
to a Board of Supervisors.[20] The city of Modesto, however, used the
device of dividing the city into two zones, one permitting laundries and
one excluding them, and in this way squeezed past the constraints of the
state constitution and the Fourteenth Amendment:

20. The San Francisco attempt foiled: *Yick Wo* v. *Hopkins, Sheriff,* 118 U.S.
356 (1886).

It shall be unlawful for any person to establish, maintain, or carry on the business of a public laundry or washhouse where articles are washed or cleansed for hire, within the City of Modesto, except within that part of the city which lies west of the railroad tracks and south of G street.[21]

Such nuisance-zone statutes spread down the Pacific coast. They were directed against laundries, livery stables, saloons, dance halls, pool halls, and slaughterhouses. In Los Angeles during the years from 1909 to 1915, successive ordinances culminated in something very like a modern land-use, structure-type zoning statute. The whole of Los Angeles was divided into three districts of specified classifications: one restricted to residences, in which only the lightest manufacturing was permitted, a second open to any sort of industry, and a third open both to residence and to a limited list of industries. The California precedents, when joined with the regulations of Washington, Baltimore, Indianapolis, and Boston in respect to fire precautions, building heights, and strictures on construction, served to create the New York Zoning Law of 1916, the prototype statute of the nation.[22]

In New York a new high-density form of land use, the skyscraper, threatened the established functioning of the low retail blocks of the city. The earliest skyscrapers, though modest by today's standards, broke the traditional relationship between street width and building height which had controlled Western building for centuries. Masonry construction had hitherto limited buildings to a maximum height of six to eight stories. Then, with the perfection in the late 1880s of steel-frame construction, structures of from nine to sixteen stories became feasible.[23] Thanks to the urban concentration effected by electric street railways, elevateds, and subways, land rent skyrocketed in downtown areas, and in response to the soaring values steel frame skyscrapers mushroomed in Chicago and New York, at first for office buildings and later for department stores and factories.

In New York the Fifth Avenue Association, a group composed of men who owned or leased the city's most expensive retail land, demanded that the city protect their luxury blocks from encroachment by the new tall buildings of the garment district. The problem was quite

21. *In re Hang Kie,* 69 California 149 (1886).
22. W. L. Pollard, "Outline of the Law of Zoning in the United States," *Annals of the American Academy of Political and Social Science,* 155 (May 1931), 15–33; John Delafons, *Land-Use Controls in the United States,* Cambridge, 1966, pp. 18–24.
23. Carl W. Condit, *American Building,* Chicago, 1968, pp. 124–30; Homer Hoyt, *One Hundred Years of Land Values in Chicago,* Chicago, 1933, p. 150.

specific. Jewish garment manufacturers had captured the national market for ready-made clothing by perfecting highly specialized methods of manufacture, and the rapidly expanding industry required more space than could be bought or rented in the congested lower East Side locale in which the Jewish firms had first located. Nearby real-estate firms thereupon assembled parcels occupied by small old buildings, which they tore down and replaced by eight- to twelve-story lofts for the garment manufacturers. By this process the garment industry had spilled over twenty blocks north of Fourteenth Street in the first decade of the twentieth century.[24] The Fifth Avenue Association feared that the ensuing decades would see the lofts invading their best properties, bringing with them lunch-hour crowds and a blockade of wagons, trucks, and carts. In short, they feared that skyscraper lofts, low-paid help, and traffic congestion would drive their middle-class and wealthy customers from the Avenue. The needs of the Fifth Avenue Association were met by joining their protests to those of other regulatory interest groups throughout the city, and a successful coalition for the passing and enforcement of zoning ordinances was formed.

It was a Brooklyn lawyer and politician who put together the ingredients that propelled the nation's zoning law and zoning policies. He was Edward M. Bassett (1863–1948), who had been serving on the State Public Service Commission that planned New York's subways. He established the practice whereby a zoning map would be drawn only after the most extensive hearings in the neighborhoods themselves, so that local landholding interests might participate. Indeed, the private property owners in the small areas of the city were in effect to draw the residential maps.[25] Such an inclusive administrative process could succeed because the rationale of zoning was aimed not at disturbing existing conditions but at projecting current trends into the future and perpetuating them. Nonconforming use of land remained, but it was hoped that adjacent majority practice would perpetuate the norm in subsequent years.

Bassett himself stressed the preservation of "the character of the district." In the suburbs zoning would protect homeowners by maintaining the uniformity of their neighborhoods, and real-estate men who held

24. Robert M. Haig and Roswell C. McCrea, *Major Economic Factors in Metropolitan Growth and Arrangement, Regional Survey of New York and Its Environs,* v. 1, New York, 1927, pp. 80–94.
25. Stanislaw J. Makielski, Jr., *The Politics of Zoning: The New York Experience,* New York, 1966, pp. 7–40.

vacant land could proceed to build upon their small tracts in confidence that the adjoining ones would be improved according to the uses specified on the zoning map. One-, two-, and multiple-family houses would spread out in orderly paths, while apartments would march along the principal streetcar lines and cluster at the subway stations. For the dealers in commercial real estate the zones stabilized the current downtown and suburban uses, leaving abundant room for the future growth of industry and commerce. Zoning in sum contravened none of the expansion patterns of the city, but it did protect all classes of residents from the most unscrupulous and speculative use of individual parcels of land. Furthermore, it encouraged uniformity of development, which by then had become the fashion of the real-estate industry. So popular was the New York Zoning Law of 1916 that it was copied by 591 cities in the next decade. Bassett himself was invited to draft a model statute for the United States Department of Commerce, and this was widely adopted after its publication in 1924.

According to this standard form, a typical zoning law consisted of three elements. First, there was a map of the city on which all private land was assigned to a particular area or zone. Second, the restrictions applying to each of these zones were itemized. They included the height, number of floors, and general size of any structure that could be permitted *in the future* to be built on land in a particular zone. In addition, the percentage of the lot area that might be covered by building, the size of yards, courts, and open spaces, and the population density were all specified. Third, calling upon the precedents of the past half century, there was a recital that this set of restrictions on private property was legitimate and constitutional because it represented the traditional exercise of police power in cities and states and that it was directed toward the protection of the health, safety, morals, and general welfare of citizens; that these principles could best be served by preventing overcrowding, facilitating transportation, conserving the value of existing property, and guaranteeing adequate light and air in all habitations.

As the years passed and the patterns of growth and decay in the city shifted from the density of the early twentieth century to the diffused multicentered megalopolis of the post–World War II era, the consequences of zoning became clear. Just as zoning had given the wealthy retailers of Fifth Avenue a means of defense against the encroaching garment factories, so subsequent zoning gave suburbanites a defense against "undesirable" activities and people. No sooner had the New

York ordinance been passed than the South seized upon the device as a way to extend its laws and practices of racial segregation. A Louisville ordinance creating zones for whites and for blacks was declared unconstitutional in 1917 in the case *Buchanan* v. *Warley*,[26] but more subtle zoning refinements continued to plague the courts until 1948. Everywhere zoning laws interacted with real-estate prices to reinforce segregation by income, national origin, and race within the cities. Stipulations in zoning ordinances that single-family homes should prevail over two-family homes or apartments, or that one-acre lots were to be required instead of quarter-acre lots, had powerful social repercussions in a society of mixed population and markedly unequal distribution of family income.[27] A land or structure limitation therefore became a financial, racial, and ethnic limitation by pricing certain groups out of particular suburbs. Italians were held at bay in Boston, Poles in Detroit, blacks in Chicago and St. Louis, Jews in New York. At times, especially during the 1920s, racial and ethnic covenants conspired with zoning to prevent "non-Caucasians" (Jews, blacks, Orientals) from even purchasing land. Such practices struck at the root of the ancient justification of American land law. By severing the connection between personal freedom and property ownership, the very being of our law which held private property to be the basis of a man's civil liberties perished. In 1948 the Supreme Court finally ruled such contracts unenforceable,[28] but the class and racial consequences of the interaction between the unequal distribution of income and zoning spread unabated.

Zoning, as planned and executed by each political subdivision of the industrial metropolis, also lashed city building to petty political divisions and produced the same conditions that later hamstrung the federal grants-in-aid program for public housing. Each city and town in the emerging megalopolis was a zoning entity. During the twenties real-estate dealers' enthusiasm for expansion and for uniformity of practice lessened the differences among suburbs. The Babbitts controlled the politics of most suburbs, and they mapped generous tracts for all kinds of new building: for modest homes, apartments, and shopping streets. Their social generosity was spurred by the knowledge that subdivision and store building offered the highest profit to the land developer. The

26. *Buchanan* v. *Warley*, 245 U.S. 60 (1917).
27. According to a recent estimate, two-thirds of the zoned vacant land in the New York Metropolitan Region now calls for one-family houses on lots of half an acre or larger, and almost half of this land is zoned for lots of one acre or larger. Regional Plan Association, *The Region's Growth*, New York, 1967, p. 68.
28. *Shelley* v. *Kraemer*, 334 U.S. 1 (1948).

real-estate man, except in a few of the wealthiest suburbs, was not the enemy of the lower middle class in their advance out of the core city but a booster who tried to promote their exodus.

After World War II the diffusion of the automobile quickened the pace and lengthened the reach of the urban middle class and even of the working class and thereby made suburbanization possible for a larger mass of people than in the twenties. A different attitude, however, now appeared among the older residents of suburban communities. Instead of seeing all growth as good, selling their property for a profit and moving on, as they would once have done, they now tried to use zoning to protect their established pattern of light settlement against developer encroachment, to defend their comfortable style of low-density living against a cheaper and more congested style. Also frequently now, a particular social group—white Protestant, Jewish, or Catholic—was resisting new classes, new ethnic groups and races. Accordingly, regulations that limit an entire town to single-family occupancy or to minimum lot sizes of one, two, or even four acres have been enacted in order to preserve intact the existing social context of lightly settled suburbs.[29] The established residents, having lost faith in the value of continuous growth, see no improvement in their towns as development robs them of their view, their orchard, or their beach, however much development may raise the value of property in general. They are in fact fighting for what they regard as their de facto rights in the unused farmlands, fields, or woods adjacent to their own land. The established have increasingly fought, and are still fighting, many of the suburban developers within the megalopolis in an effort to block the granting of variances or the alteration of old zones to include apartments and shopping centers, sometimes whole new suburbs.

By and large, suburban defenses since the Second World War have enabled a significant number of well-organized communities to limit their growth by halting or delaying development. But the cost has been high. These campaigns have added a new level of antisocial bias to the ordinary life of America. The success of one town in halting development implies an ability to ignore the legitimate needs of its neighbors. The fact that the builders of downtown skyscrapers were seizing light and air and street use from their neighbors was a salient motive for zoning in the first instance, and their behavior is now echoed on a wider

29. David S. Schoenbrod, "Large Lot Zoning," *Yale Law Journal,* 78 (July 1969), 1418–41.

scale as the wealthy and the firstcomers join hands to seal off the best land of the megalopolis from the mass of their fellow citizens.[30]

Downtown zoning was no better able to achieve a balance between public needs and private power. The first generation of zoning officials hoped that regulations to limit the height and bulk of buildings would supplement the health and tenement regulations already in effect and assure neighborhoods of decent housing. But the price and total volume of housing units available in a city proved so much more important to the erection of low-income housing than density charts setting forth future construction that the zoning rules proved irrelevant. The mortgage rate and the timing of building booms turned out to be the crucial variables in new construction, and zoning was in any case of little help to the masses of city dwellers who had to live in secondhand housing.

Also, the skyscraper could not be denied. In the 1920s downtown areas across the United States continued to boom on the basis of transit, railroad, and streetcar transportation and of inner-city manufacturing. Given the consequent high land values, real-estate firms insisted that zoning allow generous corridors or islands of blocks where skyscrapers could be built, and towers sprang up in clusters all over America. The public burdens imposed by this sustained boom in tall buildings were enormous. The skyscrapers shut off light and air from the passing pedestrian as they did from workers in the adjacent factories and offices and cast whole blocks of old-fashioned structures in the shade. The lofty height of the towers created a special microclimate of high winds in winter and sizzling streets and oven-hot masonry walls in summer.[31] The fabric of utility and municipal services so painfully assembled over the previous century had to be totally reconstructed in the downtowns of all major American cities. It is by no means clear that the costs of the new electric substations, post offices, and gas, telephone, and water lines were borne exclusively by the skyscraper builders and users. Utility rates favor the biggest consumers, and this reworking of the utility network may well have been partially financed by less impressive commercial and residential consumers.[32] Whatever the facts in respect to utilities, the

30. Seymour I. Toll, *The Zoned American*, New York, 1969, pp. 254–310; *New York Times*, August 17, 1971, pp. 1, 39.
31. Lawrence Halprin and Associates, *New York, New York: A Study of the Quality, Character, and Meaning of Open Space in Urban Design*, New York, 1968, p. 21.
32. Jack Hirshleifer et al., *Water Supply, Economics, Technology, and Policy*, Chicago, 1960, pp. 87–113; Charles F. Phillips, Jr., *Economics of Regulation*, Homewood, Illinois, 1965, pp. 351–70.

land and transportation reconstruction necessary to make these metropolitan cores workable placed a gigantic burden on the twentieth-century city. Acres of old blocks had to be encumbered with superstructures and substructures and assaulted by noise to accommodate new elevated and subway systems, and many more acres had to be leveled to permit traffic access to the central towers. This upheaval, wholly municipally financed from 1900 to 1930, went forward on a scale equal to the urban renewal of the 1950s and 1960s, and so overwhelming were the costs that for the first time in our history public works drove our major cities toward bankruptcy.

This rebuilding was disguised under the architectural slogans of the City Beautiful movement. Since the Chicago Columbian Exposition of 1893, visions of beautifying the crowded and unrelieved commercialism of the downtown areas had captured the popular imagination and kindled it by suggestions of a classical civic and cultural center incorporating an art museum, a city hall, courthouse, perhaps even an opera house. Yet the most costly elements in these schemes, and furthermore those most important for implementing the skyscraper core, were the new subways and the baroque boulevards and malls that had to be constructed to open traffic routes to the downtown areas. This was of course the case in Chicago's lakeside improvements, Philadelphia's Fairmount Parkway, or St. Louis's Market Street development.[33] In New York, land prices were too high for street reform to be undertaken, and a subway network was added instead to existing streetcar and elevated lines. When the Depression struck in 1929, the capabilities of municipal finance had been so distended by street and subway reconstruction that the cities could not meet the welfare obligations they had honored since the formation of the Republic.

Finally, since zoning was a complex of guidelines and not a positive building program in its own right, it had no power to reverse the trends of obsolescence that overtook the vast core areas of the megalopolis after World War II. In such areas zoning could not even maintain the majority practice of their residents. Some of them who had grown old with their homes now took in roomers or added apartments for added income despite zoning or the effects on abutting property. In addition, the sluggish market for aging structures often meant a considerable support at City Hall (and frequently in the neighborhoods) for variances permitting lower zoning classifications or industrial encroachment.

33. Werner Hegemann and Elbert Peets, *The American Vitruvius: An Architect's Handbook of Civic Art*, New York, 1922.

In all, zoning failed to resolve the conflict between private land-ownership and the increasing interdependence within the megalopolis. In cases in which it was effective, it insulated residential areas against newcomers of lower income, sometimes to the extent of being a de facto abridgment of classes' and minorities' civil rights. As a planning tool it did not supplement public programs for highways, housing, schools, and utilities; it simply set a seal of approval on what was being done in any case.

The reliance of American law upon the regulatory approach to city building problems, which zoning typified, meant the atrophy of the promising young discipline of city planning and has contributed to its collapse in our own time. Planning practice has clearly been ineffectual in confronting the tremendous conflicts inherent in such undertakings as national interstate highways or federally sponsored urban renewal. City planning was a contemporary of zoning; both of them emerged in the Progressive era.

Planning was compounded of European precedents and the native movement to introduce orderly management into the business of city government. The pioneers in city planning saw urban land as a limited social and economic resource, and they hoped to coordinate its orderly development with the heavy capital investments of cities—in utilities, schools, streets, fire equipment, and so on—by means of rational advance planning. Finding themselves barred by native political and legal traditions from direct participation in the development process, unable themselves to buy and sell land or to build utilities or housing, planners soon fell back into an advisory role and lapsed into mapmaking. The best that the municipalities who hired them could offer was a coordinating function, and they did do much to order the relationships among parks, schools, public works, city engineers, and private real-estate interests. The high level of amenities of the residential developments after the First World War in those cities which maintained planning offices stands as a monument to the efforts of these men. Yet in most cities land development could move ahead only in step with zoning regulations, and the preparation of the zoning maps was the peculiar province of planners. Accordingly, municipal planning staffs spent most of their time in drawing zoning maps and holding hearings on zoning changes.[34] The result has been that the profession has become chained

34. John L. Hancock, "Planners in the Changing American City, 1900–1940," *Journal of the American Institute of Planners,* 33 (September 1967), 290–304.

to its maps, and no procedures except zoning have emerged for the democratic resolution of land-use conflicts. No procedures have evolved that can take account of interests other than the traditional market evaluation of a specific structure and its lot; no procedures have arisen to arbitrate between concerns of the neighborhood and concerns of the city as a whole. In terms of justice and efficiency, the interstate highway program and the federal renewal program should have had access to both sorts of procedure, but neither sort has been or is yet available to the American metropolis.

The interstate highway system owes its inception, politics, and concerns to issues far removed from the worries of San Francisco homeowners or Fifth Avenue merchants. Its origins lay in a popular demand to lift the farmers' wagons out of the mud, and its form unfolded from the logic learned in a series of highway programs that were undertaken to end rural isolation. The coalition that launched the federal highway program was compounded of diverse elements. Among them were the urban bicycling enthusiasts who clamored for paving beyond the city limits, automobile manufacturers whose cars could fulfill the salesmen's promises only on decent roads, farm-state Representatives and Senators who personally experienced the rural mire in spring, professors in agricultural colleges who felt a continuing concern for the social isolation and economic handicaps of farm families, and highway officials in those prosperous states which had begun to take an active role in implementing and supervising county and town roadbuilding. After a series of campaigns, the joint efforts of such groups culminated in the passage of the 1916 Federal Aid Roads Act.

The 1916 act set the administrative framework for American roadbuilding in the twentieth century. The framework is worth understanding, since the authors of the act specifically debated and rejected proposals for continued county control of roadbuilding and chose instead state-wide administration. When localism does appear in highway legislation, it is tightly restrained by the much more powerful state structure. In the 1930s the federal highway program was expanded to include aid to counties for secondary road construction, but this was a minor supplement to a large and continuing federal-state administration. This turn away from extreme localism stands in strong contrast to the opposite strategy of federal housing, where, as urban renewal became ever more varied and complex, the federal effort was confined and crippled by the original local administrative framework.

The 1916 act required every state, as a condition of federal aid, to establish a state highway department to plan routes, supervise construction, and maintain the roads that federal funds helped to build. The Bureau of Public Roads of the U.S. Department of Agriculture was to restrict itself to approval of the plans of state-proposed projects, inspection of workmanship, and reimbursement of the state for 50 percent of the cost of approved roads. A formula based on population, area, and mileage of rural free delivery postal routes determined the apportionment of federal funds among the states. This administrative structure has remained and has determined the direction of state and federal highway projects ever since. The basic act of 1921 confirmed this structure and strengthened national goals by adding the provision that state highway departments should be subject to orderly scheduling in their projects so that the ensuing road system would be integrated and interconnected. From this provision there emerged in 1925 and 1926 the uniformly numbered "U.S." highway routes, and these served as the skeleton of intercity highway traffic until the interstate highways of the 1960s were constructed.[35]

Until 1944 no federal highway funds were expended on urban needs; the problem was seen as a national one, calling for the construction of thousands of miles of rural roads rather than for the paving of city streets. The only federal work done in the cities was a by-product of New Deal public works employment projects undertaken to improve state routes that passed through cities. Of course the building of a national network of two-lane, all-weather intercity roads was bound to bring with it increasing reliance on automobile transportation and therefore mounting traffic jams. At the time of the initial Federal Aid Roads Act in 1916 there were 3,618,000 buses, trucks, and cars registered in the United States; they had increased to 10,494,000 at the passage of the basic 1921 act. There were 25,262,000 in 1934, when federal funds were called for to be used in research to forecast highway planning, and 31,010,000 by 1939, when the major summary of that research appeared.[36]

35. American Association of State Highway Officials, *A Story of the Beginning, Purposes, Growth, Activities and Achievements of AASHO*, Washington, 1964, pp. 152–55, 169–77.
36. U.S. Bureau of the Census, *Historical Statistics of the United States, Colonial Times to 1957*, Washington, 1960, p. 462.

Urban Transportation

1. Horsecar, 4th Avenue near 10th Street, New York City, ca. 1865. The world's urban transportation revolution began with the introduction of horsecar service by the New York and Harlem Railroad in 1832. Twenty years elapsed before city growth caught up with the innovation, but, by the Civil War, streetcar tracks crisscrossed the streets of every major city in America. The standard specifications: two horses, a driver and a conductor; 40 passengers in comfort, up to 74 in a squeeze, five-cent fare; and an average speed of six miles per hour. *New-York Historical Society*

2. Cable Cars at 55th Street and Cottage Grove Avenue, Chicago, ca. 1902. Cable cars, introduced in San Francisco in 1873 to cope with its hills, in the 1880s moved heavy traffic along main streets leading to downtown in other cities. Horsecar networks stretched ten to fifteen miles from the city's center in a feeder system to the faster (ten to twelve miles per hour) cable lines, much as today suburban streets merge with superhighways. Unlike the high-speed highway, this modest innovation did not destroy abutting neigh- borhoods but rather nourished spines of apartments and stores along its routes. *Library of Congress*

3. Electric Streetcars on Madison Street, Chicago, 1906. For a time, the electric-powered streetcar, first put into practical operation in Richmond, Virginia, in 1887–88, and introduced in every city during the nineties, seemed the answer to big-city traffic problems. Cheaper to install than cable lines and faster than the horsecar, it could reach suburbs, or be linked in tandem and scheduled in steady streams for the central city. Its major failing was its grinding gears and pounding steel wheels, which made it the enemy of sleep on summer nights, and an annoyance all year long. By raising the sound levels of urban streets to intolerable heights the streetcars drove the rich from their customary conspicuous locations on the city's main thoroughfares. Quiet isolation became a fundamental amenity in wealthy neighborhoods and the goal of middle-class homeowners. *Chicago Historical Society*

4. A Distant Streetcar Subdivision, Altadena, Los Angeles, ca. 1890. Twelve miles from the core city, then only 50,000 inhabitants, land speculators stretched their electric car lines beyond traffic demand in anticipation of house-lot sales. The automobile, traveling on publicly financed roads, freed land developers from such expenses, thereby perpetuating the small opera- tor in city building. *History Division, Los Angeles County Museum of Natural History*

5. Downtown Traffic Jam, Dearborn and Randolph Streets, Chicago, ca. 1910. More and faster service, from horsecars to cable cars to electrics, brought greater downtown traffic and taller buildings. *Chicago Historical Society*

6. Wabash Avenue Elevated Railway, Loop, Chicago, 1907. For a brief period (in Chicago, 1892–1911) the pent-up demand for downtown shopping and business locations in the largest cities made it profitable for private firms to construct enormously expensive elevated networks. But an intown express was also an outbound express. The new els and the motor truck expanded options of location for many firms; thus the densest traffic jams in our cities' history led to the long and steady process of decentralization. *Library of Congress*

7. Elevated Construction, Willow Street near Sheffield Avenue, Chicago, 1897. Environmental choices for rapid transit were all bad. Who was to suffer the sensory destruction of darkness, noise, and dirt? The elevated placed the passenger in fresh air, above the noise, with an occasional spectacular view. Below, it spread a pall over the street, abutting houses, and work-rooms. Here, a new elevated through a Near North Side working-class district. *Chicago Historical Society*

8. Underneath the Elevated, Downtown Chicago, 1940. No neighborhood de-fense committees rose against the elevateds—in a business-dominated age, landowners anticipated higher rents from retail stores crowding the new routes to capture pedestrian trade. The alternative solution, the subway, saved the street, but cost so much to build it required municipal subsidies and shifted the discomfort of noise, dirt, and bad air to the passengers. *Library of Congress*

9. Dezendorf's Delightful Dwellings, Queens, New York, ca. 1920. For the mass of city dwellers abundant residential land opened up by streetcars and rapid transit brought light, air, and yards, but atrocious land planning caused by private profit maximization foreclosed the benefits of good low-density design (even room for off-street parking). This photograph was used by the New Deal's Resettlement Administration as a prime exhibit of common-place abuses of private subdivisions. *Library of Congress*

10. Automobile Subdivision, Whittier Boulevard near Atlantic Boulevard, East Los Angeles, 1930. Given wide streets and extensive car ownership, the price of residential land fell sufficiently to allow even marginal home buyers to obtain their long-standing goal—a free-standing house and small yard. Vacant lots along Whittier Boulevard, reserved for subsequent retail devel-opment, foretell the dreary routinization caused by new zoning ordinances of the twenties, which simply separated retail and industrial strips from interior residential grids. *Historical Collections, Security Pacific National Bank*

11. Whittier Boulevard and Lindsay Avenue, Pico Rivera, Los Angeles, 1961. The automobile main street is perhaps the ugliest feature of the modern city. In the late twenties, the concept of a limited-access highway triumphed for traffic control. State legislatures foreclosed the common-law right of abutting landowners to connect to the superhighway. Although the shopping center represents the logical next step, the automobile city awaits a similar organization of retail land for public benefit. *California Division of Highways, District VII*

12. Hawthorne Boulevard, Artesia Boulevard, and San Diego Freeway, Los Angeles, 1961. Los Angeles traffic flows comparatively easily because its freeways were built to supplement an already generous network of wide streets, unlike the narrower street grids of older Eastern cities. Here, Hawthorne Boulevard, running north and south, shows maximum development of an automobile city street—six traffic lanes, median strip division, and one- and two-lane left-turn pockets. *California Division of Highways, District VII*

13. Long Island Single-Family Houses, 40 Miles from New York City, 1967. The automobile brought the Los Angeles growth pattern to the old New York metropolis, as elsewhere. Without voter authorization of new metropolitan subdivisions with green spaces, retailing organized, highways isolated from abutting houses, and homes appropriate to all classes, races, and ages, this highway and suburban pattern encompasses the metropolis in the same antisocial, environmentally destructive way as Los Angeles. *Regional Plan Association, Louis B. Schlivek*

14. Grand Central Commuters, New York, 1969. There is no way to humanize the traffic caused by extreme population densities. Our experience shows only choices among evils. The most elaborate nineteenth-century designs demanded crowded trains, underground rides, dense pedestrian tides, even for wealthy suburban commuters. *Regional Plan Association, Louis B. Schlivek*

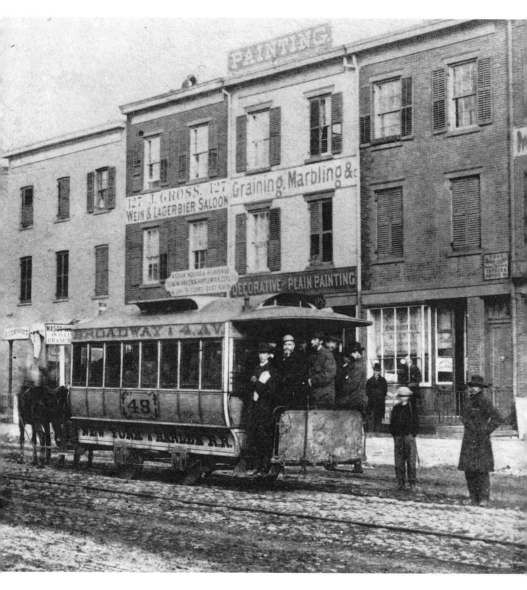

1. Horsecar, New York City, ca. 1865

2. Cable Cars, Chicago, ca. 1902

3. Electric Streetcars, Chicago, 1906

4. A Distant Streetcar Subdivision, Los Angeles, ca. 1890

5. Downtown Traffic Jam, Chicago, ca. 1910

6. Elevated Railway, Loop, Chicago, 1907

7. Elevated Construction, Chicago, 1897

8. Underneath the Elevated, Downtown Chicago, 1940

9. Queens, New York, ca. 1920

10. Automobile Subdivision, East Los Angeles, 1930

11. Pico Rivera, Los Angeles, 1961

12. Los Angeles, 1961

13. Long Island Single-Family Houses, 1967

14. Grand Central Commuters, New York, 1969

The systematic traffic research of the 1930s and its incorporation into the criteria for highway design governed the layout of the interstate highways that entered American cities in the late 1950s and 1960s. A succession of studies revealed the logic of highway traffic. In the twenties it was generally agreed that most of the traffic entering a city from outside its boundaries was passing through to destinations beyond it, an impression that nicely confirmed the wisdom of the contemporary policy of building roads between cities while more or less ignoring city congestion. Traffic engineers, however, began to station men at city intersections to ask motorists their origin and destination and learned that 80 percent of the traffic entering even a small city of twenty-five to fifty thousand inhabitants was bound for destinations within that city; for large cities the proportion rose to 90 to 95 percent.[37] Accordingly the city came to be recognized as a place of rising vehicular pressure, where the demand for driving room grew more intense as the streets approached the center. This perspective of course ran precisely counter to the availability of urban land, and it had somehow to be reconciled with the competing needs of stores, pedestrians, offices, and factories.

Further traffic counts, coupled with the discovery of reliable methods of sampling the population of a city to determine the routes most preferred, revealed the logic of intracity movement. In the central business districts, 50 to 60 percent of the entering vehicles were bound for destinations beyond the downtown core but were nevertheless forced to pass through it by the radial arrangement of the main arteries of most cities. Such information suggested that traffic jams could be eased and the demand for street space reduced if highways were planned as a belt around the downtown areas; no car then need enter the center if its destination lay elsewhere.[38]

Taken as a whole, the studies of the thirties suggested a new model for basic urban highway design—the pattern of the wheel. The downtown area would stand inside the hub, untouched by superhighways but surrounded by the new inner belt. As many radial highways as the size of the city required would be constructed like spokes from the inner-belt hub, two or three for a small city, five or six for a large one. Finally, at the outer edge of settlement, ready to accommodate the future growth of

37. U.S. Public Roads Administration, *Highway Practice in the United States of America,* Washington, 1949, pp. 53–55.
38. Public Roads Administration, *Highway Practice,* pp. 56–59.

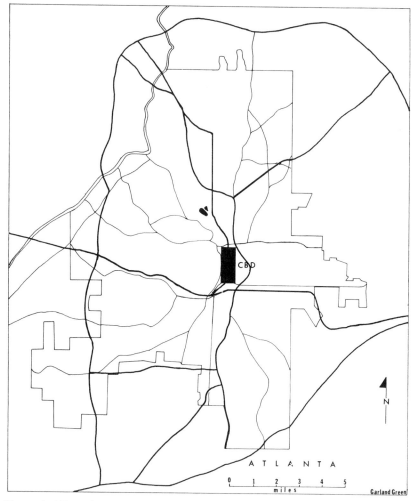

Figure I. Atlanta Interstate Wheel

SOURCE: U.S. Geological Survey, *The National Atlas of the United States of America,* Washington, 1970.

the city and to handle light intercity traffic, would be the outer-belt, or circumferential, highway.[39]

Just as traffic studies led highway engineers to the wheel model for

39. American Association of State Highway Officials, Committee on Planning and Design Policies, *A Policy on Arterial Highways in Urban Areas,* Washington, 1967, pp. 66–83.

urban roads, so studies of passenger-car speeds led them to the design specifications for the highways themselves. Tests at manufacturers' proving grounds showed the average top speed of low-priced American cars climbing rapidly. From forty-seven miles per hour in 1924 it rose to seventy-two by 1937 and 1938, and more expensive cars were capable of speeds of eighty or more. Further studies showed that the average motorist drove on the open highways at an average of forty-nine miles an hour, the overwhelming majority at less than sixty. Taking into consideration the trend toward faster cars as well as the fact that a highway represents so costly a capital investment that it should serve for twenty or more years, the engineers of the late 1930s concluded that superhighway speed limits should be set at fifty miles an hour in urban areas of heavy traffic and at seventy through open country.[40]

The decision on speed limits was the eventual determinant of the physical layout of the highway. It would have no intersections, and curves would be gentle enough to be negotiated at high speed. Traffic moving in opposite directions would be separated by median strips to prevent head-on collisions, and a breakdown lane or safety shoulder would lie at the outer edges of the lanes on each side. Lines of sight would be long and uninterrupted, and to this end grades would be moderate. Logical requirements indeed, but they were requirements that quite naturally led to the two- and three-hundred-foot right-of-way and to a wide-sweeping geometry that would inevitably conflict with the rectangular grid fabric of urban streets and buildings. Quite apart from the constraints of the topology of cities, which made the interstate highway a greedy competitor for space along the rivers and in the valleys, high speed limits made it an alarmingly disruptive force in city construction.[41]

Previously only the railroads had approached a geometry of such proportions, and their construction had preceded much American city growth; railroads had not been introduced into urban patterns already set, and subsequent city expansion could readily conform to their lines.

40. Public Roads Administration, *Highway Practice*, pp. 64–66.
41. The East River Drive in New York City, which dodges the amenities of its abutting neighborhoods, is a noteworthy exception to the usual insensitive practice of urban highway design. M. R. Werner, "A Reporter at Large: Through Thick and Thin," *The New Yorker*, 17 (April 5, 1941), 40–49; Joseph R. Passonneau, "Full Compensation and Transportation Corridor Analysis," American Society of Civil Engineers and American Society of Mechanical Engineers, *Conference on Socio-Economic Impact of Urban Freeways and Rapid Transit Systems*, Seattle, July 1971, pp. 5–6.

Nevertheless the railroads introduced an ominous precedent; peninsulas and islands of houses, factories, and warehouses were often isolated from the rest of the city by the tracks, so blighted by smoke and noise that the spaces were "lost." A survey showed that many old-time residents were not even aware of the location of these areas as the geometry of the tracks moved obliquely and indefinitely through the organization of city streets. Examples were Boston's South End and Chicago's southwest industrial districts, and indeed most cities had such railroad wastelands. Now a similar problem would be faced by more big cities and they would be dealing with mammoth transportation lines.[42]

Just before World War II, the studies made by traffic engineers in respect to the logic of the superhighway found mature expression in an analysis of a national system of turnpikes by the U.S. Bureau of Public Roads. This 1939 report, *Toll Roads and Free Roads,* compiled at the request of Congress, was the first of a series that led directly into the interstate highway program of 1956.[43] The pilot report set forth the design criteria for the restructuring of urban traffic and for the high-speed linkages of intercity movement. Also in 1939 the Futurama exhibit for General Motors at the New York World's Fair appeared and captured the public imagination as a model of the coming superhighways. Designed by the theatrical-set designer and city planner Norman Bel Geddes (1893–1958), this three-dimensional representation of a miniature countryside crisscrossed with effortless motoring impressed millions of Americans who stood in long lines for the chance to inspect it. Industry leaders and public officials pronounced the General Motors exhibit tremendous publicity for the sort of road experience that had greeted motorists only at the approaches to San Francisco's Golden Gate Bridge, on the Pennsylvania Turnpike, or on Connecticut's Merritt Parkway.[44]

World War II halted highway construction except for the building of roads to military bases and to new war plants. These strategic highways, though often hurriedly planned, did add to the nation's list of examples of limited-access superhighways, and they also broke the old formula for

42. Kevin Lynch, *The Image of the City,* Cambridge, 1960, pp. 22, 46–62.

43. U.S. Public Roads Administration, *Toll Roads and Free Roads. House Document No. 272,* 76th Congress, 1st Session, Washington, 1939.

44. General Motors Corporation, "Dinner for American Association of State Highway Officials Given by Alfred P. Sloan, Jr., Chairman of General Motors Corporation, Terrace Club, New York World's Fair, Saturday Evening, October 14, 1939," Pamphlet, Transportation Library, University of Michigan.

matching federal-state funds for financing. They set the precedent for the 90 percent federal contribution that would become the final interstate financing formula.[45]

After the war, automobile registrations leapt forward to 41,086,000 in 1948 and climbed relentlessly year after year to 65,154,000 in 1956, the year in which the interstate bill finally passed Congress. Urban traffic jams lengthened, and in the densely settled corridors of the Northeast, Midwest, and West Coast, intercity traffic pile-ups occurred daily. It was found that in sections such as these, privately financed turnpikes could profitably be built. So substantial was the saving in time for the turnpike user that he willingly paid a toll for the privilege, just as travelers had on the toll roads of the late eighteenth and early nineteenth centuries. Maine, Massachusetts, Connecticut, New York, New Jersey, Ohio, and Illinois all authorized and built turnpikes in the 1950s, and their success increased the demand for a national network of superhighways. At the same time it became clear that the toll roads carried the most remunerative traffic and that they would scarcely serve to finance a full set of national roads. Nation-wide coverage required such diverse elements as the fabulously expensive urban inner-belt and radial roads, the lightly traveled linkages of the South and West, and the intercity ties to small cities throughout the nation. Finally, after rejecting several measures which were strongly pressed by President Eisenhower, state highway officials, and groups who used the highways or supplied the automotive industry, in 1956 Congress enacted a basic Federal Aid Highway Act.[46]

The 1956 act created the interstate system. Forty-one thousand miles of limited-access highways were to be built between 1956 and 1972, and these would link all the major cities and reorganize their internal traffic according to the hub-and-wheel analogue. An exception was made for the few cities already spread out into a number of centers instead of having a single downtown area; these were to receive highways in the form of a giant grid, not a modified wheel. Los Angeles is the most dramatic example of the grid alternative.[47] In any case the total effect of the interstate program, now nearing completion, has been

    45. U.S. Bureau of Public Roads, *Highway Needs of the National Defense. House Document No. 249,* 81st Congress, 1st Session, Washington, 1949.
    46. AASHO, *Story of the Achievements of the AASHO,* pp. 181–97.
    47. California Department of Public Works, Division of Highways, *The California Freeway System. Report to the Joint Interim Committee on Highway Problems of the California Legislature in Conformity with Senate Concurrent Resolution No. 26,* Sacramento, September 1958.

to accelerate other existing tendencies toward the dispersion of the American city.

City planners, architects, sociologists, and urbanists of every sort have been debating the merits of decentralization for the past twenty-five years. Some of them argue that the loss of the dense single-centered city will be the end of our brand of civilization; others that low-density settlement will save us from the evils of urbanization. This is an important controversy, but to understand its relation to the American tradition of land management the governing factor is not centralization or decentralization but the ways in which the new roads were located. The highway program of 1956–72 could have been used to promote or to degrade new forms of centralization, but it was so radical an introduction into the urban land maps that it soon became certain that the highways would in fact create a new reticulation of their own. Regardless of whether or not we approve of the traffic relationships now emerging in every city, we can acknowledge that the interstate highways dramatized the complete failure of our land-management tradition in the face of the new challenge.

When highway engineers prepared to lay out the new urban roads, they confronted land regulations that were totally ineffective as guidelines for decisions at the metropolitan scale and equally ineffective for protecting the liberties of the city dwellers whose lives and homes would be disrupted by their work. Because city planning had been so closely tied to municipalities and their political boundaries, in 1956 no metropolitan planning agency existed for any American city. There were, to be sure, some consultative bodies—private ones such as the New York Regional Plan Association, and a few public agencies as in Atlanta, Cincinnati, Detroit, St. Louis, and Los Angeles—but no one of them had the requisite power to allocate metropolitan land for highway uses or for development by highway services.[48] Moreover, no rationale of metropolitan regional economics existed, and there was no popular consensus on what a metropolis ought to be or how it ought to function. Thus there was no way to calculate the costs and benefits of a metropolitan highway system or to set realistic goals for it. At a moment when city planning was most needed it had neither the knowledge, technique, procedures, nor power to guide the massive reworking of American urban land. There were not even any metropolitan transportation agencies to

48. Mel Scott, *American City Planning Since 1890*, Berkeley, 1969, pp. 430–52.

Figure II. Regional Interstates of Boston

SOURCE: U.S. Geological Survey, *The National Atlas of the United States of America*, Washington, 1970.

coordinate highway planning with bus routes, rapid transit, rail commuting, or airport service. Indeed, so reluctant and ill-equipped were the cities to cooperate in planning that the Federal Aid Highway Act was amended in 1962 to the effect that after 1965, transportation planning agencies were to be created in all cities having more than fifty thousand population as a condition of state participation in the interstate highway program.[49] This meant that for the first decade of its operation the interstate program dealt with state highway departments familiar with intercity road construction but faced a multitude of metropolitan civil

49. Title 23, *United States Code,* Section 134; Scott, *City Planning,* pp. 580–85.

jurisdictions for intracity construction. Most cities were made up of ten, twenty, or even hundreds of separate zoning maps, each with a distinct land policy, for each borough, town, city, and incorporated and unincorporated settlement in the county or counties that huddled within the megalopolis. In practice, then, highway planners faced the choice either of following precedents by retracing the paths of the old state and U.S. routes which ran through the cities or of establishing new paths whose alignment would be determined by their own professional judgment. They did both.

The engineers did not consciously attempt to produce a new city form, although their work had such an effect, but sought only to use the conventional practices that had emerged in their past cooperation with state highway departments and adapt these to current patterns of urban land use. The intracity goal of the new interstate highways was to relieve congestion in the central business districts according to the strategy suggested by the research of the 1930s. The inner belt, the radials, and the circumferentials of the wheel pattern were to be so placed as to cause the least possible disruption to accepted land values rather than to lead each city toward a rational new solution to the automotive era.

In the American city of the 1950s and 1960s the accepted values were the inherited values of the private market in land, according to which commercial and industrial properties were the ones that sold for the highest prices and paid the largest taxes. Hence the old order of values ordered that these properties should be shored up in worth by new highways and not be seized for the two- to three-hundred-foot rights-of-way needed to insert superhighways into existing blocks. Moreover, the areas that were least developed and often had no commercial value at all—open spaces, parks, river margins, and undeveloped farmland and woodland—became prime locations for the new roads. The fact that such land had indeed high public value as open space or as beauty spots of the city had no relevance for the engineers. In rejecting such use and value they were responding only to the pricing system of the private land market.[50] Even today, after the devastation of many urban open spaces and after fifteen years of research into highway economics, there is no accepted criterion for assessing the worth of parks, views, and land of low market value in the calculation of the costs and benefits accruing from differing highway locations.

50. AASHO, *Arterial Highways in Urban Areas,* pp. 89–91.

Thus the wheel design for urban interstate highways was the product of purely commercial values. Its first duty was seen as the alleviation of traffic pressure on the central business districts; its next to assist, by means of radial and circumferential roads, the existing shopping centers and industrial parks and to encourage the development of new ones. It was this shortsighted objective of causing the least disruption to established commercial values of the private land market that made the metropolitan zoning maps the instruments of planning. The zoning districts, which after all represented only the building uniformities of the past, became the principal determinants of the form of the new automotive megalopolis.

Interstate engineers also inherited the confusions and inadequacies of the public housing program and the inequalities of compensation law. Successive campaigns of city building had laid down concentric rings of houses in which the oldest homes naturally lay closest to the original site of the city. As time passed and the cities grew, downtown areas came to be surrounded by a thickening band of the homes of the white and black poor. The poor concentrated even more in these districts after World War II because rents were lowest there and public transportation to work most abundant. These areas were popularly denigrated by being classified as slums and legally defined as "blighted areas," with no discrimination as to the condition of individual houses or consideration of the social functions of poor neighborhoods. In these districts New Deal public housing began its clearance work, tearing down the "blight" and replacing it with new housing projects. Working in a climate of many vacancies and empty crumbling houses, the small-scale projects of the thirties and early forties ignored the effects that the razing of slums would have upon the social structure of the neighborhoods of the poor. They could afford to do so because at most they disturbed a few blocks. Nevertheless these were the projects that thenceforth stigmatized these areas, both by publicity and law, as blighted and fit only for destruction.

By an unhappy convergence of history, the interstate highway program passed Congress in an era of political reaction, so that the seizure of poor urban neighborhoods coincided with a cutback in public housing. Since the location of roads just outside the urban center was implicit in the wheel strategy of the highway engineer, the cry of "blight" urged on him the merits of taking as much of the land of the poor as he wished. Thus to rip out the houses of the poor was a transportation principle that became a public contribution rather than an act of social irresponsibility. It might have been expected that a rational and humane society would confront the repercussions of highway building on the metropolitan scale by the erection of enough public housing to compensate for the units plowed under by the highways and to place these units so that the new transportation routes could conveniently be used for job access. Instead such American housing as still went forward was confined to the political boundaries of each zoning unit. Center-city projects remained in the center city; they could not, as in London, be used to relocate the poor to give them the benefit of the new roads in reaching their new work areas. Because of the convergence, then, of the political mood, the transportation explosion, and the traditional fragmented American city, poor neighborhoods came to bear a disproportionate share of the costs and suffering that attended the reconstruction of the metropolis.

In short, the land needs of the highways were so enormous as to upset the urban housing market to the strong disadvantage of the poor. A 1968 study of Baltimore reveals how relentlessly highway construction costs there bore down upon the poor of the central city. The old core city lacked vacant land or new residential building, yet it was the principal—and indeed for blacks the only—area where low-income families could find decent housing within their price range. At the same time, racial pressures were driving an increasing number of blacks back to the central city from the suburbs, and no public housing programs were planned for the city or region to relieve the shortage of shelter. On the contrary, in ten years' time, from 1965 to 1974, Baltimore was scheduled to lose 10 percent of its existing housing to public works, equivalent to the loss from a siege or repeated bombing attacks. The prognostication therefore was for rising rents but no improvement in housing conditions.[51]

The Baltimore Urban Design Concept Team was able to loosen the vise to some extent by moving the proposed inner-belt highways a mile farther from the downtown district than had originally been planned.[52] No justice could be done, however, in respect to the poor, black or white, since neither the Department of Transportation nor the Department of Housing and Urban Development was prepared to undertake new housing projects or to compensate displaced families for the real

51. Charles Abrams, *The Role and Responsibilities of the Federal Highway System in Baltimore,* Baltimore, 1968, pp. 3, 8.
52. Passonneau, "Full Compensation," p. 12.

costs of their removal. There is some evidence from the Baltimore study and others like it that in many cities the inner-belt highways have been placed too close to their centers for traffic efficiency simply because the costs of recompensing displaced families have not been fully paid.[53] In these cases the cost estimates for land and structure takings are falsely low because the compensatory payments as specified do not include all the damage suffered by tenants, small businesses, land-contract home buyers, and owner-occupiers of substandard homes.

The specific provisions of land condemnation when considered as a whole have meant that much of the cost of urban highways has been pushed off on those who live in their path. The long period that elapses between the first rumors of the road location and the final taking of the land inevitably depresses the market value of such informally earmarked property. Sales dwindle to a trickle, public services decline, businesses leave as their leases expire, vandals attack unused buildings. In short, the neighborhood deteriorates rapidly and with it the values upon which compensation will ultimately be measured. Those who, unlike conventional-mortgage home buyers, are trying to purchase homes on a land contract—a popular method in poor neighborhoods whereby sellers retain the property title as security until the full price is paid—can lose their homes without any compensation at all. For a number of years tenants, the most numerous group of the poor, were made to vacate their premises without aid or compensation since they legally held no private property. Small businessmen did receive aid for moving expenses, but common law specifically exempted compensation for good will, even though the reputation of a business might constitute its very *raison d'être*. A 1962 amendment to the federal statute tried to alleviate this inequality by calling for states to institute relocation programs for those displaced by interstate highways, but the lack of effective coordination among social agencies which could deal with the social problems of displaced families, the low moving allocations, and the shortage of decent housing at comparable rents or prices crippled this benign goal. Finally in 1968 Congress passed a law allowing additional compensation of up to $5,000 for homeowners to help them buy new houses, and grants for two years of up to $1,500 to tenants to help them pay higher rents, but such aid could not guarantee a new home in a nearby neighborhood or make any headway against the urban low-income

53. Ibid., p. 13.

housing shortage.[54] Moreover, public-interest lawyers have charged that in the rush to initiate projects callous local authorities have ignored many of these protective measures and that the federal government has not enforced its own rules.[55]

The individual and class injustices that have marked land practices relating to the interstate highways since their inception in 1956 were an inevitable consequence of the violent disparity between the metropolitan scale of the highways and the parcel-by-parcel justice of the old law. For the well-to-do, a good lawyer and the wide choice of other homes makes relocation a comparatively harmless matter. For the poor, in whose neighborhoods highways were located with the precise aim of minimizing the disruption of high-value property, both the traditions of the property law and the workings of the free-enterprise housing market meant suffering without adequate redress. As angry citizens discovered in meeting after meeting, no mechanism in which their interests could receive adequate weight controlled highway siting. The law and the political structure of the metropolis could create city councils, condemnation hearings, and courts in which the individual or neighborhood might be heard, but at no point was the neighborhood powerful enough to achieve its goals in the face of the gigantic highway program. Occasionally an informal league of neighborhoods could arouse public anger to such a pitch that a highway would be halted, as happened in San Francisco and in Cambridge, Massachusetts, but such victories only underlined the irrationality of the whole procedure.[56]

The huge scale of the interstate highways requires national and multistate planning decisions that should be made on the basis of national goals for full employment, regional economic growth and land development, and human-resource potentials. So far no democratic method of planning appropriate to such decisions has appeared at the national, state, or metropolitan level. We have seen that city planning never developed such procedures, and when in 1965 metropolitan planning became a compulsory adjunct to highway design, no other agencies or rules for adjudicating the opposing economic and land-development

54. Anthony Downs, *Urban Problems and Prospects,* Chicago, 1970, pp. 192–227; Wallace F. Smith, "The Relocation Dilemma," *The Appraisal Journal,* 37 (July 1969), 424–32.

55. Edgar S. Cahn et al., *The Legal Lawbreakers, A Study of the Nonadministration of Federal Relocation Requirements,* Citizens Advocate Center, Washington, 1970.

56. Gordon Fellman and Barbara Brandt, "Working-Class Protest Against an Urban Highway," *Environment and Behavior,* 3 (March 1971), 61–79.

interests were forthcoming. Instead power was handed over to administrative bodies of mixed government and business interests. Perhaps it is
not surprising that no democratic planning procedures for dealing with
the highways had emerged in a society that has clung for three hundred
and fifty years to the concept that government was supposed to aid
private property and not to allocate land for the general benefit of
society.

As the late Charles Abrams has so ably pointed out, dealing fairly
with the displaced and the adjoining neighborhoods could have been an
easy task, well within the capabilities of our society, since such action
lay within the reach of conventional city planning. Both the Department
of Transportation and the Department of Housing and Urban Development have sufficient authority to build housing that will relieve the
shortages caused by urban-renewal and highway projects. Legal precedents for the joining of housing to other public works abound in the war
workers' housing of World Wars I and II, and whole towns have even
been built as in the instances of Greenbelt, Maryland, Oak Ridge,
Tennessee, and much of Cape Kennedy. Instead Congressional antipathy toward the urban poor has joined with administrative callousness to
aggravate housing shortages. Highway programs, by taking responsibility for an entire project instead of for isolated parts of it, could have
included the needs of neighborhoods adjoining the highway alignments.
It would have been necessary only to move the boundary of responsibility beyond the planting and the chain-link fence into the affected areas.[57]

The raising of such neighborhoods to modern urban standards—in
most cases at present they conform only to the standards of 1900—is a
legitimate function of highway construction and a proper use of Highway Trust Funds; neglect of this function has meant that adjacent homes
have been forced to pay the costs of the benefits enjoyed by motorists.
The standards for a decent neighborhood in regard to noise, air, traffic,
public and commercial services, and housing are well established. Such
specifications lie in the dusty files of every local city planning office, in
the desks of city inspectors and engineers. These norms, so well documented and widely agreed upon, could serve as the basis for a democratic planning process, and abutting neighborhoods could deal with
issues on which they have knowledge and competence, and over which
they have appropriate jurisdiction. In disputes between neighborhoods
and planning officials the standards could serve to decide civil suits.

57. Abrams, *Role and Responsibilities,* pp. 13–22.

Furthermore, such documentation and its relative uniformity would enable courts to act with dispatch without having to assume the impossible task of balancing the equities between an aggrieved landowner and the logic of a metropolitan highway.[58]

Because such opportunities have never been realized, local groups have served only in an obstructive role. They have never been able to insist that the building of a highway, which after all involves the rebuilding of a city, include neighborhood reconstruction. Both city and neighborhoods have suffered. From the city's point of view, the outworn values of the private land market and the outmoded traditions of seventeenth-century land law have fixed its form for a long time to come.

Long lines of disparate historical trends, including private land speculation, attempts at regulation, private controls over public building, and the Balkanization of metropolitan political units, all came together after World War II to create in American cities the worst of all possible worlds. The freedom of the individual, which had been the dominant concern of our land-law tradition, disappeared with the growing scope of the influence of all manner of highway, urban renewal, and housing officials.[59] At the same time, the benefits of mass housing and of rational urban investment, both inherent in European socialism, were rejected by an unshakable commitment to the private land market.

58. Frank I. Michaelman, "Property, Utility, and Fairness: Comments on the Ethical Foundations of 'Just Compensation' Law," *Harvard Law Review*, 80 (April 1967), 1171, 1193–95, 1224–26, 1248–58.

59. Allison Dunham, "Property, City Planning, and Liberty," and David W. Craig, "Regulation and Purchase: Two Governmental Ways to Attain Planned Land Use," in Charles M. Haar, ed., *Law and Land, Anglo-American Planning Practice,* Cambridge, 1964, pp. 28–43, 181–211.

T W O

▲ BUILDING A NATION
OF CITIES

The Engine of Private Enterprise

New York 1820–70:
commerce, canals,
and sweatshops

THE TYPICAL AMERICAN CITY DWELLER is a commuter. He lives in one place, and from there he drives or takes a bus or subway to another place, where he works. For him there are two cities: a city of homes, a city of jobs. In daily alternations he delineates two of the essential elements of city growth, for it is the interaction between jobs and homes that shapes the city. The jobs pay for the houses and in part determine their location, but in part the location of jobs is governed by proximity to the houses. The interdependence speaks of much of the growth and development of our cities. This unity between commonplace experience and basic urban structure holds out great potentialities for the democratic control of our metropolitan world, but they have remained largely unrealized. The difficulty is that most citizens see themselves as men and women coping with the city and not as participants in its building.

The sheer size and extent of our cities overwhelms us. The interminable streets of houses, stores, offices, and factories, the incongruity between slums and suburbs, the intimidation of giant office towers, the flood of traffic, the infinity of government offices engender a sense of powerlessness. Such a sense has nurtured a depressed and defensive civic consciousness. We vote, but not so often as our ancestors; we turn out, a few of us at least, to defend our neighborhoods or our children in public hearings and school meetings; we join organizations, if it is required or if it is the custom of the place. But neither the politicians nor the officers of our organizations seem able to do much to assist the family budget or to combat the dearth of good jobs, the decay of the neighborhood, the danger on the streets, the needs of a difficult child, the disaffection of young people, or the isolation of aged relatives. We do have a strong sense of home, even though many of us move from block to block or from subdivision to subdivision, and that sense can be touched by personal tragedy or by organized appeals for church and charity. It is nevertheless a circumscribed feeling and only a partial public manifestation of an essentially private life. For the most part we learn to take the job as it comes and the city as we find it.

A deep pessimism underlies this sort of adaptation to modern city life. We comfort ourselves in our helplessness by repeating the bromide that the system is at fault, that it somehow seems to work against people, not for them. On the job no one cares for good work, no one looks out for the other guy, no one wishes to take responsibility. And for all the years at school, the raises and fringe benefits, and the household gadgets, a comfortable home and a decent neighborhood are becoming harder and harder to find and to manage.

This commonplace reasoning from everyday experience is sound enough; it is the wisdom of people trying to cope with a hostile world. But it is self-regarding and self-defeating, and precludes any possibility of understanding the meaning and consequences of the catchall we use to express the generality of our experience—the system. We speak often of "the system," by which we mean a set of nearly all-powerful outside forces that control our jobs, our homes, and our lives. Neither we nor our politicians are apt to speak of the system in terms that suggest what we might do to change it.

The very fact that an urban system exists, that we do not all suffer at random but are harassed by predictable, repeated, and identifiable inter-actions, creates the possibility for intelligent action and points to the hope for change. Since the thrust of our urban history has been toward ever more inclusive organization of our cities and ever greater integration of our national economy, it is clear that we now live in a period—as opposed to earlier, more loosely structured times—when problems connected with homes and jobs can be effectively politicized. We can reasonably expect that out of the conflicts that arise over the goals and means for the creation of new forms of city life, more humane urban environments will emerge. Our urban world is now so much a "system" that it could be managed by democratic planning if we wished to turn our private complaints outward into political channels. The first step in turning outward is to understand the system we confront.

The interactions between the national economy and the urban business institutions largely determine the nature of both workplaces and residences. The detailed analysis and reordering of these interactions is an enormously complex subject requiring great expertise, but in general outline—in the broad terms in which goals and policy must be debated—it can be made clear enough for anyone who wishes to study and understand it. Moreover, a historical review is one of the best ways to begin. The different modes of business and the varying forms of cities that have existed in the past reveal the elements of our urban system like a skeleton.

To understand why American cities are as they are, we must learn to look for two sorts of activities. First, we must seek repeated relationships in the fragments of our everyday experience. Ours is a highly structured society and these repetitions are its framework. Second, we must peer out from the city itself—watch the license plates on the trucks moving along the freeway, if you will—to recognize the city as a part of a national economy. The repeated interactions between the national economy and the local business organizations create the jobs and fund the housing of the city.

First, structure. Our urban history is the history of the conflicts and possibilities wrought by the growth of the nation and the growth of the units of its organization. It is also a history of the increasing interconnectedness of these units, which stems from the development of the economy and its cities. The organization of these connections into repeated interactions is the structure of the economy and the structure of its cities. For example, one can speak of the structure of a city in terms of its land-use patterns or of its transportation networks, for both of these produce regular, repeated connections in an ordered way. In this brief history the general categories of urban structure will be two: the national network of cities and the patterns of land use within the cities themselves. The category of economic structure will be the urban business institutions—the proprietors, partnerships, and corporations.

The general trend of the past hundred and fifty years has been toward an expansion of the national urban network, both as a whole and in its parts. The number of cities in the nation has multiplied, almost all cities became larger, and the interaction among them has steadily increased. In a parallel fashion the size of business units and the interactions among them increased; small shops became giant factories, partnerships grew to corporations and then to conglomerate corporations of corporations, while the volume of business transactions, bank loans, sales, and shipments proliferated. Finally, the size of the units of land use in cities and the interactions among them increased. Mixed blocks of shops and houses gave way to specialized districts, business or residential, and whole suburbs and satellites of one class or one group of businesses emerged. Simultaneously the number of trips, messages, and exchanges within and among these enlarged areas rose in volume.

Our urban history, however, is not a simple tale of expansion. The general trend toward greater size and greater interconnectedness always contained the opposing characteristics of centralization and decentralization. Centralization looked toward the efficiencies to be realized from such expediencies as the gathering of all the steel producers into one city, such as Pittsburgh, or the unifying of many steel firms into one corporation, such as United States Steel. Decentralization looked toward the advantages of specialization obtainable from such practices as the locating of steel mills near different cities, as at Buffalo, Chicago, or Detroit, or the multiplication of the number of steel companies by having some specialize in bridges, some in rails, others in wire or structural members. In various periods of our history entirely different combinations of cities, businesses, and urban land use have appeared in response to the advantages of centralization and decentralization. In our own time we have highly centralized business organizations, highly decentralized business activities, and highly decentralized cities, and thus enjoy a wider range of possibilities for organizing both urban and economic structure than ever before.

To comprehend the boundaries of our current freedom we must look to the historical interactions among the national economy, business organization, local jobs, and local housing. The urban system that governs this set of relationships revolves around the interactions among the national economy, urban markets, and business organization.[1] For

1. I have taken this hypothesis of the relationship between city size, functional specialization, and the role of a city in the national network of cities from the modern empirical investigations of Beverly Duncan and Stanley Lieberson, *Metropolis and Region in Transition,* Beverly Hills, 1970, pp. 29–116; and Otis D. Duncan et al., *Metropolis and Region,* Baltimore, 1960, pp. 209–11, 248–75. I am also indebted to the more theoretical work of Eric E. Lampard, "The Evolving System of Cities in the United States: Urbanization and Economic Development," in Harvey S. Perloff and Lowdon Wingo, Jr., eds., *Issues in Urban Economics,* Baltimore, 1968, pp. 81–139; and Wilbur R. Thompson, *A Preface to Urban Economics,*

example, a change from small firms to large corporations affects the urban markets used by them. A few corporations may encompass the trade formerly handled by hundreds of independent salesmen or dozens of small firms. At the same time, the financial and sales power of the corporations may make it possible for them to sell bread or beer over whole regions like the Midwest or even throughout the entire nation. Similarly, the concentration of a specialty in a single city (like flour milling in Minneapolis) draws related firms to that city, creating a local enclave for wheat and flour, with attendant shipping offices, railroad yards, bag companies, and the like. If the specialty of the city is far-reaching, as is the case in flour milling, local business will be reorganized to reflect the national scale, and a few big companies will dominate the local urban economic life. Finally, changes in the national economy, signaled by a transportation change like a new railroad or natural-gas pipeline or by a new banking system such as that brought into being by the National Banking Act of 1864, may restructure both urban markets and business organization by favoring some cities over others, by aiding some firms in their search for capital or their reach for sales to the disadvantage of others. Out of these countless interactions came the jobs of the nation's cities, and the differential rates of growth of individual cities and their jobs governed the local markets for housing.

Long ago the circle of national economic conditions, urban markets, and business organizations was remarkably stable, changing only slowly over time. Consequently, prior to the nineteenth century the multiplication of cities and their growth was a comparatively slow process. But beginning in the late eighteenth and early nineteenth centuries a rapid and accelerating succession of changes in transportation and technology disrupted the stability of the past and brought about several almost total reorganizations within the urban system. New national economies, new markets, new businesses, new cities, and new urban structures have been spawned from these innovations. The angry citizens who today demand, for reasons of ecology or peace, that they be given control over science, space exploration, supersonic transport, or automobile emissions are attacking the vital sources of change in our society.

Baltimore, 1965, pp. 37–60. The use of the hypothesis for the 1820–70 period finds support in the New York data of Allan R. Pred, *The Spatial Dynamics of U.S. Urban-Industrial Growth, 1800–1914,* Cambridge, 1966, pp. 163–85; Robert Ernst, *Immigrant Life in New York City,* New York, 1949; and Robert G. Albion, *The Rise of New York Port: 1815–1860,* New York, 1939.

Transportation and technological change have influenced the urban system principally by creating opportunities for specialization and diversification. A new digger enables some farmer to specialize in the raising of potatoes, and a new road can also enable him to specialize by opening his farm to a wider market. In the same way a stitching machine for shoes, accompanied by good freight service to distant cities, may make a giant shoe factory thrive where none could have survived before. The same spectrum of changes in technology and transportation supports diversification of a city's economic activities, for if a city can reach new suppliers and new customers its merchants will be able to handle a greater variety of goods as well as a larger volume of them. The introduction of Rural Free Delivery postal service led directly to the rise of the great Chicago mail-order houses of Sears, Roebuck and Montgomery Ward—an outstanding example of a simple link between transportation and diversification. The introduction of the stationary steam engine in the 1850s made it possible for cities that had been commercially oriented to branch out into mechanized production and thus to compete along certain lines with older waterpower mill towns.

To trace the patterns made by the impact of transportation and of technological innovation upon the system of American cities, it is convenient to divide our modern history into three periods, 1820–70, 1870–1920, 1920–   , and then to describe the special characteristics of each period.[2] In each we shall examine the state of technology and transportation, because it is from a particular technological climate and a particular configuration of transportation that the form of our cities and our business institutions inevitably takes shape. From these two determinants flow the national network of cities, the condition of the urban markets, and the kind of business structure that flourishes. Finally, we shall look at the end products of the entire system—the jobs and the residential structure within the cities.

The decades from 1820 to 1870 were the years of the perfection of hand tools and horse-powered machines, the use of waterpower and steam engines, and the invention of myriad tools to perform tasks

2. This periodization is copied from the one used so successfully by Lewis Mumford in his *The Culture of Cities,* New York, 1938, pp. 495–96. In this work and its predecessor, *Technics and Civilization,* New York, 1934, Mumford elaborated a scheme first proposed by the Scottish biologist Patrick Geddes, *Cities in Evolution,* London, 1915. The geographer John R. Borchert has proposed a similar ordering of American urban history in his summary article, "American Metropolitan Evolution," *Geographical Review,* 57 (July 1967), 301–32.

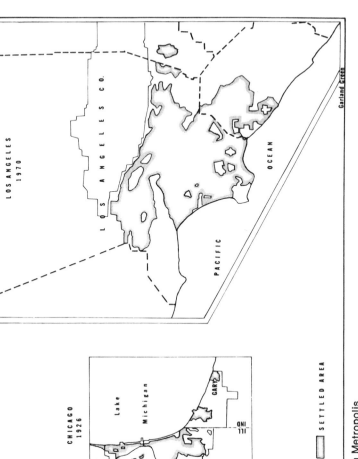

Figure III. Expanding Size of the American Metropolis

SOURCE: O. W. Gray and Sons, *The National Atlas,* Philadelphia, 1876; Homer Hoyt, *One Hundred Years of Land Values in Chicago,* Chicago, 1933; and U.S. Geological Survey maps.

formerly dependent on hand skills. But for all the new machinery, there was little mechanized production except in textiles and in some lines of ironworking. Most important, these were the years of the building of two new transportation networks, the water system of canals and steamboats, and the overland rail system. The new transportation gave rise to the big regional city and to the consequent organization of the economy around regional marketing and financial centers. Within business offices proprietorship and partnership prevailed, and in many cases the artisan competed with the sweatshop factory. Only a primitive specialization in respect to urban land existed, and the neighborhoods and districts of the big cities were highly mixed in their activities, ethnicity, and class.

In the second period, from 1870 to 1920, science and engineering reached a sufficient degree of inclusiveness to be systematically applied to all aspects of manufacture. Fully mechanized in-line factory production became the hallmark of the era. Electricity, the new energy source, replaced waterpower and surpassed steam in the flexibility of its use. The national rail network reached its ultimate limit and was supplemented locally by the electric street railway, the motor truck, and the automobile. These were the modes of production and transportation that created the giant industrial metropolis and the related multicity manufacturing belts of the Northeast and Midwest. These sprawling urban regions, organized about New York and Chicago, both produced for and marketed for the nation. Within the cities themselves everything tended toward giantism. The corporation controlled American economic life. Armies of workers, gathered into factories, attempted to unionize so that they might redress the balance of power between labor and corporate management. Urban land, responding to the pressures of intense economic organization, itself became highly specialized. The central hive of the downtown district, with its department stores, office skyscrapers, hotels, railroad stations, loft manufacturing, and warehouses, was the most dramatic outcropping of specialized land use. Other uniformities also emerged. The industrial sector and satellite, the strips that sheltered the factories and suburban mill clusters, radiated from the central city. Simultaneously, the daily movement of passengers by the electric street railway encouraged commuters to cluster by class, ethnicity, and race. Colossal scale, centralization, and segregation were the telling signs of the industrial metropolis.

In our own time, that is in the years since 1920, more far-reaching science and more sophisticated technology have multiplied products for common consumption and raised standards of living so much that more and more of the economy has turned away from farming, mining, and manufacturing into the provision of services, the seeking of international business, and the prosecution of foreign wars. New modes of transportation by express highway, airplane, and pipeline have made possible a rapid multidirectional movement of goods and people in tremendous volume. Production has accordingly been freed from a limited number of products and single locations to attune itself more finely to its markets. In the contemporary adaptation, business both builds multiple plants to capitalize on particular regional opportunities and expands the range of its products to meet specific demands of various kinds of customers. Atomic power has arrived to supplement the conventional generation of electricity, and the terror implicit in its military uses has provided an important rationalization for the undertaking of the disgraceful task of world domination.

The new high-production, high-service economy gave rise to a characteristic urban structure—the megalopolis. Three megalopolises are so far identifiable, the Northeastern, Midwestern, and Californian. These are multicity, multicentered urban regions, distinguished from the former manufacturing belts by the huge volume of exchange within them, the almost continuous low-density settlement, and the sharing of business activities among the many urban nuclei. Here layers upon layers of economic specialties facilitate the production and marketing of highly complicated products and services. Within the megalopolises, as within the nation as a whole, private and public corporate enterprise has continued to elaborate. The corporation's concentration of political and economic power, with its use of telephonic communication, cost accounting, and computers, makes for giant scale and extreme centralization. The corporation's multiple activities, its search for good marketing locations, and its allocation of responsibility to branches and divisions, however, exhibit a tendency to decentralization that resembles the proliferation of centers, government agencies, and branches in the megalopolis itself. These contradictory impulses toward centralization and decentralization suggest a potential for flexible economic planning that can satisfy many publics and diverse demands. At the same time, the vast increase in bureaucratic work in both private and public corporations has moved the white-collar worker, his employers, and his suburbs into the forefront of urban development.

In land use, the clusters of the megalopolis have become more and more specialized and segregated. Shopping strips, one-class suburbs, black ghettos, and industrial parks dot the urbanized region. Even the old industrial metropolis's downtown, so formidable a monument fifty years ago, has turned into an office and financial center, while its retailing, wholesaling, and manufacturing have been scattered all over the megalopolis. Residentially, various kinds of segregation have replaced the single-centered geographical organization of races and classes of the former era. Like the opposing tendencies within the corporation, the intensity of the social forces of specialization and segregation are countered by the vast extent of the megalopolis. The conflicts between prejudice and parochialism on the one hand and between low density and large open areas for rebuilding on the other suggest tensions that could offer a much broader range of urban choices than ever before.

To serve as examples of each period, we will focus on typical large cities in each era; New York 1820–70; Pittsburgh and Chicago 1870–1920; and Los Angeles 1920–   . Although each one will be dealt with as an archetype of its day, it should be realized that, despite remains of old neighborhoods and the persistence of past business specialties and urban styles, the power of the urban system is such that today metropolitan New York and Chicago resemble Los Angeles more than their former selves. Small cities could have served as well to reveal the skeleton of our urban system, but since we are now a nation in a state of panic over the conditions within our large cities it seemed most useful to concentrate on metropolitan history. Finally, since the history of the American urban system is a long one, it will be divided into three parts: first, the rest of this chapter, on the era of the big city; second, a chapter on the industrial metropolis; and third, a chapter on the megalopolis and the boundaries and potentialities of our urban world.

The Big City: 1820–70

No period of our history has surpassed the first half century of industrialization in its rate of change. Never again did the rate of urbanization climb so sharply. Not only did Americans conquer and settle the continent in these five decades, but their way of living on the land underwent a complete metamorphosis in which a national system of cities mobilized scattered villages and farms into a network of regional commercial and manufacturing centers. This sudden reorganization of American life, the forcing of a rural society into an urban mold, exacted a terrible toll in everyday life. Nineteenth-century urbanization and industrialization inflicted punishment and suffering on city dwellers and tore at the fabric of society in the same ways that today's neglected cities do. Never were conditions more exploitative and dangerous to human life, but they were experienced in such a scattering of small factories, stores, and houses that no sustained labor movement could be organized to cope effectively with the new discipline. Yet cities of every size boomed with the possibilities that flowed from new resources, new methods of transportation, new ways of doing business, and new ways of making things.

Technological innovations, simple machines and inventions, were directed toward the products most basic to an agricultural society. The essence of industrial design in these years lay in perfecting simple, cheap products that could be sold in quantity to farmers: clocks, food mills, stoves, oil lamps, wagons, buggies, sewing machines, and the like. Such was the proliferation of devices and techniques turned out by trained engineers and scientists, as well as by gifted mechanics and tinkerers, that the foundations for the fully mechanized economy of the future were securely laid down.[3]

Inventions of the first era, then, attacked the basic concerns of food, clothing, housing, and transportation. In agriculture, tools like axes, scythes, and shovels reached a high level of perfection, taking on the enduring forms in which we use them today.[4] Similarly our alarm clocks, as well as the coffee mill and food grinder, eggbeater, metal spoon, and ice-cream freezer of our own kitchens, replicate designs of these inventive years. By harnessing horsepower to farm tasks formerly executed by hand, a great breakthrough was achieved in extending the scope of agriculture. Plows, mowing machines, hay rakes, reapers, and threshers broke the confines of the past which had tied armies of farm workers to the seasonal preparation of the land and to the harvesting of staple crops. Continuous, almost automated flour milling and an assembly-line process of butchering and meat packing slashed labor costs and permitted the large-scale production of these key farm items. The formerly ubiquitous icebox was also an invention of these years, and at the same time the technique of cooling chests and whole rooms by ice

3. This description of the process of early technological change rests on a brilliant article of Dorothy S. Brady, "Relative Prices in the Nineteenth Century," *Journal of Economic History,* 26 (June 1964), 145–203.

4. *Sigfried Giedion, Mechanization Takes Command,* New York, 1948, pp. 141–49.

was mastered.[5] Methods providing for the safe canning of meats, fruits, and vegetables were introduced. By 1870 the United States possessed the basic components for a range of modern food products. Farm and city dwellers were alike freed from the limitations imposed by the short list of cheap all-year staples formerly available to them; to cornmeal, wheat flour, salt fish and salt meat, dried fruit and vegetables, and whiskey and beer were now added much more than merely local and seasonal supplements. One historian has underlined the change by noting that toward the end of this era the workingman could expect to find on his table such delicacies as fresh fish chowder and apple pie with some regularity.[6]

The textile and clothing industries were revolutionized by the importation of British techniques and by further advances in American inventions, and the cost of these necessities was drastically cut for farmer and city dweller alike. During the first decades of the nineteenth century, fully integrated cotton mills, performing every operation from spinning and weaving to finishing and printing, came into production in New England and elsewhere in the Northeast. They were soon followed by woolen mills and by a parallel improvement in water turbines to drive the mills.[7] In the same years the manufacturers of rifles—the most expensive tools purchased by the early nineteenth-century farmer—perfected what was then termed the "American system" of using interchangeable parts. In time the same methods enabled the machine shops of the East to invent and build milling machines and other metalworking tools which could turn out boxes of identical parts. Accordingly, when the practicable sewing machine was invented in 1846 these new techniques were at hand for its mass production and for its distribution for home and factory use. By the time the Civil War broke out, cloth and clothing were thoroughly modern machine-made products.[8]

In construction, a succession of inventions for the manufacture of hardware, windows, doors, stair parts, flooring, and uniformly sized

5. Oscar E. Anderson, Jr., *Refrigeration in America,* Princeton, 1953, pp. 14–70.
6. Brady, "Relative Prices," 192.
7. Robert B. Zevin, "The Growth of Cotton Textile Production after 1815," and Peter Temin, "Steam and Waterpower in the Early Nineteenth Century," in Robert W. Fogel and Stanley L. Engerman, *The Reinterpretation of American Economic History,* New York, 1971, pp. 122–47, 228–37.
8. Carroll W. Pursell, Jr., "Machines and Machine Tools, 1830–1880," in Melvin Kranzberg and Carroll W. Pursell, Jr., *Technology in Western Civilization,* I, New York, 1967, pp. 392–405.

lumber united with the balloon-frame pattern of nailed beams and boards to cut the costs of building.[9]

The inventions that appeared between 1820 and 1870 saved an incalculable number of man-hours, skilled and unskilled, but by today's standards the cumbersome use of the tools still required a great deal of supporting labor. A farmer had to drive the team that pulled the new reaper; each machine tool needed an operator to feed and guide it; textile mills still depended on armies of women and children to tend the looms and spinning frames. Customarily the machine at this time performed only a single step in the total process; it stitched the seam but not the buttonholes, it sewed the soles but could not form the last, it cut door parts that had to be glued, assembled, and sanded by man. Flour milling was almost fully automated, but the frequently cited meat-packing assembly line was nothing more than a way to move the work past a row of skilled men. The partial introduction of machines and the partial redesign of products, together with the small and often seasonal scale of many markets, meant that in every shop from iron foundries to shoe factories there was a considerable volume of discontinuous handwork. There was much carrying of things from one machine to the next, of setting them up for one batch and then turning to the next, and short runs of products went back and forth from machine to hand to machine.

Innovations in transport resulted in the creation of two new networks that gave the inventions a revolutionary impact, and the networks had the effect of making each invention reverberate throughout the urban system. All the elements of the urban system were themselves transformed by the new transportation, and the changes were felt in urban markets, the structure of business, and the national economy. It was transportation that made the building of a national network of cities possible even while it revolutionized the social conditions within them by vastly enlarging the economic opportunities for thousands of small businessmen.

America built its canal system in two spurts, from 1815 to 1834 and from 1836 to 1854. In the first period more than two thousand miles of canals were built to connect the Atlantic port cities with each other and with the cities and towns of what was then the West. The river steam-

9. Dorothy S. Brady, "The Effect of Mechanization on Product Design in the Course of Industrial Development," *Third International Conference of Economic History*, Munich, 1965, pp. 7–15.

boat and the canal were complementary; the steamboat made upstream travel swift and reliable, cutting the time of the journey from weeks to days and hours, and canals flowed through land formerly accessible only by difficult overland pathways. By substituting an easygoing hitch of one to three horses or mules for the straining teams of the past, freight costs were cut by 90 percent. On the Erie Canal in New York, the most successful of them all, average rates for a ton-mile of goods moving from Buffalo to New York City fell from nineteen cents in 1817 to two cents and finally to one cent after some years of operation.[10]

As the second canal boom went forward, extending existing lines and adding new Western ones, the railroad and its companion the telegraph stepped up the possibilities for high-speed travel and communications. The first railroads of the 1830s radiated from the old port cities like Baltimore and Boston to garner nearby trade. In the 1840s small cities like Albany and Binghamton in New York State made local efforts of the same sort, and big cities turned to the financing and promotion of long Western rail lines that added all-weather intercity routes to the canal connections. The railroads, unlike the state-financed canal routes, were very much the products of the cities themselves. Whether one thinks of giant projects like the Eastern Division of the Union Pacific and the Pennsylvania Railroad or of little local runs like the Albany and West Stockbridge, we find behind them Kansas City, St. Louis, Pittsburgh, Philadelphia, and Albany as prime movers as well as beneficiaries.[11]

Compared to anything that had gone before, the railroad was a wonderfully versatile transportation invention. It could cheaply join a series of small coal valleys in Pennsylvania to a canal or a larger rail complex, or it could tie together the mill towns and cities of New England. It could as readily fan out over the prairies, as it did in Illinois, opening an entire state to market agriculture. In 1840 there were three thousand miles of rails and three thousand miles of canals; by 1854 one could travel by rail all the way from New York to Chicago and St. Louis. Fifteen years later the Union Pacific and the Central Pacific

10. Carter Goodrich, ed., *Canals and American Economic Development,* New York, 1961, pp. 172, 184–85, 227–29.
11. Harry H. Pierce, *Railroads of New York, A Study of Government Aid 1826–1875,* Cambridge, 1953, pp. 115–16; Charles N. Glaab, *Kansas City and the Railroads: Community Policy in the Growth of a Regional Metropolis,* Madison, 1962, pp. 103–23.

joined to complete a transcontinental line; in a mere half century the country had undergone a thoroughgoing revolution in transportation.[12]

The powerful effect of emerging transportation upon society and its economy stemmed precisely from its ability to widen the market opportunities of everyone it served. By widening the market, that is by increasing the number of potential customers, specialization was always encouraged. Why specialization? Because in almost all cases profits may be augmented by a concentration on those crops which grow best on a given piece of land, on those products which can be made most cheaply, or on those goods most easily bought or handled in volume. For example, New York merchants trading in general metal products turned to the importation of copper or tin or railroad iron, or they became dealers in blacksmith supplies or in simple hardware for country stores.[13] The expanded grasp of the city in turn fostered rural specialization. Upstate farmers responded to the faster and cheaper transportation by switching from the few limited cash grain crops of the past to orchards, dairies, stock farms, and wool. In the process their prosperity swelled the market for manufactured goods and city services.[14]

By myriad interactions a process of development stimulated by transportation had begun. Ease of transport led to more specialized and more efficient methods of agriculture which in turn extended the markets for farm products, and the increased prosperity of the farmers gave rise to cities to supply them with a rapidly lengthening list of comforts and necessities, such as loans, hand tools, farm machinery, pots and pans, food mills, furniture, pumps, clothing, and so on and on. In this interaction lay the workings of the urban system, the truth behind the bombast of railroad Congressmen, state canal promoters, and town and city merchants, all of whom habitually hailed every road, canal, rail, or telegraph line as an "improvement."

Indeed, transportation did transform the national network of cities, changing it from a string of small commercial Atlantic coast cities into a

12. George R. Taylor, *The Transportation Revolution, 1815–1860,* New York, 1951, pp. 32–103.

13. The interaction between firm specialization and sales area is neatly documented in Elva Tooker, *Nathan Trotter, Philadelphia Merchant, 1787–1853,* Cambridge, 1955, pp. 108–31; for Trotter's competition, see Albion, *The Rise of New York Port: 1815–1860,* pp. 248–49.

14. Clarence H. Danhof, *Change in Agriculture: The Northern United States, 1820–1870,* Cambridge, 1969, pp. 4–23.

continental complex of trading centers to which were added a scattering of wholly new specialized manufacturing cities. In 1820 the nation possessed but five cities (New York, population of the present five boroughs 152,000; Philadelphia, 65,000; Baltimore, 63,000; Boston, 43,000; New Orleans, 27,000). Half a century later the leading commercial centers had grown into cities of more than a quarter of a million inhabitants. The placement of these cities reflected their functions as import-export centers joining Europe to the United States via the ocean and railroads, and as assemblers and distributors of goods through the continental United States (1870 population figures: New York, 1,478,000; Philadelphia, 674,000; St. Louis, 311,000; Chicago, 299,000; Baltimore, 267,000; Boston, 251,000). To support these six big cities, forty-five cities having populations ranging from twenty-five thousand to a quarter of a million had grown up along with them (Table 1).

The national network of six big cities and forty-five lesser ones reflected the extent of the organization of the national economy achieved

TABLE 1

	Towns 2,500–24,999		Cities 25,000–249,999		Metropolises 250,000 and larger		Total Urban Places	
	No.	% U.S. Pop.	No.	% U.S. Pop.	No.	% U.S. Pop.	No.	% U.S. Pop.
1820	56	3.58	5	3.63	–	–	61	7.21
1870	612	9.86	45	6.74	6	8.21	663	24.81
1920	2,434	15.23	263	16.00	25	19.64	2,722	50.87
1970	5,520	28.34	859	24.03	56	20.75	6,435	73.12

	Population by Size Groupings			Total Population	
	Towns	Cities	Metropolises	Urban	U.S.
1820	344,000	349,000	–	693,000	9,618,000
1870	3,933,000	2,689,000	3,280,000	9,902,000	39,905,000
1920	16,218,000	17,030,000	20,910,000	54,158,000	106,466,000
1970	57,577,000	48,829,000	42,151,000	148,557,000	203,166,000

Note: All cities are assigned population according to their changing political boundaries except New York, which is listed as one city of five boroughs in all periods. The Towns category in 1970 includes unincorporated urban fringe areas of 2,500 or greater numbers of inhabitants. Calculations were made from U.S. Bureau of the Census, *Historical Statistics of the United States, Colonial Times to 1957*, Washington, 1960, p. 14; *Fourteenth Census of the U.S.: 1920*, I, *Population*, Washington, 1921, pp. 62–75; *Statistical Abstract of the U.S.: 1971*, Washington, 1971, p. 17. Some disagreement in detail exists among these sources, and in such cases the Fourteenth Census has been followed because it gave specific listings of city populations by name of city.

during the years 1820–70.[15] All fifty-one cities constituted an integrated commercial interdependency, a hierarchy of trade governed by New York and supervised by the regional centers of Philadelphia, St. Louis, Chicago, Baltimore, and Boston. Banking and wholesale trade in farm staples and some manufactured goods were controlled by the market rates and prices in these national and international trading centers.[16] Wheat, cotton, corn, banknotes, bonds, cloth, iron, books, and all manner of goods for which there were large markets were traded in the regional centers, but with an eye to New York and ultimately to Atlantic demand and prices. Regional bankers and merchant houses maintained correspondents and agents in New York to keep them posted and to negotiate for purchases and sales. In view of these financial and commercial linkages, the United States in 1870 could be said to be an integrated national economy organized around its major city markets.

The entire economy, however, was as yet only partially organized on a national basis because manufacturing had not yet settled into the pattern whereby each specialty located in its best site, and from such a single base or cluster of bases sold its products throughout the nation. In 1870 such common items as stoves, hardware, kitchenwares, farm machinery, steam engines and locomotives, carriages, wagons, clothing, and shoes were being manufactured in cities and towns all over the United States. The network of cities reflected this fragmented and overlapping placement. The six largest of them had added a wide range of manufactures to their commercial base and were producing an extraordinary variety of goods from fur muffs and gas lights to ships and steam engines. In the duplication of effort, Philadelphia's furniture mills made the same Windsor chairs as their Boston, New York, and Chicago counterparts, while the Philadelphia weavers made a line of goods from mosquito netting to muslins, repeating the line of the textile towns in New York and New England. Such repetitiousness reflected the mixed

15. The forty-five cities in rank order were: Cincinnati, New Orleans, San Francisco, Buffalo, Washington, Newark, Louisville, Cleveland, Pittsburgh, Jersey City, Detroit, Milwaukee, Albany, Providence, Rochester, Allegheny (now part of Pittsburgh), Richmond, New Haven, Charleston (South Carolina), Indianapolis, Troy, Syracuse, Worcester, Lowell, Memphis, Cambridge, Hartford, Scranton, Reading, Paterson, Kansas City (Missouri), Mobile, Toledo, Portland (Maine), Columbus (Ohio), Wilmington (Delaware), Dayton, Lawrence, Utica, Charlestown (Massachusetts), Savannah, Lynn, Fall River, Springfield (Massachusetts), and Nashville. U.S. Bureau of the Census, *Fourteenth Census of the U.S.: 1920, Population,* Washington, 1921, p. 81.

16. Duncan and Lieberson, *Metropolis and Region in Transition,* pp. 43–58, 116.

tendencies of the times, for each big city was in part a market unto itself and produced for its own region, even while it was also a dealer in outside goods now beginning to be produced for national markets. It took perfection of the rail network and the organization of the large corporation to put an end to these anomalies.

The lesser cities reflected the same lack of national specialization in manufacturing. In the list of forty-five stood commercial cities whose principal activity lay in trading with their rural hinterlands, as had Baltimore and Boston in previous years. Such cities as New Orleans, Memphis, Indianapolis, Kansas City, Portland (Maine), and Rochester served their local regions with imported goods and traded as well in the local specialties of sugar, cotton, corn, cattle, grain, and lumber in the traditional manner of commercial cities. Their rapid growth over a half century reflected the settlement of the continent and the impact of river, canal, and rail transportation on growth and diversification. Other cities on the list represented the new industrial specializations for large-scale production: Lowell, textiles; Reading and Scranton, anthracite; Providence, machine tools; Hartford, guns; Utica and Troy, textiles and machinery. In some cases an industrial specialty contributed to a commercial city's growth, as did ironworking in Pittsburgh, meat packing in Cincinnati and Chicago, and oil refining in Cleveland. To appreciate fully the contribution of early manufacturing to the urbanization of the United States, one has only to consider the case of the still largely rural South, which had only eight cities on the national list of 1870. Although scholars disagree concerning the reasons for the retarded urbanization and industrialization in the region south of the Ohio and east of the Mississippi River, its agricultural economy in 1870 resembled an underdeveloped eighteenth-century colony and had little in common with the boom conditions of the Northeast and Midwest.[17] One can perceive the lineaments of the future growth of the two great manufacturing belts in the 1870 mixture of cities, factory towns, and commercial centers which had already grown up there.

Just as the national network of cities had transformed the lives of American farmers, so the sheer magnitude of these new cities radically affected the lives of city dwellers. The metropolises were after all five to ten times as large as the leading cities of half a century before, and it is not an exaggeration to maintain that in the years from 1820 to 1870 no

17. Douglass C. North, *The Economic Growth of the United States, 1790–1860*, Englewood Cliffs, New Jersey, 1961, pp. 4–7, 189–203.

important facet of urban life was left untouched by the rapid change in scale. Yet the setting for these changes would now appear strange to us because the cities of the 1820–70 era were so different from our own. They were cities of storekeepers and small sweatshop factories, of businesses run by one boss or a few partners, of the scattering of shops and workrooms among residences, of mixed neighborhoods of rich and poor, native and immigrant, and of strong smells and slovenly habits coexisting with stiff and polished propriety.

The enlarged markets for the sale of goods within the cities worked in two ways to change the organization of business and the nature of urban jobs. First, as the city grew so did its needs, and residentiary industries such as little local bakeries spread through the neighborhoods of the city.[18] Second, export industries were bound to multiply and expand when a city could sell to a broader region around it. For example, New York's cracker industry grew lustily to sell barrels of hard crackers far and wide to country stores and to ships' captains. In many cases local and distant markets overlapped. New York sold steam engines to shipbuilders and factories in the immediate environs even as it exported them to distant mills; it made the same line of clothing for local workingmen that it made for country stores or Southern plantations.

The new markets relentlessly favored a different kind of businessman, called in those years a contractor or capitalist, whom today we could perhaps best describe as a hustler. Inventions were important in the reorganization of business by small proprietors and partnerships, but since early machinery served at most as a substitute for a few hand tasks, the principal gains in production accrued to bosses who could organize their shopworkers for a steady production of uniform output. These emerging businessmen recruited labor from the old independent artisan shops where a complete product had been made by one man, or by a couple of men assisted by a boy or a family. They moved artisans, unskilled immigrants, women, and children into their own shops, where they could watch over them. Or they carried unfinished garments and products from shop to shop and tenement to tenement, issuing the strictest instructions for their completion. Instead of waiting for orders from individual customers to come in the door, these capitalists solicited

18. Sam Bass Warner, Jr., "The Feeding of Large Cities in the United States, 1860–1960," *Third International Conference of Economic History,* Munich, 1965, pp. 83–87.

business from wholesale merchants and produced for the expanding anonymous urban market. By a combination of hard driving, strict supervision, and a certain amount of machinery, they transformed such cities as New York, Philadelphia, and Boston from artisan towns into hives of small factories and wholesale outlets (Table 2, page 93).

The transformation went forward even in the most ordinary and unmechanized activities. Often the old and the new existed side by side. In New York there was still work in 1870 for the carpenter who followed the ancient custom of bidding on a house or two each year and doing most of the work himself, for the tailor who measured and fitted each suit individually, or for the wood carver who carried his tools from shop to shop, following his own preferences in employers. But higher rewards than a commonplace living wage awaited the man who determined to expand. A carpenter could become an entrepreneur by transforming himself into a contractor and hiring a mixed crew of men—some skilled but many unskilled—to install the new factory-produced windows, doors, moldings, and stairs. By rushing from job to job he could manage to erect whole groups of houses by his own energy and by driving his workers, and so enjoy the patronage of speculators in the city's periodic real-estate booms. He could grow wealthy while his old crew of skilled artisans and day workers would be left behind. Similarly a tailor might break down the skills of his craft into its components of cutting, basting, buttonhole making, and the like and place his unskilled or semiskilled tasks in the homes of poor women, children, and immigrants. He could prosper in the urban market for workers' ready-made clothing and could sell as well to the country stores whose merchants came regularly to the big cities to buy stock.

Well before sewing machines were invented, before tin ceilings or cast-iron store fronts were used, even before balloon-frame house construction had been popularized, the merchant capitalist and contractor came forward in the American city to reorganize its labor. These were the drivers of men who lengthened the workers' hours, abolished the holidays and self-determined comings and goings of independent artisans, broke down the craft traditions, and oriented the business of the city toward ever spiraling production and sales.[19]

19. John R. Commons, et al., *History of Labour in the United States*. I, New York, 1918, pp. 338–50; for the garment manufacture case, Oscar Handlin, *Boston's Immigrants: A Study in Acculturation*, Cambridge, rev. ed., 1959, pp. 75–77; for building trades, Brady, "Effect of Mechanization on Project Design," p. 12.

The cities of course had their inventors too, men who saw opportunity in the expansion of the day and made their fortunes by adding personal mechanisms and techniques to existing methods. In New York City, Peter Cooper (1791–1883), former wood carver, manufacturer of shears for the napping of wool cloth, and grocer, made the decision to compete with imported glue and gelatin. By careful attention to the details of manufacture and with the aid of a few inventions bearing on the processes, he was able to offer a cheaper and more uniform product than had been in use before. As New York and its markets grew, his glue boiling prospered magnificently.[20] There were many inventor-manufacturers like Cooper in the big cities of this period, such as the shipbuilding Stevens family in Hoboken in the port of New York and the machine-making Sellers brothers in Philadelphia, but invention also flourished in mill towns over the whole East and Midwest. In this era of tinkering, wherever there were machines there were inventors.

The big cities, however, did tend to have a particularly encouraging effect on inventions and in time more or less concentrated the innovators within their bounds. This encouragement was compounded of the complementary suppliers and marketing firms that surrounded them in the urban districts. Cooper, for example, had set his glueworks near the slaughterhouse of Henry Astor, where hooves were abundant and cheap. In these days before dressed meat could be shipped in refrigerator cars and indeed before there were cattle cars on the railroads for the shipment of livestock, cattle were driven to the city to be killed, and New York City was the slaughtering capital of the nation. Furthermore, the city's users of glue—shoemakers, bookbinders, furniture manufacturers, and so on—were located near at hand as ready consumers of his product, and he was thus dealing with America's largest wholesale and retail market. Although the city of this period was made up of a multiplicity of small firms—smaller in most instances than Cooper's glueworks—the clustering of complementary businesses made expansion easy.

The swelling of urban markets into a partially integrated national economy and the consequent transformation of business into a swarm of small aggressive production and marketing firms had drastic and enduring consequences for urban workers. The explosive growth of cities created something like a labor vacuum into which were sucked thou-

20. Allan Nevins, *Abram S. Hewitt, With Some Account of Peter Cooper,* New York, 1935, pp. 45–62.

sands upon thousands of rural migrants. A profound cultural shock
ensued. Native workers had to face up to the reality of competing and
coexisting with waves of foreign immigrants. To add to the difficulty of
their adjustment, depressions and periodic mass unemployment now
threatened their jobs for the first time in our history. The closer linkages
of urban work to national and international sales made each city
economy a captive of worldwide business cycles. Finally, the new
stricter discipline and the growing size of shops and factories reversed
the egalitarian trends of the early merchant-artisan city and instituted
the deep class cleavages between hand workers and paper workers, between working class and middle class.

The nineteenth-century American city was a magnet for immigrants.
From the 1820s onward, young men flocked to the city from American
farms and towns as well as from European villages, towns, and cities. In
the years before 1870, Great Britain, Ireland, and Germany supplied
most of the immigrants (Table 3, page 168). Over and over, the
story was repeated of the eager youth who, in seeking his fortune,
accepted the heightened pace of work and the endless hours of labor as
a challenge. He tried to work ever harder than his competitors, contributing his youth to the energy of the city. A tale of that period that
speaks of boys from the New England countryside makes clear the
standards of morality and behavior by which such newcomers were
judged:

> With a few dollars and a mother's prayer, the young hero goes forth to
> seek his fortune in the great mart of commerce. He needs but a foothold.
> He asks no more, and he is as sure to keep it as the light will dispell
> darkness. He gets a place somewhere in a "store." It is all store to him.
> He hardly comprehends the difference between the business of the great
> South street house, that sends ships over the world, and the Bowery dry
> goods shop with three or four spruce clerks. He rather thinks the Bowery
> or Canal street store the biggest, as they make more show. But wherever
> this boy strikes, he fastens. He is honest, determined, and intelligent.
> From the word "go" he begins to learn, to compare, and no matter what
> the commercial business he is engaged in, he will not rest until he knows
> all about it, its details—in fact, as much as his principals.
>   Another characteristic of the future merchant is this—no sooner has
> he got a foothold, than the New England boy begins to look for standing
> room for others. Perhaps he is the son of a small farmer who has
> several other children. The pioneer boy, if true blue, does not rest until
> one by one he has procured situations for all of his brothers. If he has

The Big City

Urbanscape

tioned Federal blocks to the new tall, narrow, heavy-corniced tenements of contemporary fashion. *New-York Historical Society*

23. West Washington Market, New York, 1880s. As the city's population grew, markets expanded from old neighborhood stalls, where housewives shopped daily, to specialized farmers' and grocers' wholesale distributing centers. Here, a market built in 1858. *New-York Historical Society*

24. West 133rd Street, New York, ca. 1877. Like today's suburban fringes, speculators' housing took up broken parcels of land at the city's growing outer edge. *New-York Historical Society*

25. Fifth Avenue, 116th and 117th Streets, New York, 1893. The fringe shanties of the poor. *New-York Historical Society*

Business

26. 168–172 Fulton Street, New York, ca. 1820. The shop and warehouse of the famous furniture maker Duncan Phyfe. Typical small-scale enterprise of the first era of industrialization. *Metropolitan Museum of Art, Rogers Fund, 1922*

27. 512–514 Broome Street, New York, 1935. The photographer Berenice Abbott in her *Changing New York* recorded extremes of the big-city era; two old houses towered over by a six-story warehouse, the limit of construction before the steel-frame skyscraper of the industrial metropolis. *Museum of the City of New York*

28. Coenties Slip, New York, ca. 1879. Three-to-four-story merchant warehouses and docks overshadowed by new elevated railway, whose high volume of traffic raised downtown land values until the traditional urban framework could no longer accommodate the enlarged scale of business enterprise. *New-York Historical Society*

29. Hudson Street, New York, ca. 1865. The big-city hive of small shops. *New-York Historical Society*

30. 480 Water Street, New York, ca. 1863. In the preindustrial era, barns and churches were *the* commonplace large structures. Here, a typical barnlike building serves as factory for a ship joiner making deckhouses. *New-York Historical Society*

31. Wall Street, New York, ca. 1878. A Sunday, presumably, at the heart of American finance, the small scale of early capitalist concentration. *New-York Historical Society*

Transportation

32. Coffee-House Slip, New York, 1830. Packet Lines offering abundant regularly scheduled sailings from New York to European and East Coast ports were a key to the city's mercantile supremacy. *Eno Collection, New York Public Library, Astor, Lenox, and Tilden Foundations*

33. Canal Boats, New York, 1852. Before the organization of wholesale lumber districts and grain elevators, shippers and canal boats carried small lots of farm and forest products to regional trading centers for manufacture and processing. *New-York Historical Society*

34. Highlands of the Hudson River, 1874. River artery of early industrial economy: sloops, schooners, canal boats under tow, the Albany–New York dayliner *Mary Powell* on the first New York thruway. *New-York Historical Society*

35. South Street, New York, 1880s. Square-riggers and small merchant warehouses, Atlantic links of the nation's first big city. *New-York Historical Society*

36. Grand Central Station at 42nd Street, New York, 1875. A deceptively small and elegant Paris-style hotel façade conceals the overarching power of the intercity railroad network. This new transportation system remade New York's economy into a national industrial metropolis, adding manufacturing to its established functions of finance and commerce. *New-York Historical Society*

37. Interior of Grand Central Station, New York, 1885. Such passenger train sheds were seen by contemporaries as symbols of the force of a new era. "What forces, what fates, slept in these bulks (great night trains lying on the tracks) which would soon be hurling themselves . . . through the night!" William Dean Howells, *A Hazard of New Fortunes* (1890). The French Impressionist Claude Monet painted seven scenes in and around Gare Saint-Lazare (1876–77), manifesting the same spirit. *New-York Historical Society*

38. General Motors Plant, Linden, New Jersey, 1967. Early nineteenth-century canal and railroad alignments permanently laid down the basic industrial skeleton of today's Northeastern megalopolis. Here, an auto assembly plant, fifteen miles from Manhattan along the old New York–Philadelphia transportation axis, U.S. Highway No. 1 (left) and Penn Central Railroad tracks (right). *Regional Plan Association, Louis B. Schlivek*

39. Grand Street Livery Stables, New York, 1865. The livery stable was the back-up transportation equivalent of today's truck and auto rental chains.

Their flies, manure, and smell were the bane of every neighborhood. *New-York Historical Society*

40. Greenwich Street Elevated, New York, 1867. Inventor of a cable-drawn engine, Charles T. Harvey, tries it out on the city's first el. *New-York Historical Society*

41. Greenwich Street Elevated at Ninth Avenue, New York, 1876. Typical American failure to adapt transportation innovations to the city's inherited framework. Here, old West Side working-class and industrial quarter is attacked by the new transit system. *New-York Historical Society*

15. New York, 1849

16. Boston, 1855

17. San Francisco, 1850–51

18. Broadway, New York, 1834

19. Broadway, New York, 1870s

20. Hudson Square, New York, 1866–67

21. Fifth Avenue from 28th Street, New York, 1865

22. Working-Class New York, Canal and Mott Streets, ca. 1870

23. West Washington Market, New York, 1880s

24. West 133rd Street, New York, ca. 1877

25. Fifth Avenue, 116th and 117th Streets, New York, 1893

26. 168–172 Fulton Street, New York, ca. 1820

27. 512–514 Broome Street, New York, 1935

28. Coenties Slip, New York, ca. 1879

29. Hudson Street, New York, ca. 1865

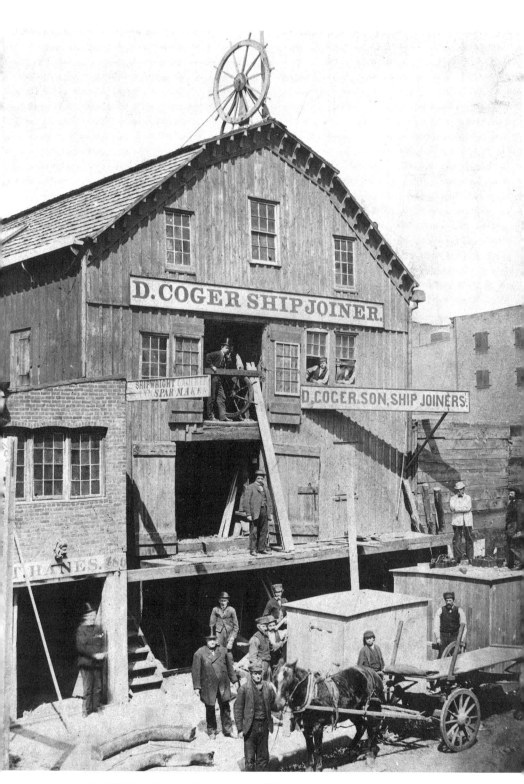

30. 480 Water Street, New York, ca. 1863

31. Wall Street, New York, ca. 1878

32. Coffee-House Slip, New York, 1830

33. Canal Boats, New York, 1852

34. Highlands of the Hudson River, 1874

35. South Street, New York, 1880s

36. Grand Central Station, New York, 1875

37. Interior of Grand Central Station, New York, 1885

38. General Motors Plant, Linden, New Jersey, 1967

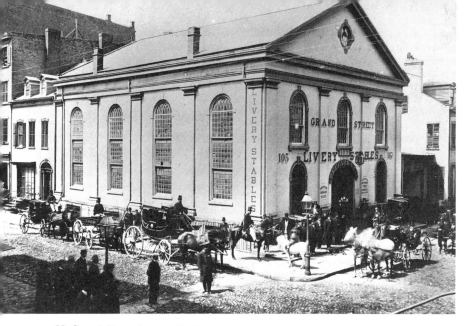

39. Grand Street Livery Stables, New York. 1865

40. Greenwich Street Elevated, New York, 1867

41. Greenwich Street Elevated at Ninth Avenue, New York, 1876

none, he has friends in the village, and ere a year, Bill, Jo and Jim have been seduced off to New York.[21]

Unlike European countries of the time, the United States was an undeveloped land of bounteous resources which sustained a severe shortage of skilled labor. It offered high rewards to men who practiced a craft, and foreign-born artisans became leaders in many of the crafts in America. German immigrants predominated in New York in such diverse trades as sugar refining, the making of pianos and guns, and in lithography. Watchcase makers came from France and Switzerland, glass cutters from Ireland; ship riggers were Swedish, machinists British.

Urban production for a widening market also implied dependence upon a national and an international economy in a way that earlier artisans had never known. There were boom times, but there were also busts, panics, and depressions that caught all America and its London bankers short of orders, money, and credit. At such times wages might plummet 30 and 40 percent in a year's time. It has been estimated that a third of New York City's work force became unemployed in the panic of 1837. The depression in the winter of 1854–55 caused such widespread misery that a relief group claimed 195,000 men, women, and children were in want.[22] With every decade the cities burgeoned and intertwined more tightly with the rest of the United States and the world, so that each swing of depression meant longer breadlines, more evictions, more pervasive suffering.

The increase in the scale of production and the reach of markets started a long process of division into two classes within the urban labor force. The new discipline of urban work harassed and enticed Americans into a permanent acceptance of a social division between hand workers and pen wielders, operatives and clerks, the blue collar and the white. The pace of market growth was so fantastic that it impelled the enlargement of family shops and those with four or five employees to establishments with a dozen, fifty, even hundreds of workers. A number of results could be seen at once: the introduction of strict discipline and the systematic exploitation of women and children, the breakdown of

21. Walter Barrett (pseud. Joseph A. Scoville), *The Old Merchants of New York City*, New York, 1865, pp. 57–58. Note that this same spirit of youthful energy for moneymaking and success also characterizes the Lithuanian immigrant Jurgis Rudkus in Upton Sinclair's anticapitalist novel *The Jungle* (New York, 1906).

22. Ernst, *Immigrant Life*, pp. 73–83.

complex craft skills into simple repetitive tasks, the drive for quantity by cutting piecework rates and by the introduction of machinery. Simultaneously a whole new class appeared—the well-to-do class of owners and partners who always enjoyed prosperity far beyond their employees and sometimes attained the undreamed-of wealth of a John Jacob Astor, a Peter Cooper, or a Cornelius Vanderbilt.

The widening gulf between classes by no means went unnoticed by contemporaries. From the first, workingmen of the largest cities protested the loss of control over their working lives, and to combat it they formed unions. In the 1820s and 1830s, early in the process of differentiation between boss and worker, some unions included masters and shopowners who sympathized with the men or were themselves oppressed by wholesale competition. The great Ten-Hour movement of the thirties appeared as a wave of enthusiastic strikes and parades and swept the Eastern coast cities. It sought relief from the unbroken sunrise-to-sunset hours that had once been only seasonal or rush practices and asked for reduction in hours without reduction in pay.

It was the depression of 1837–39 that broke the power of the workingman and his new organizations. Subsequent hard times and panics, as well as the counterorganization of employers, attacked later revivals of unionism. Only a few highly skilled unions seemed able to establish themselves permanently, groups like the printers, cigar makers, iron molders, and the members of some of the building trades. Though the union movement as a countervailing force to business reorganization remained endemic throughout the nineteenth century, everything worked against it: the steady erosion of craft skills and the consequent weakening of the bargaining power of the men, the growing influx of foreign labor and the ceaseless coming and going of all working groups in a restless search for decent wages and better conditions, the competitive and exploitative use of women and children and untrained immigrants, and the expansion of business that put more and more wealth and political influence into the hands of employers in labor disputes. The same factors worked against the men's attempts to set up producers' cooperatives and other social experiments, while the working-class political parties were destroyed by competition with another social outgrowth of this era, the urban political machine. The machine could successfully undercut the labor parties by delivering jobs and opportunities to its faithful party workers at the same time that it was giving verbal support to workers' platforms.[23] Indeed, it has long been one of the major functions of American politics to blur class conflicts in order to appeal to the broadest possible coalition of voters.[24]

The very fact that the early nineteenth-century trend toward widening social distinctions between working class and middle class was a reversal of former preindustrial tendencies made the process all the more painful. During and after the Revolution, the urban artisan had gained a growing measure of political participation and power. Jacksonian democracy rose on the momentum of these years, only to collapse as social conditions in factories, cities, and farms undermined its dependence on a vanishing social reality of independent artisans, shopkeepers, and farmers.

In the period between 1776 and 1820, America seemed to be moving toward a growing egalitarianism. In the old commercial cities of the time, cities of small shopkeepers and merchants, the lines between worker and owner were blurred despite an obvious coexistence of rich and poor and the prominence of families of long-standing privilege and influence. Then beginning in the 1820s, as business quickened and harsh methods spread, the benign trends reversed themselves and the inexorable advance of blue-collar–white-collar distinctions commenced. Despite the unions, parades, strikes, and political parties that centered on the workingman, the hand worker lost ground. He lost status, he lost assurance of employment, and he lost personal control over his work. Ensuing waves of frustration and anger broke over the city. All the big cities suffered epidemics of violence; there were labor riots, race riots, native-foreign riots, Catholic-Protestant riots, rich-poor riots.[25] New York City alone underwent a succession of riots, eight major and at least ten minor, between 1834 and 1871. The climax came in 1863 as a mixed class and race riot, begun in protest against the draft, exploded among the city's workingmen and poor Irish.

---

23. Commons, *History of Labour*, I, pp. 169–84; Norman Ware, *The Industrial Worker 1840–1860*, Boston, 1924, pp. 18–70.

24. For example, the industrialist Peter Cooper, like many Americans of his time, mixed Jacksonian antibanker, popular democratic ideas with strong antiforeign, anti-Catholic and staunch probusiness politics. See Robert P. Sharkey, *Money, Class and Power, An Economic Study of Civil War and Reconstruction*, Baltimore, 1959, pp. 276–84; and Edward C. Mack, *Peter Cooper*, New York, 1949, pp. 357–72.

25. Hugh B. Graham and Ted R. Gurr, *Violence in America: Historical and Comparative Perspectives*, New York, 1969, pp. 53–55.

Early in the morning men began to assemble here [on the West Side] in separate groups, as if in accordance with a previous arrangement, and at last moved quietly north along the various avenues. Women, also, like camp followers, took the same direction in crowds. . . . The factories and workshops were visited, and the men compelled to knock off work and join them, while the proprietors were threatened with the destruction of their property, if they made any opposition.

A ragged, coatless, heterogeneously weaponed army, it heaved tumultuously along Third Avenue. Tearing down the telegraph poles as it crossed the Harlem & New Haven Railroad track, it surged angrily up around the building where the drafting was going on. The small squad of police stationed there to repress disorder looked on bewildered, feeling they were powerless in the presence of such a host. Soon a stone went crashing through the window, which was a signal for a general assault on the doors. These giving way before the immense pressure, the foremost rushed in, followed by shouts and yells from those behind, and began to break up the furniture. The drafting officers, in an adjoining room, alarmed, fled precipitously through the rear of the building. The mob seized the wheel in which were the names, and what books, papers, and lists were left, and tore them up, and scattered them in every direction. A safe stood on one side, which was supposed to contain important papers, and on this they fell with clubs and stones, but in vain. Enraged at being thwarted, they set fire to the building, and hurried out of it. As the smoke began to ascend, the onlooking multitude without sent up a loud cheer.

The scene in Third Avenue at this time was fearful and appalling. It was now noon, but the hot July sun was obscured by heavy clouds, that hung in ominous shadows over the city, while from near Cooper Institute to Forty-sixth Street, or about thirty blocks, the avenue was black with human beings,—sidewalks, house-tops, windows, and stoops all filled with rioters or spectators. Dividing it like a stream, horse-cars arrested in their course lay strung along as far as the eye could reach. As the glance ran along this mighty mass of men and women north, it rested at length on huge columns of smoke rolling heavenward from burning buildings, giving a still more fearful aspect to the scene. Many estimated the number at this time in the street at fifty thousand.[26]

For four days mobs of workingmen and lower-class citizens broke into the stores and homes of the rich, beat and killed policemen, and fought pitched battles against the companies of police and militia. They broke into the armories, felled telegraph poles, and closed off streets by means of cobblestone barricades. The city police and the troops who were rushed back from Gettysburg quelled the riot but only after the city

26. Joel T. Headley, *The Great Riots of New York: 1712–1873*, New York, 1873, reprint, Indianapolis, 1970, pp. 160–61, 164.

had suffered casualties estimated as high as two thousand killed and eight thousand injured. If the estimates are accurate, they would make the casualties of the New York Draft Riots equivalent to the losses at Shiloh or Bull Run.[27]

Unquestionably these riots, likened by contemporaries to the uprising in Europe in 1848 and later to the Paris Commune of 1871, frightened generations of wealthy Americans. The idea of a class war between worker and capitalist, though never widely adopted despite energetic Marxist indoctrination, became an indelible part of the thinking of the wealthy at least until the Second World War. But there was a more immediate and progressive consequence of the riots: the undertaking of a systematic investigation into urban living conditions.

What were these early big cities of America like?

They were a crowded jumble of small buildings organized as yet by only the most primitive specialization of land use. Imagine a city of half a million or even a million inhabitants in which church steeples stood out on the skyline and the masts and spars of ships at the wharves could be seen above the roofs of warehouses and factories. As yet there were no giant manufacturing lofts or skyscrapers to house offices and stores, partly because the techniques for erecting such structures had not been perfected but also because there was as yet no pressing need for them. The downtown office of the mid-nineteenth century consisted of one to three partners and a few clerks. The unique downtown institutions of this era were not skyscraper banks or corporate office towers but the Merchants' Exchange and the Stock Exchange, the settings for periodic gatherings of businessmen who met each day to transact their business together. A big daily newspaper office and plant, like Horace Greeley's *Tribune,* fitted on a downtown street in a modest five-story building, one of several in a row that made up the block. The factories in which the new discipline and new machines were being introduced were for the most part small affairs. They might be housed in a floor or two of an ancient narrow building belonging to a merchant, in a basement, in a rear-yard structure of one or two stories that resembled a barn, or perhaps, in some trades like the making of cigars or clothing, in the tenement room of the worker himself.

Capacious factories and shipyards did stand at the edge of the city, but the modest spatial demand of most business enterprises meant that

27. Herbert Asbury, *The Gangs of New York, An Informal History of the Underworld,* London, 1928, pp. 169–70.

they could be served by one or a few building lots. Accordingly, every part of the city contained shops and small factories. Let us look at New York's fashionable Washington Square as examined in detail after the Draft Riots. Doctor F. A. Burrell of 22 West Eleventh Street, who conducted the inspection, reported a population of 27,587 in the area (the Fifteenth Ward), occupying almost three thousand buildings: "The style of living of the population presents every variety from luxury to poverty, and almost every branch of industry is represented." There were in fact forty-eight factories, which turned out such products as pianos, cabinet furniture, trunks, sewing machines, chocolate, carriages, photographic materials, and hoopskirts, and there was one slaughter-house and one soap and candle factory. The survey also identified 542 "stores" of all kinds and 234 "dram shops" (which we would now call bars), 23 "lager bier saloons," 17 gambling saloons, 7 concert saloons, 76 brothels, and 22 policy shops.[28] Hardly the modern bourgeois residential style.

For all its conglomeration of little buildings, the early big city was not a disorganized hodgepodge. It had an internal structure that held within the limitations of its day the potential for future elaboration. Those businesses which handled a considerable volume of goods, whether of trade or manufacture, huddled together next to the wharves because intracity freight transport was so arduous and expensive. Once the railroads, lake and coastwise schooners, river steamers, or canal-boats had been loaded, they could take their freight cheaply from one city to the next, but within the city their cargoes had to move from warehouse to warehouse by handcarts or horse-drawn wagons. A special flavor pervaded the mixed downtown areas of the period. They were districts densely settled by unprepossessing offices and stores and factories of all kinds, and even by sugar refineries and slaughterhouses, side by side with the more genteel firms that dealt in banking, law, insurance, or cloth. In St. Louis, Philadelphia, or New York, commerce encircled the port and stood on the banks of the Mississippi, the Delaware, or the East and Hudson rivers.[29]

Surrounding this characteristically mixed downtown section were two types of neighborhood, the slums and the streets of fashion. As

28. Citizens' Association of New York, *Report of the Council of Hygiene and Public Health upon the Sanitary Condition of the City,* New York, 1865, pp. 132–45.
29. Leon Moses and Harold F. Williamson, "The Location of Economic Activities in Cities," *American Economic Review,* 57 (May 1967), 211–22.

housing aged and commercial uses made living in old core sections unpleasant, landlords converted private homes into rookeries for the poor, who crowded into the tiny new rooms or into attics and cellars to be near downtown jobs. In some cases a local neighborhood served as an industrial quarter on its own, given over to shoemaking or the garment trade. These were not the huge slums of later times; they were accommodations of a lower sort than ever existed again, but they were limited in extent. Most of the poor mingled instead with middle-class families by renting rooms and apartments all over the city. Even by 1870 the characteristic residential form of the American city was not yet that of a core of poverty and an outer rim of affluence.[30]

Just beyond downtown, a street or two would be filled with the homes of the wealthy. These were the merchants, manufacturers, doctors, and lawyers who could afford valuable land and who wished to enjoy the prominence and convenience of a central address. Beacon Hill in Boston, Chestnut Street in Philadelphia, and Washington Square in New York remain as reminders of the housing habits of the rich. These early sections also marked the axes of fashion for their cities, so that when later growth and a movement to the suburbs drove the wealthy and their followers uptown and beyond the city, their new homes advanced in the same general direction that had been plotted by their inner-city streets.[31]

Outside the slum streets and fashionable blocks stretched acre upon acre sheltering mingled commercial, industrial, and residential neighborhoods that have no counterpart in our own day. Boardinghouses stood beside prosperous homes, mill workers crowded around a suburban establishment like Peter Cooper's glueworks, while the owner's home stood alone across a field from the group. Another row of houses for downtown workers might stand a block away, and back lots were universally crammed with stables and blacksmith shops and lumber yards.

30. The mixed character of the city in this era is confirmed by the journey-to-work estimates of Pred, *Spatial Dynamics,* pp. 197–213, and by comparison of activities in a slum like the Sixth Ward to an upper East Side new district like Sanitary District 22, in Citizens' Association, *Report of the Council of Hygiene,* pp. 77–80, 275–77.

31. For a systematic confirmation of earlier studies of the clustering and migration of upper-income city dwellers, see Peter G. Goheen, *Victorian Toronto, 1850–1900: Pattern and Process of Growth,* Chicago, 1970, pp. 123, 146–47; also Walter Firey, *Land Use in Central Boston,* Cambridge, 1947, pp. 74–86; and E. Digby Baltzell, *Philadelphia Gentlemen, The Making of a National Upper Class,* Glencoe, 1958, pp. 174–77.

Baldwin's locomotive works in Philadelphia, a leading enterprise of the city, was a definition point for a fine mixed white-collar and blue-collar residential section.

If the criterion of urbanity is the mixture of classes and ethnic groups, in some cases including a mixture of blacks and whites, along with dense living and crowded streets and the omnipresence of all manner of business near the homes in every quarter, then the cities of the United States in the years between 1820 and 1870 marked the zenith of our national urbanity.

4

The Segregated City

—

Chicago 1870–1920:
factories, railroads,
and skyscrapers

MOTORISTS SPEEDING ALONG the New York Thruway, their glance drawn for a moment by a fragment of stonework from an old Erie Canal lock, may find it hard to see in such small constructions the fateful determination of their own lives, but the artifacts of the second period of industrialization present no such problems of self-recognition. We live among the objects of that age—its railroad stations and yards still stand near the center of town, its rows of warehouses and factories line many of the main streets of any city old enough to have grown up in those years. Its luxury apartments, when still maintained, are widely sought after for their old-fashioned charm and spaciousness, its houses of the well-to-do are the objects of neighborhood defense against destruction by urban renewal, while its parks, boulevards, office towers, and public buildings are often the only monuments to civic pride and luxury in our cities. These structures among which we live are but symbols of our more meaningful ties to this former time. Its manufacturing belts have coalesced into our megalopolises, and many of its business institutions are today's largest corporations. The archetypal city of this era was the industrial metropolis—the city of the mechanized factory, the business corporation, the downtown office, and the segregated neighborhood.

In technological terms the progression from the first era of industrialization (1820–70) to the second (1870–1920) can be characterized as a giant leap forward in power, speed, energy, and adaptability. The

85

complex machine ceased to be an innovation and became ubiquitous. The period actually opened in 1863 in France with the invention of the Siemens-Martin open-hearth method of high-quality steelmaking, and in 1865 with the introduction of cheap Bessemer steel production in Troy, New York. With the abundance of steels came all the elaboration of engineering that distinguished the times—high-speed rails, massive bridges and viaducts, skyscrapers, battleships, and finally automobiles. Mastery of the technology of electricity made possible the application of energy in measured quantities wherever it was needed, a boon denied to the operators of the cumbersome pulleys, shafts, and belts in the preceding days when power was generated by steam and waterwheels. Now electricity could run an individual streetcar or light a lamp in one room as easily as it could illuminate a skyscraper; it could pull a mammoth assembly line or drive a single sewing machine. Moreover, electric power could be transmitted hundreds of miles from its source, thereby allowing manufacturing plants to seek their best transportation, labor, service, and sales locations rather than clinging to waterpower sites. Explorations taking place in the field of chemistry made possible the refining of petroleum, the manufacture of dyes and high explosives, and the compounding of new alloys. The repeated economic successes of technological innovations led to the institutionalization of invention itself, so that firms regularly set aside money for the specific task of discovering new tools, products, processes, and modes of transmitting energy.[1]

The ubiquity of power and machines in the late nineteenth and early twentieth centuries had profound effects on the American urban system. First the new technics encouraged urbanization in general by drawing more and more Americans into those economic roles which peculiarly favored the growth of cities. Mechanization of agriculture, mining, and lumbering freed a multitude of workers for alternative tasks in manufacturing, transport, finance, and the servicing of business. So successful were the new modes of factory production in saving manpower that in the fifty years after 1870 the ratio of Americans employed in marketing, transportation, and services, the very specialties of cities, grew more rapidly than the ratio of those in manufacturing itself.[2]

1. Jacob Schmookler, *Invention and Economic Growth,* Cambridge, 1966, pp. 199–209; Melvin Kranzberg and Carroll W. Pursell, Jr., *Technology in Western Civilization,* I, New York, 1967, pp. 357, 563–692.

2. Harvey S. Perloff et al., *Regions, Resources, and Economic Growth,* Baltimore, 1960, pp. 131, 151–61, 168.

Second, the functions of cities within the national urban network shifted. The largest cities diversified, becoming great manufacturing centers as well as places of commerce and finance. At the same time, small cities which specialized either in manufacturing a narrow line of goods or in processing regional products for the national market multiplied and prospered. These growing small cities were not, however, evenly distributed across the nation but were concentrated in the Northeast and Midwest. Because the new electrical and automobile technology built upon the skills and tools of the old iron and steam technology, the cities of these two industrialized regions stood in a favored position for making the components of the new age.[3]

Even the crudest classification of the nation's cities by size of population reveals the new trends (Table 1, page 70). Industrial diversification spurred the growth of metropolises. The 1920 national network of cities was composed of twenty-five metropolises ranging in size from New York (5,620,000) to Denver (256,000).[4] Moreover, the sizes of the cities reflected their economic diversification. The giants, New York, Chicago, and Philadelphia, were the largest manufacturing clusters in the nation in which every kind of product came forth, from the earliest mechanized goods like textiles, clothing, flour, and meat to the most modern like structural steels, petroleum, electrical machinery, and automobile parts. So powerful had been metropolitan growth that two of the twenty-five metropolises, Newark and Jersey City, were themselves adjuncts to the metropolitan district of New York. The smallest metropolises, on the other hand, added a few manufacturing specialties to the traditional regional commercial activities. Rochester concentrated on men's clothing, boots and shoes, foundries and machine shops, furniture, and optical instruments; Portland (Oregon) on lumber, foundries and machine shops, and wooden shipbuilding; Denver on railroad-car building and repair, foundries and machine shops, and slaughtering and meat packing.[5]

3. Beverly Duncan and Stanley Lieberson, *Metropolis and Region in Transition,* Beverly Hills, 1970, pp. 119–34.

4. The twenty-five metropolises of 1920 were: New York, Chicago, Philadelphia, Detroit, Cleveland, St. Louis, Boston, Baltimore, Pittsburgh, Los Angeles, Buffalo, San Francisco, Milwaukee, Washington, Newark, Cincinnati, New Orleans, Minneapolis, Kansas City (Missouri), Seattle, Indianapolis, Jersey City, Rochester, Portland (Oregon), and Denver. *Fourteenth Census of the U.S.: 1920,* I, *Population,* Washington, 1921, p. 80.

5. *Fourteenth Census of the U.S.: 1920,* IX, *Manufactures, 1919,* Washington, 1923, pp. 163–64, 1089–90, 1256.

Below the largest cities came an efflorescence of smaller ones, 263 in all. Of these, 69 were classified by the statisticians of the Fourteenth Census as sections enveloped within metropolitan districts.[6] However one divides them, into 25 metropolises and 263 cities or into 23 metropolitan districts and 194 independent cities, the difference between the two groups was a matter of the degree of specialization of economic function in the urban system.

The smaller cities were all specialists, but of two distinct kinds. One variety, processing and commercial cities, fulfilled the classic urban role of rendering financial and commercial services to its rural hinterland, bringing the goods of the nation to the farms and towns of its surrounding area. In return these cities processed and shipped the local specialties into the stream of the national and international market. Memphis handled Southern lumber and made oil from cottonseed, Tampa manufactured cigars from Cuban tobacco, Richmond made cigarettes, Sacramento canned fruits and vegetables, Tulsa refined petroleum, and El Paso, Houston, and Fort Worth built and maintained railroad cars and equipment which carried the Texas farmers' crops and livestock. In the Midwest and Northeast a second variety of small city flourished—the mill town. Here specialties were not based directly on local farms or natural resources but rather capitalized on local skills and the regional and national markets for producers and consumers goods. Albany concentrated on shirts, nearby Troy on collars; Bridgeport on corsets, brass, and machine tools; New Bedford and Fall River on cotton textiles; Elizabeth, New Jersey, on electrical machinery; Chester, Pennsylvania, on iron and steel; Allentown, Pennsylvania, on silk goods; Erie, Pennsylvania, on foundries; Columbus, Ohio, on railroad cars; Dayton on machine tools and cash registers; Toledo on glass, foundries, and auto parts; and Youngstown on steel.[7] The clustering of these specialized cities created the two manufacturing belts of the nation. One belt stretched along the Atlantic coast all the way from Maine to Virginia; the other lay west of the Alleghenies and north of the Ohio, stretching from Pittsburgh and Buffalo on the east to St. Louis and Milwaukee to the west.

It was the railroad that allowed the metropolises to diversify and the

6. *Fourteenth Census,* I, *Population,* pp. 62–75.
7. City specializations taken from listing by city in the *Fourteenth Census,* IX, *Manufactures.*

small cities to specialize, because it created the national and large
regional markets for both groups of cities. These were the years when
almost all of the nation's internal traffic moved by rail. In 1916 (ironi-
cally the year in which federal aid was first granted to highways) the
nation's rail network reached its apogee: 254,000 miles of tracks, 77
percent of the intercity freight tonnage, 98 percent of the intercity
passengers.[8]

Urban economic diversification and specialization both stemmed
from the way the railroad customarily handled its freight. Freight cars
were made into long trains at the terminals in the largest cities and were
then dispatched to another metropolitan center at a distance, with only
limited stops for the purpose of adding or dropping cars or taking on
more locomotives to climb the Appalachian range, which separated the
two manufacturing belts. In these long hauls the railroad reached its
maximum efficiency, its lowest costs per mile. A skeleton crew could
handle the moving train, whereas the terminal yards required many
more men to assemble and reassemble freight cars. Thus starting and
stopping were very costly, but the extended hauls saved on fuel. Influenced by these factors as well as by a desire to increase the volume of
traffic on long lines through the lightly settled South and West, the
railroads offered low rates for those long-haul commodities which were
specialties of any given region in the United States—oranges from
Florida, lettuce from California, strawberries from Louisiana, copper
from Montana, lumber from Idaho.[9]

Furthermore, as the railroads delivered farm products and national
resources to the freight-yard and terminal cities, they conferred upon the
metropolises choice locations for expansion in wholesale and retail
manufacturing. Accordingly, next to the urban terminals sprang up
enormous breweries, refineries, steel mills, or meat-packing concerns.
Brewing and meat packing, as well as milling, had formerly been among
the dispersed processing activities, yet now they clustered together at the
terminals in Minneapolis and St. Paul, Kansas City and St. Louis,
Chicago, Toledo, and Buffalo. The shipping advantages enjoyed by the

8. John F. Stover, *American Railroads,* Chicago, 1961, p. 269.
9. Benjamin Chinitz, *Freight and the Metropolis,* Cambridge, 1960, pp. 110–28;
David M. Potter, "The Historical Development of Eastern-Southern Freight Rate
Relationships," and Stuart Daggett, "Interregional Freight Rates and the Pacific
Coast," *Law and Contemporary Problems,* 12 (Summer 1947), 416–48, 600–620.

important terminal points likewise aided existing city industries like printing and clothing manufacture.[10]

The rail-terminal metropolises did not monopolize all the urban growth of the era; rather they formed symbiotic relationships with networks of specialized small cities, thereby allowing these cities to expand on the basis of their particular advantages. The specialized cities were in part the outgrowth of industries based on cheap resources: Manchester, New Hampshire, had long since grown up around waterpower, as had Trenton, though Trenton had access to coal and iron as well. Peoria was a new city that lived by distilling the nearby corn. Some carried old skills into the new electrical and auto age, as was the case in Providence with its machine tools or Waterbury with its brass. But these settlements, whether oriented toward natural resources or toward skills from their pasts, were all sustained and nourished by the interlacing rails that ran through the Northeast and Midwest.

The nation's coal trade also favored the Northeastern and Midwestern manufacturing belts. Coal far outweighed any other freight movement along the railroads. In the nineteenth and early twentieth centuries, coal had to be shipped from the mines of Appalachia, southern Illinois, and Missouri to the cities of the East and Midwest: huge tonnages to heat and light the cities, to make gas for cooking and lighting, to power the factories, to melt the iron, and to serve as the base for chemicals. To keep the fuel moving smoothly, the railroads had to build city terminals and extra trackage along the coal routes. This heavy investment in transportation capacity for coal set in motion a positive cycle of railroad investment, low freight rates, and high industrial investment; since the rail capacity had been justified by coal, it could be used as well for other freight. Thus, low rates and good terminal service could be offered by the railroads in these two regions which the South, Mountain, and Pacific regions could not hope to duplicate.[11]

Finally, competition policed the rate structure of the railroads of the East and Midwest. City rivalries during the years 1840 to 1860 had led Boston, New York, Philadelphia, Baltimore, and others to build rail systems. When completed and interconnected after the Civil War, they offered more than one path to many destinations; the shipper could

10. There was much contemporary objection to the rate-making advantages of the rail-terminal cities and already industrialized regions. See, for example, Charles Horton Cooley, "The Theory of Transportation," *Publications of the American Economic Association,* 9 (May 1894), 113–23.

11. Edward L. Ullman, *American Commodity Flow,* Seattle, 1957, pp. 1–19.

often choose his railroad. Cutthroat competition ensued, only to be halted by agreements among the railroad corporations themselves during the 1870s and 1880s. The corporations set standardized fares within the Northeast and Midwest that ignored precise distances and thereby eliminated slight mileage advantages of one city over another. Federal regulations confirmed these agreements until truck competition made them impossible to maintain in the 1930s.[12] For the half century of its duration this standardized rate structure of the railroads was a stimulus to intra-area traffic. So too was the fact that the volume of freight was so immense in the two lanes of greatest traffic—the Atlantic coast and the land west of the Alleghenies—that lines within these regions could add a certain amount of business without incurring the expense of additional facilities.

Thus the transportation lines and the economy grew together, the easy intercommunication among the industrial metropolises and the specialized small cities fostering the manufacture and marketing of ever more complex products. With good rail service, the lines of complementarities among firms that used to prevail only in the neighborhoods of the old big city now could be enjoyed throughout the manufacturing belts of the Northeast and Midwest. Steel could be ordered from Pittsburgh, Buffalo, Detroit, or Chicago for subway cars being built in New Hampshire, ships being built in Wilmington, generators being built in Schenectady, or harvesters being built in Milwaukee. Likewise the many parts and subassemblies for all these products could be gathered from the crisscross traffic of the regions. Though the long hauls were always the cheapest per mile, the sheer volume and frequency of such traffic, as well as the competition among the lines, kept rates down and service up, and fostered the growth of the two sprawling manufacturing belts, made up of many small cities and linked together by giant industrial metropolises. Half a century ago the railroads were laying the foundation for two of the megalopolises of our own time.

As the completed rail system extended the scope of urban markets so that all manner of products from precut beef to stone crushers could be sold nationally, the mechanized method of production came forward to take advantage of the profits to be reaped by large-scale endeavor. Thus the increase in the size of business enterprises so painfully begun

12. Pittsburgh Regional Planning Association, *Economic Study of the Pittsburgh Region,* I, *Region in Transition,* Pittsburgh, 1963, pp. 188–202.

in the earlier period continued unabated. The trend toward bigness was most dramatic among the specialized cities where giant mills concentrated on a narrow range of products. The average number of employees per manufacturing establishment exceeded a thousand in such places as Lawrence's worsted mills, New Bedford's cotton mills, Omaha's slaughterhouses, Providence's machine-tool factories, Oakland's shipyards, Milwaukee's engine plants, and Racine's farm-machinery works.

In the industrial metropolis trends were more selective, with considerable variation among cities and industries. New York and Chicago differed in scale of enterprise (Table 2) partly because New York's industrial structure had taken shape in the earlier era of small shops. Here the presence of subcontractors and small specialists discouraged the concentration of every aspect of the manufacture of a product under one roof; firms could achieve large-scale production by taking advantage of the complementary suppliers in the city. On the other hand Chicago—the new industrial metropolis, the rail center of the Midwest, and the center of a vast wholesale trade—organized around large firms and long production runs. Thus its firms, even in old industries like boots and shoes, clothing, furniture, and hardware and hand tools, were larger than New York's. In both cities, however, new industries like electrical machinery, refrigerated dressed meat, rubber products, paper and wooden boxes, steel ships, railroad cars, and steel mills showed the effects of large markets, heavy capitalization, and expensive machinery (Table 2). For such enterprises, firms of hundreds and even thousands of employees became commonplace.

The new scale of business forced a reorganization of urban business institutions. The private corporation replaced the gathering of hundreds of proprietors and partners that had characterized the former big city. As this transformation proceeded, the power of deciding what urban working conditions would be like and where urban jobs would be placed shifted from an unmanageable army of small entrepreneurs to a clearly identifiable group of corporate managers. By 1920 a planned national economy and a nation of planned cities became a possibility open to Americans.

The private corporation in the United States had its roots in the necessity for amassing capital for large undertakings. In the years from 1820 to 1870, when corporations were still a novelty, private groups had sought charters for such institutions in order to construct bridges,

TABLE 2. Average Number of Employees per Manufacturing Establishment, 1870–1967[13]

Standard Industrial Classification	1870			1919			1967		
	Chicago	N.Y.	L.A.	Chicago	N.Y.	L.A.	Chicago	N.Y	L.A.
All Manufacturing Establishments	25	20	9	48	25	23	76	40	52
372 Aircraft							147	50	409
3,352 Aluminum, rolling and drawing				20			282	50	306
371 Auto bodies and parts				32	17	12	111	35	78
314 Boots and shoes	38	26		126	59	44		71	
265 Boxes	19	18		75	38	71	88	67	72
325 Bricks	55	68	14	77	46	58	78	56	85
374 Cars, railroad		210		805		1,104	608		
28 Chemicals	11	20		24	53	19	62	63	35
232 Clothing, men's	63	22		82	25	36	47	27	40
233 Clothing, women's	55	24		30	24	28	46	30	30
36 Electrical machinery				127	82	13	199	100	115
204 Flour milling	10	34	4	67		69	128	28	37
35 Foundries and machine shops	33	35		68	39	22	52	27	22
25 Furniture	19	16		45	20	24	51	20	26
342 Hardware	33	12		45	33	7	55	40	48
331 Iron and steel works	244	41		734*			1,235*	67	141
31 Leather and leather products	21	20		78	23	8	53	41	10
24 Lumber and planing mills	31	18		32	21	32	22	12	15
2,911 Petroleum refining						29	561	140	352
27 Printing and publishing	15	33		28	17	9	45	31	22
30 Rubber products		60		43	126	12	66	41	46
3,731 Shipbuilding	27	12			1,092			91	288
2,011 Slaughterhouses and meat packing	69	3		1,140	81	452	66	45	115
21 Tobacco	9	8		4	14	11	22		

* All Illinois.

13. The purpose of Table 2 is to give illustrations of changes in manufacturing establishment size in a number of representative industries. The industries listed stand for varying degrees of removal from primary processing of resources to complex multistage products which are manufactured either for consumers or for other producers. Some industries were selected because they have a long con-

canals, turnpikes, and railroads, to establish banks, and to engage in some manufacturing.[14] These firms had a common need to raise large amounts of capital. The corporate form, with its legal devices of stock and bonds and limited liability of stockholders for the debts of the business, facilitated a wide canvass for capital. Under the contemporary partnership form of business, every partner was personally liable for the debts of the entire firm, and many a nineteenth-century businessman lost his savings and his home upon failure or from a partner's incompetence or fraud. Under the corporate form, large merchants and small investors, total strangers to each other, could club together in the confidence that each risked only his investment, not his fortune, his home, or his farm.

Although the corporate charters required a governing board elected by the stockholders, the early corporations were so small that they were not in fact managed by committees but by one or two men. The success of these firms depended on the ability of the managers to stay in contact with all aspects of the business in order to coordinate diverse activities and to direct the firm into new undertakings. As the size and complexity of American enterprises increased, however, business management passed beyond the reach of any one man's personal supervision. First with the trunk-line railroads of the 1850s, and then increasingly in production of food products, sewing machines, and farm machinery in the

---

tinuous history, like clothing, flour milling, hardware, and tobacco, and others were selected because they were peculiar to an era, like railroad cars or aircraft.

The verbal descriptions of each industrial group in the table were taken from the 1919 Census of Manufactures, and an analogous 1967 Standard Industrial Classification group was sought to match. For 1870, vaguer approximations had to be tolerated. The 1870 equivalents for the 1920 descriptions were: boxes, cigar, paper, wooden and fancy (1870) for boxes, paper (1920); drugs and chemicals for chemicals; machinery not specified, engines and boilers for foundries and machine shops; iron forged and rolled for iron and steel works; lumber planed and sawed and sashes, doors, and blinds for lumber and planing mills; shipbuilding and repairing for shipbuilding, steel. The killing of animals for shipment as dressed fresh meat was not an industry in 1870, so the packing of salt pork and beef had to be taken as the equivalent of the entire meat-packing industry of 1919.

The city boundaries are in 1870 Cook County, Kings and New York County, Los Angeles County; in 1920 the cities themselves; in 1967 the Chicago Consolidated Statistical Area, the New York Consolidated Statistical Area, and the Los Angeles–Long Beach Standard Metropolitan Statistical Area and the Anaheim–Santa Ana–Garden Grove Standard Metropolitan Statistical Area.

Ninth Census: 1870, III, *Statistics of Wealth and Industry in the United States*, Washington, 1872, pp. 639, 649, 701–704; *Fourteenth Census*, IX, *Manufactures*, pp. 122–26, 358–64, 1058–66; *Census of Manufactures, 1967*, III, *Area Statistics, Parts I & II*, Table 6.

14. George H. Evans, Jr., *Business Incorporations in the U.S. 1800–1943*, New York, 1948, pp. 10–30.

1880s, American corporations experimented with new forms of management. By the first decades of the twentieth century a centralized, departmentalized, bureaucratic form of corporate management had been established as the norm for big companies.

No sinister force withered the strength of the personal-style managers, but the increase in the size and complexity of their responsibilities overwhelmed them. In the 1850s a textile company might employ some eight hundred men, a locomotive works six hundred, but the Erie Railroad had four thousand employees, men not confined to one yard but scattered over five hundred miles of track. No one office handled the cash; hundreds of station agents and conductors took in the company's money. By the 1880s the major trunk-line railroads like the Pennsylvania had several thousand miles of track and upwards of fifty thousand employees. Nor was mere size the extent of the manager's problems. These were times of rapid technological change in railroad construction and locomotive and car design, and times of fierce competition. The manager could not hide his head in routine but had to make quick competitive decisions, perhaps whether to merge with minor roads or to cut rates in order to capture more traffic. It was a time too when unscrupulous financiers maneuvered the stocks and bonds of the railroads to found individual empires, so that many a firm was harassed to the point of destruction by external and internal security manipulation.[15]

The absolute necessity for dependable coordination of the management of daily business and the simultaneous need to meet the competition transformed the early trunk-line railroad into a modern centralized corporation. The Erie, the Baltimore and Ohio, and the Pennsylvania were all pioneers in bureaucratic innovation; between 1850 and 1880 they established the fundamental structure of the American corporation. Railroad management divided naturally into three departments—finance, operations, and traffic—each with distinct responsibilities and chains of command. Finance concerned itself with the collection and dispersal of revenues as well as with the issuance of stocks and bonds; operations controlled the movement of trains and their maintenance; while traffic was essentially a sales department, finding customers and following the course of their goods and freight

15. Alfred D. Chandler, Jr., *Railroads, the Nation's First Big Business*, New York, 1965, pp. 97–100; and Chandler, *Strategy and Structure, Chapters in the History of the Industrial Enterprise*, Cambridge, 1962, p. 38.

cars, as well as watching the costs of passenger and freight movement. Throughout this first stage of corporate development the emphasis was on centralized control, because the highest profits were found to accrue through consolidating unrelated commitments into one comprehensive undertaking.

Therefore each department and each section within it had both line and staff officers. The line officer managed day-to-day operations within his section and might deal with the movement of cars, the routine repair of a segment of a trunk line, or the disbursement and collection of funds in a given geographical area. The staff officers reported directly to the central office. They were charged with the responsibility for long-range decisions, such as whether or not to purchase new rolling stock or to establish new traffic patterns. This departmental management of a centralized bureaucracy made possible the successful operation of the great railroad complexes of the period. It also made possible the coordination of hundreds of small lines, originally built by the cities and towns, into far-flung, high-speed routes traveled by thousands of cars, which were unscrambled and rerouted in a thousand different ways on their trips into the city terminals.

The same opportunities and challenges that had organized the railroads manifested themselves a few years later in industries attempting to reach and hold a national market for their products: meat, cigarettes, flour, bananas, harvesters, sewing machines, and typewriters.[16] Problems might arise in sales, production, or supply, but since they had their origin in the grandiose scale of the enterprise, the solution was everywhere the same—toward rationalized departments in management, toward centralization of control. Gustavus Swift (1839–1903), a cattle buyer and shipper, who financed the development of the railroad refrigerator in order to sell meat butchered in Chicago in Eastern cities, found his business requirements driving him from a partnership to a modern corporation. Once he had perfected his car, he needed sales offices and refrigerated warehouses at his major destinations; he had to finance his fleet of refrigerator cars and struggle with the railroads to obtain fast service for them; and finally he had somehow to connect the purchasing and slaughtering of animals in Chicago to his sales in the East. Aided by a centralized departmental structure and by staff and line control over his operations, Swift was able to build a national business.

16. Alfred D. Chandler, Jr., "The Beginnings of 'Big Business' in American Industry," *Business History Review,* 33 (Spring 1959), 6.

He overcame consumer reluctance by national advertising and expanded into related lines of pork, veal, lamb, butter, oleomargarine, soap, glue, and fertilizer. He was eventually able even to shift to multiple plant locations (Fort Worth, Omaha, St. Joseph, St. Louis) that brought processing closer to the sources of his supplies.[17]

The necessity for management to control sales throughout many cities and possibly also throughout a number of supply locations spread the new bureaucratic corporate structure to cigarettes, flour, bananas, sewing machines, harvesters, and lighting and power utilities.

Corporate centralization also appeared in the rubber companies and in many metalworking industries during the late nineteenth century. To take full advantage of the new technology required heavy investments in machinery housed in factories capable of a tremendous volume of steady production. The consolidated plants were of course immensely more efficient than the previous small factories, but they did require a new approach to sales; the sales force had henceforth to be under the control of management as well as subservient to production. The independent salesman who worked on a commission had dominated American marketing during the nineteenth century, and his success depended on selling a few products at a high commission rather than on selling a great many at a low commission. The route to harnessing the market to the output of the giant factory henceforth lay in the adoption of national advertising to arouse consumer demand and of salaried salesmen and sales managers to close the deals, and this route proved to be the way around the old independent salesman.

Still other industries, like steel and oil, expanded in the direction of controlling their sources of supply so that production would not be at the mercy of outside forces. In almost every industry the forces for centralization, for the integration of sales, supply, and production, pressed upon owners and managers of American business, and everywhere the response took the same general direction toward vertical integration, departmental structure, staff and line responsibilities, and centralized control. The progression was always an uneven one, and some giants like U.S. Steel remained a muddle of centralized operations and semiautonomous subsidiary corporations until the 1930s. The notorious Standard Oil Corporation never attained in these years the rationalization achieved by American Tobacco or General Electric.

17. Oscar E. Anderson, Jr., *Refrigeration in America,* Princeton, 1953, pp. 50–52, 142–50; Chandler, "Beginnings of 'Big Business,' " 6–8.

Whatever the degree of formal rationalization, however, the impersonal centralized private corporation was an outstanding social fact of the era, and from it spread the ever-widening bureaucratization of American work and society.[18]

The reorganization of business institutions to suit the demands and possibilities of large-scale enterprise brought about a chain of adaptations within the cities themselves. Immense factories became normal manufacturing elements. There arose the rubber plants of Akron, the glassworks of Toledo, the cotton mills of Manchester in New Hampshire, the cash-register factory at Dayton, and together they overwhelmed the specialized minor cities of the manufacturing belts. Such factories with their ferocious rationalization were apt metaphors for the new metropolis itself, which experienced a similar heartless rationalization of its jobs and its land use. Exploitation and segregation were the dominant trends within the cities of this era. The similarities between the mechanized centralized enterprise and the industrial metropolis of the half century after 1870 were entirely apparent to their contemporaries. As the science and engineering of the time had supplied the expertise for developing products and processes, so the emerging social science uncovered the framework of the economy and the city and suggested sensible guidelines for their humanization. Indeed, the two most typical cities of the period, Pittsburgh and Chicago, were the ones in which investigators carried on the most advanced research and reached the most perceptive conclusions concerning the interconnections of the national economy, corporate enterprise, urban jobs, and urban land-use structure.

The Industrial Metropolis: 1870–1920

In Pittsburgh a team of investigators spent most of a year in 1907–1908 probing into every aspect of the city. Their goal was to relate the systematic knowledge of census and survey to the reportage of individual lives and experiences. Their hope was to arouse local action directed toward the improvement of living conditions. The reports were masterpieces in social science and journalism. The six volumes ultimately published served as the foundation for urban social science during the next twenty or thirty years, and they are still the richest

18. Chandler, *Strategy and Structure,* pp. 24–41.

available source of concrete information on the urban life of these times.[19]

The repetitive theme of the Pittsburgh Survey emphasizes the driving force of the age. It explored the centralized, rationalized, carefully planned engineering controlled by vast enterprises; the furnaces and rolling mills, railroads, mines, and ovens all interlocked in a wonderfully productive unity supported by armies of men and thousands of machines and fully able to move mountains of material over half a continent. From 1880 to 1910 an industrial metropolis based on steel, glass, and electrical machinery had sprung up from the conjunction of almost unlimited high-grade coking coal, natural gas, and the talent of a fine inventor-industrialist, George Westinghouse (1846–1914). Yet over this triumph of human energy hung a dark pall—a literal blanket of smoke that shut out the sun and seared the soil, as well as a metaphorical pall of exploitation, neglect, disorganization, and helplessness. The personnel of the giant mills was rigidly divided into classes, with college graduates at the top of the pyramid, followed by the skilled workers and finally by the mass of unskilled laborers. Corporations rewarded each class appropriately in their own view, with steady salaries and hierarchical promotions for the educated elite, high wages and fringe benefits in housing for the skilled, bitter poverty and unremitting toil for the unskilled.[20] The gulf between respectability and poverty in the corporations established the major segregation of the city, but this class separation was subdivided by further segregation within the neighborhoods of the city by race, national origin, and church affiliation.

Everywhere in the city, production was the focus of attention. Every day, men were killed and maimed by machinery; every trade injured its help without compunction. The pace was too fast, the hours were too long, and in this era it was not the cellar sweatshops or upstairs factory but the mighty enterprise that stood in the front ranks of the callous. The steel mills and railroad yards ran on a twelve-hour day, seven days a week. Yet managers ruthlessly and systematically used their power to block any counterorganization of the men. The Homestead strike of 1892 and the steel strike of 1919 were both crushed by troops and by

19. The survey first appeared in summary form in one volume, "The Pittsburgh Survey," *Charities and the Commons*, 21 (January 1909), 515–1194; the complete edition, Paul U. Kellogg, ed., *The Pittsburgh Survey*, New York, 1909–1914, 6 volumes.
20. David Brody, *Steelworkers in America: The Nonunion Era*, Cambridge, 1960, pp. 80–95, 112–24.

the illegal use of police and criminal charges, as well as by spies and scabs and the whole military, economic, and civic machinery of repression.

As the corporations sowed, so the city reaped. Old forms of poverty, fostered by neglect, persisted on and on. One of the worst of the U.S. Steel slums was Painter's Row, a district inherited from a small mill-owner forty years before and never either abandoned or repaired. Self-help was not unknown, but it frequently failed; homeowners dug wells to escape dependence on polluted water only to have their wells polluted in turn by runoff from nearby privies. Ignorant and corrupt public officials in a civic government under the thumb of political bosses and business executives fragmented political boundaries so that big companies escaped taxes, and the workman was left without community resources with which to protect his family or educate his children.[21] Pittsburgh was the perfect prototype of centralized private economic power. Its enormous productivity was based on an insane rationality that consumed men, women, and children in order to create personal ascendancy and a multiplicity of mere things.

Pittsburgh, the heavy-industry metropolis, was the cartoon for Chicago, the total urban industrial landscape. This giant new metropolis (299,000 inhabitants in 1870; 2,702,000 in 1920) was subjected to piecemeal investigation by a generation of social workers and university investigators, with the result that in time a Chicago school of social science could present a reasonably complete analysis of the workings of the economy from 1870 to 1920 and trace its effects upon the city. Whereas the Pittsburgh group had confined themselves to accurate reporting of the existing situation, the Chicago team was able to relate the growth of business in Chicago to national growth factors. They could therefore indicate how the patterns of job location and the wages of workers and office employees determined the location of housing. Finally they discovered that this placement defined much of the social and political structure of the city.

Like all the major cities of the world, Chicago owed its importance to its situation at a point where cheap long-distance water transportation met the more expensive land transport. Even more significant was the fact that at the very moment the inventions in farm machinery, the

---

21. F. Elisabeth Crowell, "Painter's Row," *Charities and the Commons,* 21 (January 1909), 899–910; Roy Lubove, *Twentieth Century Pittsburgh: Government, Business, and Environmental Change,* New York, 1969, pp. 1–19.

Industrial Metropolis

The Downtown

River Industrial Sectors

49. Chicago River, Looking East Toward Lake Michigan, 1875. Where lake schooners and canal boats (lower right) met, the city's earliest manufacturing districts began. Air-Line Elevator (left) was on the site of present Merchandise Mart. *Chicago Historical Society*

50. South Branch of the Chicago River, 1883. Chicago perfected mass processing of raw materials, animals, grain, and lumber as no city had before. Here, a two-mile wholesale lumber district. *Library of Congress*

Rail Industrial Sectors

51. Track Elevation at 23rd Street, Chicago, ca. 1907. View of work on Chicago, Burlington and Quincy Railroad shows that the railroad and industrial neighbors often formed a continuous lineal city within the metropolis. *Library of Congress*

52. Calumet Harbor–Gary Industrial Strip, 1908. Six railroads and artificial harbors for ore boats nourished a sixteen-mile strip of heavy industry, since the late nineteenth century a basic element in Chicago's economy. Here, the new Universal Portland Cement Company plant, next to the Gary steel mills (out of picture, at right), with Calumet Harbor plants of South Chicago down the tracks (upper left). *Library of Congress*

53. Western Electric, Hawthorne Works, Cicero, ca. 1910. In 1903 this manufacturing subsidiary of American Telephone and Telegraph moved its giant plant out to the fringe of the city, where land was plentiful and its operations could be served by the circumferential belt railroads that tied together all the lines of the metropolis. *Chicago Historical Society*

54. Casting Pig Iron, Iroquois Smelter, Calumet Harbor, South Chicago, 1906. A few workers in the army of hand laborers required by large-scale industry during the early and middle stages of its mechanization. *Library of Congress*

Residential Infill

55. Standard Housing, State Street near 15th, Chicago, 1868–69 (above, left). Narrow wooden buildings were one-to-a-lot in good neighborhoods, crammed one behind the other in poor sections; the unpaved street and wooden sidewalk were typical. *Chicago Historical Society*

56. Standard Housing in Brick, 1848 Bloomingdale Avenue, Chicago, ca. 1912 (center, left). After the 1871 fire, a city ordinance, only laxly enforced, required that the core city be rebuilt in brick. Half-cellar rental units ("up and down" housing) were created out of a single-family house design. *Chicago Historical Society*

57. The New Environment, 1749–59 North Whipple Street, Chicago, ca. 1912 (below, left). About five miles west of downtown, streetcars and elevated railroads opened up Humboldt Park section to the middle class and upper working class. It provided running water, public sewers, electricity, gas, paved streets and sidewalks, lawn strips and street trees, and closely set single- and two-family wooden houses. *Chicago Historical Society*

58. Rear Yards, 1754–58 North Whipple Street, Chicago, ca. 1912 (above). Urban houses are intended to make their best impression on the front street, and this plan was carried to the suburbs until the ranch house and attached garage of our time brought cars, children's bicycles, trash barrels, and impressive front entrances all to face the street. Here, an alley carries electricity, gives access for trash and service, with small businesses occupying sheds in rear yards before zoning prevented such mixed land uses. *Chicago Historical Society*

59. Nineteenth-Century Housing, 44th and Wood Streets, Chicago, 1959 (below). Industrial metropolis housing survives in working-class sections of all American cities. Here, with asphalt siding, encroached upon by cars, a "Back of the Yards" neighborhood of the 1880 standard land and housing plan. *Chicago Historical Society, Clarence W. Hines*

60. Lake Shore Drive, Chicago, 1905. The absence of railroad tracks and easy commuting to downtown shifted the focus of fashion from South Side to the Near North Side Lake Shore. The public parkway system enhanced the private amenities of the rich. *Library of Congress*

61. Going to a Band Concert, Lincoln Park, Chicago, 1907. The well-to-do always have gotten the best municipal socialism in America. Lincoln Park is the nicest and most continuously maintained and improved of all the Chicago parks. It serves the fashionable North Side. *Library of Congress*

62. Kenilworth Avenue, near Chicago Avenue, Oak Park, 1925. Seven miles west of the Loop, just outside city limits, shaded lawns and planted streets of railroad commuters, the apogee of bourgeois propriety. *Chicago Historical Society*

63. Maxwell Street near Jefferson Street, Chicago, ca. 1904–06. Effective street cleaning was one of the important goals of the Progressive Era. "Perhaps our greatest achievement was the discovery of a pavement eighteen inches under the surface of a narrow street, although after it was found we triumphantly discovered a record of its existence in the city archives." Jane Addams, *Twenty Years at Hull House*, 1910. *Chicago Historical Society*

64. Women with Market Baskets, Stock Yards District, Chicago, 1904. *Chicago Historical Society, Daily News*

65. Children on Wooden Sidewalk, Stock Yards District, Chicago, 1904. The standard of living among the poor has now risen sufficiently that, in contrast with this, today's poverty pictures show children with sneakers or shoes. *Chicago Historical Society, Daily News*

66. Family Waiting for Strikers' Parade, Stock Yards District, Chicago, 1904. *Chicago Historical Society, Daily News*

67. Packing House Workers' Strike Parade, 4600 Block, Ashland Avenue, Chicago, 1904. *Chicago Historical Society, Daily News*

68. Mob Hunting a Black Man, Chicago Race Riots, July 1919. Lacking the racial covenants, housing price barriers, and real-estate associations of the prosperous, poor white neighborhoods enforced their apartheid by violence. *Chicago Historical Society*

69. Black Victim Stoned to Death, Chicago Race Riots, July 1919. The fleeing man was cornered and killed by the mob. *Chicago Historical Society*

70. Blacks Evicted from Their Houses in the Wake of the Riots, Chicago, July 1919. With the old South Side ghetto jammed by blacks drawn to Chicago for wartime jobs, many sought houses on margins of their neighborhoods. A leader of nearby Kenilworth Improvement Association testified, "We want to do what is right. . . . But these people will have to be more or less pacified. At a conference where their representatives were present, I told them we might as well be frank about it, 'You people are not admitted to our society,' I said. Personally, I have no prejudice against them. They have been clean in every way, and always prompt in their payments. But, you know, improvements are coming along the lake shore, the Illinois Central, and all that; we can't have these people coming over here." Carl Sandburg, *The Chicago Race Riots, July, 1919. Chicago Historical Society*

71. Under the El at 63rd Street and Cottage Grove Avenue, Chicago, 1924. Despite bombings, riots, and intimidation, the Negro ghetto could not be denied. Here is its more prosperous, growing edge, having advanced fifteen blocks south since the riots. *Chicago Historical Society*

42. Pittsburgh Mill District, 1940

43. Michigan Avenue, Chicago, 1933

44. Near 12th and Jefferson Streets, Chicago, 1906

45. Working-Class Chicago, 1934

46. South Water Street and the Chicago River, ca. 1920

47. Michigan Avenue and Grant Park, ca. 1910

48. Wabash Avenue, Chicago, 1907

49. Chicago River, Looking East Toward Lake Michigan, 1875

50. South Branch of the Chicago River, 1883

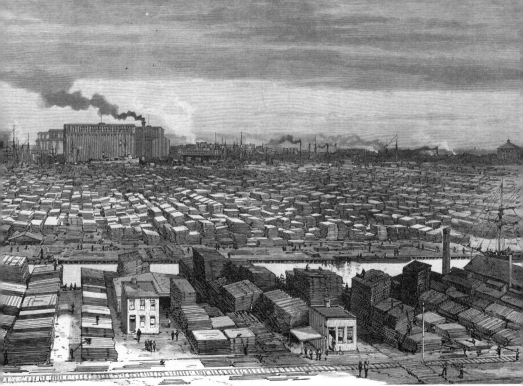

51. Track Elevation at 23rd Street, Chicago, ca. 1907

52. Calumet Harbor—Gary Industrial Strip, 1908

53. Western Electric, Hawthorne Works, Cicero, ca. 1910

54. Iroquois Smelter, Calumet Harbor, South Chicago, 1906

58. Rear Yards, Chicago, ca. 1912

55. Standard Housing, State Street, Chicago, 1868–69

56. Standard Housing in Brick, Chicago, ca. 1912

57. The New Environment, Chicago, ca. 1912

59. Nineteenth-Century Housing, Chicago, 1959

60. Lake Shore Drive, Chicago, 1905

61. Band Concert, Lincoln Park, Chicago, 1907

62. Kenilworth Avenue, near Chicago Avenue, Oak Park, 1925

63. Maxwell Street near Jefferson Street, ca. 1904–06

64. Stock Yards District, Chicago, 1904

65. Stock Yards District, Chicago, 1904

66. Strikers Parade, Stock Yards District, Chicago, 1904

67. Packing House Workers Strike Parade, Chicago, 1904

68. Mob Hunting a Black Man, Chicago Race Riots, July 1919

69. Black Victim Stoned to Death, Chicago Race Riots, July 1919

70. Blacks Evicted from Their Houses, Chicago, July 1919

71. Under the El, Chicago, 1924

perfecting of the railroad, and the unmistakable westward flow of the American population made the occupation of the Midwest profitable, Chicago rose to service this giant hinterland. By 1856, with the completion of the Illinois and Michigan Canal and ten trunk-line railroads, Chicago began its role as a major regional center. At first it functioned simply enough. Commercially it marketed the grain and animals of the new farms while managing the flow of capital out to the farms and towns of the newly settled West, and industrially it manufactured almost every item needed to run a railroad or start a farm, to build a town, to furnish a home, or to clothe a family. The geography of Chicago thus assured its future as a world metropolis. In addition, it was placed in the most rapidly rising sector of the national economy by the functions it performed in mechanized manufacturing, transportation, finance, and servicing of business.[22]

The rapid growth of all the elements that composed the city's economy in this era—factories, railroad shops and yards, banks and exchanges, warehouses, offices, department stores, and so on—forced Chicago, and indeed all contemporary American cities, into a new spatial structure: the sector-and-ring pattern of settlement. The strictness of the segregation of this urban organization and the suddenness with which it swept over American cities holds much meaning for today. On the one hand the residential segregation patterns of this era, its core of poverty and rings of rising affluence, still prevail in many cities. On the other hand the swiftness and completeness with which Americans in this era overturned their former habits suggest that in the future strong changes in transportation, job location, and housing prices could easily revolutionize what now seem to be obdurate habits of city dwellers. If we really wished to abandon our current pattern of an inner ring of poverty and black segregation, we could probably do so as quickly as we suddenly assumed it during the late nineteenth century.

In Chicago in the years from 1870 to 1920, the location of jobs was governed by the concentration of economic activity in sectors: narrow pie-shaped wedges of commercial and industrial property stretching out from the downtown business center toward farmland yet to be developed beyond the city. Between the long corridors of the industrial wedges lay vast tracts of empty land, into which settled the major part of the population in three highly segregated great rings: an inner one of

22. Homer Hoyt, *One Hundred Years of Land Values in Chicago,* Chicago, 1933, pp. 53–59.

poverty and low income marked by cheap divided houses and old apartments, a middle ring of secondhand working-class houses and cottages, and an outer ring of better-quality apartments and homes (Figure V, page 106). In addition, the wealthy and their followers, the downtown white-collar workers, occupied a long wedge of their own, cutting across the rings and running from the fashionable shops and downtown offices outward along the lines of good transportation and attractive sites. By 1920 the axis of this corridor lay along Michigan Avenue and the north shore on Lake Michigan. This generalized sketch of the spatial configuration of Chicago in this era—the radial city with a single center—can be applied to the other industrial metropolises of the time. It was a pattern to which all of them roughly conformed,[23] and it was the very same pattern which the highway engineers rediscovered for themselves in their traffic studies of the 1930s.

The central point from which the industrial sectors of Chicago fanned out lay at the meeting of lake and land traffic at the mouth of the Chicago River. The two sectors that were occupied first ran along the north and south branches of the river, which divided a few blocks inland from Lake Michigan just north of the central downtown area that was to become the Loop. City commerce and settlement commenced at this center. It burgeoned with the opening of the Illinois and Michigan Canal in 1848 and was thereafter continually re-formed and rebuilt by unremitting industrial pressure. Ever since, the river has served as an inner harbor for the handling of grain and lumber and coal, and manufacturers have been attracted by the accessibility of transport. The river banks became the industrial sinews of the city. Here Cyrus H. McCormick (1809–84) built his reaper factory, originally on the North Branch; later on the South Branch when he rebuilt after the Chicago fire of 1871.[24] As the city grew, competition for central space drove the price of inner-city land up and up, and industry edged ever outward from the center along the branches of the river, paralleled by the lines of the railroad. Other businesses not immediately dependent on the complementary cluster of small firms and support from the downtown services followed them out—Montgomery Ward to the North Branch,

23. Robert E. Park, Ernest W. Burgess, and Roderick D. McKenzie, *The City,* Chicago, 1925, pp. 47–58; U.S. Federal Housing Administration, *The Structure and Growth of Residential Neighborhoods in American Cities,* Homer Hoyt, ed., Washington, 1939, pp. 72–78, 86–104; Harlan Bartholomew, *Urban Land Uses,* Cambridge, 1932, pp. 97–102.
    24. Hoyt, *Land Values in Chicago,* p. 104.

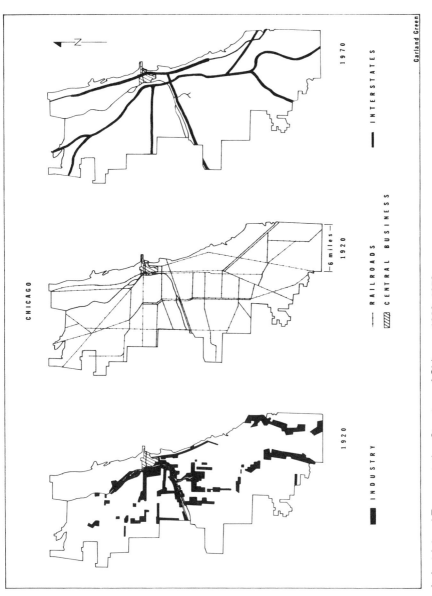

Figure IV. Industrial and Transportation Structure of Chicago, 1920, 1970

SOURCE: Homer Hoyt, *One Hundred Years of Land Values in Chicago*, Chicago, 1933; Center for Urban Studies, University of Chicago, *Mid-Chicago Economic Development Study*, Chicago, February, 1966.

machinery factories to the South Branch, while others joined Sears, Roebuck in a due-west migration from the city center.[25]

The city core itself assumed a mature form in the early years of the twentieth century. At the center, land mounted in value until it was prohibitive to manufacturing and wholesaling on any considerable scale; instead the innermost streets blossomed with skyscrapers and theaters and stores, all the full flowering of an old-fashioned metropolitan downtown. Around this center, factories and commerce threw up an immense wall of structures. The wall was composed of factories that needed minimal space and so could remain near the center by occupying multistory buildings and of wholesale houses that were dependent on downtown passenger stations, hotels, and customer entertainment.

It is clear that this era had spawned industrial sectors and a downtown far removed from the urbanism of New York in the preceding period, with its mixed commercial and residential center and informal fringes. Rather, every part of the industrial metropolis now became more rigidly compartmentalized with each year of growth. After about 1890, no neighborhood in the city of Chicago sheltered industry, commerce, and homes of all classes of citizens; segregation of industrial, commercial, and residential land became the hallmark of the metropolis.

Rail lines coming in from the West and South added two more manufacturing sectors to those created by the Chicago River and the tracks that ran parallel to it. The transportation activity itself—tending the yards, repairing cars and locomotives, building all sorts of equipment from fishplates to Pullman cars—generated an enormous volume of employment. Chicago was the nation's foremost rail-terminal city, and the prosperity of its railroads did much to build its employment base. By complementarity and the sheer expansion of urban business, these new rail sectors attracted industry. Most famous were the stockyards and meat-packing houses of the southern sector, a development of 1865 at Thirty-ninth and Halsted Streets that comprised a hundred acres of cattle pens and two hundred and seventy-five additional acres devoted to slaughterhouses and packing plants. The dependence of this gigantic operation on cattle cars and refrigerator cars forbade any but a rail location.

The stockyards forecast a special urban characteristic of the industry

25. Center for Urban Studies, University of Chicago, *Mid-Chicago Economic Development Study,* Chicago, February 1966, pp. 16–37; Hoyt, *Land Values in Chicago,* pp. 82–85.

of the 1870–1920 period—the movement of mammoth enterprises completely outside the confines of the core city. Steel mills, electrical machinery plants, car factories, all industries that needed good transportation for great quantities of shipments as well as vast open land for future expansion, followed the meat packers' example in seeking locations at the fringes of the manufacturing sectors.[26] In 1880, George M. Pullman (1831–97) built his shops and model town south of the city, and he was soon followed by steel mills, cement plants, and the whole Calumet River heavy industrial complex. The United States Steel Corporation placed a brand-new integrated steel plant in Gary, Indiana, a city constructed for the purpose in 1905 just east of the Calumet concentration. The industrial satellite city, a mill town set within a metropolitan region where workers could live and labor in their own community instead of commuting to work, was a characteristic type of the era. All such satellites owed their appearance to the configuration of rail transportation and the scale of late nineteenth-century mechanized manufacture. As Chairman Elbert H. Gary set his new mill down outside Chicago, so Westinghouse built in East Liberty on the edge of Pittsburgh and Ford built at River Rouge outside Detroit.[27]

Finally a spatial relationship between the metropolitan railroad lines and the outer industrial locations should be mentioned, less for its impact on the structure of Chicago in this era than for its future consequences. The radial Chicago form had emerged from the railroads that served the industrial sectors, which fanned out from the core of the city. In addition, however, transfer of freight from one line to another and from one sector to another necessitated interconnections. The most inclusive of these linkages were the rectangular belt lines that crossed over the city's radial trackage to pass almost entirely around the city. A map of the railroads in this period can therefore be seen as the superimposition of a giant grid, reminiscent of the early township grid pattern, upon the older radial lines (Figure IV, page 103). Moreover, where the belt lines intersected the radials, still other centers were created. This evolving multicentered layout helped to relieve the city's inner terminals from the traffic congestion that inevitably tends to plague a strongly central-

26. Harold M. Mayer, "Localization of Railway Facilities in Metropolitan Centers as Typified by Chicago," *Journal of Land and Public Utility Economics,* 20 (November 1944), 299–315.
27. Graham R. Taylor, *Satellite Cities, A Study of Industrial Suburbs,* New York, 1915, pp. 1–67, 165–93; Glenn E. McLaughlin, *Growth of American Manufacturing Areas,* Pittsburgh, 1938, pp. 127–32.

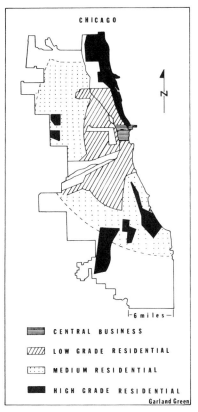

Figure V. Class Rings and Sectors of Residential Chicago, 1920

SOURCE: Federal Housing Administration, *Structure and Growth of Residential Neighborhoods in American Cities,* Homer Hoyt, ed., Washington, 1939.

ized system with all the heaviest traffic concentrated at its center.[28] After 1900 the belt lines themselves became increasingly attractive to industrial firms. Western Electric, for example, moved its plant in 1903 to Twenty-second Street and Cicero Avenue on the outermost belt line.[29]

In the years after World War II, highway engineers began to appro-

28. The strong radial quality of the alignment of tracks in American cities made freight traffic jams endemic during the late nineteenth and early twentieth centuries and brought a catastrophic breakdown during the First World War. K. Austin Kerr, *American Railroad Politics 1914–1920,* Pittsburgh, 1968, p. 40.

29. Hoyt, *Land Values in Chicago,* pp. 104–7, 213; Robert L. Wrigley, Jr., "Organized Industrial Districts," *Journal of Law and Public Utility Economics,* 23 (May 1947), 180–98.

priate the partially occupied land along the railroad corridors, and three of Chicago's four interstate highways have repeated in a rough way the radial and grid alignments attributable to the old railroads. When the next section of the interstate Crosstown Expressway is built along Cicero Avenue, the duplication of the old rail system will be complete, and Chicago will have constructed a crude grid layout of highways whose squares grow larger as one moves from the center of the city.[30] Such a pattern has proved highly efficient for the purpose of moving traffic through a multicentered network that serves multiple locations of origin and destination. It is a pattern that much resembles the one made by Los Angeles highways, a city that so fully exemplifies the era of the automobile megalopolis.

The great preponderance of urban land has always been taken up by residential lots and streets, and these miles and miles of neighborhoods filled the spaces between the industrial fingers of the metropolis. In the half century after 1870 these neighborhoods ceased to be a jumble of rich and poor, immigrant and native, black and white, as they were in the former era of the big city. Instead the neighborhoods of the industrial metropolis came to be arranged in a systematic pattern of socioeconomic segregation. The rings of residential settlement varied from inner poverty to outer affluence,[31] and this pattern of residential segregation was as characteristic of the metropolis of 1870–1920 as were its industrial sectors, its satellites, and its downtown areas.

The suddenness with which the new pattern settled upon American cities has been documented for Chicago by its social scientists. The new possibilities of cable and electric street transit worked with rapid growth and a middle-class fashion in suburban living and downtown shopping to revolutionize the social geography of the American city.

On October 9, 1871, the Chicago Fire burned out the core of the

---

30. Center for Urban Studies, *Mid-Chicago Development,* plates 13 and 14; Joseph R. Passonneau, "Urban Expressway Design in the United States: The Institutional Framework," *Systems Analysis for Social Problems,* Alfred Blumenstein et al., eds., Washington Operations Research Council, Washington, 1970, pp. 210–22.

31. The sector of the wealthy, occupying an attractive site and enjoying easy transportation to the downtown (Chicago's North Shore) is a significant exception to the ring arrangement of residential land. The reasons for a sector of the rich, not a ring, are twofold: the rich are not numerous enough to fill a metropolitan ring, and they can pay enough to control expensive land near the center of the city. The phenomenon of this sector in 1870–1920 cities has been shown to be general by Homer Hoyt, in his *Structure and Growth of Residential Neighborhoods,* pp. 112–22; and Peter G. Goheen, *Victorian Toronto,* pp. 201–13.

city and its North Side, leveling 2,100 acres of city land and destroying nearly a third of its structures. At first Chicagoans rebuilt their city in somewhat the same mixed central business and residential patterns with which they were familiar. With mortgage funds from the East, speculators rebuilt the downtown office buildings to a height of four and five stories instead of the previous two or three, while a few promoters hazarded six and even eight stories. But near the offices and stores, a block or two from the railroads, warehouses, and factories of the center of the city, many middle-class Chicagoans rebuilt their homes or settled into rented quarters or small hotels or boardinghouses in the core city.

During the 1870s the class pattern of Chicago homes bridged both the old and the new style of neighborhoods. The presence of some middle-class and well-to-do families near the downtown area recalled the old tradition, as did the outer location of many working-class dwellings. The new, however, was represented by a growing suburban fringe of middle-class families who were commuting to the downtown offices and stores.

During the next two decades the outmigration of Chicago's middle class completely reorganized the settlement patterns of the city. Instead of taking up vacant tracts in the partially built-up fringe where the working class were also settled, as had been the practice in the past, the middle class skipped over that ring entirely and settled itself in its own districts beyond. In Chicago the specific location of the ring of middle-class settlement had been determined by the building of a series of parks and boulevards in imitation of New York's Central Park and Baron Georges Haussmann's Paris boulevards. Finally mass suburban living was made possible by a succession of transportation improvements during the years from 1887 to 1894. Cable lines, electric surface lines, and elevated rapid transit all were introduced. Simultaneously, a uniform five-cent fare with one free transfer facilitated commuting.[32]

In this way Chicago's residential pattern by class had been fully set by 1894. The Loop was surrounded by decaying structures waiting to be taken up for commercial and industrial uses as the downtown expanded. Beyond this section, abandoned by the middle class, was the belt of working-class housing, close to jobs in the core city and close to the industrial sectors. Into the inner area poured the immigrants, native and foreign, and their poverty and consequent overcrowding of existing

32. Hoyt, *Land Values in Chicago,* pp. 104–7, 429.

homes transformed twenty-year-old middle-class houses and workers' cottages into the slums of the core city.[33]

With this new urban segregation of classes by housing, the core of poverty, and the rings of rising affluence, the working class came to assume the city-building role the middle class formerly performed. In the teens and twenties the working class, in order to find land to build upon or to rent, had to expand into those suburban areas which the middle class had already partially occupied, just as the middle class had earlier taken up vacant land in the mixed fringe of the old premetropolitan city. As their members moved outward they had to buy land that had already advanced in price in anticipation of suburban development. Often they found subdivisions of small lots which bore the charges of full city improvements, such as streets and curbs and sidewalks, city water and sewers, and gas and electricity, and which had to be built upon in conformity with modern building codes. The cheap working-class dwelling, the tiny wooden house or shack often built by the owner upon undesirable fringe land, now became a legal as well as an economic impossibility. Such housing returned only after World War II, with the trailer parks and self-help housing that occupy edges and pockets of the megalopolis. For most of the workers of the city the entrapment of the early twentieth-century housing pattern endured, and the loss of the single-family cottage which had been the staple of Chicago workers since long before the fire was never recovered.[34] From the first decades of the twentieth century dates the relentless shortage of decent detached homes for the blue-collar class and the widespread use of two-family and three-flat structures; by 1915, statistics showed that single-family homes had fallen to 10.8 percent of all new construction in Chicago.

The street railway, elevated in the Loop section, further influenced the makeup of metropolitan neighborhoods by nourishing the whole central-city retailing complex. Millions of men and women could now be carried cheaply in and out of the core to work and to shop. Although rows of stores sprang up along the streetcar lines and at the transfer points to serve the neighborhood, these stores faced intense competition from the shops of the Loop. Well-to-do women formed the habit of

33. For documentation of inner-ring housing conditions, see Edith Abbott and Sophonisba Breckinridge, *The Tenements of Chicago 1908–1935,* Chicago, 1936, pp. 72–169.

34. Hoyt, *Land Values in Chicago,* p. 231.

shopping as a form of daily entertainment; for the women of the middle and working classes the seeking of bargains and major purchases in downtown stores became a focal point of their lives. To a degree perhaps not equaled since the 1830s and the heyday of the Broadway promenade in New York City,[35] the downtown district became *the* city for Chicagoans. It was the place of work for tens of thousands, a market for hundreds of thousands, a theater for thousands more. Yet for a city like Chicago, a metropolis of two million, even though its newspapers, tall buildings, and advertisements may have cried out for civic pride and unity, a downtown could not re-create the recognitions and sociability of a city of three hundred thousand like old New York. Instead the metropolitan downtown functioned as the symbol of unity and pride for a mass of individuals.

Chicago sociologists of the early twentieth century spoke of their fellow city dwellers as isolated individuals, cut off from each other by a screen of thousands of impersonal commercial contacts.[36] Surely the downtown and its crowds looked that way; so too did the Chicago novelists report it.[37] But the monumentality of the lake front and the Loop and their power as symbols misled the novelists. The sociological studies that have come down to us do not show a mass of two million discrete individuals but rather a highly fragmented society tightly structured along economic lines.

The scholars' reports gave the clue to the new social linkages: workers were tied to mills and foremen within them; immigrant laborers were tied to *padrones* and sweatshop bosses; office girls had been organized in clerical pools or became personal servants for the men they served; store clerks were at the mercy of buyers and merchants. The people of Chicago were systematized by work relationships and bound into a gigantic metropolitan economic web. The Chicago studies made plain how much of the city dweller's life was ordered by the sway of the boss, the foreman, and the buyer.

35. John A. Kouwenhoven, *The Columbia Historical Portrait of New York,* Garden City, 1953, p. 145.
36. Robert E. Park, "The City: Suggestions for the Investigation of Human Behavior in the City Environment," *American Journal of Sociology,* 20 (March 1915), 577–612.
37. For instance, Theodore Dreiser's Carrie Meeber in *Sister Carrie* (New York, 1900) and James T. Farrell's Studs Lonigan and his friends (New York, 1932–35) are overwhelmed by the early twentieth-century downtown environment which they experienced from the street. Inside the skyscrapers conditions were portrayed as more human, if also more vicious; cf. Henry B. Fuller, *The Cliff Dwellers* (1893).

In addition social investigations revealed that, despite basic economic ties and the class rings of residential settlement, no metropolitan
class consciousness had emerged. In the residential districts there was
further fragmentation by race, religion, and ethnicity.[38] Local politicians did their best to manipulate this configuration for their own ends,
but it was a fragmentation without a uniform political direction. Harvey
Zorbaugh's wonderful 1923 study of the near North Side of the city
showed the cleavages. Here within a few square blocks lived the city's
artists and writers and bohemians. There were streets of young people
from the farms and small towns of the Midwest living in roominghouses
and trying to find a place for themselves in the life of the city, as well as
an enclave of Italian immigrants and a Persian colony, flanked along the
lake edge by a narrow strip known as the Gold Coast and occupied by
Chicago's oldest and wealthiest families. Such a district had not produced even district-wide power groupings, to say nothing of class
consensus or political programs. Experiments by settlement-house
workers or citizen volunteers to transform the district into a single social
and political entity failed because the residents' significant ties were to
their jobs, their homes, their ethnic groups.[39]

One extremely influential group, however, did live in the district and
enjoyed city-wide ascendancy—the wealthy Anglo-Saxon Chicagoans of
the Gold Coast. These families owned, controlled, or worked as professionals with the leading economic units of the city. For them the downtown and its towers were the effective center of the city. From the
windows of their skyscraper offices they could look over the roofs of the
city, and from their desks they could read the reports of the far-flung
factories, shops, banks, and properties of the metropolitan region. It is
no accident that the Commercial Club, whose members were the
wealthy Chicago businessmen, should be the first to propose a city plan
for the entire metropolis.

Zorbaugh concluded his study of social fragmentation by saying that
the new industrial metropolis contained only one group who had the
entire city as their focus, the men of the Gold Coast, and that therefore
upon that group would depend the future of any program requiring city-

38. A recent study of elections in Chicago shows that, except for a few issues
which particularly attracted the middle class, voting behavior was linked to ethnicity, not to class. See John M. Allswang, *A House for All Peoples,* Lexington, 1971,
pp. 182–212.
39. Harvey W. Zorbaugh, *The Gold Coast and the Slum,* Chicago, 1929, pp.
182–220.

wide attention. Though an admirer of the generosity and wisdom of some of the Gold Coast families—indeed he thought them the city's only hope—Zorbaugh went on to point out that the structure of social relationships in the new metropolis was such that this elite could know nothing of the daily existence of the country boys and girls, the Sicilians, the Persians, and the bohemians who lived a few blocks away.[40] Remarkably, since the study was firmly rooted in the academic style of his day, Zorbaugh ends by describing the structure of the industrial metropolis in terms that parallel our modern assessment of the corporation which had made the industrial metropolis possible. He could have described his Chicago as Alfred Chandler did the early twentieth-century corporation:

> Yet the dominant centralized structure had one basic weakness. A very few men were still entrusted with a great number of complex decisions. . . . Because these administrators had spent most of their business careers within a single functional activity, they had little experience or interest in understanding the needs and problems of the other departments or of the corporation as a whole. As long as an enterprise belonged in an industry whose markets, sources of raw materials, and production processes remained relatively unchanged, few entrepreneurial decisions had to be reached. In that situation such a weakness was not critical, but where technology, markets, and sources of supply were changing rapidly, the defects of such a structure became more obvious.[41]

Yet change, within the city and within the network of cities, had always been the essence of the American urban system. Even as downtown skyscrapers piled ever higher in the boom of the twenties, the breakup of the overcentralized, oversegregated industrial metropolis began.

40. Ibid., pp. 261–79.
41. Chandler, *Strategy and Structure,* p. 41.

5

The New Freedom

—

Los Angeles 1920– :
bureaucracy, racism,
and automobiles

OUR GREAT URBAN CONGLOMERATIONS offer to the mass of people who inhabit them an illusively wide range of choices, whether of a way of life or of work among a diversity of social institutions. A high level of choice has always been a peculiar attraction of cities, and the wealthy have long flocked to them to enjoy the stimulation of variety and the satisfactions of freedom of personal expression. Even in colonial times the planters of South Carolina built town houses in Charleston, and mill owners and mining czars moved to New York and Chicago to escape the constrictions of the towns in which they had founded their fortunes. For the masses, however, whether white-collar or blue-, urban life was always severely constrained by long working hours, tight schedules of time and commutation, and the strict conformity required to hold a steady job, advance a career, or belong in a "nice" neighborhood. As a nation we have not yet traveled far from these conditions, and the blacks and the poor still struggle within this old framework to be admitted to the freedom of our cities. These are the unique qualities and terrible failures of our urban areas. Nevertheless in many basic structures of today's cities there is the potential of a range of personal choices and social freedoms for all city dwellers if we would only extend the paths of freedom that our urban system has been creating.

In brief, since 1920 the basic technology, transportation, urban markets, business institutions, and land-use structures of the growing national network of cities have all expanded by means of successive inventions and investments until the entire elaborate modern urban complex has begun to reveal an increased potentiality for personal and social choices. The automobile did not by any means initiate the suburbanization of the American city, but it did enable suburbanization to take on a new low-density, multicentered form. Neither did the truck build the nation's manufacturing belts, but by lengthening the distance of cheap short-haul freight traffic it did enable the manufacturing belts to be reorganized into the far-flung communication regions we now identify as megalopolises. The corporation was very much a product of the nineteenth century, but its lusty growth in the soil of national urban markets brought decentralization with it, thereby placing more authority and autonomy in the hands of some of its employees. The turn of the national economy toward services from production began with the introduction of machine manufacture, but in our own time the proliferation of urban services has promoted and sustained a giant middle class without forcing it into a single role of corporate bureaucracy.

During the past half century these extensions from the past have mired our society in a series of contradictions and confusions which we must now come to understand if we are to find policies that will enable us to realize humane solutions. Every component of the forces that bear upon the American urban system, as well as the system itself, harbors twin potentials—for mass repression or for the expansion of popular freedoms. Science and technology can be directed toward war and manipulation or toward services for everyday living; the multiple ways of modern transportation can be either an escape route for the affluent or a means of expanding everyone's horizons; the service economy can be directed toward world domination or toward everyday human needs; the national network of cities can be linked only to the enrichment of local business and political elites or can become the foundation for broadened employment and equalized living standards; the reach and complexity of urban markets can be tied only to private profit or can provision a universal public; private and public corporations can be instruments for bureaucratic control or levers to release personal and group autonomy; the abundant land of the megalopolis can be restricted to the present unequal contest between the classes and races or can become the site of humane physical environments. Our history shows that the capacity of the American urban system for war production, private profit, and inequality, and for the ignoring and infliction of deprivation and suffering is seemingly limitless and certainly enduring. What is new in our time is the enlarged potential of the system to promote the freedom of all the groups within it.

The trend toward the institutionalization of science and technology, well begun in the nineteenth century, has matured in full corporate form in the years since 1920. Private business has sponsored laboratories, universities have established science and engineering faculties, the federal government has financed and carried out massive scientific and technical investigations. This institutionalized effort, bolstered by motives of commercial profit, the conquest of diseases, and military competition, has produced an extraordinary acceleration of the preceding century's discoveries and inventions. Direct communication by telephone had been the previous era's only supplement to the indirect transmission of messages by letter, telegraph, photograph, newspaper, magazine, and book. Now mass-communication modes followed one upon the other, first movies, then radio, and finally television. Three complete transportation systems—the automobile, the airplane, and the pipeline—were added to the familiar rail and water networks. Mechanization matured into a harvest of small specialized tools from electric drills to oscilloscopes, while factory machinery grew in size and complexity to embrace complicated multistage production. Sophisticated machines capable of limited self-correction, often guided by computers, carried out automated sequences of manufacturing and processing. White-collar work, formerly geared to pens and pencils, typewriters, adding machines, and filing cabinets, was mechanized by the computer and by a host of machines for printing and sorting, copying and recording, and mailing. To serve production needs, science and technology created materials of every conceivable kind from metals and plastics to drugs and compounds. Atomic power, a whole new energy system, came into being.[1]

So overwhelming was the power and scope of the expanding knowledge and technical achievement in the United States and other advanced countries that nature itself came to be approached as a man-made artifact. Just as a building stands or falls at the whim of human decisions, so now a lake persisted or became a swamp, a plant or animal species multiplied or died out, depending upon the fiat of man. Nor did man himself escape the reach of scientific enterprise. The social sciences

1. Melvin Kranzberg and Harold W. Pursell, Jr., *Technology in Western Civilization*, II, New York, 1967, pp. 37–52, 309–34.

(especially macroeconomics, market and opinion research, and group and individual psychology) have subjected all levels of society to systematic management and have placed human life under the threat of manipulation.

Yet in the onrush of science and technology each set of tools, each product or technique, held within it recurrent possibilities for a conflict between autonomy and control, centralization and decentralization, personalization and standardization. For example, the making of an automobile required great precision and heavy investment for complicated mass production. As a result the auto worker was habitually subjected to degrading discipline and a stultifying simplification of his tasks.[2] The dignity and independence implicit in the worker's pride in his suburban home were radically contradicted by his working conditions. Similarly the freedom he experienced in his daily drives through the city, for shopping and visits to friends, found no counterpart in the exigencies of his job.

Radio has imposed a form of tyranny in its national propagation of politically manipulated news programs and commercial advertisements, but it also has been an important medium of expression and communication for special publics who make and consume classical music, rock music, black culture, and Bible evangelism. Computerized cost accounting and inventory control have served both to draw decision-making from branch sales offices and factories to the central office and to allow greater branch autonomy. The computer's ability to keep track of complex information and to monitor a multiplicity of distinct programs enables the home office to decentralize decision-making with the assurance that it can keep track of what is happening in its diversified undertakings. Finally, the new social sciences have shown that they are powerful at all levels of society. They can subdue business cycles that formerly scourged all highly developed countries, or they can provide the rationale for the grossly inequitable manipulation of economies; they can enhance the productivity of small groups of workers or mitigate the stresses of racially torn schools and housing projects; they can relieve the mental suffering of individuals. Yet the conflicts of the uses of science and technology pervade the social sciences as well. The question returns and returns of whether social science will become the servant of centralized national government and private and public corporations

2. Robert Blauner, *Alienation and Freedom, The Factory Worker and His Industry,* Chicago, 1964, pp. 89–123.

and be turned to the control of society, or will nourish the autonomy of small groups and promote individual freedom and happiness.

The elaboration of the new transportation system was the most direct instrument for the multiplication of men's choices. Automobiles allowed rural migrants seeking jobs in the city to keep in touch with the countryside and the folks back home, freed urban workers from the necessity of living next to their factories or in central city slums, and gave businessmen an unprecedented choice of locations and complementary services. Production and marketing could devise numberless combinations of diverse services and suppliers and use them within and between the metropolitan regions. Key improvements in transportation lay along two quite different paths. The first set of improvements was directed to lengthening the range of short-haul traffic; the second multiplied the modes of long-haul traffic so that long-distance shipping reflected more specific adaptations to products and passengers than had former all-purpose rail systems and hence were capable of a higher degree of efficiency.

The change in the costs of short-haul transportation was probably the single most important factor to influence the dispersal of job locations within the modern metropolis. Intracity freight movement had formerly been dependent on men and boys who carried parcels in handcarts or on horse-drawn wagons, and its slow pace and high costs had restricted business users of freight service to rail locations in the manufacturing sectors or near the central terminals of the inner city. Small firms were crowded around a downtown post office or inner-city freight yard; more expansive firms with a steady traffic in whole carloads of material could and did settle on spur tracks in the outer rail sectors.

Slowly the truck and automobile loosened and broke these constraints. In the first thirty years of the twentieth century the motor truck, with its obvious advantages in speed and cost over horse teams, was introduced.[3] Although it offered a more efficient alternative to the railroad, the truck did not as yet alter existing rail patterns, because its full realization awaited highway improvements. It is true that during the twenties streets on the periphery of the metropolises were paved and intercity roads improved by the U.S. Route system. Had not the Great Depression intervened just then, a pronounced outward industrial movement would doubtless have got under way in the thirties. As it was,

3. Leon Moses and Harold F. Williamson, "The Location of Economic Activities in Cities," *American Economic Review*, 57 (May 1967), 214–15.

dispersion awaited the building of war plants on the fringes and the postwar manufacturing and housing boom.

By 1948, when wartime shortages had been overcome and the United States had returned briefly to a civilian economy, the truck and automobile did at last free many firms from traditional central locations. Trucks of all sizes could move up to a third of the load of a standard railroad car quickly and cheaply to any destination within a hundred and fifty miles. Overnight trucking service could serve points from two hundred and fifty to three hundred miles apart, and since the perfecting of diesel trucks in the fifties the ranges for both daytime and overnight hauls has been lengthening. Thus a location on any major highway became an excellent departure or terminal point for any except the heaviest freight users, such as lumber mills, foundries, and sugar refineries. At the same time, the widespread private ownership of automobiles released all but the lowest-paid third of the work force from dependence on the streetcar and rapid-transit lines, which were still running radially from suburbs to downtown. Like the freight, workers could now travel in their own cars in any direction through or beyond the metropolis. The result since World War II has been a steady and substantial outmigration of firms and, even more significant, the placing of new enterprises wholly outside the bounds of the central core of each metropolis.[4]

In old cities like Boston, the circumferential highway, built around the fringes of the city and designed to tie together the roads radiating out from the center, has become the axis of industrial growth. In fast-growing cities like Los Angeles, fingers of manufacturing crept out for thirty and forty miles from the old central core. The original industrial development there had taken place at a close knot of rail lines in the southeast sector of the city. As the metropolis became a major national manufacturing region, freeways paralleled the old rail network, and industry stretched farther and farther in every direction to create employment opportunities all over the city.[5]

Despite the advances in transportation, firms that required the most immediate complementary interaction remained at the core. The metropolitan center has retained the firms that depend upon transient eddies

4. Benjamin Chinitz, *Freight and the Metropolis,* Cambridge, 1960, pp. 120–27, 130–57.

5. Los Angeles Chamber of Commerce, *Industrial Development Map, Los Angeles Five County Area,* Los Angeles, 1969; Los Angeles Regional Transportation Study, *Base Year Report 1* (December 1963), p. 36.

of fashion, such as the garment trade, publishers, and art dealers. The center has also been partially rebuilt with office towers to house the headquarters and regional offices of the great corporations that need the traditional cluster of bankers, lawyers, and accountants and the more recent public-relations and advertising firms. But the downtown has failed to capture even a majority of the office and commercial growth of the metropolis. Some stores have followed their customers to the suburbs; others have found that office routine, sales, and professional services can be performed as effectively in suburban shopping centers as in the urban confines.[6]

The benefits accruing from the changing patterns of work locations were obvious and substantial. With the improvement of metropolitan highways, immense tracts of industrial and residential land opened for use and the cost of urban sites fell. Employer and employee alike gained over their 1920 condition. The employer could easily purchase from and sell to firms within a radius of fifty to four hundred and fifty miles of the megalopolis, and he could furnish or obtain daily service within a fifty-mile radius of the metropolis itself. Similarly the employee found an extensive range of jobs inside the fifty-mile radius, and he could live almost anywhere within the metropolis and still take advantage of the widened job market.[7]

In terms of the physical form of the city, this freedom from spatial restrictions offered an unprecedented array of urban arrangements for all degrees of population density. The highway interchange could support areas crowded with row houses, factories, and apartment and office towers, which could yet be wholly encircled by forests or fields; suburban streets and freeways could sustain a uniform spread of houses and lawns and tree-lined streets, interspersed with shopping strips or centers and industrial parks. Unfortunately, for reasons having to do in large part with organization of the land and real-estate market, the great variations in urban design that might have been feasible under the transportation revolution have not been fully exploited in America.

The principal drawback of the evolving pattern lay in its entrance fee: private ownership of a car. Young people, old people, poor people could gain access to metropolitan jobs only by means of a private

6. John F. Kain, "The Distribution and Movement of Jobs and Industry," in *The Metropolitan Enigma*, James Q. Wilson, ed., Cambridge, 1968, pp. 1–32.

7. Stanley Lebergott, "Tomorrow's Workers: The Prospects for the Urban Labor Force," in *Planning for a Nation of Cities*, Sam Bass Warner, Jr., ed., Cambridge, 1966, pp. 124–33.

automobile or through a car pool. In the homes of low-wage and unskilled workers, a decent income can be earned only when two members of the family work. For the wife, the finding and reaching of jobs, often widely scattered in the metropolis, has proved extremely difficult. Transport networks have tended strongly to reinforce racial segregation in employment and housing by confining the poor, especially poor women, to a depressed inner-city labor market.[8] In the core of most cities the old 1870–1920 public transportation system is still maintained; at the core too are the decaying slums that still house the black and white poor. Here manufacturers can find a large reservoir of low-skilled workers. As a result a cycle of underpaying jobs, constricted transport, and ghetto living has settled upon many of our old metropolises. In New York City proper, manufacturing wages fell behind those of Birmingham, Alabama;[9] elsewhere the women and the old and the poor await the perfection of a public transportation system that, by imitating the highway patterns of today's diffused metropolis, will let them participate in the society as full-fledged members.

Advances in long-haul transportation over the past fifty years have reinforced the nationalizing accomplishments of the earlier rail lines, which the new systems supplement. In the exploitation of natural resources, oil and gas pipelines bring cheap fuel to cities thousands of miles from the Oklahoma and Texas wells in a volume that railroad freight could never have handled. Improvements in the Midwestern river system have revived barge traffic in coal, grain, cement, and other bulk commodities so that the old Ohio-Mississippi route is again functioning as a carrier of cheap resources as it did before the Civil War.

Since World War II the long-haul truck has combined with air freight to sustain the national manufacturing economy by moving small quantities of goods quickly and inexpensively. Parts for a broken machine, a tub of a particular chemical, a broken instrument being returned to its manufacturer for repair—all these can be shipped between the most important centers in the nation in a matter of hours. Long-haul truck service supplements air freight by allowing firms with less than full rail carloads to ship materials and semifinished goods directly from one factory to another within a day or two and to do it

8. John F. Kain, "Housing Segregation, Negro Employment, and Metropolitan Decentralization," *Quarterly Journal of Economics,* 82 (May 1968), 175–97.
9. Nathan Glazer and Daniel Patrick Moynihan, *Beyond the Melting Pot,* Cambridge, 1963, pp. 299–300.

more cheaply and with greater dispatch than on the railroad's old circuitous less-than-carload routing. Altogether, the addition of truck and airplane facilities and the more specialized barge and pipeline service to the old rail network has meant a burgeoning of the paths and volume of American traffic. Goods move swiftly and cheaply within the cities of the old manufacturing belts of the Northeast and Midwest and within the new southern California region. Moreover, despite the long distances involved, shipments travel easily back and forth between the manufacturing regions and the growing metropolises of the South and West. The transcontinental production of aerospace components, especially in Massachusetts, Connecticut, New York, New Jersey, Missouri, Texas, and California, has been an outstanding example of present possibilities.

The proliferation of technology and transportation has strongly influenced both the national economy and its network of cities. The continued application of science and technology to agriculture and mining has brought an increasingly dramatic decline in employment in that sector of the economy and a concomitant strong outmigration from the rural United States. The sheer productivity of mechanized manufacture, despite the multiplication of products and the vast increase in the volume of factory-made goods for producers and consumers, has allowed the ratio of the labor force engaged in that sector to fall slightly too. Trade, services, transportation, and government have become the hallmarks of today's economy because two-thirds of the labor force is engaged in these activities. Science, technology, and transportation have made possible the service and military economy that now obtains.[10]

The changing focus of the national economy has meant a corresponding adjustment in the network of cities. Urbanization in general was encouraged because the growing trade-service-transport-government activities were themselves the specialties of cities. Thus the population of the United States, North and South, East and West, grew increasingly metropolitanized. Ports and trading centers, on both coasts and along the Great Lakes and in the South, prospered in particular. If we measure the size of cities solely in terms of the inhabitants within their formal political boundaries, Houston rose to be the nation's sixth most populous city, Dallas the eighth, and San Antonio passed Boston and St. Louis, while the size of Memphis, New Orleans, Seattle, and Phoenix each exceeded that of Pittsburgh—the archetypical city of the former

10. Harvey S. Perloff, et al., *Regions, Resources, and Economic Growth,* Baltimore, 1960, pp. 234, 465.

era of the industrial metropolis.[11] The simple tabulation of the size of cities according to their political boundaries highlights the importance of the new trading cities (Table 1, page 70), since their growth countered the outmigration of population from old core cities like New York, Chicago, and Boston. By these additions to the list of cities of metropolitan size, the category was able just to maintain the same proportionate share of the nation's population from 1920 to 1970. Beyond serving as a general encouragement to urbanization, the new economy instilled vigor into the small cities and towns—places of 2,500 to 249,999 inhabitants. These were the building blocks of the new economy, and their share of the population rose to 52.4 percent (Table 1, page 70). Such cities and towns were found everywhere in the nation and made up the constituent elements of the 243 Standard Metropolitan Statistical Areas classified by the census. Some like Arlington and Richardson (Dallas), Hollywood (Miami), Mesa (Phoenix), Overland Park and Independence (Kansas City), and Bloomington (Minneapolis-St. Paul) contributed to the metropolitanization of the West, Midwest, and South. Others were beneficiaries of the continued growth of the basic manufacturing regions of the nation: Orange and Garden Grove (Los Angeles), Joliet and Oak Lawn (Chicago), Warren and Livonia (Detroit), Kettering (Dayton), Framingham (Boston), Norwalk, Piscataway, and Bay Shore (New York), Willingboro (Philadelphia), Catonsville (Baltimore), and Silver Spring (Washington).

The complexity of manufacturing in the new economy was compatible with the dispersal of urban population from old central cities, but at the same time it fostered a concentration of population within large multicity regions. Thus the old manufacturing belts of the Northeast and Midwest, and the new one in southern California, prospered as the urbanized manufacturing regions of the United States.[12] The major trend in manufacturing locations since 1920 has been to seek sites near

11. The rank list of cities in 1970 according to their political boundaries: New York 7,895,000; Chicago 3,367,000; Los Angeles 2,816,000; Philadelphia 1,949,000; Detroit 1,511,000; Houston 1,233,000; Baltimore 906,000; Dallas 844,000; Washington 757,000; Cleveland 751,000; Indianapolis 745,000; Milwaukee 717,000; San Francisco 716,000; San Diego 697,000; San Antonio 654,000; Boston 641,000; Memphis 624,000; St. Louis 622,000; New Orleans 593,000; Phoenix 582,000; Columbus 540,000; Seattle 531,000; Jacksonville 529,000; Pittsburgh 520,000; Denver 514,000. *Nineteenth Census: 1970, Number of Inhabitants, Final Report PC(1)-A1*, Washington, 1971, Table 28.

12. Perloff et al., *Regions, Resources and Economic Growth*, p. 462; Beverly Duncan and Stanley Lieberson, *Metropolis and Region in Transition*, Beverly Hills, 1970, pp. 154–242.

the final markets for consumer goods and to search out effective placement in the midst of regions where producers' goods can be bought and
sold easily. Both trends favored the old manufacturing belts because
these were huge agglomerations of individual consumers and also buyers and sellers of producers' goods. The mass migration to southern
California and the succession of wars since 1941 have transformed that
region into another such belt. The diffusion of population and enterprise
within these three regions has altered their former patterns of mill town
and industrial metropolis established in the railroad era. The megalopolis, a gigantic continuous band of urbanized territory with towns, cities,
and metropolises embedded within it, is the emergent urban manifestation of the new economy and new transportation. The Boston–New
York–Washington megalopolis has functioned at least since 1950 as a
regional city; the Pittsburgh–Cleveland–Detroit–Chicago megalopolis
seems to be a recrudescence of the old Midwestern manufacturing belt
but in a form that favors growth along the path of the region's largest
metropolises; while the third, stretching from San Diego through Los
Angeles to San Francisco, has become recognizable as a growing entity
only in the last decade.[13] The megalopolises are of about equal length.
Each of them extends 454 to 470 miles, and all of them are abundantly
provided with transportation. They are in every case industrially diversified and encompass thousands of specialized firms so that the benefits of
complementarity obtain for almost any economic enterprise, from steel
mills to toy manufacture, throughout the regions.

The channeling of national metropolitan growth into the formation
of the three megalopolises has had two effects upon the organization of
urban business: first, corporate enterprise has expanded and altered its
management form; second, the service economy has nurtured an enormous class of urban professionals and small businessmen—retailers,
furniture dealers, doctors, lawyers, insurance agents, and every kind of
home and business service establishment. Both developments contain
possibilities for a more humane urban society and equally for the further
concentration of power exercised for the benefit of a minority.

The large corporation, as it added more products and services
and reached ever farther afield for customers, was forced to abandon its

13. Jean Gottmann, *Megalopolis, the Urbanized Northeastern Seaboard of
the United States*, Cambridge, 1961, pp. 150–213; Constantine A. Doxiadis, *Emergence and Growth of an Urban Region, The Developing Urban Detroit Area*, Detroit, 1966–1970, I, pp. 75–113; III, pp. 25–51.

traditional centralized, departmentalized form. Instead it adopted various adjustments that resulted in a general way in a hierarchy where a central office of staff executives assessed and assisted a series of semi-autonomous divisions. This decentralized, divisional structure owed its origins to a management crisis of the 1920s. In the four cases that have been studied in detail (General Motors, Du Pont, Standard Oil of New Jersey, and Sears, Roebuck) a growing diversity of operations finally broke the centralized form. General Motors made many different models of cars—unlike Ford with its Model T—and also turned out refrigerators, electrical equipment, and an extensive line of parts and accessories. Du Pont branched out in the first years of the century from gunpowder and blasting materials into chemicals and paints. Standard Oil of New Jersey undertook international oil prospecting, oil transport, and refining, along with the domestic and foreign marketing of a full range of petroleum products from automobile gasolines to fuel oils and the old staple, kerosene. Sears, Roebuck, already a profitable mail-order house, in 1925 established a national chain of retail outlets to offset declining sales and to reach out to the growing suburban markets.[14]

In each case diversity of operations brought financial losses and crises in management. In each case the solution proved to be reorganization of management in such a way as to break up departmental structure. Before this time the vice-president of each central office had concentrated on one major phase of the business—production, sales, development, or finance—and the day-to-day decisions had originated with him and his staff in the central office. The crisis in management arose when these executives could not distribute the flow of products among the departments, when production poured out more items than the sales force had orders for, when the executives, oriented each to his own specialty, could no longer intelligently allocate staff and capital among the departments.[15]

The multidivisional structure instituted in the big diversified corporations during the 1920s assigned the central office to staff service for the entire corporation but relieved it of everyday decisions, which were now passed down to divisional heads. Each division—at Du Pont, divisions were respectively responsible for paint, dyestuffs, explosives, films, and so on—had a general manager to supervise production, sales,

14. Alfred D. Chandler, Jr., *Strategy and Structure, Chapters in the History of the Industrial Enterprise,* Cambridge, 1962, pp. 289–302.
15. Ibid., p. 71.

and personnel. The central office evaluated the success of each division in relation to the others, either granting increased budgets or cutting back an operation on the basis of its individual performance as it related to prospects for the entire corporation. The staff of the central office also conducted studies in market research, engineering, and design, and in its own accounting department it strove to assure the prosperity of the complete enterprise. If the performance of one division showed low profits, the central staff either closed out the operation or stepped in to reorganize it. In short, the role of the central office resembled that of an investment banking house, placing corporate capital as best it could among the divisions or using accumulated profits to purchase related independent firms and thereby to add more products or even divisions to the undertaking. For its part each division, its partial autonomy assured by an annual budget, was free to purchase materials wherever it could find them and was no longer restricted to contracts made by a central purchasing office. It could assemble its own sales force, locate plants and warehouses, and until the arrival of national industry-wide unions could make its own terms with local labor.[16]

In the United States, World War II initiated an almost uninterrupted thirty years of intensive demand for industrial products. That war and the succeeding wars in Korea and Vietnam stimulated arms production while the government policy of cold-war military rivalry with the Soviet Union and China spurred naval, air, and space research and weapons production on a scale of wartime magnitude. During the same years the elaboration of science and technology in the United States, Europe, and Japan brought forth a steady stream of consumer products, such as tape recorders, dishwashers, gasoline lawn mowers, paints, and drugs. The combination of both domestic and foreign military and consumer demand encouraged corporations to diversify by taking up additional sales regions and new products, and in time this always meant the adoption of a decentralized form of operation.

Today's business structure reflects these historical solutions. The strength of the corporate form as an institution for managing accumulated capital is attested by the sheer giantism of American corporate enterprise. The smallest corporation on *Fortune's* 1971 annual list of the nation's five hundred largest had 7,850 employees, the largest were as big as nineteenth-century cities: General Motors had 696,000 em-

16. Peter F. Drucker, *The Concept of the Corporation,* New York, 1946, pp. 46–68.

ployees, Ford Motor Company 432,000, General Electric 397,000, International Business Machines 269,000, Standard Oil of New Jersey 143,000. Among the retail chains, Sears had 359,000 employees, A&P 120,000; American Telephone and Telegraph employed 773,000; Consolidated Edison, the electric monopoly for New York City and nearby New York counties, 23,726; the Southern Pacific Company had grown to 42,000, United Airlines to 66,000, the Prudential Life Insurance Company to 59,000, the Bank of America to 36,000, the First National City Bank to 37,000. Such immense institutions could be managed only by committees and decentralized forms of governance.[17]

Decentralization today takes a number of forms. The semiautonomous divisional style of the 1920s is favored by the new conglomerates, which are aggregations of capital assembled by a team of central-office executives who seek to purchase independent businesses for profitable investment. If the newly acquired business proves to be well managed, its executives continue their work as an autonomous division of the conglomerate. This is true for instance, of Litton Industries of Beverly Hills, California, a firm that began in 1954 in electronics and now deals in typewriters, calculators, office furniture and equipment, surgical instruments, X-ray machines, motion-picture cameras, and automatic revenue-collecting machines, and also operates paper mills, printing plants, and Great Lakes shipping lines. It manages its diverse affairs through fifty separate divisions, each largely autonomous.[18]

The reach to the ultimate consumer has meant market-oriented decentralization for manufacturing firms as well as for retailers. The goal of management has been to adjust production to sales as closely as possible and thereby to reduce losses sustained by the accumulation of unwanted and slow-moving inventories. Abundant long-haul transportation enabled manufacturing firms to maintain specialized production plants, each located for its specialty's best advantage, where components could be manufactured and then assembled into the final product near the final markets. Cheap intracity transportation encouraged such a strategy; one sales-warehousing-assembly plant could serve an entire metropolis or a cluster of them. Thus a famous brand of St. Louis beer no longer travels by refrigerator car from a single brewery to scattered urban markets but is brewed in Tampa, Newark, Houston, and Los

17. "Fortune Directory of the 500 Largest Industrial Corporations," *Fortune,* 83 (May 1971), 170–204.
18. *Business Week* (April 16, 1966), 175–185.

Angeles and marketed regionally from these points. Chevrolets are assembled at Arlington (Texas), Baltimore (Maryland), Doraville (Georgia), Janesville (Wisconsin), Leeds and St. Louis (Missouri), South Gate and Van Nuys (California), North Tarrytown (New York), Willow Run (Michigan), and Wilmington (Delaware).[19] Here, then, were some of the multitude of plants and offices that have sought sub-urban locations since World War II. Retail chains like Sears, Roebuck and Montgomery Ward have evolved a commercial style that they call metropolitan management. A metropolis like Los Angeles may have a dozen retail stores belonging to one of these chains, each store located in a regional shopping center. The sheer volume of Los Angeles sales, as well as the peculiarities of that particular market as opposed to the Chicago or New York demands, justified the establishment of a metro-politan management team responsible for operations in that area. For general merchandising, unlike the distribution and sales of a limited range of products like automobiles or beer, the metropolis has proved to be a more feasible unit than the sprawling megalopolis.[20]

In these cases of decentralization it is easy to see how a measure of public responsibility could be introduced into the national corporate structure. The special interests of the metropolis or megalopolis in employment, plant, office, and store location, and the need of workers and managers for autonomy, could be expressed in management com-mittees of public officials and employees without disrupting the effi-ciency of the corporation since the current dispersal of the company mirrors the structure of the national network of cities. Other recent management forms, however, are less easy to accommodate to urban requirements.

The huge scale involved in the production of aircraft and of military needs, power plants, and the complexity of other large contracts has moved some firms toward project management, in which teams of engi-neers and executives are formed around a particular job. They seek the contract and coordinate the work of design and production divisions and other departments of the parent company with outside firms who become subcontractors. Sometimes called "matrix management" be-cause the men responsible for the single contract are given budgets and authority that cut across the lines of regular organization structure in the corporation, this form reintroduces centralized power into all branches

19. *Ward's Automotive Reports,* August 10, 1970.
20. *Fortune,* 82 (May 1970), 231–45.

of industrial enterprise. Though the device is effective (indeed insisted upon by the U.S. Air Force, which wants a single group to call upon for each major contract), it creates frequent conflicts within the firms that use it.[21] It also promotes urban and regional irresponsibility. Once the contract is secured, the project is insulated from all concern for such issues as working conditions within the offices and plants either of the parent company or of its subcontractors, and these become problems solely of divisional and departmental managers. The project is freed from concern for local employment or for the ecological consequences of the aircraft, power stations, or factory complexes it builds, since the project team's task is directed only to getting the job done. A consequent social irresponsibility is spreading throughout American corporations.

On a smaller scale, makers of highly competitive mass consumer products are using product managers to take charge of a single item, like Procter and Gamble's Crest toothpaste. Also, venture teams of designers, engineers, and marketing specialists are being formed to search for and test new avenues for the investment of a corporation's accumulated capital.[22] As in the project, the venture team is not responsible to the division, the department, or a geographical area but only to the national headquarters, where the criterion is profit alone.

The outcome of five decades of these contradictory decentralized and centralized business trends is a mixture of benefit and condemnation for the urban worker and city dweller. Thanks to the sheer growth of big business, industrial work, which in the preceding century was the scene of the most unrestrained exploitation of workers, has now become bureaucratized. Planned production, market power, and manipulation even out the employment season for corporate workers so that they can be reasonably sure of an approximate yearly income. National unions, such as the United Auto Workers, represent their members as they confront the giant corporations in conflicts over wages, local plant discipline, mechanization, and working conditions. The countervailing union power, however, suffers all the problems of responsibility that confront its corporate adversary. The key issues revolve around working conditions in the individual plants, and they find their expression in the union locals. In recent years large national and international unions have proved cumbersome and inadequate to negotiate these issues for their

21. Franklin Moore, *Management & Organization*, forthcoming edition.
22. Mack Hanan, "Corporate Growth Through Venture Management," *Harvard Business Review,* 47 (January-February 1969), 43–61.

members. Strikes that have been settled to the satisfaction of the central union office and the corporate headquarters have dragged on for weeks and months in scattered plants around the country. Moreover, most unions have been reluctant to enter in a positive way into the decisions of plant location and production design and prefer to content themselves with a responsive role, approving or disapproving each individual innovative machine or job description. Yet the high level of modern technology offers many alternative paths to efficient production. The assembly line is not the only way to make cars, cut meat, or assemble TV sets.[23] Although no group or institution in the nation, the megalopolis, or the metropolis takes as its charge the establishment of more humane working conditions, the riots and strikes of the past and the boredom, absenteeism, and local union rebellions of the present repeatedly emphasize that working conditions are and always have been one of the three or four determinants of the quality of urban life.

White-collar workers, although not usually unionized, have profited most from the trends of the economy over the past half century. Opportunities abounded as white-collar jobs rapidly increased. Large-scale production and sales required more and more research, engineering, cost accounting, advertising, and promotion, and the white-collar force has accordingly advanced at a reasonably regular pace in the nation's corporate bureaucracies. Scientific management, especially for middle management, has also come to the aid of the white-collar worker. Social scientists have demonstrated that when decisions must be made in an environment of rapid change, efficiency is promoted by individual and group autonomy, open communications from those lower in status to those above, and a general climate of trust and cooperation.[24] Modern business thrives in situations of rapid change, and management jobs have accordingly multiplied, much to the pleasure and profit of the middle-class city dwellers who work in them. The problem for the city and the society as a whole has been that these benign and inherently more pleasurable working roles have not been extended more widely. Bureaucratic routine and mechanized production are the rule for most tasks in American business and government, and they are successful after their fashion. Autonomous, responsible white- and blue-collar

23. American Academy for the Advancement of Science, Symposium on Technology of Humanizing Work, *New York Times,* December 28, 1971.
24. Rensis Likert, *The Human Organization: Its Management and Value,* New York, 1967, pp. 3–44; Warren G. Bennis and Philip E. Slater, *The Temporary Society,* New York, 1968, pp. 53–76.

work for nonmanagers will not become generally available until the masses of office and factory workers insist upon it. In fact, so long as Americans regard their working hours as an unavoidably unpleasant period by which they purchase evening and weekend pleasures, they will not find the civility and autonomy in their jobs that they insist upon in their leisure and home environments. One need only contemplate the human impairment and cultural poverty of a large industrial city like Detroit to appreciate the enormous costs of our present methods of doing business.

The disadvantages of today's style are notorious. Although our plants, offices, and schools may be less harsh than their predecessors, more uniform and equitable in their treatment of people, less authoritarian and more temperate, a fog of boredom tinged with resentment fills the factories, salesrooms, and offices of the metropolis.[25] Much work is dull routine. Much work in sales and supervision consists of selling one's own personality and manipulating those of others. Indeed, some of the new findings in social science have been used to manipulate employees for the benefit of management. Thompson Ramo Wooldridge Systems, for instance, is currently using T-groups, a technique of social psychology, as a means of reducing payrolls.[26] In the factory, close tolerances and repetitive tasks make for ceaseless discipline without the compensating psychological release that might be provided by control over one's pace or by self-determination through one's craft. Everywhere there is an acceptance of real personal powerlessness and a dependence upon the pecking order of bureaucratically defined jobs.[27] Sociologists speak of the alienation of the modern American; radio and television trumpet the fun culture. The advertising and market manipulation that ensures the corporate worker's position seeks also to alleviate his alienation by urging him to deaden his complaints in repeated consumerism.[28]

Like the bureaucracies that have preceded our own—the Vatican, the Manchu society, and France under Louis XIV—our corporate society has come under attack for its seamless irresponsibility. By a

25. Survey Research Center, University of Michigan, *Survey of Working Conditions, November 1970,* U.S. Department of Labor, Employment Standards Administration, Washington, 1971.

26. *Business Week* (March 20, 1971), 44–50.

27. C. Wright Mills, *White Collar, The American Middle Classes,* New York, 1951, pp. 77–111; Blauner, *Alienation and Freedom,* pp. 15–34.

28. Jules Henry, *Culture Against Man,* New York, 1963, pp. 220–231.

balance of internal conflicts among vice-presidents, division managers, and unions, the corporation grows and adapts to its surroundings. But, guided as it is by the profit motive, it is helpless to control itself for purposes other than its own growth. The automobile chokes the air of the cities, numerous products are dangerous to health, the very processes of modern industry and agriculture poison the rivers and seas of the world. In trying to combat the evils of such irresponsible self-serving, regulatory government agencies have mushroomed throughout the twentieth century. In the nineteenth century the development of the private railroad corporation was soon followed by the creation of state railway boards and the Interstate Commerce Commission. Yet over the years bargaining between bureaucrats and corporate lawyers, coupled with the shifting of personnel back and forth between industry and government, has softened regulation. Both industry and government have accommodated themselves to the sharing of power and to a common limitation on outside responsibility.

Just as Americans have failed to make full use of the flexibility of the dispersed metropolis, so they have failed to realize the social opportunities of the corporate society. The modern corporation has all the organized power necessary for the democratic and socially responsible organization of its enterprise. The capacity of the central staff to control accounting, planning, engineering, product design, market research, and capital allocation demonstrates that our society could manage the whole range of planned production. The successful splitting of the centralized firm into semiautonomous divisions suggests that the worst features of mindless uniformity could be overcome by giving more divisional authority to workers and regions where the corporation operates. In the last half century, while the corporations have been maturing, the missing element has been the urge on the part of citizens to make the private corporations public. Yet it seems clear that if we are to regain control of our society we must find ways to make our corporations into public enterprises.

Underlying the whole issue of the relationship between private corporations and urban life runs the unanswered question of legitimacy. What are the legitimate goals of these ubiquitous institutions and to whom should they be held responsible? Hitherto Americans have subscribed to the belief that the function of private enterprises was to make money for their managers and investors. Over the years unions and government regulations have defined limits within which this activity should take place, yet neither unions nor government agencies deny that profit is the ultimate justification for corporate endeavor. Corporations are now too important to society to be allowed to continue in this limited direction; profit should be but one test of their effectiveness. So long as profit remains the ultimate measure of achievement, the products and services of corporations will fail to build a humane society because they will take on only those tasks in the society which are profitable and will indeed rush toward those that are most profitable to the exclusion of essential considerations. Thus in the midst of urban racism, poverty, and neglect, unemployment, housing shortages, malfunctioning education and health services, world starvation, and a host of other social ills which call out for attention, General Mills has decided that its future prosperity lies in developing a line of games and hobbies.[29] The decision may be logical enough, given the company's past organization, present talents, and the likelihood of a large middle-class market, but it hardly sets in motion an activity to which society at the moment needs to devote its managerial talent or inherited capital. So it is down through the list of corporate contributions to our consumer society. Most products are harmless, and each of them is useful and satisfying in its own way, yet the sum of all the new cosmetics, cake mixes, lawn foods, appliances, home and office furnishings, and sports cars constitutes a vast misapplication of human resources and accumulated capital. The high but extremely uneven standard of living which the corporations have helped to create represents—like the corporations themselves—an appalling default in bringing about the humane and inclusive urban society that might be appearing.

The already large class of professionals and small businessmen has expanded with the rising standard of living, and the shift of the economy into retailing and services has helped to screen private corporations from public notice. For example, in metropolitan Los Angeles in 1967 there were 801,000 proprietors and employees engaged in operating small shops and services: lumber companies, hardware stores, groceries, restaurants, gasoline stations, clothing, furniture and appliance and drug stores, motels and laundromats, dry cleaners, travel and real-estate agencies, bowling alleys, and so forth. The same year, 982,000 persons were engaged in manufacturing enterprises, but they were laboring in establishments with an average of fifty-two employees, while the re-

29. Hanan, "Corporate Growth," *Harvard Business Review,* 47.

tailers were working in establishments that averaged 7.3 and the service people five.[30] In other words, besides the highly organized manufacturing workers in the modern metropolis stands a group of workers, almost as numerous, who follow the working patterns of the early nineteenth-century city. This modern petty-bourgeois class is deeply antisocialist, and it regards all social regulation and control as a threat to its personal and economic freedom. As C. Wright Mills observed some years ago, this class of professionals and businessmen defends the managers of large plants and offices in the local chambers of commerce and before local government agencies.[31] It uncritically supports the use of public money for the assistance of business as a boon to prosperity and progress, obstructing all efforts toward local and regional planning which might deny a firm its desires. As a class it opposes national economic planning unless it takes the form of public works, tax write-offs, and subsidies. Thus today's urban business institutions present an ugly paradox—the corporate form holds a real potential for successful public ownership or public management, while the growing retail and service sector continues in the mold of the ideology of the early nineteenth century. The corporation is susceptible to dedication to public goals; but the second group, although it could be a key element in a revived localism, is opposed to every effort to make public goals the aim of successful economic enterprise.

The form of the corporation has always been and will continue to be determined by the ways in which the society and the economy are developing. We stand at a moment of unique opportunity. If strong steps are not taken now to socialize these institutions, it seems probable that the personnel of government and private management will merge into interlocking bureaucracies placed beyond the reach of democratic supervision. Such at least is the tendency today; it is the meaning of the outcry against the military-industrial complex and the reason for the frustration of consumer and ecological reforms. If we fail to socialize soon we will have lost, through foolish devotion to our cherished myth of private property, a historic opportunity to gain social responsibility for and democratic control of the building of our society and its cities.

30. U.S. Bureau of the Census, *Census of Business, 1967, Retail Trade: California, BC 67-RA6* (Washington, 1969), Table 4; *Census of Business, 1967, Selected Services; California, BC 67-SA6* (Washington, 1970), Table 4.
31. Mills, *White Collar*, pp. 44–54.

The Megalopolis: 1920–

Los Angeles, city of war material, swimming pools, and smog, wonderfully exemplifies the urban consequences stemming from the change in structure of the national economy and its institutions. It is par excellence a city of the past half century. In 1920 the city proper had grown to be the tenth largest in the nation, about the same size as Pittsburgh (Los Angeles, 577,000; Pittsburgh, 588,000), and its metropolitan population had reached almost a million. Thanks largely to the prosperity and land rush of the twenties, the metropolitan area sustained a population of 2,785,000 on the eve of World War II, and the wartime infusion of business and workers raised this figure to 9,475,000 in 1970.[32] Today Los Angeles is the second largest cluster of population and the third largest manufacturing center in the United States (Chicago Consolidated Statistical Area 7,612,000; New York CSA 16,179,000). It has now become the economic capital of the Pacific and the Southwest, the heart of the fast-growing San Diego–San Francisco megalopolis.

Like all great American cities, Los Angeles grew not by accretion of economic functions taken from other cities but by being geographically located in the center of new developments. Chicago rose with the settlement of the Midwest, Los Angeles with the waves of migration to California and the Southwest. Moreover, new resources and industries fired its growth. The railroads, the prairie farms, the forests of Michigan and Wisconsin, and Lake Superior ore had made Chicago a center for transportation, food processing, lumber, steel, and machinery. Similarly oil, a warm sunny climate, and the airlines made Los Angeles the capital of petroleum refining, of the national distribution of fruit and vegetables, and of movies, as well as the focal point of the nation's aircraft, aerospace, and war-research industries. Migrants added banks, stores, and residentiary industries of all kinds, and the local specialties encouraged complementary industries, until by the fifties the city was functioning as

32. Since the Los Angeles metropolis spread out so rapidly, it is impossible to represent the city by one set of boundaries. A reasonable approximation of its population comes from using Los Angeles County in 1920, population 936,000, and sticking with that definition to show the boom of the twenties, and then adopting for 1970 a definition of the Los Angeles Standard Metropolitan Statistical Area plus the Anaheim–Santa Ana–Garden Grove SMSA, plus the San Bernardino SMSA.

The Automobile Metropolis

72. Downtown Los Angeles Freeway Circuit, 1970. Because of the speed and ease of automobile travel, a conventional retailing, office, and manufacturing core became but one center in a network of scattered concentrations. *California Division of Highways, District VII*

73. Looking Toward the Downtown from the Convention Center, Los Angeles, 1971. As in all American cities, the new corporate office towers symbolize the increasing bureaucratization of the urban economy and provide the dynamic element in the refashioning of old city cores into more narrowly specialized office and government centers. *Mason Dooley*

74. Raymond Avenue, Los Angeles, 1971. The near-universal cultural goal of a city of private homes shaped the potential of the automobile into the reality of Los Angeles. *Mason Dooley*

75. Stone Canyon, Sherman Oaks, 1970. Although Los Angeles' housing styles have been widely copied, the informal garden characteristic of California modern has generally been employed to intensify the inward-turning, private-family orientation of traditional American urban housing styles. *Mason Dooley*

76. Japanese-Americans Awaiting Removal to Concentration Camps, Los Angeles, 1942. The special contribution of Californians to American white racism was their fear of and hostility to Orientals. Wartime panic and xenophobia climaxed decades of earlier discrimination. Today's legacy is a precedent which threatens every American's civil liberties, and the permanent loss of a lively Japanese component in the culture of the metropolis. *Library of Congress*

77. Boyle Heights, Los Angeles, 1971. The trickle-down housing market in the Mexican-American east side. The low density of typical twentieth-century Los Angeles building has saved the city from the worst sanitary and overcrowding effects of earlier styles of slum housing. *Mason Dooley*

Elements of Growth

78. Main Street, Los Angeles, ca. 1875. Los Angeles began like all American cities with a shopkeepers' street of drygoods stores, livery stables, saloons, and hotels. View from the Plaza south toward the present downtown core. The Santa Ana Freeway now crosses Main Street beyond the first intersection. *History Division, Los Angeles County Museum of Natural History*

79. "Parking Lot" at Long Beach, 1905. The first of Los Angeles' special assets was its climate, but the cost of a horse and carriage for a time preserved urban recreation spaces for exclusive middle-class use. *History Division, Los Angeles County Museum of Natural History*

80. Streetcar Beach, Long Beach, ca. 1920. Street railways brought mass commercial exploitation of the Pacific shore, partially overcome by the subsequent extensive development of public automobile access beaches. *History Division, Los Angeles County Museum of Natural History*

81. William Fox Studio, Western Avenue and Sunset Boulevard, Los Angeles, 1927. Continuous sunshine drew the new movie industry from its earlier metropolitan New York locations. *History Division, Los Angeles County Museum of Natural History*

82. Del Rey Oil Fields, Los Angeles, 1930. The oil boom of the twenties added a second impetus to the city's growth, starting it on its path to industrial diversification. *History Division, Los Angeles County Museum of Natural History*

83. Ford Assembly Plant, Long Beach, 1929. With the take-off of Los Angeles in the twenties, growth begat growth, and national firms began to locate regional plants in the metropolis. *Historical Collections, Security Pacific National Bank*

84. Union Pacific Industrial Area, Vernon, 1924. Modern zoning laws intensified the rail orientation of American urban industry by specifying such land for factories only. In Los Angeles old rail alignments continue to function as the skeleton for industrial expansion. *Historical Collections, Security Pacific National Bank*

85. The earlier railroad-sponsored industrial development has reached in our own time the ultimate form of a planned satellite city. Here 35 miles from the downtown, developers have laid out a 4,000-acre tract with 350 firms and multiple transportation service: the San Diego and Newport freeways, Orange County airport, and a spur of the Atchison, Topeka and Santa Fe. *The Irvine Company*

Centers

86. Hill and 9th Streets, Downtown Los Angeles, 1924. Far more dispersed than its predecessors, the central cluster grew until World War II in the conventional form of a multipurpose, retail, office, government, theater, hotel, wholesaling, and manufacturing center. *History Division, Los Angeles County Museum of Natural History*

87. Republic and New High Streets, Los Angeles, ca. 1925. As in all cities, the immigrant quarters appeared at the fringe of the downtown. Here, the Mexicans have taken over shops and houses abandoned by their Yankee predecessors. *History Division, Los Angeles County Museum of Natural History*

88. Beginnings of the Civic Center, Los Angeles, 1940. Since the early twentieth century, huge and expensive government buildings were deemed to foster citizenship and heightened civic pride. Los Angeles refashioned its downtown with arid malls and colossal government offices, monuments to bureaucratization. The first stage: City Hall, 1927 (left), U.S. Court House, 1937 (right). *History Division, Los Angeles County Museum of Natural History*

89. A Quarter of a Mile from City Hall, Los Angeles, 1936. Mexican-American slum housing at the industrial fringe of the downtown. *Library of Congress*

90. Brand Boulevard, Glendale, ca. 1926. Typical suburban subcenter eight miles from the downtown with the Pacific Electric Railway's "big red cars" stopped on the main street. Until left-turning automobiles clogged the streets and grade crossings, a 1,200-mile electric interurban system enabled Los Angeles to function as a single suburbanized, low-density, multicentered metropolis. *History Division, Los Angeles County Museum of Natural History*

91. Manchester Avenue and Santa Ana Freeway, Anaheim, 1965. Shopping centers with big stores and specialty shops, service roads, and freeways have solved automobile traffic circulation problems, but fail as social institutions because private developers cannot profitably offer low-rent space. *California Division of Highways, District VII*

92. Westwood Village, Wilshire Boulevard, Los Angeles, ca. 1965. Wilshire (lower left to right) connects a line of high-income settlements running from the old downtown through Hollywood and Beverly Hills to Santa Monica. A continuous downtown, it is lined with stores and parking lots and at intervals with specialized apartments and office subcenters. Here is the University of California node (upper center); note the large proportion of street and parking area. *History Division, Los Angeles County Museum of Natural History, Spence Air Photo*

Homes

93. Working-class Housing, 55th and Alameda Streets, Los Angeles, ca. 1930. Relative cheapening of land brought by the automobile meant a slight enlargement of the most inexpensive house lots, a bit more open than

comparable rapid-transit-and-street-railway-dominated Chicago and New York mass housing. *Historical Collections, Security Pacific National Bank*

94. Yards in Colon Street, Wilmington, 1945. The extra increment of land allowed working-class housing to age well. Garages could be converted into rentals and still meet minimum sanitary and fire safety standards; garden fragments could survive even in the lowest-income neighborhoods. *Mason Dooley*

95. Whittier Boulevard near Atlantic Boulevard, East Los Angeles, 1924. Sub-dividers continued to follow the standard American grid street and rectangular house lot practice used to parcel out the nation's land since the westward movement began. *Historical Collections, Security Pacific National Bank*

96. Whittier Boulevard, Belvedere, ca. 1924. Main street became the endless shopping strip. *History Division, Los Angeles County Museum of Natural History*

97. San Vicente Boulevard at Crescent Heights, Los Angeles, 1929. The prosperous middle class fared little better than the mass at the hands of private real-estate developers. Expensive houses, in English cottage, Spanish and American colonial styles, crowded the small rectangular lots. *History Division, Los Angeles County Museum of Natural History*

98. Sunset and Beverly Boulevards, Beverly Hills, 1924. Only the wealthy benefited from the garden potential of southern California suburbs: hill sites, large grid lots adapted to streets following contours of the land, small parks and extensive street plantings preceded the luxury-home buyer. *County of Los Angeles Regional Planning Commission; Spence Air Photo*

99. Court, 1st Street, Boyle Heights, Los Angeles, 1971. The only useful innovation of Los Angeles urban architecture was the mutiple-family courtyard. It began as a mean small-apartment barracks set in a U shape along a single walk, filling an entire rectangular lot. This primitive practice continues today in the cheapest motor courts. *Mason Dooley*

100. Court, Pinafore Street, Baldwin Hills, Los Angeles, 1971. Since World War II middle-income families have been attracted to an expanded court design, now often in a hollow square, two and three stories high, requiring several rectangular house lots. Peripheral parking, central garden and swimming pool are standard amenities, a kind of apartment design that overcomes both the social isolation and parking problems of the more land-conserving apartment blocks of Eastern cities. *Mason Dooley*

101. Apartment Towers, Avenue of the Stars, Century City, Los Angeles, 1971. In marked contrast to the courts, which will decay humanely, Los Angeles developers erect on expensive and fashionable land luxury apartment towers, which maximize isolation of tenant from tenant, and tenants from the surrounding city. In half a century, when today's mortgages are paid off, the city as a whole will inherit heavy social costs as these structures decay into the worst kind of slum rookeries. *Mason Dooley*

72. Downtown Los Angeles Freeway Circuit, 1970

73. Looking Downtown from the Convention Center, 1971

74. Raymond Avenue, Los Angeles, 1971

75. Stone Canyon, Sherman Oaks, 1970

76. Japanese-Americans Awaiting
    Removal to Concentration Camps,
    Los Angeles, 1942

77. Boyle Heights, Los Angeles, 1971

78. Main Street, Los Angeles, ca. 1875

79. "Parking Lot" at Long Beach, 1905

80. Streetcar Beach, Long Beach, ca. 1920

81. William Fox Studio, Los Angeles, 1927

82. Del Rey Oil Fields, Los Angeles, 1930

83. Ford Assembly Plant, Long Beach, 1929

84. Union Pacific Industrial Area, Vernon, 1924

85. Irvine Industrial Park, 1971

86. Hill and 9th Streets, Downtown Los Angeles, 1924

87. Republic and New High Streets, Los Angeles, ca. 1925

88. Beginnings of the Civic Center, Los Angeles, 1940

89. A Quarter of a Mile from City Hall, Los Angeles, 1936

90. Brand Boulevard, Glendale, ca. 1926

91. Manchester Avenue and Santa Ana Freeway, Anaheim, 1965

92. Westwood Village, Los Angeles, ca. 1965

93. Working-Class Housing, Los Angeles, ca. 1930

94. Yards in Colon Street, Wilmington, 1945

95. Whittier Boulevard, East Los Angeles, 1924

96. Whittier Boulevard, Belvedere, ca. 1924

97. San Vicente Boulevard, Los Angeles, 1929

98. Sunset and Beverly Boulevards, Beverly Hills, 1924

99. Court, Boyle Heights, Los Angeles, 1971

100. Court, Baldwin Hills, Los Angeles, 1971

101. Apartment Towers, Century City, Los Angeles, 1971

a widely diversified metropolis given over to manufacturing, commerce, service, and war production.[33]

During the twenties and thirties, irrigated agriculture, oil discoveries, the motion-picture boom, and waves of Midwestern and Texan migrants seeking a pleasant place to live and work swelled the city's size. Oil revenues in part financed the construction of an ocean port at Long Beach, and favorable rail connections to the Southwest and the East (the city lies a few miles closer to Chicago than San Francisco does) made Los Angeles a preferred site for warehouses and branch plants of national corporations. During the twenties, for example, both Ford and Goodyear built Pacific plants there, and many other firms followed suit. But the city was handicapped by the circumstance that its factories were some two thousand miles from the western edge of the Midwestern manufacturing belt at St. Louis. Therefore the sectors of the metropolitan economy devoted to general machinery and metalworking—sectors of vital importance to a fully elaborated industrial region—did not develop during these years. Los Angeles in 1940, for all its impressive size, was not yet committed to manufacturing.[34]

Thirty years of almost continuous hot and cold wars ended this anomaly. Tremendous aircraft orders from the federal government not only caused that particular industry to shoot ahead, but federal sponsorship of aerospace research and all sorts of war material fostered supportive manufacturing, until today the city is the only fully diversified manufacturing region outside the belts of the Northeast and Midwest. To be sure, Los Angeles still has its agricultural, aircraft, electronic, and movie specialties, just as Chicago still concentrates on steel, machinery, and printing and New York on garments, leather, printing, electrical equipment, and national offices, but since the 1950s a full range of complementarities has been available in Los Angeles to boost further expansion.[35]

Three special characteristics of the Los Angeles metropolis stand out by comparison with the earlier examples of New York and Chicago:

33. Perloff et al., *Regions, Resources, and Economic Growth*, pp. 462, 465, 471–75.

34. Frank L. Kidner and Philip Neff, *An Economic Survey of the Los Angeles Area*, Los Angeles, 1945, pp. 1–26; Robert M. Fogelson, *The Fragmented Metropolis, Los Angeles 1850–1930*, Cambridge, 1967, pp. 108–34.

35. U.S. Bureau of the Census, *Census of Manufactures, 1967, Summary Series: General Summary MC 67 (1)-1*, Washington, 1970, Table 2; *Census of Manufactures, 1967, Area Series: California, Illinois, New York, MC 67 (3)-5,-14,-33*, Washington, 1970, Table 6.

its high degree of spatial freedom, its potential for a more equitable and inclusive class and racial society, and its growth in response to deliberate federal programs.

The land-use and transportation structure of Los Angeles gives glimpses of a more humane environment than we have yet enjoyed. The special factor of the city's social geography is its low density of settlement, the ease and scope of movement of the overwhelming proportion of its citizens, and its comparative lack of domination by a single downtown area. It has thus escaped the rigid core, sector, and ring structure of business and residential occupation that tyrannized the industrial metropolis and from which older cities are only now beginning to extricate themselves. Los Angeles is an amorphous metropolis, and vast tracts of it have a rather uniform low-density settlement of five to twenty-four persons per acre. Along the Pacific in the Santa Monica and Long Beach areas and in a crescent of housing from Santa Monica through Beverly Hills to the old core city there are apartment houses and multiple-dwelling neighborhoods that resemble those in Chicago or New York. Also scattered through the metropolis, especially along its shopping strips, stand many of the motel-like courts that are the contemporary slum-tenement style of the American city; but the single-family dwelling has long been the glory of Los Angeles and the expression of its design for living. Sixty-four percent of all its occupied housing in 1967 was given over to single-family dwelling units.[36]

The plan for a metropolis composed of single-family houses did not emerge from the drawing boards of freeway engineers; their constructions followed an already entrenched preference of the Angelenos. During the twenties three social factors had converged to establish the Los Angeles plan: the cultural preference of Americans for detached private homes, the need to supply water for burgeoning land development, and the sheer pleasure and freedom bestowed by the automobile.

Three out of four of the army of migrants who came into southern California during the early part of the twentieth century were white native-born Americans from the cities to the east and from the farms and small towns of the Midwest.[37] City dwellers and farmers alike brought with them an ingrained tradition of the single-family house as

36. Los Angeles Regional Transportation Study, "1967 Origin-Destination Survey, Summary of Findings," Draft, November 18, 1970, p. 31.
37. Stephan Thernstrom, *The Growth of Los Angeles in Historical Perspective: Myth and Reality,* Institute of Government and Public Affairs, University of California, Los Angeles, 1970, pp. 8-11.

the measure of a home and of Main Street or suburbia as the measure of satisfactory living. The American has often had to share his housing with others—in rented rooms, in two-family houses, in tenements of three, six, or more flats—but given the opportunity he has customarily sought a house of his own. Moreover, just as in the case of Chicago's middle class, in the Los Angeles region no thirst for the big-city life of skyscrapers, restaurants, and theaters has tempted him to sacrifice the privacy of a tree-shaded lawn and garden for apartment luxury or for the urban habits of the nineteenth-century inhabitants of European or American industrial cities. In sum, people came to southern California seeking a warm, sunlit, home-town city.

To provide these amenities in the first decades of the twentieth century in the face of the aridity of Los Angeles, residential property carried high land-preparation costs and so had to be developed in tracts of considerable size. An expensive water supply had to be meshed with public transportation to a degree unheard-of in the modest subdivisions common in Eastern cities. Speculators capitalized on the situation by building a wide-range complex of electric interurban streetcars. They hoped that their initial investment in lines that stretched from twenty to thirty-five miles out from the downtown area would be justified by massive profits from future land development and ensuing heavy traffic on their routes. Los Angeles in 1920, compared to other cities of the period, was extraordinarily extended into large-scale suburban development.[38]

The automotive boom of the twenties carried these trends toward diffusion to modern proportions. The general ownership of automobiles and their use in commuting allowed developers to open up smaller tracts beyond walking distance from the interurbans. When these lines began to lose money from competition with automobiles and when traffic jams in downtown Los Angeles became intolerable, the municipality called for the construction of a rapid-transit system to alleviate traffic, revitalize the street railways, and save the downtown. Other cities had voted for subways in the twenties, but Los Angeles did not follow the precedents; its citizens voted down the proposals. Their city was so new and open that they had no image before them of a desirable downtown, and they had no habit of listening to the appeals of downtown business leaders.

38. Fogelson, *Fragmented Metropolis,* pp. 85–107; Kelker, De Leuw & Co., *Report and Recommendations on a Comprehensive Transit Plan for the City and County of Los Angeles,* Chicago, 1925, plates 12, 18.

Then, too, their tradition told them that happiness lay in another style of life.[39]

During the Great Depression the public transportation system cut back its service, and after World War II the interurban lines closed down; today the public bus lines handle a small volume of passengers— 400,000 fewer than in 1939. Without the discipline of street railways, commerce drained from the core city to spread out along strips of land like Wilshire Boulevard. Suburban towns like Glendale and Pasadena established their own downtowns, and suburban shopping centers and office clusters have sprung up to form a multicentered metropolis.[40]

The key decision in the determination of the spatial freedom of its residents came in 1939, when the Los Angeles Freeway plans were settled into a multicentered pattern. A failing public transit, serious traffic jams, and a new state statute that permitted construction of limited-access highways had prompted the City of Los Angeles to commission still another study of its transportation problems. The Works Progress Administration of the federal government carried out a traffic census, and on the basis of these findings the City of Los Angeles Transportation and Engineering Board made its recommendations; freeways would be the solution to the region's traffic difficulties. The unusual multicity and multicounty membership of the advisory board may have accounted for its metropolitan orientation. Besides Los Angeles officials, representatives from such scattered places as Glendale, Beverly Hills, Redondo Beach, Huntington Beach, Whittier, Pasadena, and the San Fernando and San Gabriel valleys sat on the board. The 1939 plan called for limited-access express highways to be laid out in the form of a giant grid, which would be capable of carrying automobile traffic both into and out of the overcrowded Los Angeles central business district and would guide it across the city without the necessity of its going through the downtown area. The principal justification for this plan was the board's recognition of the already highly dispersed character of the region. Many of its alignments were to follow the much-traveled state highways that crisscrossed the area. The report may well have reflected too the politics of the Transportation Board itself. Although no record survives of its discussions, it seems highly probable that the members

39. Reyner Banham, *Los Angeles: The Architecture of Four Ecologies,* New York, 1972.

40. Fogelson, *Fragmented Metropolis,* pp. 164–85; Pacific Southwest Academy of Political and Social Science, *Los Angeles, Preface to a Master Plan, Publication 19,* Los Angeles, 1941, pp. 47–53, 161–68, 173–88.

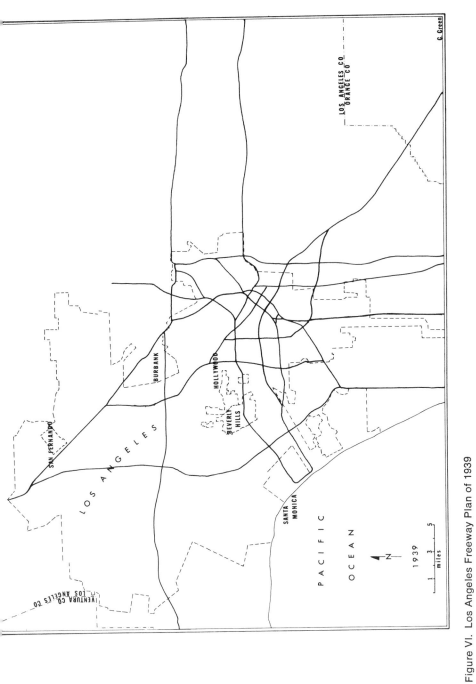

Figure VI. Los Angeles Freeway Plan of 1939

SOURCE: City of Los Angeles, Transportation and Engineering Board, *A Transit Program for the Los Angeles Metropolitan Area*, Los Angeles, December, 1939.

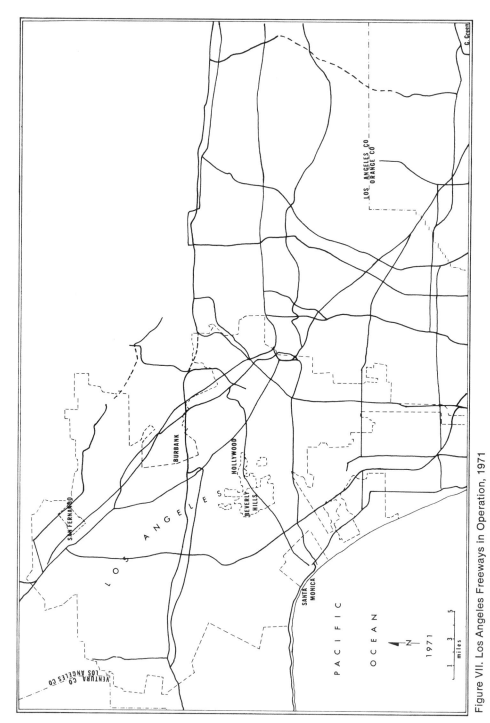

Figure VII. Los Angeles Freeways in Operation, 1971

SOURCE: California Department of Public Works, Division of Highways, *District VII Freeway and Expressway System Map*, Los Angeles, January, 1971.

from the more distant areas would not have accepted the conventional hub-and-wheel design that was at this time being proposed for old American single-core cities, since such a plan would have drawn business away from their own centers. The board did expect, however, that Los Angeles would eventually grow to be a conventional single-centered city and that in time commuter railroads and subways would be required.[41]

The 1939 proposal for freeways derives its historical importance from the fact that it was subsequently adopted and adapted in a succession of plans and projects. The first undertakings, begun in 1940 with the Pasadena Freeway, all converged on the downtown (the Hollywood, San Bernardino, Santa Ana, and Harbor Freeways), thereby beginning a radial scheme for serving the downtown, but wartime and postwar planning studies continued to repeat the basic grid strategy of the 1939 report. Then in 1956, when the federal government passed its Interstate Highway law, the California legislature set up a committee to establish routes for the state. The routes that were then adopted incorporated the 1939 proposal for a grid system of metropolitan freeways, and many such highways have been built in the ensuing years.[42] The grid is still being extended at its outer margins in order to keep up with the spread of the metropolis, and it is being added to at the center to relieve traffic congestion further, but for many years now Los Angeles has enjoyed a transportation system that permits its residents to move swiftly from subcenter to subcenter over the entire region without having to go through the downtown or any lesser center.[43]

The social consequences of the multicentered, low-density metropolitan region are manifold and are important to our urban future. First and foremost was the increase in the job choices offered the urban resi-

41. City of Los Angeles, Transportation and Engineering Board, *A Transit Program for the Los Angeles Metropolitan Area,* Los Angeles, December 1939; "California Highways . . . 1964," *California Highways and Public Works,* 43 (November-December 1964), 5–12.

42. Los Angeles Metropolitan Parkway Engineering Committee, *Interregional, Regional, Metropolitan Parkways,* Mimeographed March 30, 1946, Los Angeles Regional Transportation Study Library, pp. 1, 5; "Freeway Development on Highways of California," *California Highways and Public Works,* 24 (January-February 1946), 30–34; "Report from District VII," *California Highways and Public Works,* 37 (January-February 1958), 2–16; California Department of Public Works, Division of Highways, *The California Freeway System, Report to the Joint Interim Committee on Highway Problems,* Sacramento, September 1958, p. 18.

43. California Department of Public Works, Division of Highways, *District 7 Freeway and Expressway System Map,* Los Angeles, January 1971.

dent. In 1967 there were three automobiles for every seven persons in the Los Angeles region; 41 percent of the households had access to one vehicle, 44 percent had access to two or more vehicles, and only 15 percent of the households lacked a car.[44] Such a distribution of automobiles and freeways gives the Los Angeles employee the widest choice of job opportunities ever possible in an American city. An hour's drive from any point in the region makes hundreds of possible employers accessible. A man can live in the San Fernando Valley and work in the old industrial sector of southeast Los Angeles, or he can commute from the old core-city neighborhoods to the new steel mills at Fontana. These are extreme commuting distances, to be sure, but recent studies show that blue-collar workers in particular are crisscrossing the whole area in search of the best jobs.[45] In the past urban workers were pinned down to living next to their mills, or they purchased their economic freedom by commuting from crowded core-city working-class and slum districts along the radial lines of the streetcar system. These journeys were long, the cars crowded and slow, and transfers and waits in the cold and wet often necessary. Such trials cannot be compared with the ease of an hour's run today in a private car or car pool. In Los Angeles most commuters go directly from their home to the company parking lot, and the majority travel alone; more than 70 percent of all weekday automobile trips are taken by a single driver.[46]

To this economic freedom must be added the social advantages that have accrued to the Los Angeles public. The greater number of car trips are not work-related at all but are undertaken for social or recreational purposes or for shopping. Thus scattered friends and relatives, long shopping strips and outlying shopping centers, the Pacific beaches, and national parks are all within easy reach of most families. At the same time the city is able to grow by continuing to build in its low-density popular single-family or low-rise apartment-court style.

Like all American cities, the Los Angeles automobile metropolis does not extend its amenities equally to all its residents but reinforces sharp differences governed by class and race. Boyle Heights, an early twentieth-century neighborhood in East Los Angeles, offers some of the attractions of small-town life to its Mexican-American residents. Watts

44. LARTS, "1967 Origin-Destination Survey," p. 33.
45. Lawrence E. Maxwell, "Residential Distribution of Occupations in Los Angeles," unpublished M.A. thesis, University of California at Los Angeles, 1966, pp. 60–64, 70, Map 5.
46. LARTS, "1967 Origin-Destination Survey," pp. 39–41.

and the black ghetto have many of the same features. Yet the poor, lacking cars and perhaps also fearful of their reception in other parts of the metropolis, do not travel over large sections of the region as residents of the San Fernando Valley might do.[47] Women and old people especially suffer from a dearth of cars. The women thus lack access to jobs that would boost family income, and to essential shopping and health services. For the men, transportation doesn't seem to be the problem. Once they find employment they seem to be able to purchase cars on time.[48]

The solution to the disadvantaged position of those without cars is neither difficult nor expensive, but like all our cities Los Angeles remains heedless of the needs and suffering of its poor, its blacks, its Mexican Americans, and its old people. After the Watts riot the transportation problems of the poor were made plain, and the state of California, with federal funding, set up a demonstration project in southeast Los Angeles to attempt to deal with the problem. A social science team intervened in behalf of the poor in several ways. They became the spokesmen of the neighborhoods before the bus companies; they waged campaigns to have route maps printed and distributed and to persuade the companies to post the schedules at the bus stops. They discovered that the last bus might leave a factory's gates a few minutes before the men finished their daily shifts; they discovered routes that could be instituted or altered to reflect the commuting habits of the residents. It seems clear from the findings of this team that the cost cutting of private and public bus companies should be monitored in every city by a political agency representing the transportation interests of those outside the circle of the automobile world. The altering of existing public transportation, however, was not sufficient. The women needed short runs along shopping strips and to shopping centers and they needed long trips in every direction to reach scattered job sites. To this end the experiment rented buses for some new regular routes and also used station wagons and cars for a kind of metropolitan taxi service

47. City of Los Angeles, Department of City Planning, *The Visual Environment of Los Angeles,* Los Angeles, April 1971, pp. 9–11; this seems to be a worldwide phenomenon in modern cities accounted for largely by the failure of old rapid-transit systems to keep pace with the growth of cities. "Cars or Busses?" *The Economist,* 240 (August 14, 1971), 48–51.

48. State of California, Business and Transportation Agency, *Transportation-Employment Project, Interim Final Report,* Los Angeles, January, 1970, pp. 15, 27–30, 98; U.S. Department of Labor Statistics, *Employment and Unemployment in East and South Los Angeles, Regional Report No. 14,* San Francisco, 1971, p. 21.

to jobs at such widely dispersed destinations as Lockheed in Burbank, Douglas Aircraft at Long Beach, Torrence, and Santa Monica, American Electric at La Mirada, and Sergent-Fletcher in El Monte. The cost of these services was high, but could have been much reduced if established permanently. The demonstration project was a success, but in 1971, when the funds were gone, predictably the grant by the federal government was not renewed and the service closed down.[49]

Judging from this experience, a few millions of dollars a year spent in maintaining an agency to represent the carless and offer its own flexible small-bus service would redress the worst of the access problems attendant on Los Angeles' unequal distribution of family income. To be sure, those without cars are the ones who suffer most from low wages, from job discrimination against women, old people, blacks, and the ill-educated, and from regional and national callousness toward the unemployed and the underemployed, but even a modest effort would be far more useful to the poor than the currently fashionable enthusiasm for rail lines. Railroads by their very nature offer high-volume service only along their own narrow strip. Los Angeles is neither a linear nor a radial city; it is a multicentered city that calls for multidestination public transportation.

Finally, although Los Angeles does not have the problem of choking traffic jams and hard-to-reach areas like those of New York, it does have a serious air-pollution problem. In view of the enormous investment and great social success of the freeways, it seems foolish not to try to eliminate the smog in similar terms. Surely the technology of the moon era is capable of manufacturing low-emission engines as an alternative to the present disgraceful pollution created by Los Angeles' 4.5 million automobiles.

Since all of the metropolises and the three megalopolises of the United States are growing into the form of Los Angeles, it is important that we understand the social potential of this diffuse layout of building. The open character of Los Angeles has resulted in a land-use structure more favorable for the achievement of racial and class justice than any that has so far existed in any large American city. This structure is only a potential for justice, however, and remains far from realization.

Los Angeles is no better than most cities when it comes to racial discrimination, segregation, and disadvantages for its poor. The county

49. California Business and Transportation Agency, *Interim Final Report*, pp. 85–90.

population is 10.8 percent black, 13.5 percent of Spanish surname. The isolation of blacks is almost as extreme as in Chicago. The Mexican Americans are less rigidly segregated from the Anglo Americans than are the blacks, but nonetheless they are highly segregated.[50] When the frustration of the black community exploded with the Watts riots of 1965, a national chain reaction was set in motion, and since that time there have been a number of Mexican-American riots expressing the conflicts of another disadvantaged community. All the hostility and failings of our society, so fully documented in 1968 by the Kerner Commission and in other reports, are part of Los Angeles as well. But if it wishes to build a more inclusive society, it has a special advantage in the availability of land for redevelopment and in abundant fringe land for new construction. The prerequisite for making good use of the land in terms of its society is a commitment by the national government and the Los Angeles public and its officials to make a decent house and neighborhood open to every resident. With such a commitment, new housing can become the framework for an inclusive urban society, rejecting the city's present mechanism for class, racial, and ethnic segregation.

The original low density of Los Angeles' construction has saved it from mortgaging its future. Its built-up areas are not so crammed with structures that new construction in old areas brings serious dislocation of present residents, as is the case in Chicago or New York. There is vacant land all over the Los Angeles region. This land is in the form of weedy lots and unused spaces, some large enough for development in their own right, some requiring some demolition of adjacent houses. If public agencies were to build on five-acre tracts they would find land, either vacant or sparsely occupied, by the hundreds of parcels all over the city. Such land is ideal for the design and construction of low-rise apartments, two-family housing, and town houses. In other words, existing styles of housing could become the basis for a massive public housing program that would not disrupt the physical fabric of the city. Federal programs for land clearance, housing, and rent subsidies allow such housing to be offered today to the fourth of the Los Angeles population who cannot afford decent housing at present prices. Such

50. Los Angeles County, Human Relations Commission, "Population by Major Ethnic Grouping, Los Angeles County, 1950, 1960, 1970, Projection for 1980," *HRC Research,* June 1971; Leo Grebler, Joan W. Moore, and Ralph C. Guzman, *The Mexican-American People,* New York, 1970, pp. 274–78; City of Los Angeles, Community Analysis Bureau, *State of the City, Conditions of Blight and Obsolescence,* Los Angeles, 1970, pp. 72–73.

federal programs, however, would have to be so funded as to allow for a large-scale and sustained undertaking.[51]

At least three important social consequences would be derived from such a small-parcel program. First, the chronic shortage of low-income housing would be relieved. Second, the abundance of scattered sites would enable blacks, Mexican Americans, and the poor to choose to settle either near their present neighborhoods or in new distant sections of the city. The degree of social pioneering undertaken by any family would be according to their own choice and would not depend on the decision of public authorities. Third, the five-acre tracts would have to be designed to fit into the styles prevailing in their environs or else face strong local opposition. Perhaps this requirement that design attain at least the levels of popular taste would save the projects from the degradation of some of the philanthropic architectural styles that now stigmatize public housing.

At its fringes the Los Angeles freeway brings large tracts of vacant land within the reach of commuters. This same situation prevails in the Eastern and Midwestern megalopolis and all metropolises. Here publicly sponsored or managed new towns of 50,000 to 200,000 residents could be used as a device for increasing the residential options of black and low-income families. The key advantage of the new-town concept, or entire-city building scheme, over the conventional suburban subdivision lies in its coordination of public facilities with employment and housing. The new town can be built around industries to provide jobs for a range of skills and classes. The schools and health services can be built in the beginning so that the residents do not create unnecessary conflict by overloading small local community services. Finally, because these would be large projects, the social engineering of building at all class levels would become feasible. Los Angeles is currently building a beautiful new town at Irvine. Its extent is 53,000 acres, and it will ultimately hold 430,000 inhabitants.[52] It has jobs, recreation, an airport, and community facilities laid out in such a way that the native California land form is undisturbed. It is a brilliant example of the advantage of large-scale new-town development over the spread of subdivisions. Despite all this, Irvine is a social scandal—an all-white, upper-middle-class enclave. It is exactly the sort of project that at once shows the high

51. Regional Planning Commission, County of Los Angeles, *Environmental Development Guide*, Revised Draft, Los Angeles, September 1, 1970, pp. 64–75.
52. *Irvine World News*, April, 1970.

potential of the new metropolis and its bigoted, class-bound failure to realize that potential.

Finally, Los Angeles should be understood as an outstanding example of regional and national planning. Its port at Long Beach, its interstate water-supply system, and its national parks and forests are excellent examples of well-designed and coordinated large-scale planning. Its war-stimulated growth is of interest precisely because it demonstrates an important but as yet little exercised capability of the federal government to influence the prosperity of a metropolitan region. The Los Angeles experience shows that we have depressed cities and depressed regions only because we have chosen to let them go unattended.

Several principles governing a successful national urban policy can be derived from the federal sponsorship in Los Angeles. First, federal orders for products and services, direct intervention in the construction of plants, and long-term aid in the building of water and electric facilities encouraged and sustained its growth.[53] In the case of huge aircraft orders and the subsequent erection of aircraft plants with federal funds, the investment helped an industry that had already taken root to settle in more firmly. The additional contracts in the fields of aerospace and war material were instrumental in bringing the blossoming electronics industry into the city from the East.

Second, the magnitude of orders and assistance exceeded any later federal attempts to foster business in depressed areas through favored purchasing, small-business loans, and Office of Economic Opportunity programs. Aside from the money spent for war material, tools were being forged here for a national policy directed to urban growth and regional employment guidance, but our low-key use of these tools and our compulsion to tie them to the Congressional pork barrel have rendered them ineffective.[54]

Third, the federal infusion of capital into the area continued over a long period—at least thirty years—without serious interruption, so that the war specialties of Los Angeles have been consistently nourished.

Fourth, the Los Angeles case showed that special institutions could be used to upgrade a regional labor force that had been neither particularly skilled nor outstandingly intelligent. The government sponsored here the foundation of nonprofit research and development corpora-

53. Kidner and Neff, *Survey of the Los Angeles Area*, pp. 101–3.
54. Lloyd Rodwin, *Nations and Cities, A Comparison of Strategies for Urban Growth*, Boston, 1970, pp. 222–35.

tions, such as RAND and the Systems Development Corporation, to supplement the educational and research capabilities of the California Institute of Technology, the University of Southern California, and the University of California. These additional institutions, by attracting scientists and engineers to the region, did much to accelerate the city's movement into higher levels of technology, and at a pace more rapid than would have prevailed if the city had depended only upon its universities and the technical staffs of resident aircraft and electronic concerns.[55] In the Boston metropolitan region, similar paramilitary institutions helped raise the level of a management and labor force formerly connected to the dragging textile industry, and it seems probable that the Houston Manned Spacecraft Center will have the same effect in Texas. These instances suggest that the federal government could create research and service institutions for civilians as a device to upgrade the industries and labor forces of such places as Atlanta, Chicago, Detroit, and New York.

Fifth and finally, the federal investment in Los Angeles, moved by an unconscious planning wisdom, supplemented and stimulated an existing trend. There was no effort to reverse the path of popular migration or to go against the locational trends of the economy as might have been the case in such places as Appalachia or East St. Louis, Illinois. It is obvious that to roll with the economy, to relieve temporary distress, and to help people to move is a prerequisite for national urban programs.

What the federal effort in Los Angeles lacked was self-conscious dedication. The United States has the tools to plan its regional and national urban growth through the twin job-awarding devices of the giant corporation and the federal budget. Since World War II the magnitude of the corporate and federal effort has in large measure determined the national location of jobs;[56] it has designated the industries and places where jobs would be plentiful and where they would be sparse. The depressed condition of the core of New York City is a casualty of the federal and corporate concentration on war just as surely as the prosperity of Los Angeles is its hero. If we are to mitigate the appalling human waste and suffering of our cities, both institutions must be made

55. Christopher Rand, *Los Angeles, The Ultimate City,* New York, 1967, pp. 72–100.

56. Murray L. Weidenbaum, *Federal Budgeting, The Choice of Government Programs,* Washington, 1964, pp. 4–22; Douglass B. Lee, Jr., and John W. Dyckman, "Economic Impacts of the Vietnam War: A Primer," *Journal of the American Institute of Planners,* 36 (September 1970), 298–309.

to act as self-conscious agents of urban reordering. The federal government must follow European examples by adopting a carefully considered, politically viable policy for urban growth so that the modernization of our cities and our economy can go forward more humanely; the
corporations must be socialized to the point at which they can be held
accountable for the public consequences of their behavior. Like the
legitimate demands for decent work, comfortable housing, and an open
inclusive society, the promise of today's economy and its cities will not
be realized unless the American public demands that government and
business serve the goals of a humane society.

THREE

▲ THE PAST IN THE PRESENT

6

The Inheritance of the Neighborhoods

—

Processing migrants by class,
race, and religion;
four-part cultures

ONE OF THE REMARKABLE QUALITIES of the American metropolis is the cultural consensus which runs throughout its neighborhoods. For cities so vast, composed as they always have been of migrants from every circumstance of life, the presence of this consensus is an extraordinary historical event well worth understanding for its own sake. Yet the cultural uniformity of the American metropolis, a legacy from the past, has further significance in that it holds the potential of great service to the future. It is the best foundation we have upon which to build powerful and sustained urban plans and policies.

Current social science studies show that our cultural consensus runs far deeper than the common factors of television, automobiles, and the consumerism of the mass media. It is rooted in the behavior and aspirations of millions of American families, rich and poor, black and white. In the everyday behavior of urban families can be seen the commitment to the basic values of an equalitarian private competitive life which is manifested in a common residential style of loyalty to relatives, friendly visiting of neighbors, pressing for the education of children, concern for family health, the use of housing and neighborhoods as the expressions of family status, high tolerance for interfaith marriage, and an openness of membership in churches and other local institutions. The frequent complaints against our urban style of living, the income striving, lack of close communities, the rapid movement of families from place to place,

153

and the exclusionary tactics of many suburbs are but the concomitants of this same consensus.

Working against this common culture, both its openness and its near-universal private family expectations, are two deeply ingrained attitudes which are endlessly reinforced throughout the metropolis: the tradition of white racism and the differential rewards of capitalism. The former poisons every neighborhood and institution, the latter segregates the city into clusters of families of similar class attainment and delivers the power and destiny of the modes of urban growth into the hands of the well-to-do. By their overwhelming purchasing power and control of most of the political, economic, and social institutions of the city, the upper income groups always have controlled and still do control the allocation of the city's resources and the determination of its patterns of development.

Thus today we do not face an urban crisis brought on by some sudden disaster; we suffer from a heightening of a chronic urban disease. Our situation deserves to be called a disease since most of its symptoms—poverty, slums, self-serving public institutions, violence, epidemics of drugs and diseases, misappropriation of land, and despoiling of the environment—grow upon a healthy body of everyday behavior and aspirations. The cure for these social ills rests upon a public willingness to give the highest priority to the commonplace values of everyday life. Urban crises of the past have been answered by reforms which appealed to the cultural uniformities of the city, and such partial successes show the soundness of such a strategy. But because our political, economic, and social institutions have remained in the hands of the white and the well-to-do, who have chosen to interpret our common culture primarily in terms of rewards for those who succeed and punishments and neglect for those who fall behind, the major causes of our urban maladies have gone unattended. By stressing the value of private competition in the cluster of American aspirations, the well-to-do have legitimized their behavior. At the same time, the losers, in order to understand what was happening to them, have depended upon this same orientation to validate their personal experience. This overwhelming priority for family striving has continually submerged the other behaviors and attitudes of our culture, and therefore the other needs and aspirations have been unable to sustain any enduring efforts to allocate the political, economic, social, and physical resources of the city for the benefit of all its citizens.

Since the existence of a common urban culture is of the utmost importance to any hopes for democratic planning, the history of the process whereby a diversity of migrants became a common people is well worth understanding. This chapter will summarize that history and review some of the recent social science literature on the uniformities and variations now extant in the neighborhoods of the metropolis. The ensuing chapters will show how this culture has fared in respect to two of its universal needs and aspirations: housing and health care. As this story shows, it is the overwhelming of our common culture by the structures of unequal power and wealth which constitutes our chronic urban disease.

The interactions among the economy, the internal structure of cities, and the patterns of migration have produced a common culture whose variations can be interpreted in terms of class and religious identification. Current social science suggests that about 90 percent of the American population can be classified by noting people's class and socioreligious attitudes. Most of our city dwellers have a common American culture but differ according to whether they are upper class, middle class, working class, or lower class. They also differ according to whether they are white Protestant, white Catholic, white Jewish, or black Protestant.

The origins of class attitudes are easy enough to account for. Just as the unfolding economy produced our segregated urban structure, so each day it sifts and grades its members, rewarding some more highly than others. Some men, like Marquand's top executives, inherit or earn large personal fortunes; others push their families forward into power and affluence by means of long years of education and the common striving of a young husband and wife, the sort of steps stressed in Whyte's *Organization Man;* still others, like Henry's Bill Greene, can see only a limited future and while teen-agers give up the struggle and spend their lives in routine hard work and domestic comfort. Finally, there are those for whom the economy of the city is essentially closed, men like Liebow's Tally or Harrington's other Americans.[1]

Out of the repetition of thousands of such similar personal experiences come the basic class dimensions of our culture and the common

---

1. John P. Marquand, *Point of No Return,* Boston, 1949; William H. Whyte, Jr., *The Organization Man,* New York, 1956; Jules Henry, *Culture Against Man,* New York, 1963; Elliott Liebow, *Tally's Corner,* Boston, 1967; Michael Harrington, *The Other America,* New York, 1962.

attitudes and behavior of the upper class, the middle class, the working class, and the lower class.

Yet if one restricted oneself to interpreting the conditions and conflicts of the modern city only in terms of class, the outcome of most elections would be wrongly predicted, and strife over housing, zoning, bussing, schools, police, traffic, and taxes would be unintelligible. The reason that class is an inadequate key to the modern city is that, superimposed on the class-graded cultural variations of Americans, lie the broad bands of their racial and religious identifications: white Protestant, white Catholic, white Jewish, and black Protestant. These religious loyalties derive from our population history. We are a nation of immigrants, and these four socioreligious allegiances have matured out of the process of adaptation of immigrants to the circumstances of American urban life. Over time these loyalties absorbed the immigrant's previous ties to the village, the region, the ethnic group, the religious denomination, or the nation, so that now all but a small fraction of our citizens identify themselves to a greater or lesser degree with the four broad socioreligious orientations.

All American families share a remarkably uniform urban experience, an experience compounded of class, ethnicity, and religion. The pattern is migration, followed by the ghetto or the slum or just hard times in the city, and this is succeeded by the eventual emergence into a stable income position, be it good or bad (and for many it is good), then the church and the suburb. Behind the migrations lay tribes, villages, or family farms, depending on whether the family memory went back to Africa, Europe, or the rural United States. But as each family lives through its experiences in this country, each one passes through the acid of the city which burns off the special qualities of the past. In this corrosive environment Sicilian villagers became Italians, and Italians became neighborhood Catholics; Alabama farm boys, black and white, became slum family men, and family men became builders of Baptist or Methodist churches.

This sequence was, and still is, the sequence of the urbanization of our rural migrants. Put most crudely, one brings to the city an extremely localized culture. After some years in the city the culture becomes broader than the former village or town; it becomes ethnic. The most enduring ethnic cultural institutions in American cities have proved to be the churches, so that over the years or generations ethnic loyalties become merged into religious loyalty. Simultaneously job, income, housing, and neighborhood teach the class structure of the city, so that in time—for some a few years, for others a generation or two—a class and religious culture determines the orientation of all city dwellers. This is a simple model to cover a complex urban and population history, but it seems to order the sequences of the past hundred and fifty years in such a way as to make the contemporary city intelligible.[2]

1820–1870

The population history of the country during the first period of urbanization and industrialization had four notable characteristics. First, the native population prospered and moved westward to fill the continent. At the same time, Americans began sharply to control the size of their families so that population growth after the middle of the nineteenth century no longer depended solely on native reproduction. Second, millions of immigrants from Germany and Great Britain came to join the native population in its westward migration, and they also adopted the new style of the small family. Third, the collapse of the Irish economy expelled millions from that country and added a heavy stream of Irish to the transcontinental flow (Table 3, page 168). They too followed the predilection for family limitation. Fourth, interaction between evangelical Protestantism and Catholicism—especially of the Irish variety —formed two basic elements in American urban culture, the broad Protestant and Catholic allegiances.

At least until 1870, when the standard of living commenced its steady rise in both the United States and Europe, the story of our population and its immigrants was the story of poor farmers, poor peasants, and poor artisans accustomed to subsistence living, who in moving were seeking an opportunity for a decent living for themselves and their families. The sheer abundance of cheap farmland enabled the

2. There is an extensive literature devoted to this model which I have used to build this cultural history: Ruby Jo Kennedy, "Single or Triple Melting Pot? Intermarriage Trends in New Haven 1870–1940," *American Journal of Sociology,* 49 (January 1944), 331–39; Will Herberg, *Protestant, Catholic, Jew,* New York, 1955; Gerhard Lenski, *The Religious Factor: A Sociological Study of Religious Impact on Politics, Economics, and Family Life,* New York, 1961; Oscar Handlin, "Historical Perspectives on the American Ethnic Group," *Daedalus,* 90 (Spring 1961), 220–32; Seymour Martin Lipset, *The First New Nation,* New York, 1963; Milton M. Gordon, *Assimilation in American Life,* New York, 1964; Nicholas J. Demerath, *Social Class in American Protestantism,* Chicago, 1965; Mark A. Fried, "The Role of Work in a Mobile Society," in *Planning for a Nation of Cities,* Sam Bass Warner, Jr., ed., Cambridge, 1966, pp. 81–104.

great mass of the nation's white farmers to support large families and for their children to survive. In this era, as always in our history, the rural areas supplied a disproportionate number of the nation's children; even today rural births consistently outrun those in town or city. Moreover, until the twentieth century the death rate among children in American cities was always higher than in the countryside.

Up to 1840 almost all population growth stemmed from natural increase, white and Negro, and although the birth rate fell steadily during the nineteenth century, until 1860 it still continued to exceed European rates. From then on, American birth rates declined in the same general ratios as those of England, France, and Sweden. Scholars do not yet understand the cause of this decline; but it is a long-term historical trend participated in both by natives and immigrants, with only a few very short exceptions and slight reversals. For the moment, all that can be said is that Americans and Europeans limit their families as they become urban industrial peoples.[3]

The native population established the directions for the streams of continental migration which the immigrants followed. Prior to 1870 Americans moved westward in roughly parallel bands: migrants from New England and New York filled the upper Midwest; families from the Southeast settled the lands from Alabama to Texas; and people from Virginia and Pennsylvania settled in Kentucky, Tennessee, and Missouri, and in southern Ohio, Indiana, and Illinois. With the coming of the railroad and the rapid development of the Midwest, settlers from the entire North and Midwest overran the plains, mountain, and Pacific regions.

Slavery was an effective barrier against mass European immigration into the South, but millions of Germans, English, Scots, Welsh, and Irish joined the westward movement in the fifty years after 1820. Farm counties in the Midwest were as rich an ethnic patchwork in those years as the blocks of Manhattan.

Historians of the era have fully documented the special ethnic contributions brought by these immigrants to the first stages of our urbanization and industrialization. In the mill town of Lowell, Massachusetts, there was an "English Row" of houses belonging to calico printers from

3. Conrad and Irene B. Taeuber, *The Changing Population of the United States,* New York, 1958, p. 294; Susan E. Bloomberg, Mary Frank Fox, Robert M. Warner, and Sam Bass Warner, Jr., "A Census Probe into Nineteenth Century Family History: Southern Michigan 1850, 1880," *Journal of Social History,* 4 (Fall 1971), 26–45.

Lancashire; English and Scottish workers supplied the skilled labor in the cotton and woolen mills of New England and New York; the woolen weavers and knitters of Philadelphia and Lowell, as well as those of Thompsonville, Connecticut, were Scottish. In the 1820s, English, Scottish, and Welsh miners opened up the anthracite mines of eastern Pennsylvania, Maryland, Ohio, Illinois, and what is now West Virginia. Cornishmen, seeking lead, were the first foreigners to settle in Wisconsin; they also dominated copper mining in the Upper Peninsula of Michigan, and they cut the first railroad tunnels through the Berkshire Hills. The early history of American labor inherited many of its distinguishing features from the British tradition. The great "Ten-Hour" strikes of the big cities, when skilled artisans turned out in vast numbers to demand shorter hours and higher pay, the first fraternal organizations like the Masons or the Odd Fellows, and many of the workers' insurance and benefit funds were in most places initiated by English and Scottish immigrants.

No city or town north of the Ohio River was without a German quarter, and many of the small towns were composed almost entirely of Germans. In the big cities German peasants suffered from poverty and slum housing as severely as did the thousands of Irish peasants and were as cruelly exploited in the cheapest trades. Like the English, however, the skilled among them maintained their tradition of workingmen's associations which flourished in all manner of clubs, benefit associations, and labor organizations.

The new people also brought with them the conflicts of the British Isles. Cornish and Irish mobs—the "pasties" versus the "codfish"—fought pitched battles in the copper country of upper Michigan; the rooms of the New England textile mills were segregated to the disadvantage of the Irish; English and Irish Protestants brawled and rioted in every city; and the murders by the Molly Maguires were an echo of less drastic Irish attacks on their British colliery foremen.[4]

Yet many of the qualities peculiar to the various immigrant cultures were soon lost. Those which could easily be absorbed, like labor unions and lager beer, disappeared into the general cultural scene, and individual manifestations were ground off in the cultural clash between Protestant and Catholic. The 1820–1870 migrations of German and

4. Rowland T. Berthoff, *British Immigrants in Industrial America 1790–1950*, Cambridge, 1953, pp. 30–87, 185–92; Robert Ernst, *Immigrant Life in New York City 1825–1863*, New York, 1949, pp. 61–98.

Irish Catholics met a special kind of Protestantism when they landed—
not an established state religion but a collection of thousands of small
congregations. But for all its fragmentation, Protestantism flourished
during these years and developed into a general Protestant-American
consciousness.

A blend of the colonial institutional inheritance with later religious
enthusiasms gave the Protestantism of the years between 1820 and 1870
its particular character. Late eighteenth-century colonial Americans had
not been churchgoers. Theirs was probably the most secular of all our
cultural periods, and scholars estimate that only 10 percent of the
population at most belonged to any church at all. Simultaneously the
Revolution gave rise to the apprehension that established churches were
agents of monarchical tyranny and laid down a tradition that our nation
would be one without state-supported churches. All Protestant denominations were in effect compelled to become voluntary, competitive
organizations. Except perhaps in the case of the Quakers and some
pietists, Protestantism was oriented toward bringing in the unchurched,
and most congregations for the sake of their own survival had to adopt
not an exclusive but a recruiting mission.[5]

Our colonial history was marked by continual strife along denominational lines—among Anglicans, Quakers, Presbyterians, Congregationalists, Baptists, Methodists, and pietists of various kinds. Some of
the confrontations were of course plainly rooted in the home countries,
as in the cases of German pietists or Scotch-Irish Presbyterians, but
many were not. When Massachusetts Congregationalists persecuted
Quakers or Baptists, or when Connecticut Congregationalists expressed
their disapproval of Methodists, they were discriminating against their
own kind.

The evangelical drives for membership dampened interdenomina-
tional conflict and eroded doctrinal lines. Most late eighteenth- and early
nineteenth-century American Protestants believed that the individual
had to discover God, not vice versa, and that there were rewards and
punishments in this world and the next for good Christian behavior.
Accordingly waves of evangelism, with ministers welcoming the unchurched into Protestant fellowship, swept the country from 1795
through the next half century or more.

A millennial hope that the spread of Christianity and of liberal

5. Sidney E. Mead, *The Lively Experiment: The Shaping of Christianity in
America,* New York, 1963, pp. 16–37, 103–33.

human institutions would bring the Kingdom of God to the United States suffused the era. The means, of course, were individual, "an elevated state of personal holiness."[6] Churchgoing grew more popular. Simultaneously Protestantism became more and more unified both in doctrine and practice, and no deterrent stood in the way of intermarriage between members of different denominations. When conflict arose with Catholic immigrants, a generalized Protestant sentiment defended the voluntarism and individualism of their way of life and warded off Catholic incursions into Protestant control of political organizations and public institutions for education and welfare.

As always in America, the blacks had a separate history. At the time of the Revolution there were no Negro congregations in Northern cities. Blacks attended white Protestant churches, although sometimes, as in Philadelphia, they were segregated to a balcony. In the early nineteenth century the growing emancipation and democratic sentiment in the small black colonies of the Northern cities engendered a move toward self-determination for Negroes in religious matters, so that by the 1840s every city had its black churches and fraternal organizations. The full flowering of this black urban culture nevertheless awaited the substantial migration of blacks to Northern cities, which began in the 1890s.[7]

The massive migration of Germans and Irish from 1830 to 1870 changed the religious composition of the nation. Since the seventeenth century America had been a Protestant country, whether or not devoutly or secularly so; now it became a Protestant-Catholic nation. By 1870 Catholics constituted the largest single religious group, about 40 percent of the churchgoers, and such has been the balance of immigration ever since.[8] A drastic leap in numbers, however, did not immediately imply a unified American Catholicism. Instead, Catholicism during this era was able only to discover and lay down the institutional framework on which later generations would build a Catholic culture for all classes. Until

6. Quote from Reverend Edward Beecher in Timothy L. Smith, *Revivalism and Social Reform in Mid-Nineteenth Century America,* New York, 1957, p. 225.
7. Leon F. Litwack, *North of Slavery: The Negro in the Free States 1790–1860,* Chicago, 1961, pp. 187–213.
8. In the absence of reliable data there is an unavoidable vagueness in estimates of past religious involvement. Lipset, who focuses on attendance, suggests a constant level of participation, while Edwin S. Gaustad, who works from church membership, proposes a rising religiosity. I have chosen the latter method because it is comfortable with the accounts of evangelical revivals during the first half of the nineteenth century. Lipset, *First New Nation,* pp. 160–71; Gaustad, *Historical Atlas of Religion in America,* New York, 1962, pp. 110–11.

then, the poverty and fragmentation of the Church and its immigrant membership outweighed every extraneous consideration. Yet in facing poverty, fragmentation, and the contemporary Protestant attack, the foundation of a broad cultural unity was formed.

A nineteenth-century American Catholic, whether immigrant or native-born, inevitably bore an inherited reputation for having advanced the traditions of "popery," which had been the bogy of Great Britain for two hundred and fifty years and had made Catholics the object of deep-seated national prejudice there. Through English colonists and the colonial wars against the French this prejudice was transferred to America, and Catholics of whatever origin were stamped as a negative reference group in the early Republic. Events overseas made matters worse. The campaign in England to remove the last civil penalties from Catholics spawned a deluge of anti-Catholic literature that poured across the Atlantic until the passage of the Catholic Emancipation Act in 1829. At the same time, Protestant ministers and organizations were single-mindedly seizing on anti-Catholicism to inspire popular enthusiasm for affiliating with a Protestant church. The American Bible Society not only published anti-Catholic tracts but even launched a campaign to spread the King James Bible among Catholics. The campaign naturally aroused an angry response among the American bishops. Furthermore the stubborn refusal of poor immigrants to accept the free Bibles gave rise to a widespread belief that Catholics were opposed to the Bible—a conviction that was to play a prominent part in the public-school and nativist controversies of the forties and fifties. Finally, well-known Protestant ministers began to preach anti-Catholic sermons as part of their proselytizing efforts. The Reverend Lyman Beecher of Boston delivered three Sunday sermons in as many churches on August 10, 1834, speaking out violently against Catholicism and its regular clergy and further inflaming an already explosive situation in that city. He and his fellow ministers may be said to have contributed directly to the first burning of a convent in the United States, which took place on the following day. All this fervor, anger, and prejudice preceded (or dated from the very start of) the great wave of German and Irish Catholic immigration. When that tide appeared, the nation's cities, large and small, entered upon three decades of anti-Catholic rioting marked by the burning of churches, orphanages, and convents.[9]

9. Ray A. Billington, *The Protestant Crusade 1800–1860*, New York, 1938, pp. 32–76.

The frequency and virulence of Protestant attacks did not automatically unite the largely impoverished mass of native American, French, German, and Irish Catholics. In 1820 the church was a weak and scattered organization made up of parishes from the old French empire at New Orleans, St. Louis, and Detroit, from the old colonial parishes in Maryland and their more recent offshoots in Kentucky, and of churches in most of the Eastern cities. Because there was but one major facility for training diocesan priests here, St. Mary's Seminary in Baltimore, priests had to be recruited from France, Germany, Italy, England, and Ireland, and they brought with them the diverse national styles endemic to European Catholicism.[10] In addition, no strong hand existed to enforce unity. During the long colonial years of intolerance and penalties against Catholics and of official neglect by the English bishop who had formal charge, priests here evolved an independent collegial style for the management of their common affairs. Perhaps fortunately for Catholicism in America, in view of the variety of backgrounds of the new waves of immigrants, the early nineteenth-century Church depended upon the initiative of scattered bishops who coped with their growing dioceses as best they could. Differences among them had to be reconciled by occasional provincial meetings, most frequently held in Baltimore, where the bishops gathered to legislate for the American Church. In its decentralization and widespread use of democratic and federal forms both within dioceses and among them, the Church of these years reflected the general political thrust of its era.[11]

By 1870 the Catholic Church had four and a half million members. Its parishes were scattered across the land from city slums to Midwestern farm counties, along the banks of every railroad and canal from the Atlantic to the Pacific. Such massive growth forced the Catholic Church into a position not unlike that of its Protestant opposition. The sheer necessity of building churches at a rate rapid enough to bring the Mass within reach of the incoming tides of newcomers necessarily delivered much of the power of the organization into the hands of the parish. Popular church-building priests and successful fund-raising congregations became the models of the day. Although Catholic immigrants

10. John Tracy Ellis, "A Short History of Seminary Education: Trent to Today," in James M. Lee and Louis J. Putz, eds., *Seminary Education in a Time of Change,* Notre Dame, 1965, pp. 46–57.

11. James Hennesey, "Papacy and Episcopacy in Eighteenth and Nineteenth Century America," *Records of the American Catholic Historical Society of Philadelphia,* 77 (September 1966), 175–84.

varied a great deal in their use of the Church, some depending upon it solely for its sacraments and others, especially Germans, bringing with them a custom of a village church and related clubs and societies, one can see in this emphasis on fund raising and on the building of churches and parochial schools the beginnings of the transformation of many a European church into the typical American Catholic parish of bingo, basketball, and building funds.

The ethnically fragmented hierarchy and parishes and the pressure for church building were manifested in a particular movement of localism—trusteeism—during these years. The trustee movement surfaced in open conflict immediately after the Revolution when local congregations asserted their right to appoint priests and control parish budgets in place of the bishop. In New York, Philadelphia, New Orleans, Norfolk, and Buffalo certain parishes resisted all attempts at discipline for as long as forty years. The difficulties had many dimensions, but the ethnic one proved to be the most obdurate. English priests had been the first to staff the American Church, and trustee clashes took the form of battles between American parishioners and the customs of French priests who fled here from the French Revolution, or between newly formed Irish congregations and native and French styles. Irish-German confrontations fired by English-language conflicts arose in the North and Midwest.[12]

To cope with these conflicts—and they remained bitterly divisive throughout the nineteenth century—the Church was compelled to adopt the rule that special churches for single nationalities might be established within the boundaries of the parishes established for each diocese. Moreover, the bishops endeavored to maintain harmony by calling regular meetings of all the parishes under their supervision. This episcopal compromise, later repeated when Catholics from Southern and Eastern Europe arrived, made it possible for the Church to maintain a troubled unity during the great migrations of the late nineteenth and early twentieth centuries.[13] So successful were these devices in enabling the Church to stay in contact with newly arrived immigrant groups that

12. John Tracy Ellis, ed., *Documents of American Catholic History,* Milwaukee, 1956, pp. 155–58; Thomas T. McAvoy, *A History of the Catholic Church in the United States,* Notre Dame, 1969, pp. 93–122; John Tracy Ellis, *American Catholicism,* rev. ed., Chicago, 1969, pp. 45–50.

13. Theodore Maynard, *The Story of American Catholicism,* New York, 1941, I, pp. 219–28; John Tracy Ellis, *The Life of James Cardinal Gibbons, Archbishop of Baltimore, 1834–1921,* Milwaukee, 1952, I, pp. 331–88.

when the twentieth-century Church began to speak for all the urban poor in political and philanthropic affairs, the general public found this representation acceptable.

Perhaps even more important for future Catholic culture than the halfway house of the ethnic Church was the establishment of parochial education. The beginning of the parochial system is customarily dated from the opening of a school for poor children in 1810 by Sister Elizabeth Seton at St. Joseph's Parish in Emmitsburg, Maryland. She employed the Sisters of Charity, of whom she was the American founder, to staff the school, and she operated it with free materials and without tuition for the children of the area. The basic formula of an elementary school attached to every church was seized upon by the most ambitious bishops as the best chance for the survival of Catholicism in Protestant America. In 1884 the Council of Baltimore adopted it as the official task of all dioceses. Thus, unlike in Europe, where universal education was yet to be established as a national norm, and where state funds and long-established endowments supported both churches and schools, American Catholic communities faced a double burden of creating a network of schools and churches sufficient to serve the waves of immigrants flooding in from abroad. The sheer poverty of some Catholic communities, like that of Boston, doomed the effort to failure in these first decades. Elsewhere, especially in German-settled cities where the desire for foreign-language teaching lent an additional impetus for local support, and in dioceses of aggressive bishops who successfully solicited funds and teaching orders from Europe, a rough approximation of the goal was attained before the Civil War.[14] Despite the universal emphasis of the parochial-school drive for a free education for every Catholic child, such a massive and relentless fund-raising effort imposed its class mark on Catholic education because it firmly anchored the parochial system to the parents of children of the working class and middle class, the very members of each urban parish who were making their way most successfully.

The building of the parochial system, begun on a large scale to meet the needs of the immigrants' children in the 1840s, had two consequences for American urban culture. First, it began the secularization of the public schools, dominated until that time by Protestants; second, it helped to build a characteristically American style of Catholic culture.

14. Harold A. Buetow, *Of Singular Benefit, The Story of Catholic Education in the United States,* New York, 1970, pp. 60–63, 108–54.

During the forties, Bishop John Hughes of New York and Bishop Francis Kenrick of Philadelphia pressed for the abolition of Protestant teaching in the public schools and for municipal or state aid to parochial schools. An explosion of antiforeign, anti-Catholic prejudice, resentment, and rioting greeted these demands. In every state where Catholics sought funds in the mid-nineteenth century they were refused. Not only did this outcry tend to draw German, Irish, and American Catholics together, but the gigantic effort required to build and to maintain thousands of schools committed each parish to an enduring social task: the education of children. The goal of literacy, both Catholic and secular, for any child who presented himself at the school door meant that the Catholic Church was as securely tied to the task of Americanization through education as were the contemporary public schools. Moreover, because the building and financing of its schools rested with the families of the parish, the values of the Church itself became tied to the hopes and values of child rearing which its neighborhood supporters possessed.[15]

1870–1920

The migrations of native Americans during the second era of urbanization and industrialization reflected some specific changes in the economy. The last years of the nineteenth century and the first two decades of the twentieth have been characterized as the "golden age of American agriculture."[16] It was a time when skillful farmers, using new techniques taught by the agricultural colleges and extension stations, prospered as world prices rose for American staples. The contemporaneous completion of the railway network opened up the high plains, Florida, the Southwest, and the Pacific coast so that every variation in soil and climate was utilized by farmers universally bound to national and international marketing systems.

The completion of the westward movement did not however halt the migratory habits of our restless people. After 1870 systematic information becomes available for the state-by-state migrations of the native-born. There was no settling down. In any given census since 1870,

15. Vincent P. Lannie, *Public Money and Parochial Education,* Cleveland, 1968, pp. 247–58.
16. Allan G. Bogue, *From Prairie to Corn Belt,* Chicago, 1963, pp. 280–82.

one-quarter of the population was living outside the state of its birth.[17] Moreover, this documented migration followed the time-honored pattern of the common people: young men, women, and families moved because they were seeking the places where economic opportunity seemed the best. Although in 1920 there were more farms and farmers in the United States than ever before or since, modernization of the economy had already begun to drive many Americans off the land.[18] The young people especially were aware of a choice between farm and city; many of them were sick of farming and began to pour into the cities and towns of the Midwestern manufacturing belt. The Lynds' first *Middletown* book records the transformation which such shifts from a rural to an industrial society entailed for a small Midwestern city. But the country people also poured into the great cities of the era, helping to build such metropolises as Pittsburgh, Chicago, Cleveland, and Detroit.[19]

During these same years, international immigration reached its flood but did not retrace the patterns of native population flow to the degree that it had in previous years. Only Scandinavians, Bohemians, and some Germans continued to move out onto the farms to swell the westward migration of the natives. Most Europeans were concentrated in the cities and towns of the Northeastern and Midwestern manufacturing belts, thereby settling themselves in the forefront of the urbanization of the era.[20]

Historians refer to the migrations of 1870–1920 as the years of the "new immigration," that is, the coming of the Russians, Poles, and Italians as opposed to the "old immigration" of Germans, Irish, and British (Table 3). The shifts in origins and ratios of European migrants reflect the interaction between the modernization of Europe and the industrialization of the United States. For Europe as a whole there were periods of heavy excesses of births over deaths, and these were of course the times of large population gains. When the children represented by these gains reached adulthood, mass migrations took place from rural

17. U.S. Bureau of the Census, *Historical Statistics of the United States, Colonial Times to 1957*, Washington, 1960, p. 41.

18. The 1920 returns reported 3,366,510 farmowners. *Historical Statistics*, p. 278.

19. Robert M. Fogelson, *The Fragmented Metropolis, Los Angeles, 1850–1930*, Cambridge, 1967, p. 69; Robert S. and Helen M. Lynd, *Middletown*, New York, 1929.

20. David Ward, *Cities and Immigrants, A Geography of Change in Nineteenth-Century America*, New York, 1971, pp. 65–81; Brinley Thomas, *Migration and Economic Growth*, Cambridge, England, 1954, pp. 133–34.

TABLE 3. Immigration by Countries and Continents, 1821–1970 (In Thousands)

	Total	Great Britain	Ireland*	Germany	Other Central Europe†	Russia-USSR	Italy	Asia	Canada	Mexico	Balance of World
1821–30	143	25	51	7	n.a.	—	—	—	2	5	53
1831–40	545	76	207	152	n.a.	—	2	—	14	7	87
1841–50	1,713	343	781	434	n.a.	1	2	—	42	3	107
1851–60	2,598	424	914	952	n.a.	—	10	41	59	3	195
1861–70	2,215	607	436	787	8	2	12	65	154	2	142
Subtotal 1821–1870	7,214	1,475	2,389	2,332	8	3	26	106	271	20	584
1871–80	2,812	548	437	718	73	39	56	124	384	5	428
1881–90	5,247	808	656	1,453	354	213	307	68	393	n.a.	995
1891–1900	3,688	272	389	505	593	505	652	71	3	n.a.	698
1901–10	8,795	526	339	341	2,145	1,597	2,046	244	179	50	1,328
1911–20	5,736	341	146	144	902	922	1,110	193	742	219	1,017
Subtotal 1871–1920	26,278	2,495	1,967	3,161	4,067	3,276	4,171	700	1,701	274	4,466
1921–30	4,107	330	221	412	215	89	455	97	925	459	904
1931–40	528	29	13	114	32	7	68	15	109	22	119
1941–50	1,035	131	27	227	38	4	58	32	172	61	285
1951–60	2,516	209	64	346	182	47	188	150	275	319	736
1961–70	3,322	230	43	200	99	16	207	431	287	443	1,366
Subtotal 1921–1970	11,508	929	368	1,299	566	163	976	725	1,768	1,304	3,410

* Includes both Northern and South Ireland
† Austria since 1861, except 1938–45, Hungary since 1861, Czechoslovakia and Yugoslavia since 1920. There is no long unbroken time series available for Poland. U.S. Bureau of the Census, *Historical Statistics of the United States*, Washington, 1960, pp. 56–59; U.S. Department of Justice, Immigration and Naturalization Service, *Report of the Commissioner: 1970*, Washington, 1971, pp. 63–64.

areas into European cities and beyond to America. The impact of the baby booms of 1825 and 1840–45 in Western Europe had propelled the tides of German, Irish, and British migrants. In later years as railroads and urbanization stimulated the Eastern and Southern European economies, similar population booms swelled rural populations there. The birth surge of 1860–65 appeared in the American immigration peak of 1880–84; the surge of 1885–90 in the peak of 1902–15.[21]

The migrants came to this country in tremendous numbers only when jobs were plentiful here; if hard times prevailed they settled in European cities instead. Such alternative destinations for European rural migrants stemmed from the fact that the nineteenth-century cycles of building activity and capital investment were not the same for Europe and America. Until World War I the United States was a substantial importer of capital from Europe, and accordingly it had to compete with European opportunities for investment in industrial ventures and urban real estate. Capital sought first one continent and then the other depending upon the expectations for most substantial profits. These capital flows alternately encouraged and impeded employment in the United States. The flow of capital created boom years from 1878 to 1892 and from 1897 to 1913 and opened up many new jobs, and hence there were surges in immigration. Toward the end of the nineteenth century, as cheap steamship passage made the crossing of the ocean easy and safe, skilled workmen often moved between England and the United States, following the crests in wages and employment in their particular crafts. The statistics of net migration, which show departures as well as arrivals from abroad, confirm the employment-opportunity–migration sequence.[22]

There were two immediate results of this pulsating flow of peoples from Europe. The continued flood of unskilled workers directly influenced the development of mechanization in American industry, while the interaction between the origins of immigrants and the increasing urbanization of the United States determined which groups were to advance with certain elements of the economy. With immigration bringing in tides of unskilled labor to the nation, industry before the Great Depression had always to adjust to a plentiful supply of cheap unskilled labor and to a concurrent shortage of skilled workmen. The result was

21. Thomas, *Migration and Economic Growth*, pp. 155–58.
22. Taeuber and Taeuber, *Changing Population of the United States*, pp. 67–70, 202–13.

to give our technology a particular cast: the most complicated processes were mechanized first, in contrast to European practice, in order to conserve highly skilled and paid craft workers, and were mechanized in such a way that they could be carried out by men with very little training. Gradually an industrial style of high mechanization developed. It did not always present the cheapest solution, as twentieth-century competition with German manufacture made plain, for Germany used highly skilled techniques coupled with less mechanization, but it became an enduring part of American industrial culture.[23]

The second consequence of the shifting origins of European migration was that it aroused considerable alarm among both native Americans and children of the older immigration. To be sure, those native-born who moved to the cities, factories, and offices of the nation had a strong competitive advantage over most foreigners. They often possessed more formal education, some savings, and connections with well-placed relatives. Above all, they were members of the dominant culture. Studies of social mobility show that the native-born and their children moved more easily into white-collar jobs than did the immigrants or their children. Yet during the 1870–1920 years native Americans were disproportionately concentrated in the farms and small towns of the United States, and their apprehensions that they were being left behind contained some measure of truth.

For example, national statistics show that the children of English and Irish immigrants achieved high-status positions more rapidly than the native population did simply because their parents had settled in greater concentrations in the cities; and since in the half century after 1870 these were the locations of widest opportunity, the immigrant child had a better chance for education and for an eventual high-status position. In 1900, 5.7 percent of all white Americans were illiterate as opposed to only 1.6 percent of the children of immigrants. In that census year the ratios of whites in professional and clerical positions and in government employment summarize the differential effects of migration, urbanization, and social mobility: 14 percent of all Americans appeared in these categories but 22.6 percent of the children of both British and Irish immigrants. Because of their traditional rural position

23. Sigfried Giedion, *Mechanization Takes Command,* New York, 1948, p. 38; John A. Kouwenhoven, *Made in America: The Arts in Modern Civilization,* New York, 1948, pp. 13–42.

in the economy, native Americans as a whole were indeed being left behind.[24]

Conditions prevailing in the new mill towns and metropolises of the late nineteenth and early twentieth centuries also conspired to shake the confidence of both native and "old immigrant" stock. The men there had acquired the urban industrial skills of their day and counted on the continuation of the nineteenth-century world, where the continual arrival of fresh unskilled immigrants signaled not only expansion of the job market but also promotion and advancement for earlier comers. Under this mode of growth in the economy, natives and old immigrant groups had become the skilled hands, the foremen, the bosses of the new incursions of rural migrants. The repetition of this sequence of events had meant that for at least the previous century immigration and social mobility had had no grounds for conflict.

In the 1890s the scale of the city and of industry reached swollen proportions, and the scope and possibility for the social and economic mobility of the ordinary citizen seemed to narrow. Although studies by historians seem to show that the chances for individual advancement did not in fact decline during the years after 1890, nevertheless a feeling was prevalent that a man's chances to get ahead had dwindled with the coming of the giant metropolis and the factory. For the first time, the waves of European immigrants appeared as a threat: perhaps to the workers of the time, certainly to their children. As unions became fearful for the jobs of their members, the men lost confidence in the future for themselves and their children.[25]

Concomitantly an ugly rise in ethnic stereotyping swept the nation. Racial prejudice, anti-Semitism, anti-immigration sentiment, and the inflated patriotism of World War I with its phobia against Communism combined to pass in 1921 an immigration law that set limited quotas based on the ethnic mixture of the population as it was found to exist in 1910. So it was that fear of the industrial structure and of the metropolis that housed it, augmented by jealousy between rural and urban dwellers, ended the century-old pattern of migration, industrialization, and urban-

24. Taeuber and Taeuber, *Changing Population of the United States,* p. 187; Thomas, *Migration and Economic Growth,* pp. 141–54; E. P. Hutchinson, *Immigrants and Their Children 1850–1950,* New York, 1956, pp. 203–16.
25. John Higham, *Strangers in the Land,* New Brunswick, 1955, pp. 158–233, 300–330; Stephan Thernstrom and Richard Sennett, eds., *Nineteenth Century Cities: Essays in the New Urban History,* New Haven, 1969, pp. 125–64.

ization. The atmosphere since the twenties has been a miasma of antiforeign sentiment. The paradoxical result of the 1921 law and its
subsequent revisions was to close immigration from peasant countries
and to encourage the entrance of skilled workers and professional men
from the more advanced countries, thereby exacerbating competition for
the most prized jobs. Our nation with its high levels of skill and education thus continued to draw the trained sectors of population away from
those nations that had the most crying need for modern skills.[26]

During the last years of the nineteenth century, the black population
of the United States began to move from its historic place in the rural
Southeast. The special qualities of Negro migration in America have
been twofold: it has been small compared to both native-white and
European migrations, and it is a migration that has taken place under
severe handicaps, because for many years it proved difficult for blacks to
escape from their home territory.

Like earlier migrants, the blacks followed existing transportation
routes, pursuing the cheapest paths. Negroes from Maryland to Florida
came by coastal steamer and railroad to the cities of the Northeast.
Negroes west of the Alleghenies moved up the Mississippi by rail on the
Illinois Central, Gulf Mobile and Ohio, and the Wabash to St. Louis,
Chicago, Cleveland, and Detroit. The pioneering settlers were young
people who ventured north to seek a place in the small ghettos that had
existed in every city since before the Civil War. The availability of jobs
in Washington, D.C., fostered a large colony there of blacks from Virginia and the upper South, while industrial and service jobs in Philadelphia and New York attracted blacks along the Atlantic. As in other
migrations the pioneers sent back letters of encouragement, sometimes
money and tickets, and the channels of migration opened and began to
flow, pulsating with the rhythms of urbanization and economic growth.
During both World Wars this normal migration was spurred by the
active labor-recruiting policies of the steel mills and other large firms in
need of quantities of cheap labor. Indeed, the precedent for the recruit-
ment of black Southern labor lay in the nineteenth-century practices of
those companies who had imported gangs of laborers from Italy and
Eastern Europe.[27]

26. Taeuber and Taeuber, *Changing Population of the United States,* p. 70.
27. Carter G. Woodson, *A Century of Negro Migration,* New York, 1918, pp.
147–92; Gilbert Osofsky, *Harlem: The Making of a Ghetto,* New York, 1963,
pp. 17–34; Constance McLaughlin Green, *Secret City: A History of Race Relations*

Although the total volume of black migration remained small until World War II, it was enough in the early years to create in New York, Chicago, and St. Louis black ghettos that would nurture the beginnings of a modern urban American Negro culture. The Harlem Renaissance in New York began with the first waves of late nineteenth-century northward migration.[28] The timing of the start of black migration, however, proved to be disastrous. Negroes began arriving in large numbers in Northern cities exactly at the time when the great swells of fear and prejudice had begun to break over America, indeed over all the European world as well. The bitter race riots of East St. Louis in 1917 and of Chicago in 1919 testify to the anger and brutality of the climate into which the native blacks were moving in their search for opportunities in the cities of the North.[29]

The cultural effects of these new sources and differential patterns of migration immediately manifested themselves. The coming of the Jews from Eastern Europe and of the black Protestants from the South completed the roster of elements that compose our modern urban culture: white Protestant, white Catholic, white Jewish, and black Protestant. Yet since each of these socioreligious clusters consisted largely of recent rural migrants, American and European, the cultural life of each group evolved around its adjustments to new urban conditions. Each group accordingly developed pronounced old-value and new-value wings.

For the white Protestants the important cultural event of the years from 1870 to 1900 was the formation of a liberal, urban middle-class movement—the social gospel—extending laterally across all denominations. The movement reflected a self-conscious attempt on the part of Protestant ministers and laymen to comprehend and make some adjustment to the realities of their day. It drew upon the millennial enthusiasm of the earlier evangelical era but transformed it into a secular optimism based on the efficacy of social reform. It drew also upon the past emphasis on individual religious responsibility but transformed it into a

in the Nation's Capital, Princeton, 1967, pp. 119–93. The greater difficulty of blacks in moving out of their home states in the South can be shown by comparing white and nonwhite migration from Alabama and Virginia for the years 1870 and 1910: Everett S. Lee, Ann R. Miller, et al., *Population Redistribution and Economic Growth, United States 1870–1950*, I, Philadelphia, 1957, pp. 249, 293, 299, 343.

28. James Weldon Johnson, *Black Manhattan*, New York, 1930, pp. 58–125.

29. Elliott M. Rudwick, *Race Riot at East St. Louis,* Carbondale, 1964; Carl Sandburg, *The Chicago Race Riots July 1919*, New York, 1919; William M. Tuttle, Jr., *Race Riot, Chicago in the Red Summer of 1919*, New York, 1970.

call for an active citizenship informed by Christian ethics. The modern
American Christian, according to the social gospel, was to address
himself to the affairs of the world, to work as an individual and to join
others in his congregation in combating such evils as child labor, exploitation of women, Negroes, and workingmen, and the social pathology
of slum housing, alcoholism, and unregulated immigration.[30]

Institutionally the movement became apparent in interdenomina-
tional organizations like the Federal (later National) Council of
Churches of Christ in America (1908), in the founding of settlement
houses and the development of social work as a profession, in church-
sponsored investigations of major strikes, and in a vast amount of debating and pamphleteering.[31] Conceptually the social gospel enlarged the
old reformist wing of American Protestantism and brought this branch
of the culture up to date by leading it into sympathetic contact with the
realities of Protestant, Catholic, and Jewish working-class and lower-
class life. Of course the old axes of conflict still existed within Protestantism. A strong draft of nativism blew through many of the Americanization programs of progressive settlements, churches, and public
schools of the day. The temperance and antiprostitution campaigns, so
important in these years, were at once real issues of social liberation
and continuations of early nineteenth-century Protestant-Catholic war-
fare over alcohol, dancing, and Sabbath observance.[32] Yet for all this
persistence of old habits of thought the social-gospel wing of Protestantism initiated the very important task of establishing a modern liberal
middle-class sentiment that could build bridges to the three other
contemporary urbanizing cultures.

The great majority of both rural and urban Protestants were not in
any case followers of the social gospel. In these years urban Protestantism lost much of its older working-class base and became very much
a middle-class suburban phenomenon. Moreover, the new rich of the
city dominated many congregations with their conservative blend of self-
righteous capitalism and old-fashioned insistence that poverty was a
manifestation of unworthiness and sin.

    30. Henry F. May, *Protestant Churches and Industrial America,* New York,
1949, pp. 163–203.
    31. C. Howard Hopkins, *The Rise of the Social Gospel in American Protes-
tantism 1865–1915,* New Haven, 1940, pp. 257–327.
    32. Samuel P. Hays, "History as Human Behavior," *Iowa Journal of History,*
58 (July 1960), 193–206; "The Social Analysis of American Political History,
1880–1920," *Political Science Quarterly,* 80 (September 1965), 373–94.

For Catholicism the years from 1870 to 1920 were also ones of liberalization. In Europe the liberal-national revolutions and the rise of Catholic unionism and Christian socialism drove the hierarchy into a degree of accommodation with the modern world. The deep suspicion of and hostility to humanitarian reform that had marked many Papal and American Catholic attitudes in the earlier era now gave way to a sense that the Church ought to interest itself in the problems posed by industrialization and the urban masses. Pope Leo XIII's 1891 encyclical *Rerum novarum* on the relations of capital and labor and the work of James Cardinal Gibbons on behalf of the Knights of Labor marked the new trend.[33]

As Irish and German Catholics rose in large numbers from immigrant poverty to positions of success and affluence, the Catholic Church became an all-class, fully organized institution in the United States. These were the years of cathedral building in every major urban diocese, the years of the widespread establishment of the parish elementary-school system and, following the trends in public education, the opening of parochial high schools. The Church began to train its own priests, and although a continuing shortage required European recruits, the Catholic Church in America became a highly integrated organization dominated by native-born descendants of Irishmen and Germans.

Much of the liberalization of Catholicism derived from the personal experience of its membership. As millions of Catholics moved out from the poverty of the central city to the new working-class settlements and middle-class suburbs, they settled in mixed Protestant-Catholic communities. The needs of the parish for church and school building and the associational style of middle-class Americans caused Catholic clubs and societies to multiply as they did at neighboring Protestant churches. The charitable work of the Society of St. Vincent de Paul and the fraternal organization of the Knights of Columbus proved immensely popular.

Catholicism did not, on the other hand, become absorbed in the social gospel in the same way that contemporary Protestantism had done. The social gospel was after all a movement of middle-class people, often with small-town backgrounds, who were trying to come to grips with the strangeness of the industrial metropolis. Catholic liberalism in these years most commonly took the form of speeches made by Irish and German politicians and priests in behalf of the working classes and

33. Ellis, *American Catholicism,* pp. 101–104; Ellis, *Life of Gibbons,* I, pp. 486–546.

lower classes of the city. They spoke not as social investigators but as representatives. Theirs was not a movement of discovery and accommodation but a call for recognition and a demand for a more just share of the fruits of the society. Many Irish and German politicians prospered and in their success were as callous, corrupt, and conservative as the Presbyterian steel barons of Pittsburgh. But there were others who used their success to represent their constituents, men like Martin Lomasney of Boston or Charles F. Murphy of New York. These politicians joined with settlement-house workers, Protestant ministers, Jewish philanthropists, and union leaders to carry the important social legislation of the day through city councils, state legislatures, and Congress. By 1920, though the Church was full of conflicts between new Slavic and Italian ethnic groups and the established Irish and Germans and though many Catholics and priests were as doubtful as ever of the efficacy of reform and as fearful of liberalism and socialism, the success of millions of urban Catholics in moving into positions of comfort and power produced a sense of widespread personal optimism to reinforce the liberal tendencies of some political and religious leaders.[34]

For the Jewish immigrants, whose massive migration during the late nineteenth and early twentieth centuries made Jewish culture a permanent element in American life, the polarization between old-fashioned ghetto and village ways and modern urban life had commenced in Europe. German liberal Judaism and German and Russian anarchism and socialism traveled across the Atlantic to foster progressive movements among Jewish immigrants and the small Jewish communities that already existed in Eastern and Midwestern cities. There was probably not a reform effort in any big city in the United States after about 1880 that did not include at least one Jewish member. Indeed, the American version of the charitable tradition of the Jewish ghetto soon proved to be a major urban cultural bridge. Even in the face of rising anti-Semitism during these same years, Jewish philanthropists served on most metropolitan committees for child care, unemployment relief, and hospital and community fund drives, as well as on those directed to race relations and social legislation. Thus the Jewish philanthropist became a permanent element in metropolitan elite life.

34. Rudolph J. Vecoli, "Prelates and Peasants, Italian Immigrants and the Catholic Church," *Journal of Social History,* 2 (Spring 1969), 217–68; William V. Shannon, *The American Irish,* New York, 1963, pp. 114–63; McAvoy, *History of the Catholic Church,* pp. 263–390.

But for most Jews, the 1870–1920 decades were years of struggle with immigration and poverty. Just as the Irish and German slums had been symbols of poverty and exploitation in the earlier mixed commercial and industrial city, so the Jewish slum of the metropolis epitomized urban life of the "new immigration."[35] The tenements of New York's lower East Side, housing thousands of little sweatshops where Jewish immigrants labored on suits, overcoats, trimmings, dresses, and shirts, have become, thanks to liberal Jewish and Protestant writing, classic statements of the American immigrant experience. The raw exploitation of these industries was finally brought under control only by means of the organization and repeated strikes of the workers in these crafts and by the passage of restraining legislation.[36]

Because Jews located in the largest cities, where economic opportunities were then the most abundant, because they had a strong cultural imperative toward education at a time when the economy demanded the skills of formal education, and because their culture seemed so compatible with individualistic capitalism, Jewish immigrants rapidly took their places in the middle and upper levels of the class structure. Indeed, the story of the continuous struggles of these immigrant parents to provide their children with education, better jobs, and a better future has become today the controversial model of social and economic mobility. It is against this model that current arguments for cultural pluralism for Negroes, Chicanos, Indians, and old ethnic groups are being debated.[37]

Finally, the small black ghettos of Northern cities in these years laid the foundations for what would later become a revolution in black and white culture. Since job discrimination held so many Negroes in permanent poverty and race prejudice crowded blacks into expensive all-Negro communities, their liberalization and urbanization could not be borne on a wave of rising affluence and integration of the members of the culture,

35. Jacob Riis, *How the Other Half Lives,* New York, 1890; Hutchins Hapgood, *The Spirit of the Ghetto,* New York, 1902; Abraham Cahan, *The Rise of David Levinsky,* New York, 1917; Moses Rischin, *The Promised City: New York's Jews 1870–1914,* Cambridge, 1962.

36. Melvyn Dubofsky, *When Workers Organize, New York City in the Progressive Era,* Amherst, 1968, pp. 67–85.

37. Nathan Glazer and Daniel Patrick Moynihan, *Beyond the Melting Pot,* Cambridge, 1963, pp. 24–85; Lee Rainwater and William L. Yancey, *The Moynihan Report and the Politics of Controversy,* Cambridge, 1967, pp. 43–94; Mary G. Powers, "Class, Ethnicity, and Residence in Metropolitan America," *Demography,* 5 (1968), 447–48; Caroline Golab, "The Immigrant and the City: The Polish Experience in Philadelphia 1870 to 1920," Temple University Conference on the History of the Peoples of Philadelphia, April 2, 1971.

as had been the case for Catholics and Jews. Rather black culture had to accommodate itself to the fact of ghetto poverty and the capabilities of a small elite whose actions were narrowly circumscribed by the discrimination of the outside white society. Despite this confinement, the ghetto years of the first waves of migration from the South between 1890 and 1920 were a time of extraordinary cultural growth: the Negro churches adapted to the rush of migrants and participated in the general liberalization of Protestantism, while a parallel secular flowering established a modern definition of black Americans as a people with a unique art, history, literature, and music.

Before these migrations, when Negro clusters in Northern cities were small, the churches had served as community centers. They were the principal sources of black news, the cement that held clubs and lodges together, the bases for political action, and the links between the tiny black elite and the generality of low-paid black workers and servants. Rapid growth of black blocks to entire urban ghettos after 1890 inevitably destroyed such small-scale social unities. Though the web of discrimination hampered Negroes in a thousand ways, a small business and professional elite grew with the ghetto, thereby fragmenting the community's secular and religious leadership. Ministers had to share their role with doctors, teachers, newspapermen, government workers, politicians, and liquor and gambling operators, while at the same time large and successful congregations set themselves apart from the proliferation of store-front churches which sprang up to meet the needs of the new migrants. The extreme poverty of urban Negroes has forced black Protestantism to cope with far more extreme institutional divisions than its white counterpart, and it maintains to this day its character of a few large well-established churches surrounded by a sea of informal evanescent one-room congregations. Nevertheless all the features of white Protestantism prevail: a core belief and practice which allows blacks to move easily from one church to the next, the insistence among respectable families of every income that Sunday school is essential for children's education, the mixture of classes in each denomination, and the widespread participation in ancillary clubs, entertainments, and lectures.[38]

Thus the twentieth-century liberalization of black Protestantism

38. St. Clair Drake and Horace R. Cayton, *Black Metropolis, A Study of Negro Life in a Northern City,* New York, 1945, pp. 412–23, 495–525.

went forward in the general climate of American religious practice, constrained only by the facts of ghetto poverty and the inescapable demand that ghetto Protestantism, like all ghetto institutions, serve the race. In the three decades after the Civil War, Negro ministers had participated in the fight to obtain the vote for Northern Negroes, to desegregate Northern city schools, and to seek full citizenship for the race. With the rise in the late nineteenth century of a new urban humanitarianism among Protestant and Jewish churchmen and philanthropists, the black elite absorbed and adapted the social gospel to its own race purposes. On the white side, slum missions gave way to settlement houses, social surveys, and reform politics, thereby building a new bridge toward the black leaders. The result was the formation of two new permanent organizations, the National Association for the Advancement of Colored People (1909) and the Urban League (1911), which embodied the spirit and technique of the new social consciousness. Although for a time in Southern cities white and black governing boards had to sit separately, with the spread of their chapters into every large city these new organizations formed a liberal interracial core which led the civil-rights campaigns throughout the nation until the 1960s.[39]

A unique cultural flowering also accompanied the 1890–1920 migrations and the growth of urban ghettos. In view of the poverty of Negro city dwellers and the small base of support which the elite could offer to black theater and arts, the Harlem Renaissance was a remarkable achievement of black liberation. A handful of poets, actors, dancers, painters, writers, and musicians fashioned a coherent heritage and modern image of a black American: a free man in the midst of oppression whose culture stretched back to Africa and Jerusalem. The discrimination against blacks in the entertainment, commercial-art, and publishing industries and their virtual exclusion from universities forced most Negro artists to depend upon the inadequate resources of the impoverished ghetto or to leave the black world altogether. As a result the cultural stream which the Harlem Renaissance opened early in this century was choked to a mere trickle. Only jazz, which could be nourished in the ghetto while meeting universal outside demand, flourished.[40]

39. Drake and Cayton, *Black Metropolis,* pp. 46–51; Arvarh E. Strickland, *History of the Chicago Urban League,* Urbana, 1966, pp. 6–35; Allan H. Spear, *Black Chicago, The Making of a Negro Ghetto 1890–1920,* Chicago, 1967, pp. 54–89.

40. Johnson, *Black Manhattan,* pp. 182–230, 260–84; Harold Cruse, *The Crisis of the Negro Intellectual,* New York, 1967, pp. 11–95.

1920–

When the boom in the world market for agricultural products collapsed in 1921, the historic drive of Americans to cultivate their land on independent family farms collapsed with it. Troubles for the small farmer had been accumulating for years. Failure to secure credit for new machinery and new methods had driven many into mortgage foreclosure and tenancy, and competition from large-scale operators harried others. The discrepancy between what the ordinary farmer could earn by his labor and what his son or daughter could make in a city office or factory drew young people increasingly away from the land. Now as twenty years of depressed farm prices began, a term longer than anyone's savings or mortgage could sustain, farmers, white and black, gave up in droves and sought a new chance in the mill towns and cities. New Deal and subsequent agricultural legislation, far from helping the small farmer, brought new and highly productive irrigated land into competition and put capital into the hands of those who were already the most successful; the strong waxed rich and the weak were driven off the land.[41]

From Texas to Minnesota, thousands of Midwesterners gave up and moved to the Pacific; it was said that Los Angeles was Iowa transplanted. The textile, lumber, chemical, and petroleum industries gave employment to Southern farmers, while the continued expansion of the automobile industry in the Midwest absorbed many thousands from there and other regions. In this great exodus the rural American suffered all the exploitation and punishment of slum living that migrants from abroad suffered earlier. The shanty and trailer camps of Willow Run, thrown together for war workers, or the Appalachian North Side of Chicago today bear the marks of conflict between the rural style of life and that of the modern industrial city with its low pay, uncertain income, and harsh discipline.[42]

Beginning with World War II the blacks of the Southeast were finally able to participate fully in this national pattern, and they poured

41. Stanley Lebergott, "Tomorrow's Workers: The Prospects for the Urban Labor Force," in Warner, *Planning for a Nation of Cities*, pp. 124–40.
42. Harriette Arnow, *The Dollmaker*, New York, 1954; Todd Gitlin and Nanci Hollander, *Uptown, Poor Whites in Chicago*, New York, 1970.

out of the old Confederacy into Northern and Pacific cities.[43] There they have faced in our own time, as in previous periods, two special obstacles that have never confronted their white counterparts. Job prejudice consistently held down newcomers and older residents alike and excluded even the skilled and qualified from jobs commensurate with their abilities. Moreover, prejudice blocked Negroes from the traditional practice of one man's using his established position to make room for his friends, relatives, townsmen, and fellow ethnics. Employment restrictions closed down the historical process of urbanization whereby newcomers advanced either through job improvement or accumulation of property. Housing prejudice, far in excess of any that existed in respect to Jews or poor families of any sort, closed vast areas of the city to Negroes, and the black ghettos could often only expand by violence or by the purchase of housing at exorbitant prices. There had been ghettos and prejudice before in American cities, but the rapid growth of communities of Negro migrants in the North and the relentless job discrimination heightened the segregation. The outcome has been the emergence of an unprecedented situation in American cities: vast quarters are occupied exclusively by the members of a single race or origin.[44]

These special barriers against blacks made the Negro ghettos of the Northern cities a distinct departure from the slums where foreign immigrants or rural white natives lived. With housing choices and job access both severely curtailed, black ghettos became huge basins of poverty and low-income housing. They were very far from being "ports of entry," stopping places for the first years or the first generation, as twentieth-century Italian slums had been.[45] There the population repeatedly shifted as the more successful members followed jobs into industrial sectors or managed to purchase a house in a decent working-

43. These shifting patterns of urban migration among cities can be followed in Donald J. Bogue, *Population Growth in Standard Metropolitan Statistical Areas 1900–1950*, Housing and Home Finance Agency, Washington, 1953; and Karl E. and Alma F. Taeuber, *Negroes in Cities*, Chicago, 1965, pp. 139–44.

44. Sam Bass Warner, Jr., and Colin B. Burke, "Cultural Change and the Ghetto," *Journal of Contemporary History,* 4 (October 1969), 173–87; Stanley Lieberson, *Ethnic Patterns in American Cities,* New York, 1963, pp. 44–91; Taeuber and Taeuber, *Negroes in Cities,* pp. 31–68.

45. Humbert S. Nelli, *Italians in Chicago 1880–1930, A Study in Ethnic Mobility,* New York, 1970, pp. 22–54; Sister Mary F. Matthews, "The Role of the Public School in the Assimilation of the Italian Immigrant Child in New York City, 1900–1914," in Silvano M. Tomasi and Madeline H. Engel, *The Italian Experience in the United States,* New York, 1970, pp. 125–41.

class district. But newcomers kept pouring into the black ghettos and were kept there by the whites. Consequently our modern ghetto resembles the classic European one. Spatially and socially it is a microcosm of the metropolis, where the poor crowd into the oldest housing of the quarter and the skilled and more prosperous huddle together at the newer periphery.[46] All classes of blacks form an exploited community, as did the Jews in the ghettos of Europe, and they make up an isolated colony in the host society.

Furthermore, sizable black migration is a recent phenomenon, coinciding with the economic faltering of the old core cities in which blacks had to settle. Bad economic surroundings served as the unfortunate reinforcement to job prejudice, and both exacerbated the problem of the impoverishment of black migrants, of whom there were already a disproportionately large number as compared to white migrants.[47] The American Jewish ghetto had stemmed from specialization in the garment industry; the Irish, Italians, and Poles prospered in the construction trades attendant on the industrialization of booming cities. But blacks arrived to find both prejudice and an environment of low-paying, sluggish industries. This economic geography of the decentralizing metropolis creates for Negro migrants yet another hardship: the black ghetto is a residential place, not a mixed settlement of industry, commerce, and homes. Lacking skilled migrants or much employment of its own and blocked by the prejudice of bankers, insurance companies, wholesale outlets, and retailers, black capitalism can hope at most to serve the ghetto itself. Until the metropolis is opened, the skills, leadership, and capital of the black community are in the wrong place, at the wrong time, to participate in the profits of the growing metropolis.

Concurrently with urbanization, a number of events conspired to diminish the importance of overseas migration. Successive restrictions in this country and abroad prevented people from coming to the United States or leaving their own country. The United States excluded the Chinese in 1882, the Japanese in 1900, and then in a succession of laws in 1921, 1924, and 1929 set restrictive quotas that choked down the flow of population from Asia and Southern and Eastern Europe. The unemployment of the Great Depression followed and closed the United

---

46. Donald R. Deskins, Jr., "Race, Residence, and Workplace in Detroit, 1880 to 1965," *Economic Geography,* 48 (January 1972), 79–94.

47. John F. Kain, "Housing Segregation, Negro Employment, and Metropolitan Decentralization," *Quarterly Journal of Economics,* 82 (May 1968), 175–97.

States to those who were seeking improvement over the economic conditions in advanced European countries. American immigration restrictions and those of Germany, Italy, the Soviet Union, and Great Britain trapped thousands of political prisoners, especially Jews, who by nineteenth-century practices would have sought asylum in the United States. Rejected by their own country and refused by ours, millions met their death in prisons and concentration camps.[48]

Since World War II, German and Italian migration has revived to a great extent (Table 2, page 93), and it is expected that the 1968 relaxation of quota restrictions will bring in Eastern Europeans and Asians once more. Under the restrictive policies of the 1920s the major foreign influx up to now has been from Canada, Mexico, and the Caribbean. Except for the French Canadians in New England, the Canadians have melted into the native population like the British before them. The Mexican, however, is the prototype of the immigrant of today. Although a few special characteristics, especially a propensity to large families, the proximity of the parent country, and the historically unique practice of many southwestern agricultural laborers dwelling in cities instead of out on farms, differentiate Mexican immigrant life from nineteenth-century precedents, much repeats the past. Like the Irish peasants before them, Mexicans work in the lowest-paid, nonunion, marginal small firms; like the Irish they are employed in seasonal gangs as railroad, construction, and farm laborers; like the Irish they do the heavy, unrewarding labor on the streets and in the homes, hotels, restaurants, and food-processing plants of the American city.[49] Again like the Irish peasants before them, the Mexicans have been the object of prejudice and persecution, facing additionally the racial antipathies directed in the United States against any nonwhite. But the Mexican experience in the West and the Puerto Rican experience in the East have taken on a special quality ascribable to the nature of the giant cities they entered. More than for any previous groups, theirs is the unseen migration because theirs is the era of the megalopolis, made up of rigidly segregated cities and metropolises. As a result the browns may live by the thousands in a city and yet go unnoticed by their fellow citizens. In the mid-nineteenth century the Irish could not have been thus ignored; they lived in every-

---

48. Maldwyn Allen Jones, *American Immigration,* Chicago, 1960, pp. 278–307.
49. Leo Grebler, Joan W. Moore, and Ralph C. Guzman, *The Mexican-American People, The Nation's Second Largest Minority,* New York, 1970, pp. 13–33, 205–47.

one's alley, attic, and cellar, and mixed in among the families of middle-class native Americans. Again the structure of the present economy is such that the Mexican's manual labor and service exist at the margins of our advanced technology in industry and commerce: he can be replaced by a machine; he can be kept on at less than a living wage because often he has no other job choices. When Chicano families do break through the barriers of poverty they settle, like the blacks, in class-graded ghettos and replicate on a small scale the divisions of the larger society, yet like the blacks they are denied the opportunities for dispersion that are open to whites.[50] So it was that Los Angeles, the twentieth-century metropolis, expanded with new slums and a new people of slum dwellers, and New York, the oldest metropolis, found its slums filled with yet another new people, the Puerto Ricans.[51]

The cultural consequences of the low level of foreign migration for the past half century have been to permit the unification of domestic cultures along the lines of their class and religious attributes, undisturbed by major incursions of new ethnic cultures. At the same time, the high rates of migration within the country have subjected these cultural components to the pressures of a metropolis continually being restructured into diffuse suburban patterns. In general these two demographic trends of urbanization and suburbanization have brought the leveling out of the white socioreligious groups—Protestant, Catholic, and Jewish —into a bourgeois culture consensus and the fostering of a nationalist component in black Protestantism.

Looking back from today's perspective on the fate of the liberal social gospel, one can see that it contributed to the general secularization of Protestantism and to the continued trend toward the transformation of Protestant churches into middle-class social institutions. The strong call for ministerial and lay action issued by the early social gospel was accepted, but through widespread acceptance it lost its millennial imperative to build a better kingdom here and now in the United States. Instead it turned into a benign tincture for the social education of the ministry and for the encouragement of civic committees in every congregation. In time the social gospel became absorbed in the progressive domestic morality and politics of many Protestants. It became a part of

50. Margaret Clark, *Health in the Mexican-American Culture, A Community Study,* Berkeley, 1959, pp. 14–52; Carey McWilliams, *North from Mexico: The Spanish-Speaking People of the United States,* Philadelphia, 1949, pp. 175–258.
51. Oscar Handlin, *The Newcomers: Negroes and Puerto Ricans in a Changing Metropolis,* Cambridge, 1959.

their concern for the decent treatment of women and children, a clean, healthy environment, good schools, effective charity, a humane settlement of the conflicts between capital and labor, even for a sympathetic attitude toward pacifism.

The weakness of these trends lay in the marginal position of working-class and lower-class participation. Protestantism, the congregation of the faithful gathered to hear the Word, has always been the prisoner of its adherents. The well-to-do in each congregation have always specified the location of the church, decisively influenced the selection and tenure of ministers, upheld the missions, and controlled the addition of new programs, whether for Sunday schools or the introduction of a basketball team. The almost complete suburbanization of the white middle class and upper middle class after 1920 quickened the momentum of these trends, which had been in motion since 1870. Protestantism has been carried on to the suburbs; even the wealthy fashionable downtown churches, which for years had attracted a metropolitan following, have been faltering.

It has been estimated that for the past century the churches of every major Protestant denomination have moved once a generation to follow their congregations. Now situated as they are in all-residential suburbs without the stress of offices and factories, without blacks, browns, or the poor, is it any wonder that the concerns of modern Protestant churches have become the concerns of the middle class, the upper class, and the working class which aspires to middle-class ways? The lower class and the working class have been left to fall back on their own devices.[52] Their patterns are more secular and familial, less preoccupied with middle-class voluntary organizations, but in the past fifty years an old style of evangelical Protestantism has flourished among them. The Bible store front and the organized churches of Jehovah's Witnesses, Nazarenes, and the Holiness groups have multiplied, but neither by membership nor by influence can these class variants yet be called alternatives to the dominant suburban trend of middle-class modern Protestantism.[53] Dwelling in the suburbs, the place of homes and domestic issues, Protestantism has become the medium for the concerns of the family as a residential unit. The settlement house of the social-gospel era, which had been so essential to an earlier generation's discovery of the city, died out

52. Gibson Winter, *The Suburban Captivity of the Churches*, Garden City, 1961, pp. 39–76.
53. Demerath, *Social Class in American Protestantism*, pp. 4, 198–99.

or became an anachronism in both the aging core city and in the suburbs.[54] Now, as continued black migration threatened the all-white suburb and its schools, civil-rights issues polarized Protestant congregations. As repeated wars threatened the children of the suburbs with military service peace movements sprang up, and the isolated domesticity of the suburban wife gave rise to a new set of moral imperatives in the women's liberation movement. Thus modern moral polarities overlay the basic middle-class preoccupation with home, children, safety, and order.

Catholicism had reached a similar destination by the 1950s though it had traveled a different path. Conflicts with recent immigrants continued to divide the Church until the emergence of a large second and third generation of Poles and Italians after World War II indicated that the largest immigrant groups had grown used to the ways of American Catholicism. The first-generation Poles, dependent on their parish church as the center of community life, fought for independence from territorial parishes dominated by the Irish, and indeed many Poles left the Church to found a separate national church. The southern Italians, whose males were quite unaccustomed to support the established Catholic Church in their home country, and the Italian immigrants from the former Papal States, who were strongly anticlerical, failed to follow the Irish and Poles in active parish building. Rather they remained hostile to and ill-served by the Irish-dominated Church. Only the passing of time and the Americanization of Italian Catholicism in the second and third generations brought ultimate accommodation and harmony.[55]

With ethnic conflicts quieting with each year after 1920, an international reaction within the Catholic Church itself hastened the diversion of the American branch from its working-class connections. The liberal Irish bishops of the late nineteenth century were men who spoke in behalf of the working class or who protected outspoken priests who did, but they were also interested in centralizing U.S. Church politics and were proponents of a vigorous national Church with definite self-determination vis-à-vis Rome. These same men had been frequently in conflict with new immigrants because of their insistence on episcopal power, their questioning of the credentials of immigrant priests, their

---

54. Studs Terkel, *Division Street: America*, New York, 1967, pp. 29–38.
55. Richard A. Varbero, "Immigrant Culture and Urban Forms, Philadelphia's South Italians in the 1920's," Temple University Conference on the History of the Peoples of Philadelphia, April 2, 1971; William I. Thomas and Florian Znaniecki, *The Polish Peasant in Europe and America*, New York, 1927, II, pp. 1523–49.

hostility to new national parishes, and their lack of sympathy for variant styles and practices of Catholicism. Yet as vigorous Americanizers and as representatives of a large urban working class—as well as of a growing middle class—they participated enthusiastically in American nationalism. They energetically supported World War I with public appearances, ministry to the troops, and charity campaigns. At the end of the war the National Catholic War Council issued a platform for the future that endorsed all the progressive notions of the day, and indeed the statement would have done credit to the American Federation of Labor. Unions, cooperatives, public housing, everything short of socialism was recommended.[56]

Yet this working-class nationalism was the legacy of a dying generation, and its leaders passed away in the teens and twenties. They had been socially too liberal for the Papacy and too demanding of autonomy for the American Church. So fearful of this liberal nationalism had the Papacy become that only in 1908 did America cease to be directed by the Curia's Congregation of Propaganda as a missionary land. In 1921 the National Catholic Welfare Council was all but abolished because it seemed a dangerous structure and, as a national body of mixed lay and clerical affiliates, posed a potential threat to the strict hierarchical organization of the Church.[57]

The wave of conservatism that swept over the world after World War I swept with it the Catholic Church and its American clergy. Within the Church, reaction took the form of increasing repression of "modernism," by which was meant the irregular views and practices spontaneously springing up throughout the modern Catholic world. The conservative hoped to suppress cultural variations in the regulation of marriage, customs among the religious orders, governance of the Church, and in theological writing and speculation. Bishops were encouraged to master and enforce the Canon Law of 1917, which itself fostered a narrow clerical legalism. It provided for the strict seminary training of priests and active censorship of books and magazines, and required clergy who wished to speak in public or write for general audiences to do so only with episcopal permission. Furthermore, it demanded that the laity send their children to parochial schools and that noncomplying parents be disciplined by their bishops. Finally, both clergy and laymen were making popular a new style of worship—fre-

---

56. McAvoy, *History of the Catholic Church*, p. 375.
57. Ibid., pp. 454–56.

quent attendance at church accompanied by a regular reception of the sacraments—and a campaign was launched for the daily receiving of Communion.[58]

The long-term consequence of this insistence on orthodoxy and devotionalism was to hasten the removal of American Catholicism from working-class and lower-class contact and sympathy. The new imperative for parochial education implied that it would join the prevailing trend toward the establishment of separate high schools, so that the expansion of the parochial system meant not only additional elementary schools but a large secondary network also. During the twenties an enormous program of school building was launched and attendance increased dramatically, but the new parish schools could never handle more than a fraction of the poor of the mill town and metropolis. The new schools, like the old, were vehicles for the middle class and for working-class aspirants to the middle class just as much as the public educational system was, and indeed when prosperous Catholics went to the suburbs so too did the new schools.[59]

Recent studies say that the assimilation of Catholic immigrants is complete as a major social event and that Catholics are now as fully dispersed among the class positions of the nation as the members of any other group.[60] In the cities this distribution among the units of the national class structure has resulted in vitality in the suburbs but decay in the central city, where the inner-city territorial and national parishes and schools have lost attendance and support. Currently lay opinion is exerting pressure for the closing of inner-city churches and parochial schools, which serve few whites and many blacks and are costly to maintain. The working-class Catholic family is having difficulty in supporting the more expensive and ambitious parochial schools in its neighborhood, while the middle class and upper middle class urge the creation of country day schools and a network of elite Catholic schools and colleges to match the private educational system of the well-to-do

58. Ibid., pp. 390–94.
59. Andrew M. Greeley and Peter H. Rossi, *The Education of Catholic Americans,* Chicago, 1966, pp. 199–221; Andrew M. Greeley, *From Backwater to Mainstream, A Profile of Catholic Higher Education,* New York, 1969, pp. 85–98.
60. Edward O. Laumann, "The Social Structure of Religious and Ethnoreligious Groups in a Metropolitan Community: A Smallest Space Analysis," *American Sociological Review,* 34 (April 1969), 186; Stephan Thernstrom, "Religion and Occupational Mobility in Boston, 1880–1963," in Robert W. Fogel, ed., *Quantitative Methods of Historical Analysis,* Princeton University Press, forthcoming.

Protestants. At the same time, the management of colleges, schools, and hospitals has made the administration of the dioceses themselves so elaborate that many more clergy are working in administration today than fifty years ago. Here again it is the wealthy or middle-class layman who assists on episcopal boards and committees and dominates the post–Vatican Council II parish councils.[61] For these reasons, an international movement for strict orthodoxy found its American expression in the context of suburbanization and middle-class dominance. The Catholic Church has always thought of itself as an institution of families and a supporter of family life, but the economic and social progress of its constituency has made it, like the Protestant churches, an institution of middle-class families.[62]

The signal success of Jewish immigrants and their children meant the rapid *embourgeoisment* of this denominational group. No longer can the American Jew be characterized as a socialist, a union organizer, and an activist in working-class politics; the liberal charitable trend of German-based Reform Judaism has become the model. Urban and industrial conditions have eroded or destroyed Orthodox practices for most Jews, and a range of adaptations from Conservatism to Reform now obtain. There is some evidence that both modes are receiving an increasingly associational, as opposed to the older kinship, emphasis and that the structure of suburban Judaism is becoming more and more similar to the Protestant style, with the congregational services as the core social institution. It has long been the custom of Jewish families to cluster in the metropolitan region more than other denominational groups, and their related tendency to turn to their fellow Jews for most of their friendships has fostered the expansion of Jewish community institutions.[63] No other group in the American city sponsors so wide a range of charitable institutions. No group is more domesticated, more centered on the care and nurture of family life. What effect the continuing demands of Israel will have upon American Judaism is still

61. W. Lloyd Warner, et al., *The Emergent American Society,* I, *Large Scale Organizations,* New Haven, 1969, pp. 442–62; *New York Times,* March 19, 1972, Section E, p. 7.

62. A recent study of the relationships between the Catholic hierarchy and Mexican Americans in the Southwest reveals a practice of missionary work which reflects the general social gospel approach of American Christianity. Grebler, et al., *Mexican-American People,* pp. 443–79.

63. Laumann, "Social Structure of Religious Groups," 182–97; Lenski, *Religious Factor,* pp. 76–79; Warner, *Emergent American Society,* I, pp. 462–83.

unclear. What is clear, however, is that in two or three generations a diverse and fragmented conglomeration of German and Eastern European Jewish peasants, artisans, and city dwellers has been transformed into a unified, predominantly middle-class cultural group.

The persecution of Negroes and the impoverishment of the black community make it impossible for black Protestantism to follow the orientations of the white middle class.[64] The continued hostility of the white world has meant that black Protestantism has always spoken for a people as well as for congregations of the faithful. The periodic surges of black nationalism during the twenties and the sixties served to exalt the racial component in black religion. Church leadership of and participation in the civil-rights movement was an unprecedented development for modern Christianity. Denied participation in the general social rewards of the modern city, the culture of black Protestantism has never been suburbanized, and its contemporary attitudes differ more widely from white religious cultures than the white ones differ among themselves.

Thus during the past fifty years the slackening of foreign migration and the changes in urban religions have turned our ethnic history into the history of classes and religions. Recent sociological studies have demonstrated that these broad allegiances function both as a common national culture and as a set of variations on the theme of family life. The statistics of each study show two tendencies. The fact that the tables report heavy percentages of white Protestants, white Catholics, white Jews, and black Protestants following similar patterns and sharing common beliefs gives the historian evidence of the emergence of a national culture. The fact that the same tables also show differences in the percentages, differences of a range from 46 to 75 percent, also tells the historian of the presence of important socioreligious habits.

The common denominators in the habits and points of view of Americans of all religious loyalties are impressive. The basic custom is commitment to familialism. Although the commitment to and interaction with kin varies somewhat by class and religious identification, the family invariably remains the first object of loyalty. The common national manifestation of this loyalty is the visiting of relatives; many see at least one relative once a week, many more at least stay in touch

---

64. Kenneth B. Clark, *Dark Ghetto, Dilemmas of Social Power,* New York, 1965, pp. 171–86; Joseph R. Passonneau and Richard S. Wurman, *Urban Atlas: Twenty American Cities,* Cambridge, 1966, maps of St. Louis churches 1910–60.

with kin.[65] Such familial orientation, even in the face of a high degree of intracity and intercity mobility, must be recognized as a crucial dimension in the analysis of the modern city and in designs for its future. Here in familialism lie the roots of some of the urban dichotomies—well-ordered neighborhoods and acres of neglect, the weakness of organizational power in working-class and lower-class neighborhoods and the difficulties of bringing tenants together for purposes of defense. Perhaps too the failure of police protection and the confused state of public education can be ascribed to familialism and the lack of meaningful local community life. The modern city family has become a tiny island of escape in a sea of fragmented and bureaucratized individuals.

Next in importance after relations with kin, but on a lower scale of frequency and intensity, comes the universal predilection to visit with neighbors. Again there are variations according to class and denominational identifications, but "neighboring" is a basic urban American style among all classes. (It is severely constrained, however, when families must live in apartment houses.)[66] In the past as at the present moment, it has strengthened localism and local institutions, but it has also proved to be a weak and uncertain reed for any decentralized management of the city, whether at the hands of early twentieth-century Midwestern Progressives or today's New York City reformers.

Relics of historical cultural conflicts still persist. Whites, solidly racist, are more interested in avoiding the integration of their residential blocks than in keeping Negroes out of their children's schools.[67] Of the four large socioreligious groups, white Protestants tend to be most critical of the others.[68] These habits of thought are pallid remnants of the old nativist tenet that the United States was and ought to be a Protestant country and that Protestantism was *the* American culture. A number of events have stopped the historic mills of Catholic-Protestant conflict and difference. The white Protestant group's attempt to force its own liquor laws upon the nation failed with Prohibition, and much of the aggressiveness of Protestantism lost its legitimacy in that failure. Long-standing conflicts over the status of women, issues that reached back

65. Bert N. Adams, *Kinship in an Urban Setting,* Chicago, 1968, pp. 163–75; Herbert J. Gans, *The Levittowners,* New York, 1967, pp. 201–206; Bennett M. Berger, *Working-Class Suburb,* Berkeley, 1968, pp. 64–73.

66. Edward O. Laumann, *Prestige and Association in an Urban Community,* Indianapolis, 1966, p. 72.

67. Lenski, *Religious Factor,* pp. 71–73; Norman M. Bradburn, et al., *Side by Side, Integrated Neighborhoods in America,* Chicago, 1971.

68. Lenski, pp. 63–64.

even to the Abolitionist era, have died down with the suburbanization of
the Catholic housewife and her participation in the peculiar freedoms
and constraints of this modern environment. Finally, Catholics and
white Protestants have been intermarrying at a steady and substantial
rate.[69]

There is an emphasis on churchgoing among all denominational
groups. Church attendance rises with class status and according to the
length of time the individual has lived in America, and the third generation goes to church or temple more often than the first or second.
Moreover, there is a core of belief that all Christians share. Modern
surveys show that American churchgoers accept most of the proposi-
tions of a Christianity which says that God watches over us like a
Heavenly Father; He answers prayers; He expects weekly worship. Most
of them also believe that Jesus was God's only son and have faith in the
rewards and punishments of a life after death. Such a consensus has
preserved Protestant congregationalism in the midst of competition and
change, and it has enabled the Catholic Church to bury ethnic differences. Such a consensus has gained strength from the urban churches'
decades of stressing the familial and orthodox aspects of Christianity in
preference to encouraging devotional enthusiasms and religious particularism.[70]

Beyond this evidence of an unfolding national cultural consensus,
the studies show the presence of important differences by class and
differences by religious identification. The class segregation of the
modern city is mirrored in the surveys' reports of variations in the class
attitudes within religious groups. They testify to the correspondence of
the structure of the city and its culture. At the same time, religious
identification is shown to be an important and continuing quality of
urban life.

Few members of any of the four socioreligious groups were heedless
of kin or neighbor, but their loyalties did tend to make some difference.
For example, along the axis of cultural issues that runs from participation in associational life as against communal life, most Protestants were
more interested in voluntary organizations and neighborhood—that is,
they were more associational—than Catholics, who were more concerned with kin. Jews did even more visiting with relatives, but were less
aware of their neighbors than Catholics. This is not to say that urban

69. Lenski, pp. 38–39, 54–55.
70. Lenski, pp. 56–57.

Protestants are nonfamilial and that Catholics and Jews are familial; the reports indicate only variations in central tendencies. The surveys also reveal differences by class, and participation in associational life rises in all denominations as class position rises. The well-to-do are the organization men in America. Perhaps this report reflects the fact that the urban working class has lost its early nineteenth-century fondness for clubs and associations as work has become bureaucratized and neighborhood life has been broken up.[71]

To the extent that these variations by denomination and class have been tabulated, they throw considerable light on the everyday problems that dominate our segregated metropolises. In local elections, in black-white confrontations, in planning-board and zoning hearings, in P.T.A. meetings and school elections, the differences among the religious groups are tremendously important. The spectrum of views that they bring to commonplace problems and the variations in popular attitudes common to certain neighborhood or suburban populations are the elements that carry elections and determine administrative decisions. For example, white Protestants are more concerned with controlling "sin" than are Catholics or Jews or black Protestants. As for divorce, Negro Protestants are largely unconcerned, having fewer among them who oppose it than the white Protestants do, but Catholic communicants are opposed to it. All Christian denominational groups tend to oppose keeping stores open on Sundays. The patchwork of such variations affects many areas: sex education in the schools, licensing of bars and package stores, and the night and Sunday hours of great suburban shopping centers. Yet still another cultural position has its surprises: non-churchgoers of whatever religious orientation are quite uninterested in any of these issues! Such surveys suggest that our urban culture is a consensus closely woven from class and religious threads.[72]

A fascinating section of the studies is given over to information about attitudes in respect to personal autonomy as opposed to discipline. Even simple questions about home and children uncover issues that can vex local politics and education and that are symptomatic of the current state of the classes.

First, all classes and religious groups restrict the size of their families, and the variations from large to small numbers of children follow the cultural groups from black Protestant to white Catholic, then

71. Lenski, pp. 216–18, 243–47.
72. Lenski, pp. 193–98.

white Protestant, and finally Jewish. The differences, even in the metropolises, among the groups are not significant. Second, as to women's role in raising children, families did not vary widely in their attitudes by class, but when Catholic and Protestant mothers were asked if child rearing was "burdensome," 60 percent of the Protestant mothers but only 47 percent of the Catholic mothers replied affirmatively.[73] Perhaps here we can find in today's city a reflection of the Protestant women's liberation movement, which has been active in America since the early nineteenth century. Perhaps too this greater dissatisfaction of Protestant families with the child-rearing role encourages club and associational activity.

Such basic behavioral attitudes expand into local issues such as police protection and education. When city dwellers were asked whether intellectual autonomy or obedience was more to be desired in school-children, religious loyalties were identifiable. Jews and the Protestants, white and black, tended to put a higher value on intellectual autonomy than did Catholics. But the families' class status had even stronger repercussions. The upper class and the middle-class Jews, Protestants, and Catholics were all decidedly in favor of intellectual autonomy for their children, but the working class and lower class attached far greater importance to obedience. In the related issue of the enforcement of discipline, few white Protestants favored physical punishment, preferring the use of guilt or shame. Among the working classes—both white Catholic and black Protestant—there was division on the issue, although many of them favored the use of physical punishment as a means of controlling ten-year-olds in school.[74] Here one can detect echoes of both religious and demographic history. The Catholic repression of the years from World War I to the 1950s stressed authority, discipline, and orthodoxy. At the same time such an approach to the world was rein-forced by the fact that there were a disproportionate number of working-class families in urban Catholic schools. The similarity of black Protes-tant and white Catholic attitudes here seems to reflect the Negro's disadvantaged position in the general society.

The exploration of American attitudes toward such issues as child rearing and education holds some promise of linking our past history to the everyday cultural and political confrontations that trouble our neigh-borhoods and suburbs. Even this pilot report, from a Detroit survey,

73. Lenski, pp. 221, 235–39.
74. Lenski, pp. 221–26, 232–35.

shows that the family, school, and neighborhood betray the effects of a sense of powerlessness on the part of the working class and lower class. Should we wonder that class lines are followed more often than those of the religions? After all, the working class and lower class are the ones whose members have the least freedom in today's city. They are subject to bureaucratic control by unions, factories, and offices; their hours are the most strictly regulated and their tasks the most standardized; they are the ones who bring home the smallest or most variable paycheck with which to exercise the personal freedoms of leisure.[75] Finally, they are the ones who live in the most crowded districts, walk the most dangerous streets, deal with a mass of the most unsupervised children who attend the worst schools. It is not surprising that after fifty or a hundred years of such conditions so many working-class and lower-class Americans distrust intellectual autonomy in their children, demand obedience, and use physical punishment. Orderly behavior, not flexible self-discipline, is what has constantly been demanded of these families. Lacking personal autonomy or participation as equals in institutions which do have power, many city dwellers share a dependence on discipline and authority. They may call for more police, but they will not turn out for a P.T.A. meeting on the free classroom.

Out of such class and socioreligious differences—small variations for the most part, but representative of convictions deeply held and often the product of long history and overbearing social pressures—the American city must find strength and support. And the preconditions for abundant support for strong democratic planning are there. The history and present state of American urban culture meet three basic requirements for democratic planning: common cultural goals, a tolerable range of variation within the culture, and a process of change which could be activated to let more of those outside the culture join the mainstream.

In order for a democratic nation of giant cities to plan for the allocation of its wealth, for the control of the growth of its cities, and for the distribution of its jobs and services, its politics must be undergirded by a broad consensus on the goals to be sought. To plan means at the very least to set goals toward which sustained public projects and

75. An earlier Detroit study which divided the population according to its job security showed that modern liberal child-rearing practices appeared disproportionately among those families with safe bureaucratic jobs. Daniel R. Miller and Guy E. Swanson, *The Changing American Parent*, New York, 1958, pp. 116–44.

private enterprise can work. If regional divisions, class differences, and racial and national conflicts tear at the political fabric, then long-term agreed-upon goals cannot be set and planning must be the activity of a powerful, even dictatorial minority. In the United States such divisions do not obtain, and a social underpinning of sufficient unanimity exists so that an open democratic politics could be expected to manage the setting of goals and resolution of conflict inherent in large-scale national economic and regional planning. Broad agreement has been our cultural circumstance at least since the twenties, if not for much longer. What has been missing in the past, and is still absent, is a popular willingness to raise the demands of our cultural aspirations of everyday life to a status equal to our traditional capitalist drives for wealth and power. Until as a nation we are willing to subject our political, social, and economic institutions to these demands, the potential for democratic planning of our cultural consensus will remain untapped, and common life in the city will remain the creature of the higher priorities of capitalist competition, and now of imperialism as well.

The narrow range of diversity within our class and socioreligious cultures also holds out the promise that national planning may be teamed up with decentralized decision making, and suggests that local interpretations of goals for national well-being will not be extreme. A Washington or state-capital policy when filtered through the myriad metropolitan governments and administrative agencies will not meet such a range of conflicting local demands as to lose its coherence. We are therefore in the fortunate position of being able to contemplate democratic planning structures that will combine broad national objectives with state and local decisions so that the variety within the culture may find expression in the politics of the ward, the neighborhood, and the town.

Only in the relationships between whites and blacks does our common culture need to be challenged. As both history and today's television demonstrate, white Americans if left to themselves will oppress their black fellow citizens. The recent civil-rights movement shows that local actions supported by national political coalitions can overcome such oppression. The country will have to continue to spend its political energy and capital to discipline both public and private institutions and even to take affirmative federal action if white racism is finally to be conquered. One important reward for such an effort will be the increasing possibilities for local autonomy as the need for central bureaucratic control over racial affairs relaxes.

Finally, the very historical process by which our cultural consensus was reached reveals the mechanism for gaining a more inclusive democratic society. In years past, poor migrants from the rural United States and overseas came to the cities; and in time, either through the institutions of the inner city itself or by further migration to the suburbs, they became absorbed in the general class and socioreligious culture. For the millions who survived this process, the new culture provided a way for coping with the realities of American urban life. Yet the social pathologies of the city were never less than they are today, probably much worse, and millions of persons were disabled or destroyed by alcoholism, crime, disease, despair, desertion, and insanity. The single most important difference between the lower incidence of pathology among those who made it into membership in the city and those who did not was the difference between those families who could earn a living wage and those who could not. If every American who wanted a job could get one, and if every employed person received wages sufficient to support himself and his family or herself and her dependents, the disproportionate social pathologies of our ghettos and slums would disappear. Such a full-employment, living-wage policy would not solve all our urban problems by any means, but our history tells us that it would enable all Americans to participate in our culture as full-fledged members of the society and thereby it would build a firm foundation for both national and local democratic planning.

7

Coping with the Urban Environment

—

Public crises and private benefit;
the response of charity,
reform, and science

THE PROBLEMS OF HEALTH and housing in today's American cities are often perceived as belonging to two quite different domains. One cluster of problems relates to the fundamental inequality of our citizens and is manifested in the inability of inner-city poor whites and blacks to obtain the levels of health care and of a safe sanitary environment that were achieved by the majority of their fellow urban dwellers half a century ago. A second cluster of problems concerns the inability of more prosperous white Americans to obtain the kind of preventive care, day-to-day medical service, and supportive physical and social environments to which they should be entitled by modern medicine and modern physical planning. Because of the segregated structure of the metropolis and the class and racial politics of health and housing, the two problems are now dealt with as isolated issues. We debate welfare, clinics, public housing, and urban renewal for the inner city; we also debate voluntary insurance, aid to the medically indigent, community hospital service, group practice, the housing shortage, and improved planning and sub-division control for the suburbs. Yet because the entire metropolis or megalopolis is part of one national urban system and is dependent in most of its parts upon the workings of that system, the two clusters of problems are in fact inseparable: the failure of the health-delivery institutions to meet the acute needs of the inner-city poor is tied to the failure of the preventive services to meet the needs of the outer-city

198

majority; today's housing crisis of the slum is a product of yesterday's planning failure of the suburbs.

Although the death rate in American cities varies systematically by race and class, with the poor and the black having the shortest lives, the gap is small and would disappear as a by-product of the modernization of health and housing services as a whole. Today's problems rest in the context of a stable incidence of mortality and a widespread expectation of a long life. The difficult issues of our own time turn around the universal experiences of city dwellers as they live out a more or less common life span. The urgent agenda of both inner city and suburbs speaks to the quality of life as we all undergo generally inevitable traumas, accidents, communicable diseases, confusions, criminal assaults, and physical disabilities from birth to death. The quantity and quality of available housing is inextricably tied to well-baby, pediatric, communicable-disease, drug, and accident services for young people and their families; community planning is linked to mental-health, accident, and chronic-disease care for middle age; and the placement, design, and supply of housing are crucial ingredients of geriatric care and social services to the old. The failure of the modern city to realize its potential in these fields is as much a product of the workings of the urban system as is its failure to distribute its wealth equitably in respect to family income and full employment.

The gap in health and housing between potential and realization can be understood in two ways: in terms of class and in terms of institutions. First, the construction of housing (and therefore the available urban stock of housing) has always depended on the capital resources and rent-paying abilities of city dwellers. It has always reflected the differential distribution of income in the city, and it has been dependent upon the fashions and abilities of the upper one-third to one-half of the population. Similarly, medical services have been closely bound to patients' ability to pay, to the class ambitions of doctors, and to the philanthropic styles of the rich, so that the health of the urban population as a whole has always mirrored the class structure of the city. Second, in institutional terms our provisions for both housing and health take their basic configuration from the pre-1920 era of the industrial metropolis. The real-estate and housing industries and their regulatory monitors assumed most of their current form in response to the problems and capabilities of the old crowded metropolis. Similarly, the modes of American medicine—public-health institutions, acute-care hospitals, private doctors—arose in the late nineteenth and early twentieth centuries when such a structure suited the financial resources, scientific progress, and personnel capabilities of that era. Considering the advances in social science and medical science since 1920, one might reasonably expect that American society would have moved more rapidly away from these inherited constraints, but the painfully slow advance in these key elements of a humane environment can be attributed to the interactions between class-based financing and the power relationships of the accompanying institutions.

During America's first century of rapid urbanization, the years from 1820 to 1920, our urban environments polarized about two extremes. In the early nineteenth century the health of city dwellers depended upon the amplitude and adequacy of the traditional design of individual houses, upon the purity of family and neighborhood wells, the happenstance of open lots, and the variations in care of backyard and basement privies. Booming growth and mass migrations relentlessly pressed against this almost universal big-city environment, placing all citizens in continuous jeopardy from fire and disease. Innovations in transportation, municipal sanitary services, plumbing, heating, lighting, and to a lesser extent in the design of housing created a new environment for one-half to two-thirds of the urban population. By the 1890s the disparate trends of urban growth had become apparent. At one extreme stood the new urban world of single-family houses, row houses, two-families, and apartments, where an unprecedented part of the population enjoyed equally unprecedented security and a rapidly rising standard of living; at the other extreme stood the old big-city world of overcrowding in rooms and obsolete structures, faulty or nonexistent plumbing and heating, firetraps, fever nests, and malfunctioning integration of public and private sanitary systems. The potentials of the new environment and their unavoidable tensions with the old combined to call forth the housing practices and health programs of the industrial metropolis. The same potentials and tensions also set for our own era the basic institutional structures that still determine our housing supply, public health, and private care systems.

The safer and more wholesome urban environment sprang from a series of complementary events in transportation, public services, site planning, mechanical inventions, and home design. The succession of transportation innovations, from the introduction of horse-drawn streetcars in the 1830s to the electrification of street railways in the 1890s and the supplementing of public transit by the automobile after 1910, had a contradictory environmental effect. As possible commuting distances lengthened with each transportation advance, the supply of land expanded exponentially, thereby relieving what would otherwise have been an intolerable pressure upon land within the reach of pedestrian journeys to work.[1] The fact that fringe land around each booming city grew at a rate even more rapid than the city's population made possible a lowered density of many new residential environments in the industrial metropolis.

For housing built after about 1880 a new minimum standard prevailed. In most cities the standard manifested itself in miles upon miles of small wooden freestanding houses set back by a tiny lawn from the dirt and dust of the street, each separated from its neighbor by a narrow side yard and boasting a rear yard often as deep again as the house itself. The cumulative effect of forty years of such construction was to free the middle-class and typical working-class Americans from the dangers of alley housing, boardinghouses, and jerry-built conversions typical of the high land values of the big city of the early nineteenth century. Even in the nation's largest cities, where land costs were high and multistory housing prevailed, the opening of new land brought salutary effects. The universal two-family structures, the three-deckers of New England, and the flats of Chicago, though they crowded the land by today's standards, at least guaranteed no windowless rooms, and two exits—front and back stairs—in case of fire. Philadelphia's and Baltimore's row houses gained in amenity when builders stopped squeezing them into courts and rear alleys and began to lay them out instead in strips fronting only the main streets. The perspective of mile upon mile of houses of the industrial metropolis presents a dreary aspect to today's viewer, but in the essential ingredients of light, air, and fire safety the structures represent an important advance over the earlier practices of urban land crowding. Only in the inner-city tenements of every city, and especially in the crowded centers of New York and Boston, did the industrial metropolis's new transportation fail to improve the environment of large numbers of its citizens.[2]

1. Sam Bass Warner, Jr., *Streetcar Suburbs: The Process of Growth in Boston 1870–1900*, Cambridge, 1962, pp. 62–64.
2. Lawrence Veiller, "Housing as a Factor in Health Progress in the Past Fifty Years," in Mazyck P. Ravenel, ed., *A Half Century of Public Health*, New York, 1921, pp. 323–34; Robert W. DeForest and Lawrence Veiller, eds., *The Tenement House Problem*, I, New York, 1903, pp. 131–70.

A contrary tendency of transportation innovation controlled the inner city. The ability of electric-powered surface transportation to deliver ever more thousands of commuters to the downtown sent the price of centrally situated parcels of land skyrocketing, thereby raising the rents for close-in housing to higher and higher levels. For the poor, confined by their job-access needs to the center of the city, this effect of transportation improvement on rents proved an insurmountable barrier to their realization of the benefits of modernization. For the well-to-do a modest move uptown and the purchase of new building designs and mechanical services in the form of firewalls, fire barriers, central heating and lighting, and a full complement of sanitary equipment secured the safety of their town houses. In addition, the invention of a wholly new structure, the fire-resistant steel-frame multistory apartment house with elevators and generous light and air shafts, allowed the inner-city middle class to attain the minimum benefits of suburban environmental safety in the face of high-density urban living.[3]

Not more orderly land use alone, but light and air in conjunction with a more dependable water supply and waste disposal, made the early twentieth-century urban environment the safest form of mass habitation yet built. The mode of construction of water-supply and sewerage systems divided the responsibility between municipal capital on the one side and the individual installations of middle-class homeowners and home builders for the middle-class market on the other. For the majority of city dwellers this division of responsibility proved to be a workable partnership for the raising of living standards. Yet the unnecessary exclusion of perhaps a third of urban Americans in the 1920s from these standards may be laid to a lack of public attention to the inevitable class shortcomings that would spring from such a division.

The mode of construction of waterworks and sewerage in the United States arose out of the traditions and exigencies of the mid-nineteenth-century city. Sheer numbers, onrushing growth, and the crowding of land broke down the earlier small-town checks against fire and communicable disease. In every American city devastating fires swept whole blocks of valuable downtown districts. The Chicago Fire of 1871 was

---

3. Sigfried Giedion, *Space, Time and Architecture*, Cambridge, 1941, pp. 298–303; Reyner Banham, *The Architecture of the Well-Tempered Environment*, Chicago, 1969, pp. 29–70; John A. Kouwenhoven, *The Columbia Historical Portrait of New York*, Garden City, 1953, p. 444; Nathan Silver, *Lost New York*, Boston, 1967, pp. 138–43.

but the most celebrated of a half century of conflagrations.[4] Contaminated wells, overused and ill-tended privies, overcrowded buildings and rooms, and shiploads of undernourished and sick immigrants simultaneously brought epidemic waves of cholera, typhus, and yellow fever which swept the downtown districts of the poor, seeped into hotels and public places, and frightened all classes of city dwellers. Those who could afford to commute or leave their jobs fled the city during periodic epidemics, and the well-to-do adopted the habit of spending summers in distant suburbs in order to escape the season of greatest danger. Although public toleration for fire and disease stood at a much higher threshold in 1840 than in 1920, the desire to mitigate these trials found daily reinforcement in the sheer lack of reasonably clear water in many parts of the city. Water peddlers' wagons moved through the streets of New York selling spring water to housewives so they could brew a palatable pot of tea or coffee. A clouded and murky pail was often the best that a backyard well or neighborhood pump could offer for the family washing. By the 1840s the merchants' fear of fires and the desire for household convenience reached a pitch that overcame the universal distaste for taxes and heavy public expense.[5]

During the 1840s and 1850s the major cities of the nation built reservoirs, aqueducts, and pumping stations, and laid water mains through almost every street. Yet no sooner had these giant municipal undertakings been completed than the abundance of water clogged the haphazard neighborhood sewers and flooded the streets, alleys, and backyards of the city. And the threat of epidemics did not disappear. According to contemporary theory, stagnant water, putrefaction, and bad odors were the breeders and carriers of disease. Repeated statistical investigations by doctors and laymen established an incontrovertible correlation between the incidence of infection and inadequate sanitation. Thus from the 1850s to the 1870s cities shouldered the heavy burden of constructing their initial unified sewer systems to match the waterworks of the previous decades.[6]

    4. Paul M. Angle and Mary Frances Rhymer, *The Great Chicago Fire*, Chicago, 1971.
    5. Nelson M. Blake, *Water for the Cities*, Syracuse, 1956, pp. 100–120; Bayrd Still, *Mirror for Gotham*, New York, 1956, pp. 97, 103–04.
    6. John Duffy, *A History of Public Health in New York City, 1625–1866*, New York, 1968, pp. 408–18; John Henry Rauch, "The Sanitary Problem of Chicago, Past and Present," and Ellis S. Chesbrough, "The Drainage and Sewerage of Chicago," American Public Health Association, *Public Health Reports and Papers, 1877–1878*, 4 (Cambridge, 1880), 3–17.

Both halves of the sanitary system again rested upon the divided responsibility of public and private effort. The division of labor seemed perfectly natural to the age. It minimized public costs, especially when complete systems had to be constructed from scratch, and at the same time it continued the long-standing tradition by which each property owner shouldered the responsibility for the improvement of his own buildings. The public water effort stopped with the laying of water mains in the streets and placing of hydrants from which householders could draw water and to which fire pumps could be attached. Any abutter who wished to tap the main in the street for service to his house, store, or factory could do so, but he had to bear the expense of the connection as well as to pay for his own plumbing and fixtures. Similarly, the sewer ran underground through the street, available to those who chose to make a direct connection to it.[7]

The immediate consequence of this division of labor and responsibility was to hobble the effectiveness of the sanitary system. Homeowners and landlords whose tenants could afford a moderate increase in rents rapidly installed the water tap at the kitchen sink and the flush toilet, the essentials of the new environmental safety. Bathtubs, long considered a luxury, gained popularity more slowly.[8] At the growing fringe of the city the financial partnership of public and private effort placed even more expense on the individual household. Here costs were allocated according to the traditions of beneficial assessment—that is, owners of land abutting a street were charged for a share of any public improvement that raised the value of their land. In opening up new land, the purchaser of each lot had to pay for all or some very substantial fraction of the costs of laying of the water mains and sewers, as well as for the house connections and equipment. The effect was to both raise the amenity level and the costs of new construction beyond pre-plumbing levels. For its part the city waterworks and later metropolitan water and sewer boards endeavored to keep up with suburban demand by building new (and rebuilding old) water mains, pumping stations, and trunk-line sewers.[9] It was a costly race in pursuit of new development, and some

7. Donald G. Hagman, *Urban Planning and Land Development Control Law,* St. Paul, 1971, pp. 358–60.

8. Gordon Atkins, *Health, Housing, and Poverty in New York City, 1865–1898,* Ann Arbor, 1947, pp. 110–11; Blake, *Water for the Cities,* pp. 270–71.

9. Blake, *Water for the Cities,* pp. 265–81; Roger David Simon, "The Expansion of an Industrial City. Milwaukee 1880–1910," Ph.D. Thesis, University of Wisconsin, 1971, pp. 109–18.

modern authors who have reviewed the pricing of water contend that the total effect was to encourage not only suburbanization but also the commercial and industrial waste of water.[10]

Whatever the merits of alternative pricing schedules might be, there can be no doubt about the long-term environmental effects of the municipal-private partnership. By 1920 the middle class both within the city and in the suburbs had attained a newly safe and salubrious environment, while the working-class families who inherited old middle-class neighborhoods, or rented newly constructed multifamily housing of their own, reaped the same benefit. The poorest third of the population, however, was left out or lagged badly behind, suffering either from the complete absence of the new facilities in their homes or from limited plumbing facilities used by too many people.[11] The water rates could easily have been used to install and maintain the necessary faucets and toilets, thereby overcoming some of the worst effects of the unequal distribution of personal income in the society. The public costs would have been relatively slight and the gains in health substantial. All that was lacking was the popular willingness to make available to all the minimum standards of decent middle-class and working-class life.

Because the lower-income half of American urban families had to find their housing in the structures vacated by the upper half, the new environment of the 1880–1920 years is the old environment of today's cities. These former growth rings are now the gray areas of today's metropolis—the Brooklyns and Bronxes of New York, the West and South Sides of Chicago, the East Sides and Hamtramcks of Detroit.[12] The weaknesses of a previous style of environmental progress have ripened into contemporary problems. It therefore repays us to identify the inadequacies of the past so that we will not repeat the same behavior.

The most serious failures of the 1880–1920 environment stemmed from faulty land practices. The structures themselves now suffer from inevitable obsolescence and aging, but many could be brought up to

10. Jack Hirshleifer, James C. DeHaven, and Jerome W. Milliman, *Water Supply, Economics, Technology, and Policy,* Chicago, 1960, pp. 107–13.
11. The first national housing census, taken in 1940, revealed the slow and imperfect progress of standard sanitary equipment. In Los Angeles County 13 percent of the dwelling units lacked private baths or had plumbing in need of major repair, in Chicago it was 25 percent, in New York 16 percent. U.S. Bureau of the Census, *Sixteenth Census: 1940, Housing,* I, *Data for Small Areas,* Pt. 1, Washington, 1943, pp. 71, 146, 366.
12. Bernard J. Frieden, *The Future of Old Neighborhoods,* Cambridge, 1964.

current acceptance by sustained national prosperity and a steady attention by homeowners and municipalities. In the boom after World War II
an extraordinary modernization of American housing went forward, and
so it could again.[13] The social and economic consequences of bad land
planning, however, confront today's householder and public official with
extremely costly and painful choices.

The ugliness of these old areas stems directly from the habitual land
crowding of the past and from its use of uniform grid streets and narrow
rectangular lots. Yesterday's developer, like today's, sought his profit by
putting together a land-house package in which modish ornament and
late-model fixtures were combined with a generous house size. The
structure conforming so nicely to fashion was the sales item, and the
land beneath it was skimped so that the total price could be held down
and the lot-house package marketed to as wide a custom as possible.
Actually there was much good sense in this strategy. Buyers could easily
compare one standardized house with another, and the developer could
save little on his houses by alternative designs or by cutting corners in
construction. On the other hand, much could be gained by the developer
who shopped in the metropolitan market for land. Land always ranged
widely in price, in accordance with numerous variables, so that the
developer who took his profit by marking up the land in the lot-house
package rather than by alienating the buyer by radical alterations in the
structure enriched himself, while he simultaneously catered to a mass
middle-income market.[14]

The consequences of this strategy in private development have been
an array of relatively generous structures and pinched and inflexible
land divisions. From such practices came the handkerchief front lawns,
dark and narrow side yards, garage-lined alleys, solid blocks without
parks or playgrounds, and the apartment-walled streets that are common
to all our cities. In their day such areas were to achieve aesthetic success
through the softening of awkward structures by means of trees planted
between sidewalk and street and the visual merging of one tiny lawn with
its neighbor. Although each lot might be small, the overall effect of the

13. Bernard J. Frieden, "Housing and National Urban Goals," in James Q.
Wilson, ed., *The Metropolitan Enigma,* Cambridge, 1968, pp. 174–96.

14. Robert Whitten and Thomas Adams, *Neighborhoods of Small Houses,*
Cambridge, 1931, pp. 38–55, 70–78; Harland Bartholomew, *Urban Land Uses,*
Cambridge, 1932, pp. 21–69; President's Conference on Home Building and Home
Ownership, John M. Gries and James Ford, eds., *Planning for Residential Districts,*
I, Washington, 1932, pp. 108–110.

block would be the relief of repeated buildings by continuous bands of green. Moreover, land covenants and later zoning ordinances against particular uses were designed to protect the residential grids from the encroachment of commerce and industry by confining these activities to a corner store, strips along the main thoroughfare, or bands on each side of railroad tracks.

Over time such expectations and achievements have been severely eroded by the coming of the automobile and also by the inherent rigidity of the social and economic requirements of the land plan. These grids were not designs for future growth and inevitable change; they were static layouts, and this in a country with a long history of racing urban transformation. Sheer crowding of the streets and yards by automobiles since World War II has destroyed the trees, hedges, and lawns, and since side and rear yards were small (or nonexistent on apartment blocks) cluster parking could not be introduced except by tearing down some houses and apartments. With the coming of the automobile the old residential areas of American cities have irrevocably lost their earlier pleasant qualities.

Such crowded and unwalled land presupposed adequate incomes and a neighborhood consensus for the private maintenance of what were in function the public amenities of the block. Children had continually to be restrained; lawns, hedges, and trees tended and replanted; janitors, tenants, and homeowners had to be fussy about trash; home businesses and car repairs had to be excluded; and the city had to be vigilant in its cleaning, policing, and planting if the fragile green strips were to be preserved. Declining incomes of old people, lowered wealth of successors to the first settlers, crowding by the poor, small businesses, multiple occupancy, multiplication of automobiles, loss of political status at City Hall, and impoverishment of municipal governments made such a demanding neighborhood performance impossible of perpetuation. High walls and enclosed gardens and courtyards in the European manner would have enabled American residential neighborhoods to be used more comfortably by people of varying incomes and ways of life, but to modernize our inherited gray areas in such patterns and also to make room for automobiles would require a heavy investment, to say nothing of tearing down structures to make parking places. All in all, such modernization will demand an investment in landscape construction which far exceeds that allotted to our common open urban and suburban styles.

Residential areas are not alone in suffering from the real-estate practices of the past. The developer's goal of selling every last lot meant that commercial and industrial strips were cut up and filled without regard for a reserve of space needed for the future. Today narrow strips of stores laid out to serve pedestrian and streetcar traffic cannot be readily adapted to automobile traffic. No land was set aside for commercial and industrial expansion, so that firms that prosper in old sections of the metropolis must move, much to the detriment of the local economy, to find adequate space. The inner city and gray areas thus become, by a kind of anti-Darwinian selection, the sites of the old-fashioned and least successful enterprises.[15]

Finally, the new environment of 1880–1920 was more a machine for social mobility than a model for urban communities. The sociability of Americans, especially housewives and their children, did create friendly neighborhoods within the ever-expanding grids of streets and houses, but these important interactions took place despite, not because of, the land plans. The shopping strips, scattered churches and schools, and grid streets did not focus the paths of neighboring and daily errands in a way that made it possible for groups of people living within the same few blocks to know or recognize each other. This absence of widespread acquaintanceship caused by disparate daily paths has hindered the informal policing of old urban and suburban neighborhoods. Such sociability networks as did establish themselves were hardly a match for the contrary impulse toward anonymity which American mobility patterns foster. We use housing as an expression of family status and affluence, to move out when we move up, or to shift houses in a restless search for better jobs. The inevitable consequence of these habits has been very high levels of neighborhood turnover, with all the social stresses and threats to stable property maintenance and values that such behavior entails.[16]

15. Edgar M. Hoover and Raymond Vernon, *Anatomy of a Metropolis,* Cambridge, 1959, pp. 45–57; Norton E. Long, "The City as a Reservation," *Public Interest* (Fall 1971), 22–38.

16. The anonymity and irresponsibility of life in most city neighborhoods lay at the heart of Jane Jacobs's well-justified but misdirected attack on recent inner-city rebuilding programs, *The Death and Life of Great American Cities,* New York, 1961, pp. 29–88; yet this social pattern seems to be the product of a very long-standing habit of Americans of moving frequently from neighborhood to neighborhood and city to city; see Stephan Thernstrom and Peter R. Knights, "Men in Motion: Some Data and Speculation about Urban Population Mobility in Nineteenth-Century America," *Journal of Interdisciplinary History,* 1 (Autumn 1970), 7–35.

The instability of residential property, the customary failure of builders to lay out or maintain a gardenlike neighborhood, and the universal lack of community solidarity led some wealthy nineteenth- and twentieth-century Americans to experiment with communities planned to overcome these failings and to protect suburbs from the usual processes of urban growth. The earliest experiment, Llewellyn Park, New Jersey (1853–69), had a single-gated entrance which opened to a sinuous ribbon of streets laid out along the contours of a hilly site. Four hundred acres were subdivided into one-acre sites abutting an interior fifty-acre park. The park was to be controlled and maintained by the homeowners as common land. Thus the enjoyment of a country gentleman's park in the then-popular romantic style became possible for several hundred families, each of whom was responsible individually for the upkeep of only one acre.[17] A similar design for sixteen hundred acres in suburban Chicago was laid out by New York City's Central Park designers, Frederick L. Olmsted and Calvert Vaux, in 1868–69. Here an entire residential community was contemplated. The commuters' railroad station and the town stores served as the community center, while curved streets sunk below the grade of the house lots, reserved parkland, and subtle alterations in the Des Plaines River created the garden effect. In this case the subdivision—Riverside, Illinois—constituted a single political unit, so that the regular political machinery of local government could be employed for the maintenance of public spaces and for the policing of the subsequent development of the town.[18]

The enthusiasm for golf, which seized the rich in the late 1880s, offered new devices for community planning of wealthy subdivisions. The golf club with its expensive lawns and plantings could serve as a park in its own right and also as a barrier to later encroachment by smaller houses and apartments. It could in addition serve as a powerful mechanism for controlling the social unity of the area, and with such merits the golf club became the most widespread tool of suburban community design in the American metropolis. Its failings of course lay in the substitution of private club for public community and in the extreme class, race, and ethnic segregation it inevitably imposed.[19]

17. Christopher Tunnard, *The City of Man,* New York, 1953, pp. 183–202.

18. Julius Gy. Fabos et al., *Frederick Law Olmsted, Sr., Founder of Landscape Architecture in America,* Amherst, 1968, pp. 47–55.

19. Foster R. Dulles, *America Learns to Play: A History of Popular Recreation in America 1607–1940,* New York, 1940, pp. 241–43; Allen Backler, "The Location

The largest and most successful of all these upper-income residential communities has been the Country Club District of Kansas City, begun in 1905. One firm has since continued to develop a succession of subdivisions that fan out from the axes of two main streets that join at a shopping center. An extensive list of covenants between the developer and the purchaser—including for many years covenants against black purchase—and active homeowners' associations have been used to control the siting of the houses and the type of structure built and to maintain the public services of the streets and district.[20]

In 1911 the Russell Sage Foundation attempted to demonstrate in its Forest Hills, Long Island, project that these examples of design of suburban communities for the wealthy could be adapted for middle-income housing. The experiment, taking place within the municipal boundaries of New York City, attracted a great deal of attention and was a considerable success in the field of design, but it also conclusively proved that the conventional subdivision was more profitable. The lesson Forest Hills taught the infant city-planning profession was that the community planning features of curvilinear streets, cul-de-sacs, playgrounds, parks, and unified shopping centers would be adopted by subdividers only if local government regulations required them. This lesson has been well learned, and much of the superiority of post-1920 suburban subdivisions over their predecessors comes from the imposition of such rules for land platting by professional planners employed by the local governments of the American metropolis.[21]

In particular the neighborhood unit scheme, derived from nineteenth-century planned community experiments and advocated by Russell Sage Foundation executive Clarence Perry, proved a flexible device. The neighborhood unit idea, modeled in part at Forest Hills, was an institutional and traffic design program for promoting the social organization of new suburbs. Each neighborhood was to be defined by one primary school, situated in a central park. The borders of the neighborhood were to be set off by main traffic arteries. In this way only neighborhood-serving and local residents' traffic would move through the area, while

---

and Distribution of Residential Areas: The Elite of Detroit, A Case Study," Ph.D. Thesis, University of Michigan, 1971, Ch. VI.

20. U.S. National Resources Committee, *Urban Planning and Land Policies* (*Supplementary Report of the Urbanism Committee,* II), Washington, 1939, pp. 83–85.

21. National Resources Committee, *Urban Planning*, pp. 104–109; Mel Scott, *American City Planning Since 1890,* Los Angeles, 1969, pp. 90–91.

the schoolchildren and their after-school play would bring resident families into contact with one another. Service stores were to be so placed as to make for social unification, and the daily round of errands would also promote acquaintanceship. In varying modifications the neighborhood-unit idea for suburban planning has been promoted by professional planners and widely adopted in middle-class subdivisions across the nation.

Gans's study of Levittown, New Jersey, demonstrates that school, street, and errand planning do not make communitarians out of America's nuclear and highly mobile families, but such designs do reduce traffic accidents and provide an informal atmosphere in which to raise children.[22] Only in cases where subdivisions of limited class range have coincided with local political boundaries do strong suburban communities seem to develop in the metropolis. In such cases the positive effects of the promotion of public facilities, high levels of maintenance, and innovative municipal services manifest themselves, but so also do the negative effects of racial and class exclusiveness. For the preponderance of Americans, neither the old grids nor the community-planning experiments of the nineteenth century seem to create an adequate urban environment—an environment able to roll with the social impacts of a rapid rate of urban development and at the same time to fill the gap between family isolation and the goal of an open democratic community life.

If the environment of 1880–1920 is the physical inheritance of our cities, it was the medical responses of that same era that fashioned the basic set of institutions established to protect the health of our urban populations. The staying power and rigidity of this legacy derives from its extraordinary successes in its own time. Armed with new scientific discoveries and techniques, these medical institutions scored an undreamed-of victory over the epidemic and mortality crises of the nineteenth-century city. Simultaneously doctors, hospitals, dispensaries, and public-health units offered a broad range of acute-care services which met many of the day-to-day needs of the upper two-thirds of the population. Such remarkable accomplishments so raised the status and popularity of doctors and their institutions that not until our own time have the shortcomings of these arrangements from the past come under scrutiny. Yet today's problems were also those of the years of first

22. Herbert J. Gans, *The Levittowners, How People Live and Politic in Suburbia,* New York, 1967, pp. 153–216.

triumph: a badly skewed delivery of health-care services that favored city dwellers, whites, men, and the well-to-do; an arrested environmentalism that neglected nutrition, housing, community, family life, and preventive care; narrow specialization and bureaucratization which dehumanized the patient; an overemphasis on drugs, surgery, and advanced instrumentation which drew scarce resources from the essential, if less heroic, long-term physical and mental therapies; a general self-satisfaction on the part of the medical fraternity which isolated it from a range of overlapping professions in education, engineering, planning, and social science.

The sustained contagious-disease and mortality crises of giant nineteenth-century cities manifested themselves most ominously in the old environment, the quarters of the poor untouched by or only partially improved by the new patterns of city building or the new sanitary services of the 1880–1920 metropolis.[23] Here society had proved unwilling or unable to extend its environmental remedies, but fortunately the nation was spared the endless recurrence of the ancient disabilities of great cities because the discoveries of medical science were able to deal with a select list of disease and thereby reach out to protect almost the entire urban population. In addition, such was the new wealth of these cities that the adequate-income majority was able to purchase a greatly enlarged range of services for its routine health care.

In the 1820s, at the onset of rapid urbanization, American cities were virtually defenseless against both epidemics and the normal incidence of disease. The art of medicine could do little but set bones, amputate limbs, pull teeth, vaccinate against smallpox, and assist births. The few drugs doctors prescribed were unspecific and often given in debilitating dosages. Worse still, the contemporary custom of drawing blood and purging bowels was actually injurious to the ill. In these early nineteenth-century years the best medical care consisted of commonsensical home nursing by relatives and the family physician so that nature's own cures could most effectively take place. For the ordinary citizen the comfort of one's own family and the attendance of the solo practitioner were the normal recourse in times of accident or sickness.[24]

For those outside the ministrations of family comfort, the largest

23. Stephen Smith, *The City That Was,* New York, 1911; DeForest and Veiller, *The Tenement House Problem,* I, pp. 261–327.
24. Bernhard J. Stern, *American Medical Practice,* New York, 1945, pp. 19–44; Richard H. Shryock, *The Development of Modern Medicine,* New York, 1936, pp. 248–72.

cities like Philadelphia, New York, and Boston had established hospitals open to migrants, sailors, the old, mentally ill, and the sick poor. Despite good intentions, extreme class segregation inevitably undermined these institutions. As custodians of outsiders and castoffs, these early hospitals fell far short of contemporary home standards. Except in the few hospitals staffed by Catholic orders, nurses were those with the lowest status and little opportunity for other employment and were sometimes even superannuated prostitutes and former felons. Only when the middle class itself experienced hospital conditions, as thousands did as soldiers and volunteer nurses during the Civil War, did the importance of hospital nursing impress itself on the consciousness of the mainstream of the society. Hospital funds were always short, rooms overcrowded, bedding dirty; in the absence of special operating rooms and anesthesia, the screams of the patients echoed through the wards. Under such conditions, alcohol, then a major hospital remedy, was perhaps the most humane prescription. In the early nineteenth century, hospitals deserved their popular reputation as places where shiploads of sick immigrants were dumped, and where the poor and the unfortunate went to die.[25]

A more successful institution of these early years was the dispensary, a neighborhood clinic where medicines and advice were given to poor patients. Since dispensaries held no resident patients, they escaped some of the effects of ward contagion. They were cheap to run, and they also enjoyed a measure of public support as the one medical institution that could help the city in its continuing struggle against smallpox. The common council of New York, for instance, frequently voted funds to the dispensaries for immunization, but popular distrust of vaccination limited their effectiveness. Though charities, the dispensaries rose above some of the worst degradation of philanthropy because the needs of the medical profession elevated the quality of their services. There were few medical schools in those days and even less clinical supervision, so that ambitious young doctors who wanted to extend their apprenticeship sought dispensary positions much as today they seek hospital residencies. With such diverse roots of support, city dispensaries multiplied during the years before the Civil War; New York's first dispensary opened in 1791, and by 1866 there were ten.[26]

Altogether, family nursing, the private practitioner, the hospital

25. Duffy, *Public Health in New York City*, pp. 481–505.
26. Ibid., pp. 506–511.

and the dispensary were but a tenuous defense against accident and disease. Today the national death rate stands at about 9.5 per thousand inhabitants; in 1900 it was 17.2; in New York prior to the Civil War, so far as records tell, it fluctuated between 26.1 and 40.7. Infants and children dwelt in greatest jeopardy, suffering about two-thirds of each year's deaths. Yet public concern did not then, nor did it earlier, focus on childbirth and child care, or even on the major day-to-day causes of adult death and morbidity: tuberculosis, typhoid, and dysentery.[27] The public accepted these diseases as the hazards of life itself, though statistics seem to show that in the nineteenth-century urban environment such dangers to life increased with city size.[28] Rather it was the dramatic summer incursions of epidemics of yellow fever, Asiatic cholera, and to a lesser extent typhus (a disease the well-to-do could ignore as the special providence of poverty-stricken immigrants) that mobilized public opinion.[29] These epidemics called forth the nation's earliest environmental public-health programs: quarantines, emergency and immigrant pesthouses, disinfection of the rooms and houses of the stricken, and attacks on nuisances and filth.

Although the causes of the epidemics were unknown at the time, European sanitarians had conclusively shown (and American investigators confirmed) that overcrowding and bad sanitary conditions were correlated with a high incidence of such cases. Landmark studies were Lemuel Shattuck's *Census of Boston* (1845) and his *Report of a General Plan for the Promotion of Public and Personal Health* (1850), John H. Griscom's *The Sanitary Conditions of the Laboring Population of New York* (1845), and the American Medical Association's multicity investigations of 1849. The net effect of these measures and of the water and sanitary constructions which accompanied them seems to have been to stem the potential for an ever-rising death rate, which unattended urban growth would have unleashed. Until the new medical science arrived high mortality could not be turned back, but the early environmentalists did at least succeed in holding the half-dozen largest cities of 250,000 to 2,000,000 inhabitants to levels of safety commensurate with those of less than 100,000.[30]

27. Ibid., pp. 534–35; Monroe Lerner and Odin W. Anderson, *Health Progress in the United States,* Chicago, 1963, pp. 11–15.
28. Stuart Galishoff, "Public Health in Newark, 1832–1918," Ph.D. Thesis, New York University, 1969, pp. 7–8.
29. Duffy, *Public Health in New York City,* pp. 446–47.
30. Shryock, *Modern Medicine,* pp. 219–33; Harry Wain, *A History of Preventive Medicine,* Springfield, Illinois, 1970, pp. 276–78.

The rapid succession of medical discoveries which began to accelerate after 1870 led to a proliferation of medical institutions whose innovative services were as important to urban living as the sanitary engineering of the former big-city era had been. The discoveries of bacteriology made possible the specific identification of an impressive list of common diseases like pneumonia, typhoid, tetanus, dysentery, whooping cough, tuberculosis, and numerous wound infections. Parallel discoveries in chemistry, pathology, and endocrinology allowed the effective intervention by doctors in a considerable number of both children's and adults' illnesses. Thanks to the new science, by 1900 the profession of medicine was rushing forward from its previous statistical observations and commonsensical nursing toward active intervention both in individual cases and in the urban environment. The new capabilities manifested themselves in traditional and novel forms alike: in the private practice of the single physician, in the totally refashioned institution of the voluntary hospital, in the expanded private and municipal public-health clinics and dispensaries, and in new regulatory programs.[31]

For the majority of urban dwellers, the most obvious gift of the new science appeared in the augmented effectiveness of the neighborhood physician. In 1900, solo practitioners' training and equipment were still quite primitive. Nevertheless those who kept abreast of recent discoveries could carry a few efficacious drugs and vaccines in their black bags, by now knew enough pharmacology to avoid the destructive dosages of unspecific drugs, owned a small table-top laboratory where they could perform a few simple urine and blood tests, had a systematic method for examining patients to detect their symptoms, and possessed sufficient knowledge and technique of asepsis to treat minor injuries, deliver babies, and handle contagious disease without endangering their patients.

Furthermore, now that the scientific foundations of medicine had been established beyond cavil, it became possible to standardize the norms of competence and to extinguish the professional conflicts that had raged among believers in various causes of disease and different methods of therapy. The nineteenth-century hodgepodge of quacks and of physicians trained in commercial medical schools as well as in universities was soon placed under strict licensing and educational standards. By 1920, city dwellers who could pay a private doctor's fee could expect

31. Ravenel, *Half Century of Public Health*, pp. 71–72; Shryock, *Modern Medicine*, pp. 318–27.

a fair level of competence in the treatment of a considerable list of common diseases and injuries. This new effectiveness, achieved in the lifetime of one generation, raised the status of the family physician to a position of extraordinary popularity. The private practitioner became that legendary figure of healer, father, and family guardian which enabled the medical profession to defend itself against major reform in our own time.[32]

In the late nineteenth and early twentieth centuries a wholly new kind of institution, the voluntary general hospital, served as the social agent of medical progress and the adjuvant, teacher, and disciplinarian of the private city physician. By ceasing to be merely the repository for the unfortunate and becoming instead the home of the new advanced practice and the servant of the middle class, it moved from the periphery to the center of medical care. In the years after the Civil War, everything about the hospital changed. The discovery and perfection of techniques of asepsis made it a reasonably safe place to go for treatment of serious illness or severe accidents. Surgery became reliable and effective. With the growth of science and the shift in hospital clientele, nursing ceased to be the resort of undesirables or a province of religious orders. It matured instead into a suitable lay occupation for those educated middle-class and working-class girls who were seeking independent roles in a society that had formerly offered little outside the factory, shop, school, or home. Finally, the hospital became the center of scientific progress. Only the large hospital could afford the expensive equipment and laboratories required for complicated techniques; only the large hospital could provide the variety of cases essential to research and medical education. These science-based changes in the hospital engendered a new fusion—the union of university medical schools, voluntary general hospitals, medical researchers and specialists, private practitioners, and their middle-class clients.[33]

Such a fusion was a reflection of the social structure and economic power of the industrial metropolis. The fabulous fortunes of the late nineteenth and early twentieth centuries were represented on the governing boards of general hospitals and universities. The urban rich, as yet but minimally taxed for public programs, expressed their enthusiasm for

32. I have been guided in my basic structural approach to the history of American health services by the excellent lectures of Odin W. Anderson which he has published in a small book, *The Uneasy Equilibrium, Private and Public Financing of Health Service in the United States 1875–1965*, New Haven, 1968.
33. Henry E. Sigerist, *American Medicine*, New York, 1934, pp. 204–29.

the new science, and often their gratitude for medical care, by endowing chairs of medicine and furnishing the capital for new universities, new hospitals, and numerous additions to existing facilities. On these boards representatives of wealthy families met with fashionable practitioners and distinguished specialists to determine the broad policies of medical schools, hospitals, and research. Here lay the source and direction of pre–World War I medical capital. The middle-class patient, too, made his contribution. Hospital fees began to be levied for service, and these fees provided a major fraction, or even the entire funding, of the day-to-day operation of the hospital. The working class and the poor, here as in the city at large, were subject to means tests to set the degrees of remission of their charges. Moreover, as charity cases they were subject to crowding, segregation in the wards and outpatient clinics, and a cheapening of service that paralleled their outside lives as residents of the city and as low-income consumers. Nevertheless, analogous to the rising living standards of the industrial metropolis itself, the new general hospital did give the poor access to an unprecedented level of medical care.[34]

The economic formula of the new voluntary hospital, altered by the omission of expensive charity, research, and training by proprietary hospitals but emulated in the best municipal hospitals by the substitution of the city's funds for the wealthy donor, proved so successful that hospitals multiplied at exceptional rates in the late nineteenth and early twentieth centuries. In 1873 there were only 178 hospitals in the United States; by 1909 there were 4,400; by 1918, when the number of non-federal institutions peaked, there were 7,000.[35] A totally unplanned growth, which was the outcome of the potentials of new science and the wealth of industrialization, had produced the social structure of the hospital-based medical profession that has proved to have serious consequences for our own time. In the early years, when research was first lifting the veil of ignorance and when new techniques and new hospital practices constituted such tremendous advances over what had prevailed, the gifts of the rich and the making of decisions by the wealthy and the professional elite seemed natural and beneficent. Yet the failure of the American medical structure to represent either the middle-class or low-income patient in what were in fact public policy decisions has badly distorted our medical undertakings.

Ever more expensive research, ever more elaborate techniques, and

34. Anderson, *Uneasy Equilibrium*, pp. 26–36, 52–56.
35. Ibid., pp. 28–30.

the concentration on surgery at the expense of long-term care for the old were some of the most obvious results of the exclusive representation of wealthy donors and the medical elite. Environmental and preventive measures, chronic diseases, dentistry, the day-to-day rendering of service, and what might be termed throat-stick medicine have been relatively neglected. Moreover, with the rapid advance of science the solo practitioner became more and more closely allied to the hospital because it was the source of personal prestige and advanced knowledge and technique. As a result, neighborhood practice almost disappeared from poor districts, and the working class has come to be dependent upon the accident of location of hospital outpatient facilities. In 1920 the future of increasing medical specialization and the class, racial, and neighborhood consequences of the hospital structure of American medicine were only beginning to be perceived, but the seeds of our current difficulties had been sown.[36]

Not that the industrial metropolis ignored the public-health possibilities of the new science; it pursued them vigorously, constructing the institutional framework and practices that still supplement our practitioners and hospitals. Indeed, the totality of environmental services and health-care institutions succeeded at last in bringing an end to the historic linkage of large cities and death. In New York, despite its gigantic size, and despite some of the most densely crowded wards in the world, the death rate had already by 1900 been brought below its lowest nineteenth-century levels, and it continued to fall in the big cities almost every year thereafter so that in our own time urban and rural death rates have at last converged. But at such a moment we face a familiar historical crisis—the institutions of the past fail to adapt to the needs of the present. As our health concerns have shifted from mortality to morbidity, we begin to experience all the failings of our old health-delivery structure.[37]

The discoveries of bacteriology reinforced the nineteenth-century campaign of urban sanitarians. Water departments introduced filtration and chemical purification in the early years of the twentieth century. The identification of both human and animal tuberculosis bacilli led to the testing of herds and the certification and pasteurization of milk, which

36. Edward H. L. Corwin, *The American Hospital,* New York, 1946, pp. 166–74.

37. Ravenel, *Half Century of Public Health,* pp. 101–2; Lerner and Anderson, *Health Progress,* pp. 105–13.

had been a major source of child-killing infections. The precision of modern chemistry, coupled with the new large-scale marketing of meat, food products, and drugs, made it possible for the federal government to augment ineffective municipal market inspections by nationally enforced standards for purity in foods and drugs that moved in interstate commerce. The ability of the new science to explain how vaccination gave immunity even made it possible for cities and states to overcome hoary public prejudice and to institute safe, effective, compulsory smallpox vaccination for schoolchildren.[38] Finally, by shifting the focus of attention in the campaigns to remedy the ills of slum housing, the new science brought the regulatory effort to its peak and logical stopping place.

The "fever nest" slum blocks, with their high incidence of cholera and typhus mapped by the early sanitarians, had spurred the public to establish municipal boards of health and to support their pioneering programs for the removal of nuisances and for cleanup and disinfection. In New York such expert reforms had been given impetus by the frightening experience of the Draft Riots of 1863, and the city enacted the nation's first tenement-house regulation. But when quarantine measures ended the plagues, the working-class and middle-class voters lost their fright and with it their enthusiasm for aggressive public-health measures. Housing reformers were forced to fall back more and more on appeals for public support on the grounds that overcrowding led to drink, crime, and prostitution, rather than urging a community of interest in safety from disease.[39] The threads of moral horror and the community of health have always been intertwined in American housing proposals, and the early twentieth-century tuberculosis and well-baby campaigns did aid housing reform by contributing a set of causes for which there was broad popular experience and sympathy.[40]

As a result of the intensification of the sanitary attack on slum housing, by World War I all of the nation's large cities had modern housing codes specifying permissible room density, ventilation, and sanitation. These laws were an important achievement in ensuring that all future construction would conform to decent minimum standards. But regulation of housing cannot by definition expand the supply of housing, and indeed it tends to raise rents when it is enforced. Also, it offers no

38. Ravenel, *Half Century of Public Health,* pp. 136–59, 211–19.
39. Jacob Riis, *How the Other Half Lives,* Sam Bass Warner, Jr., ed., Cambridge, 1970.
40. DeForest and Veiller, *Tenement House Problem,* I, pp. 447–70.

remedy for the common situation where poor tenants and poor landlords meet. Much slum property is owned by slum dwellers, not by rich corporations. Many slum owners scrape their way into a heavily mortgaged landlord status. Neither they nor their tenants welcome the news that costly repairs must be undertaken to bring their old buildings up to modern standards. The nineteenth- and early twentieth-century housing-regulation movement was after all the achievement of sanitary specialists and wealthy philanthropists, both of whom were unwilling to disturb the basic property and income relationships of the society. Therefore however well-meaning, and despite its long-term contributions, the regulatory movement often appeared in poor neighborhoods as an exercise in harassment of the poor, against which petty bribes and aid from the ward boss in inducing inspectors to wink at violations were the best defense.[41] Housing reform shed some of its early philanthropic incubus thereafter, and in the thirties it picked up labor support when it was recast in the form of public construction and appeared as an aid to full employment for building-trades workers.

The wealth of the industrial metropolis and the efficacy of the new science also enabled the cities of the nation to establish a series of institutions that would offer specialized medical services to supplement the basic system of private practitioners and hospitals. Unfortunately for the public welfare, the urban health-delivery system was weakest in low-income areas, as housing regulations also had been, and it was in these areas that the incidence of disease and accidents rose most sharply.

Infants and children of the poor lived in the greatest danger. In the summer of 1893, Dr. Abraham Jacobi and the philanthropist Nathan Straus opened a milk station, where boiled milk and advice on infant care were offered free to mothers of slum children. The immediate success of the project in preventing deadly summer fevers led to imitation and the rapid maturing of municipally managed well-baby clinics. Soon clinics for tuberculosis and venereal disease were added to the public list.[42] The new medicine encouraged the multiplication of dispensaries, both in the old form of the freestanding clinic located in a poor neighborhood and in the new form of the outpatient departments of public and voluntary general hospitals.

    41. Edith Abbott and Sophonisba Breckinridge, *The Tenements of Chicago, 1908–1935,* Chicago, 1936, pp. 478–82; Lawrence M. Friedman, *Government and Slum Housing,* Chicago, 1968, pp. 40–41.
    42. Wain, *Preventive Medicine,* pp. 252–63.

By 1920 New York City possessed 228 dispensaries and clinics. There were 60 baby-health stations; 21 tuberculosis clinics; 12 venereal-disease clinics, only two of which offered treatment; 26 municipal single-purpose clinics for treatment of eyes, teeth, rabies infection, and occupational hazards; 34 independent dispensaries; 65 outpatient departments of hospitals; four children's dental clinics in schools; and even six dispensaries for college students. A fourth of New York's eight thousand physicians put in some of their time staffing these institutions, at which approximately 1,250,000 patients were treated annually.[43] Although these statistics of institutional growth, doctor participation, and patient use were impressive when held against the light of the preceding half century, the deficiencies of these supplements to private fee-paying doctor and hospital care had already revealed themselves. They were second-rate charitable supplements and as such were bound to atrophy in a society that honored self-help and responded most positively to fee-paying patients.

The entire list of clinics and dispensaries was not regarded by doctors as a group of institutions on their way to the provision of complete neighborhood care. Instead they were viewed as charities for the improvident and the unfortunate or as a restricted concourse of specialists who would not compete with the private doctor's general practice. The New York dispensary law required that all patients be subjected to a means test to determine medical indigency before treatment, granting exceptions only for a few contagious diseases, notably tuberculosis and venereal disease. Numerous studies were conducted, as in welfare today, to detect cheating by patients who could afford to pay the normal rates. The baby-health stations could administer only to well babies, while sick babies had to be taken to a general practitioner, dispensary, or outpatient department of a hospital. The public acquiesced in these constraints, and the network of supplementary institutions was used by the working class and the poor as their means of access to specialists and to doctors essential in cases of serious accidents or of sicknesses they could not neglect.

The whole charitable nature of these institutions prevented their maturing into adequate general-care centers. The doctors who staffed them were either ill-paid or, in the majority of cases, contributed their services. Dispensary and clinic work carried no prestige; such jobs were

43. Edwin H. L. Corwin, "The Dispensary Situation in New York City," *Medical Record,* 97 (January 31, 1920), 180.

either the doctor's tithe or were sought by young men hoping for an entrée to a regular hospital appointment by way of clinic duty. Although dealing with a public which suffered special hardships from the loss of working hours or days, only 2.5 percent of the total New York clinics' time was scheduled outside the normal business day. Patients had to wait in long lines. There was a shortage of supplementary personnel for the routing of patients, follow-up of cases, handling of records, and the offering of social services. Diagnosis was weak, records fragmentary and often illegible; tests were neglected and treatment haphazard. "Among cases of syphilis studied in only 50 percent was an indication found that the patient had been given the proper treatment," one study reported. Even the outpatient departments of general hospitals, where the latest equipment and laboratories at least existed within the same building, suffered because such facilities were planned and scheduled for resident patients. The outpatient service was the stepchild of the hospital, its trustees, its administrators, and its doctors. All in all, despite its lusty growth from 1870 to 1920, the system of clinic and dispensary was poor man's medicine.[44]

The important public consequences of this charitable incubus lay in the withdrawal of popular support for all kinds of group and socialized medicine. As in the case of public housing, promising reforms directed to the social consequences of the unequal distribution of personal income went unsupported by working-class organizations because of their experience with services which departed from the normal private market form. In medicine the urban dispensary and clinic did not grow into a successful neighborhood or district institution, and the campaigns for health insurance faced opposition or apathy from organized labor. Similarly, the federal government's promising demonstration of non-charity public housing during World War I died as suddenly as it appeared. In both cases small groups of professionals and intellectuals had demonstrated that they had fully mastered the logic of the industrial metropolis's housing and health structures, but many more years of investigations, reports, and social failures would be required before major segments of the public would mobilize for change.

The extreme shortage of housing near war plants and navy yards forced a reluctant federal government into its first venture in civilian public housing. Prior to the war the housing-reform movement had been

44. Ibid., 181–85.

Planned Housing

102. Row House Yards, South and Iranistan Avenues, Bridgeport, Connecticut, 1919. The U.S. Housing Corporation employed the most advanced land-planning practices of its day. On an expensive 25-acre site, using the smallest two-bedroom units of any project, designers mixed a colonial American building style with contemporary English Garden City site planning to provide these generous garden spaces. *National Archives*

103. War Workers' Housing, Madison Street, Waterbury, Connecticut, 1919. English cottage version of contemporary suburban styles employed by the federal government in its first public housing venture. These duplexes, pairing five- and six-room units, were erected for skilled brass workers. *National Archives*

104. War Housing Twenty Years Later, off Lincoln Street, Bath, Maine, 1940. Because the sites were well planned and the architecture met the local consensus about what constituted decent housing, the U.S. Housing Corporation's work remained popular and aged well. *Library of Congress*

105. Country Club Plaza, Kansas City, ca. 1930. Since 1905 the J. C. Nichols Company has been managing the nation's only continuously planned residential development. The basic strategy has been to follow the city's growth by subdividing land in an ever-widening triangle. Houses and lots are sold, but the company keeps the shopping centers it builds. This is the first (1923), at the intown apex of the development triangle. Nearby apartments helped to get the shopping center started. *J. C. Nichols Company*

106. Grand Drive from 53rd Terrace, Country Club District, Kansas City, ca. 1914. Following contemporary examples of other upper-middle-class suburbs, especially Roland Park, Baltimore, the company gave special attention to site preparation and landscaping. Small parks, winding streets, and generous plantings are its hallmarks. With each subdivision Homes Associations are formed to maintain the local common grounds. *J. C. Nichols Company*

107. Belinder Avenue, Country Club District, Kansas City, 1963. Uniform setbacks of the houses, careful plantings and maintenance produce the epitome of the American residential street. Photograph taken twenty-five years after first development. *J. C. Nichols Company*

108. Parking Garage, 47th Street, Country Club Plaza, Kansas City, ca. 1948. By keeping title to the shopping centers the developers can control and

finance continuous modernization. Here a former parking lot was converted into a free parking structure for 400 cars. In contrast to the pains of urban renewal, the Country Club Plaza stands as a convincing argument for municipal ownership and management of the commercial and industrial land of the metropolis. *J. C. Nichols Company*

109. Homestead Country Club, Country Club District, Kansas City, 1954. Since full-amenity development to high standards can only be profitable for middle-to-upper-income families, the entire Country Club District is a city planning triumph but a social disaster for Kansas City. Only public financing and control of land and housing development could have prevented the inevitable side effects of class and racial segregation. *J. C. Nichols Company*

110. Public Housing, Holyoke, Massachusetts, 1941. Controls against giving too much to the poor reduced New Deal housing to levels below that of the World War I projects, thereby ensuring that the gap between the rewarded poor and the middle class would widen disastrously once the Depression ended. Nevertheless, in small cities across the nation where land costs were low and projects not too large, substantial gains were made over local slum conditions. Compare these new two-story row-house apartments to the four-story wooden tenements in the background. *Library of Congress*

111. Subsistence Homesteads, El Monte, Los Angeles, 1936. A Resettlement Administration demonstration project of farm homes for clerks and industrial workers employed in the city. The three-quarter-acre lots and locally designed five-room houses successfully captured a broad popular demand. Two thousand families applied initially for the planned 140 units. Houses were ultimately sold to their occupants without loss to the government because the project was sensibly located along one axis of metropolitan growth. *Library of Congress*

112. Ida B. Wells Housing Project, Pershing Road and Martin Luther King Drive, Chicago, 1942. Typical New Deal big-city federal housing project— barracks for 1,655 black families. White antipathy to public housing outside the established ghetto forced enlargement of the project in 1955 and 1961 so that it is now an all-black philanthropic city of 12,000 inhabitants. *Library of Congress*

113. Lakeview Terrace, Whiskey Island, Cleveland, ca. 1936. Local housing authorities, unwilling and unable to see housing as an opportunity to let the poor move to modern neighborhoods and closer to the growing sectors of the metropolitan economy, frequently repackaged the poor in old slum sites. Here, 620 families were settled in an industrially impacted neighborhood. Subsequently an interstate highway has further blighted one edge of the project. *Urban Archives, Temple University*

114. Lafayette Park, Detroit, ca. 1962. A 164-acre urban-renewal project one mile east of the downtown. Conceived first in 1949 as a public housing program, it was redesigned when urban-renewal legislation offered a tax-hungry city the opportunity to clear land and build for the wealthy. Low-income property on the site was leveled without adequate relocation measures and luxury row houses and apartment towers were built. Completed 1971. *U.S. Department of Housing and Urban Development*

115. Prefabricated Housing Experiment, Akron, Ohio, 1971. Mistaking a social and economic problem for a technological one, the U.S. Department of Housing and Urban Development recently launched a high-publicity program for factory-made homes. Scarcity and costs of well-prepared land, class and racial segregation, and the financing of adequate social and educational services to housing, not the structures themselves, have been the real problem. *U.S. Department of Housing and Urban Development*

116. Scattered-Site Public Housing, Mount Clemens, Michigan, ca. 1964. Occasionally public housing meets the popular norms for decent living. Here 160 units for blacks, whites, and the elderly were mixed within a small metropolitan satellite city's urban-renewal program. Eight sites were scattered over 485 acres so as not to disturb the existing neighborhood fabric. Tenants paint their own apartments and keep up their own lawns and gardens. Problems so far: kitchens too small, not enough closet space! *U.S. Department of Housing and Urban Development*

102. Row House Yards, Bridgeport, Connecticut, 1919

103. War Workers Housing, Waterbury, Connecticut, 1919

104. War Housing Twenty Years Later, Bath, Maine, 1940

105. Country Club Plaza, Kansas City, ca. 1930

106. Country Club District, Kansas City, ca. 1914

107. Belinder Avenue, Country Club District, Kansas City, 1963

108. Parking Garage, Country Club Plaza, Kansas City, ca. 1940

109. Homestead Country Club, Country Club District, Kansas City, 1954

110. Public Housing, Holyoke, Massachusetts, 1941

111. Subsistence Homesteads, El Monte, Los Angeles, 1936

112. Ida B. Wells Housing Project, Chicago, 1942

113. Lakeview Terrace, Whiskey Island, Cleveland, ca. 1936

114. Lafayette Park, Detroit, ca. 1962

115. Prefabricated House Experiment, Akron, Ohio, 1971

116. Public Housing, Mount Clemens, Michigan, ca. 1964

fully occupied with building regulations, the brand-new controls of zoning, and experiments with philanthropic and limited-dividend model-tenement housing. Continental and British examples had begun to attract attention in advanced professional circles, and Massachusetts had tried a small experiment, but to most Americans governmental construction of houses seemed to represent a dangerous step toward socialism and a direct threat to the genius of the Republic.[45] Despite successive reports of an inability to attract and hold skilled workers without the provision of some decent accommodation for their families, Congress delayed authorization of public war housing. The fact that such an undertaking resembled German socialism more than anything else made it doubly unpalatable to Congress. Yet skilled workers would not tolerate for long the boardinghouses, barracks, and made-over garages that unskilled men and women accepted. Therefore, five months before the Armistice, a public-housing program for skilled workers was at last authorized, subject to the strict condition that all housing so built be sold to private persons at the war's end. Two federal agencies, the Emergency Fleet Corporation and the U.S. Housing Corporation, under-took the rush task and together they built or subsidized the construction of more than fifteen thousand dwelling units at seventy-nine project sites across the country.[46]

The final report of Frederick Law Olmsted, Jr., planner of Forest Hills and manager of the Town Planning Division of the U.S. Housing Corporation, is of exceptional interest because it demonstrates that pro-fessionals had early thoroughly understood the mechanisms and limita-tions of the private housing market and the remedies needed to maximize the social benefits of private construction. The report also shows that the U.S. Housing Corporation had demonstrated how a model public-housing program should be managed if the government should ever have wished to move beyond the limitations of the private market.

First, the summary report recognized the basic trickle-down nature of American housing. New housing is built for the middle class and the upper levels of the working class, and all others inherit what is vacated by these. Thus the quality of housing in a given city depends directly upon its quantity. If there is a shortage of housing, Olmsted stated, then those least able to pay rents must double up and occupy unfit structures,

45. Scott, *American City Planning,* pp. 170–74.
46. Miles L. Colean, *Housing for Defense,* New York, 1940, pp. 9–26, 156–57.

and the immediate result is "slum conditions unfavorable to that self-respecting family life upon which the security of our democracy rests."[47]

Second, he recognized local housing conditions to be a national and not a local problem, because of the crucial role played by the national flows of mortgage capital. Thus during the years from 1914 to 1918 rising building costs and more lucrative opportunities for investment elsewhere had driven capital away from new construction, so that a housing shortage existed even prior to our entry into the war in 1917. As a permanent remedy for the inevitable periodic shortage of money for home construction, Olmsted recommended federal intervention in the capital-supply market along the lines that had recently been followed by the 1916 Farm Loan Act. Under this program the government lent money to local cooperative banks, and they in turn extended cheap long-term mortgages to farmers. In 1933, with the crisis of the Great Depression, the Home Owners Loan Corporation was created exactly along such lines. This act, plus subsequent New Deal additions, established the basic American housing strategy: to encourage the private trickle-down housing market through government intervention and government support for the supply of mortgage funds.

Olmsted noted that the U.S. Housing Corporation had "dealt but little with the more difficult problem of satisfactory and economical housing for the families of unskilled and relatively low paid workers."[48] Yet looking back on the pioneering work of this agency and assessing its accomplishment in the light of America's subsequent public-housing disasters, one can appreciate these World War I construction projects as model programs that defined the basic conditions under which any successful public-housing policy must proceed. The essence of the corporation's work lay in its adoption of a contemporary consensus for standard new housing. In designing for skilled workers who were engaged in a common patriotic enterprise, the corporation's program was not obliged to lower its standards to a level below that of private housing. It did not have to avoid offending the sensibilities of private tenants and home-owners by offering less than the equivalent housing to its recipients of public welfare. On the contrary, the central office in Washington set normal prevailing standards, called together mixed planning and archi-

47. Frederick Law Olmsted, Jr., "Lessons from Housing Developments of the United States Housing Corporation," U.S. Department of Labor, Bureau of Labor Statistics, *Monthly Labor Review,* 8 (April 1919), 32.
    48. Ibid., 31.

tectural teams, and turned them loose to do as good a job as they could. The result varied from the ordinary to the excellent. Many projects used the latest traffic, curvilinear-street, park-reservation, and community-center devices of the best English Garden City and wealthy American garden-suburb practice. Taste was not regimented. There were Colonial and Tudor houses in the East, stone houses in Ohio, Spanish stucco in California, and neat wooden bungalows in the state of Washington.[49] Moreover by a strong emphasis on site planning these projects enjoyed the lasting advantage of having their utilities, streets, and services finished and located in a way that would enhance the long-term use and maintenance of the homes, instead of leaving newcomers stranded and struggling for city services, as had so often happened in low-cost outlying private developments and would occur later in public housing.

When the federal government did finally enter on public housing during the New Deal, it violated (except in its three controversial Greenbelt towns)[50] the basic World War I conditions of success. Instead of building to the standard of middle-class private consensus it built second-class philanthropic housing. By so doing it drove off local architectural and planning talent, erected obsolete structures that would have to be lived in for fifty years, and stigmatized the beneficiaries as second-class citizens.[51]

The health-insurance reformers of the pre–World War I era also displayed a competent perception of the shortcomings of the existing medical structure. The remedies they proposed, like those of the U.S. Housing Corporation group, were essentially conservative—designed to use government to make the private system more effective, not to institute a novel public organization. The health-insurance movement began in Europe and was carried to America by intellectuals, and accordingly it was never a campaign of the medical practitioners. It commenced with a concern for the maintenance of income for injured workers' families, and then as it gained momentum it moved on to proposals for insurance against everyday medical expenses. As the campaign progressed from legal and industrial reform to contact with medical practitioners and conflict with private insurance companies, it encountered a paranoid counterattack which defended the recently developed institutional struc-

49. U.S. Department of Labor, *Report of the United States Housing Corporation*, Washington, 1919, 1920, 2 v.

50. Joseph L. Arnold, *The New Deal in the Suburbs, A History of the Greenbelt Town Program 1935–1954*, Columbus, 1971, pp. 83–103.

51. Friedman, *Government and Slum Housing*, p. 18.

ture of medicine as if it were the last bastion of American free enterprise and the most sacred of the nation's ancient traditions.

The first phase of reform, employers' liability laws and workmen's compensation insurance, advanced smoothly because it proved itself able to gather adherents from all the concerned parties successively— reformers, labor unions, industrialists, and insurance carriers. Under the old common law, each individual worker had been held to have assumed the risks of accident and disease inherent in his occupation. If he suffered injury or disability in the course of his employment, he had to pay his own expenses or else initiate a lawsuit to prove not only that he was without fault but that his employer had in fact been negligent in the operation of his business. The expense of these suits, the callousness of the age, and the imbalance of power between worker-plaintiff and boss-defendant made such a recourse uncertain and the awards niggardly.

Yet the accident and disease rates in such large industries as textiles, steel, glass, mining, chemicals, and railroads added scandalously to the local relief rolls. In 1885 Alabama enacted an employer liability law making manufacturers responsible for their employees' injuries. Other states followed, and they simultaneously established numerous commissions to investigate European schemes for insuring workers' wages against days lost because of occupation-related disease and injury. These studies uncovered a mutuality of private interest. Manufacturers, by devoting increased attention to guards on machinery, the handling of materials, dust control, and prevailing shop conditions, could increase the productivity of their crews. The incidence of accidents and disease proved calculable, and it was found that insurance companies could write policies at reasonable rates and workers could benefit by an administered schedule of payments for lost wages, injuries, dismember-ment, and even death. Maryland passed the first workmen's compensa-tion law in 1902, and by 1920 forty-two states had followed. Though a highly successful advance, workmen's compensation always suffered from the weaknesses of its original consensus. As an insurance program it never covered all workers and, since employer and carriers both had an interest in low and stable payments, compensation schedules in America have recompensed workers for only a small fraction of their real costs. Although provisions for medical charges were added to the original wage-based cash benefits, the restriction of the program to work-related health problems seems to have prevented practitioners from perceiving this insurance scheme as a threat to private doctor-patient relationships. Hospitals did, however, receive direct payments from insurance companies for treatment of accident cases, and this innovation seems to have softened hospital administrators toward insurance schemes in general.[52]

Again it was Europe that pioneered in payments for sickness and accidents not related to the job. Here the issue concerned income maintenance for workers' families when the wage earner could not work, payments for medical care, and funeral expenses. As early as 1883 Germany had begun contributory employer-employee local insurance funds, and in subsequent years the number of industries to undertake such coverage was steadily expanded. Great Britain followed a parallel course in enacting in 1911 a National Insurance Act, which established compulsory unemployment and health insurance. Workers were to receive some measure of protection against the inevitable occurrence of periodic unemployment as well as some assistance to defray the costs of health maintenance. A special feature of the British scheme was its accommodation of existing benefit associations and insurance companies. The government promulgated a list of approved insurance societies, and these were to receive the joint payments of workers, employers, and the government. Local boards of doctors, insurance representatives, and government officials were to oversee the payments.[53]

Reformers in the United States were primarily academicians organized in the American Association for Labor Legislation. In 1914 the Association reported on its studies of European precedents and opened a campaign for medical insurance at the federal and state levels. The Association did not contemplate total unemployment compensation. The reformers hoped to insure industrial workers against the expenses of childbirth, accidents, sickness, and funerals so that the working class could become full-paying patients of the private medical-care system. As in Great Britain, government, employer, and employee would all contribute to funding the compulsory insurance pools. The AALL report also allowed self-employed persons not covered by the legislation to join such programs on a voluntary basis. Either state or private insurance carriers were envisaged as insurers, and the schedule of payments was to

52. Roy Lubove, *The Struggle for Social Security, 1900–1935,* Cambridge, 1968, pp. 45–61; Anderson, *Uneasy Equilibrium,* pp. 57–59.
53. Lubove, *Struggle for Social Security,* pp. 67–68.

be administered by employer-employee boards supervised by the government. The report also expressed the hope that such an insurance scheme would encourage physical examinations, early diagnosis, and such general preventive health practices as well as finance the care of acute illness.

From 1916 to 1920, bills for federal investigation of health insurance and bills for state programs were put forward. The American Hospital Association and the three nursing associations reviewed the question and issued reports calling such a step inevitable and urging hospital administrators to be sure that the scheduled fees were adequate even as they prepared for increased case loads. The National Association of Manufacturers, pleased with its workmen's compensation experience and safety-first campaigns and impressed by German business practice, expressed itself at first as favorable and then moved to a position of supporting private insurance only. Organized labor offered weak support at best along with some opposition, with the A F of L executive committee unable to agree on a position. President Samuel Gompers testified before Congress that such schemes would lead to federal spying on the homes of workingmen. The treasurer and a vice-president of the same union testified in favor, as did the railroad conductors. The poor quality of medical service offered by practitioners working for British insurance funds there created unfavorable publicity, but the medical insurance campaign here did not in any case call for group practice or any other alteration in the delivery of medical care. The low quality of American clinic practice may also have entered the minds of union leaders, since one of their major goals at the time was to achieve full equality of status for the American workingman.[54]

But the violent opposition came from a coalition of private insurance companies and doctors. One insurance executive campaigned full-time against the legislation. Once again the war inflated the specter of German socialism. "When compulsory health insurance enters the United States, Socialism will have its feet upon the throat of the Nation," he said.[55] In 1917, private insurance companies had written industrial policies covering in some way 37,500,000 workers. Conservative doctors in the American Medical Association repudiated the early stand of its leadership in favor of insurance and in a fit of wartime xenophobia voted the "do-gooders" out of office. Everywhere the state

54. Anderson, *Uneasy Equilibrium,* pp. 59–88.
55. Ibid., p. 79.

bills were defeated and the isolated reform intellectuals faced heated doctor, insurance and even Christian Science opposition.[56]

The turning back of medical insurance proved more than a temporary setback for an idea whose time had not yet come. The campaign took place during the wave of reaction that swept the country during and immediately after World War I. In this climate the American Medical Association, an institution that had begun its organized life with an advanced survey of urban slum conditions, confused the conservative reform of insurance with public medicine and nailed itself to an intransigent defense of the institutional system of American medicine as it obtained in 1920.[57] The Association's permanent resolution on state medicine, one just recently modified, forbade support of government programs of any kind except those already in existence for charity, mental health, communicable diseases, and military care. This legacy from the years of the first half century of rapid progress has cost the nation dear, the rural areas even more than the cities. It has cost the public and doctors alike. For years large numbers of American citizens have been denied access to decent medical services, and the medical profession itself has been denied the adjustments and steady evolution that would have attended the public insurance reforms. Instead of medical problems, our cities now face a medical crisis.

56. Lubove, *Struggle for Social Security,* pp. 76–90.
57. Anderson, *Uneasy Equilibrium,* p. 90.

8

The Neglect of Everyday Life

---

*Pouring new money
into old institutions; housing
and health care*

THE HISTORY OF URBAN HOUSING and health since 1920 is a history of both arrested development and rapid growth. Our twentieth-century campaigns for social justice have failed to redress the inequalities characteristic of the industrial metropolis. Yet despite this social and political lag the city itself has continued to grow and to change with the unfolding of the national economy so that in our own time it confronts a twofold crisis. On the one hand we continue to struggle with the old issues of sufficient diet, decent housing, adequate medical care, and a safe environment for the lowest third of our citizenry, while at the same time new demands, called forth by the conflicts and expectations of a high standard of living, bureaucratic work, government services, and suburban living, pour in upon the city. The new metropolises and megalopolises of the post-1920 era are both the weary settlements of unanswered poverty and the conflict-ridden arenas of mass luxury and privilege.

The full reasons for the arrested development of housing, health, and other American social programs demand sustained political analysis for explication, but two obvious trends suffice to frame the past half century. First, the late development of the labor movement, legitimized only in the mid-thirties, and the consequent failure of the labor and urban reform movements to coalesce have contributed to the heavy middle-class bias of our urban programs and weakened all attempts to

serve the lowest third of the population. Second, the preoccupation of
the nation and its leaders with great national crises, first the Great
Depression and then a continuing series of hot and cold wars since
1941, has distracted the nation's talent, energy, and wealth from the
tasks of building a humane and just urban society at home. In the last
three decades we have systematically neglected the needs of everyday
life for a national career of war and imperialism.

Although we had wealth enough for full employment and a living
wage for all able-bodied citizens, although we had plentiful resources for
the world's most ambitious public-housing program, although we had
educational and research institutions aplenty to seek new drugs and
therapies while also manning a full complement of institutions for acute,
chronic, and preventive care, we did not do any of these things. All our
social programs that touch urban life have been tentative, held to ex-
perimental levels for long periods, and when finally adopted as permanent national programs they have been underfunded and extended only
to a small fraction of the population they ought to serve.

A brief list of the angry groups in today's television news recalls the
dual nature of the urban crisis: blacks, working-class whites, middle-
class women, soldiers, students, and suburban homeowners. If there
were but a single environment with a single set of problems, the energy
behind the grievances of these groups would long ago have transformed
the politics and programs of the nation. But blacks and many working-
class white families suffer the old failure of the city to deal with racism,
full employment, adequate wages, and decent housing and health care,
while the women, soldiers, students, and homeowners suffer from the
new failure of the society to deliver on the promises of its wealth and
freedom.

The present generation of Americans thus confronts a double
burden—it must solve the old job, food, health, and shelter problems
while simultaneously addressing itself to the conflicts and potentials of
an extremely wealthy, bureaucratic, mechanized society. This arduous
task compounds so many ingredients. White racism, mass middle-class
privilege, and elite class power are milled together with the interdependencies of a high-energy, high-technology, thoroughly urbanized society.
If the task is vigorously undertaken, the society should be able to catch
up with itself by ending the old injustices and should also be able to
keep pace with the ever-unfolding sets of problems and possibilities that
urban and economic growth will bring. At the very least our present

situation is much improved over that of 1920: the nation is now much wealthier, and we have the benefit of knowing what remedies to take because we can learn from the experience of the partial programs undertaken during the past half-century. The most severe test now, as always, is the question whether the public and its leaders are willing to shoulder the burden of ending the failings and injustices of the system.

In terms of housing the United States already operates a sufficient range of public programs to redress the grievances of the bottom third of the urban population while simultaneously adapting to the new possibilities and demands of the more prosperous two-thirds. Together, the major housing and planning devices of insured mortgages, subsidized public housing, and urban renewal could transform our cities. For the past thirty-five years, however, underfunding, narrowly circumscribed and antisocial goals, and plain bad administration have prevented this set of tools from relieving our metropolitan-wide housing crises. Indeed, rather than aiding the modernization of our cities and enlarging the inclusiveness of our society, these programs directly interfere with wholesome metropolitan growth and pile governmental injustices upon the heap of private prejudice and exploitation.

The most successful and largest of all the public measures has been the national mortgage-insurance program. Born of the banking crisis of the Great Depression, the Federal Housing Administration's mortgage insurance quickly assumed a major role in helping marginal buyers to homeownership because it fitted in so neatly with the existing organizations of private moneylending, construction, and sales. Since its first full elaboration in the late thirties, FHA mortgages have covered about a fifth of all the privately owned nonfarm housing units of the nation. During World War II and the recent money shortage the federally insured fraction rose to 45 percent and 35 percent respectively.

The circumstances surrounding these programs' origins determined their subsequent history. In 1925 the post–World War I housing boom began to slacken as private capital took flight from mortgages to seek higher returns elsewhere. As a result the costs of housing rose and the number of building starts declined steadily as more and more thousands of American families on the margin of home purchase were squeezed out of the market. The financial collapse of 1929 then delivered a final blow to an already weakened building industry. National banks and trust companies emptied their mortgage portfolios to cover depositors' runs on cash accounts. Savings banks and building and loan associations, institutions which specialized in home mortgages and which lent money for long terms, typically for fifteen years, found themselves in deep trouble. The savings and loans, however, possessed important political assets. They could and did pose in Washington as innocent local small businessmen, the friends, neighbors, and servants of hard-pressed homeowners, and thereby received prompt and sympathetic action from the national government. In 1932 the Home Loan Bank Act stemmed part of the banking crisis by establishing twelve regional banks for the purpose of lending money to the 12,000 savings and loan associations across the country, thereby preserving the assets of their twelve million depositors and saving the 7,700,000 mortgages on which they had made loans.[1]

Yet the financial collapse was so deep that during 1932 and 1933 mortgage foreclosures continued unabated, reaching a peak of a thousand a day. This prolonged crisis made irresistible the pleas for an extension of aid to all banks rather than to just savings and loan companies. At the same time the extreme pressures of unrelenting unemployment (half to two-thirds of the unemployed males were workers in construction and related building-materials industries) fused in official government thinking the plight of homeowners, bankers, and the unemployed. This fusion brought forth the New Deal housing program— mortgage insurance to aid the banker and the homeowner and federally subsidized construction of public housing to increase building trades' employment. A set of remedies addressed to national economic problems, these measures have powerfully affected the growth of American cities ever since.

First as a bankers' program, the giant FHA loan system had a decidedly conservative charge: it was to concern itself with investments which were economically sound by the current tests of the private market. It was thereby to limit its social reform to aiding the lower middle class and upper working classes in their attempts to borrow money for homeownership or to aid that large segment of the population by guaranteeing the mortgages of builders of apartments and rental units in an appropriate range of rents. Though the total volume of FHA activity had tremendous and enduring impact upon the American city, most particularly by hastening the flight of the white middle class from the central city, open and formal concern for social reform was shunted

1. William L. C. Wheaton, "The Evolution of Federal Housing Programs," Ph.D. Thesis, University of Chicago, 1953, pp. 9–27.

to other departments of government. The New Deal generally, and the FHA in particular, fully accepted the racial practices of the private society. The FHA always stayed away from the inner city and gray areas and it even connived with fire insurance companies in their refusal to insure housing in black slums.[2] Far from leading, it tagged behind in racial change. Thus it was not until a year after the Supreme Court decree of 1948 declaring racial covenants on land unenforceable that regulations were promulgated forbidding the issuance of new insured mortgages on such property. Only on November 20, 1962, did a reluctant Kennedy administration issue Executive Order 11063 directing all departments of government to take affirmative action against racial discrimination.[3] For the mortgage market this order meant a timid enforcement of a FHA prohibition against new mortgage money for segregated housing developments.

Extreme caution has also marked the standard-setting functions of the agency. As a partner of private bankers, the FHA has not conceived its role to be that of the protector of the mass of mortgage borrowers, and it has therefore never pressed the consumer's interest in lowering fees for title searches, extra bank charges, and lawyers' services.[4] A similar tendency has characterized the agency's construction and land-planning policies. Quite naturally the first concerns of the FHA were to see that mortgages it insured rested on houses that conformed to the current consensus for adequate construction, and periodically these specifications have been reviewed to keep pace with changing fashions in housing. Yet the structure itself, as miles of decayed inner-city neighborhoods and half-finished and ill-equipped new suburbs witness, is at most half the cost of a decent home. The landscaping, drainage, streets, utilities, shopping centers, schools, hospitals, clinics, playgrounds, parks, public transportation, and highways require an investment at least equal to, if not far in excess of, that in the dwelling unit itself. Moreover, in the long term, say the thirty-five-year term of a FHA mortgage, the quality of these public services has more to do with the sustained value and utility of a house than do minor variations in its quality. Yet the FHA has not moved far toward using its power of awarding or withholding credit to

2. National Commission on Urban Problems, *Building the American City, House Document No. 91–34* (91st Congress, 1st Session), Washington, 1969, pp. 99–102.

3. Martin Meyerson and Edward C. Banfield, *Politics, Planning, and the Public Interest,* Glencoe, 1955, pp. 29–55.

4. Wheaton, "Federal Housing Programs," pp. 34–35, 67–69.

influence the coordination of public services with land development at the expanding edges of our metropolitan regions. Overcrowded schools, inadequate drainage, poor street and highway layout, and bad siting of structures are the hallmarks of the lower middle-class and working-class suburbs financed by the agency. The "tickey-tackey" of our new metropolitan regions, to use the current snobbish phrase, is more the product of inadequate public services and bad land planning than poor building practice.[5]

The local-bank focus, especially the local savings and loan association focus, of the federal insurance program also hampers its promotion of good vacant-land development. The local savings bank is the principal supplier of credit to the small underfinanced builder who assembles a parcel and runs up a few houses for quick turnover. The added efforts of such builders (those building less than twenty-five houses a year) contributes approximately two-thirds of each year's new suburban construction. Yet such men have neither the capital, interest, nor political power to plan large-scale coordination of public and private facilities. As a result, federal insurance underwrites a series of small ventures whose combined effect is rapid urban growth, but rapid urban growth at a standard far below the capability of the total capital invested in land, mortgages, and public facilities which this work requires.[6]

In sum, the FHA mortgage-insurance system and parallel Veterans Administration programs have proved tremendously helpful to the emerging middle-class families of America, although they have not served this class nearly as well as they might. The very fact that 60 percent of metropolitan dwellers occupy homes that they own testifies to the popularity and success of the strategy. The plentiful financial resources and high volume of construction which the American housing industry periodically attains have inspired much envy in European countries where chronic housing shortages persist.[7] With our federal

5. National Commission on Urban Problems, *Three Land Research Studies, Research Report No. 12,* Allen D. Manvel et al., eds., Washington, 1968, pp. 1–3, 19–25; National Commission on Urban Problems, *How the Many Costs of Housing Fit Together, Research Report No. 16,* Elsie Eaves, ed., Washington, 1969, pp. 1–8, 52–54.

6. George Lefcoe and Thomas W. Dobson, "Savings Associations as Land Developers," *Yale Law Journal,* 75 (July 1966), 1277, 1283.

7. Commission on Urban Problems, *Building the American City,* pp. 94–107; U.S. Bureau of the Census, *Statistical Abstract of the United States: 1971,* Washington, 1971, p. 675; Martin Pawley, *Architecture versus Housing,* New York, 1971, pp. 41–43, 75–79; Ministry of Housing and Local Government, *Report of*

mortgage insurance and concurrent interest and property-tax deduction,
which subsidize the middle- and upper-income home buyers and co-
operative-apartment owners, we have pushed the limits of massive
government assistance to private housing. As a nation we have reaped
the full benefits of a trickle-down housing market: no severe housing
shortages for the upper two-thirds of the urban population and rapid
new construction for the upper half.

Not only has the great mass of working-class successors to secondhand housing benefited; even the poor can count some gains. The
decline in density of most areas of the inner city brought about by the
rapid distention of the metropolis has meant that the greatest part of our
city dwellers can now afford private housing without doubling up. Thus,
except for the worst black inner-city ghettos, city apartments meet the
occupancy rules that were first laid down about 1900, and single-family
and two-family homes in run-down neighborhoods can be used as such
by low-income families without the need to take in boarders or share
with other families. This drop in crude density also ramifies through
many aspects of public health: it reduces the dangers of contagious
diseases; it gives the poor some of the personal privacy that hitherto had
been a luxury of middle-class life; it makes housekeeping easier and
neighborly neglect or sloppiness of less consequence. Finally, with the
decline in density the buildings themselves last longer, even though
repairs may be neglected. The poor can now use up their structures with
a lower rate of decay than in earlier times of overuse.[8]

The social costs to the city and the nation, however, have outweighed such benefits. FHA conservatism in land planning has meant
the laying down of thousands of neighborhoods which now must be used
for a century whether we like them or not, and they are neighborhoods
which failed to meet the best commonplace standards of our own time.
There is even evidence today that by taking the indirect approach of
increasing mortgage credit rather than by building itself, the federal
government may unwittingly have inflated building costs to such a

---

the Committee on Housing in Greater London, Sir Milner Holland, chmn., London,
1965, pp. 200–225.

   8. Amos Hawley, The Changing Shape of Metropolitan America: Deconcentra-
tion Since 1920, Glencoe, 1956, pp. 34–74. For recent trends and a projection of
a small rise in the density of central cities, National Commission on Urban Problems, The Challenge of America's Metropolitan Population Outlook, Research Report No. 3, Patricia L. Hodge and Philip M. Hauser, eds., Washington, 1968, pp.
17–18; National Poverty Areas, Research Report No. 9, Allen D. Manvel, ed.,
Washington, 1968, pp. 2–13.

degree that many marginal families it hoped to aid are now priced out of the market. More serious still, government mortgage insurance and tax subsidies have vigorously promoted the racial segregation of the metropolis. The government now faces the herculean task of undoing its own work, of having American city dwellers unlearn the habits and attitudes of class and racial segregation which government policies have been consciously and unconsciously teaching them since 1935.[9] It is a task at which the nation may well falter because of the weight of political habit and precedent which these policies have saddled upon homeowners, tenants, builders, bankers, government officials, and Congressmen. Over the past thirty-five years the nation has grown comfortable, even proud, of its commitment of billions of dollars in tax exemptions and government insurance for the benefit of the upper two-thirds of the population. We have grown accustomed in the housing field, as in so many others, to using government to give the most aid and service to those among us who need it least. Such a habit of government, the very essence of promoting a trickle-down housing policy, flies in the face of a goal of building a more inclusive society. Although aid to marginal home buyers is a useful policy when used in combination with a massive public-housing program, the latter has failed in its purpose because of habits of class greed, racial animosity, and majoritarian self-satisfaction which mortgage insurance and tax exemptions have long nourished. With the upper two-thirds of the population attended to, how was the lowest third to be heeded?

Since 1934 the federal government has administered a small program of housing aid to the low-income families of the nation. Much has been learned from these experiments and past errors have been eliminated by corrective legislation, especially in the basic acts of 1949 and 1968. The requirements for a decent housing program for the ill-housed third of our urban fellow citizens are now known. All the legislative shortcomings, except the correction of the disorders of the local property tax, have been rectified. It only remains for the general public to vote the necessary funds and for the public and its administrators to pursue the task with good will and energy.

Inexcusable class, racial, and commercial antagonisms have dogged American public housing from its inception, and to these antagonisms must be ascribed the most serious and enduring failings of the programs.

9. Karl E. and Alma F. Taeuber, *Negroes in Cities: Residential Segregation and Neighborhood Change,* Chicago, 1965, pp. 31–68.

Initially prejudice against such work was overcome by the sheer collapse of the construction industry, which served to bring labor unions and urban reformers together. Labor wanted construction jobs, while the reformers wanted to clear some of the slums which they had without avail been trying to exorcise by regulations. From 1934 through 1937 the Public Works Administration of the federal government built 22,000 low-rent units in fifty projects about the country on the make-work justification.[10] Court opposition, a diffuse but nonetheless widespread sentiment that direct federal construction somehow impinged too closely on local government and the sanctity of the home, and fears of real-estate dealers and bankers of price-cutting competition forced changes in the federal participation. Alarm over a monstrous federal bureaucracy was overcome by a grants-in-aid system for the benefit of locally managed housing authorities. Local landlords and real-estate interests were placated by a formula which required that public-housing families must be sufficiently poor so that they could afford rents no higher than 20 percent below those prevailing locally for safe, sanitary shelter. Reformers were given their goal by a provision that for every new low-income unit built, a dilapidated one must be rehabilitated or demolished. Beyond these political bargains the essence of the new program lay in the degree of federal support: the government would contribute the capital sufficient to build the project, the tenants must through their rents pay enough to carry the interest, depreciation, maintenance, and operating costs.[11]

Such a compromise system set some of the long-lasting failings of federal low-rent housing. The support formulas meant that the very poor could not afford to live in public housing because the rents to cover maintenance and management were too high for them. Families whose income rose above the maximum had to leave the projects for private slum housing because of the 20 percent differential which had to be maintained between the top of public housing rents and the bottom of the private market. The rules tying subsidized rent to the personal income of families were so written that if a family's fortune rose its rents could not also float up to fair market values while they continued to occupy their apartment. Instead the most economically successful families were forced out of the projects regardless of their personal prefer-

10. Robert Moore Fisher, *Twenty Years of Public Housing, Economic Aspects of the Federal Program,* New York, 1959, pp. 82–91.
11. Ibid., pp. 92–125.

ences. In Europe the common practice is to allow families settled in public housing to remain and pay market-equivalent rents if they so choose.[12] The 1968 revisions of the federal laws have finally begun tentative steps to end these antisocial income policies.

There have been other unfortunate aspects of our housing program revolving around such issues as lack of tenant participation in project management, harassment of tenants to enforce income and conduct rules, lack of social services and community facilities, neglect of space for large families, poor siting, and so forth. But most crippling of all, because these shortcomings permeate all aspects of public housing from the corridors of the apartment houses to the Housing and Urban Development Department offices in Washington, have been the interacting failures of low-volume construction, segregation, and bad design.[13] Since the goal of the 1949 act of "a decent home and a suitable living environment for every American family" has never been popularly accepted as a right of citizenship either by the victimized poor or the fearful affluent, a terrible incubus of philanthropy has plagued public housing and steadily brings on it cycles of sickness. With public housing perceived as a burden and an expression of charity rather than a right of all and an investment in the human capital of the city, both local and federal governments have consistently scrimped, saved, and limited the program. Underfunding has meant cut-down design programs, high-rise jungles, and low-rise projects which do not even match the standards of World War I workers' housing. When an occasional good design comes forward, it must be built against the weight of bureaucratic regulations and popular prejudices and is rarely imitated. Good architects and aggressive administrators have been driven off by red tape and low morale. As residents of ill-designed and ill-managed facilities, tenants have often felt little responsibility for their quarters and resented the public stigma of institutionalized charity. Underdesign meant that children soon overran such amenities as were provided, with shattered trees, worn-out grass, broken windows, and a periphery of derelict cars confirming the passing citizen's view that "those people" didn't deserve decent housing. As undeserving poor and black citizens, project dwellers must be restricted to the old slum neighborhoods, or as in Boston, be put out next to the city

12. Lawrence M. Friedman, *Government and Slum Housing, A Century of Frustration,* Chicago, 1968, pp. 106–13.

13. National Commission on Urban Problems, *More Than Shelter, Social Needs in Low- and Moderate-Income Housing, Research Report No. 8,* George Schermer Associates, eds., Washington, 1968, pp. 68–87.

dump, and not allowed to settle in the suburbs. Thus even after the federal policy of deliberate racial segregation was rescinded in 1949, segregation of public housing has continued because the housing projects we have built in our large cities stereotype the poor and the black in a way that reinforces all the fears and prejudices of working-class and middle-class Americans. Thus underfunding brought poor design, poor design fed segregation, segregation fostered the social and economic failure of projects, and failure justified underfunding. Round and round the cycle went, constantly eroding what was potentially one of the most useful tools of American urban policy.

With the post–World War II FHA-funded housing boom, organized labor lost interest in public housing; those construction jobs weren't needed any longer. Underfunding, bad design, and repeated reports and observations of the social pathology of projects drove off the urban reformers' support. In 1957 one of the most perceptive supporters of public housing, Catherine Bauer, summarized the reformers' dismay.

> Public-housing projects tend to be very large and highly standardized in their design. Visually they may be no more monotonous than a typical suburban tract, but their density makes them seem much more institutional, like veterans' hospitals or old-fashioned orphan asylums. The fact they are usually designed as Islands—"community units" turning their back to the surrounding neighborhood which looks entirely different— only adds to this institutional quality. Any charity stigma that attaches to subsidized housing is thus reinforced. Each project proclaims, visually, that it serves the "lowest income group."[14]

Though Congressional support has continued on the momentum of the past, within most large cities opposition to public housing has mounted. Detroit has only 8,200 units and has not undertaken a new project for some years; Philadelphia, Boston, Houston, Los Angeles, and Washington all have under 16,000 units for metropolitan populations well in excess of a million inhabitants. Only New York has pursued public housing vigorously, and the pathologies of that city's projects are accordingly the most visible to the nation.[15] The central city's courtship of the middle-income and wealthy taxpayer puts the final stigma on public housing. After a generation of construction, from 1934 to 1970, only 893,500 units were completed and in operation around the

14. Catherine Bauer, "The Dreary Deadlock of Public Housing," *Architectural Forum*, 106 (May 1957), 141–42.
15. Commission on Urban Problems, *Building the American City*, pp. 113, 164.

country. Of this total 143,400 were for the benefit of the elderly.[16] Less than 2 percent of our metropolitan population occupies such structures. Bad as it is, the popularity of public housing tells of the hard choices the poor must make. For most spaces there are long waiting lists. The projects are not catchbasins of abject and defeated poor, but are used by low-income families much as Americans use their private housing. The annual turnover rate, the coming and going of families, is only somewhat less than the general national norm. Finally, because of the relatively small number of units the poor have had to bear the brunt of the social and economic dislocations attendant upon giant highway and urban-renewal land clearances since World War II. In no city did public housing even approach the volume of destruction of the stock of housing from which the poor had to choose.[17]

The 1968 act has ended most of the formal barriers to a decent American public-housing program. If new court decisions in the states reduce municipal dependence upon the local property tax, the last institutional justification for excluding the poor from any neighborhood will be removed. What remains is clear enough. To end the sick self-defeating cycle of low volume of construction, segregation of sites, and institutional design, the public, both the victimized third and the fearful upper two-thirds, must come to think of all Americans as members of one society. They must come to believe that every one of us has a right to "a decent home and a suitable living environment." Surely such a principle is one of the essential elements in a minimum definition of the meaning of an affluent democracy. Once that spirit is accepted, public housing can easily be attached to urban-renewal reconstruction and the building of new towns.[18] Most importantly of all, it can be located on vacant sites in the suburbs and the new centers of our ever-enlarging metropolitan regions. When public housing ceases to be a grudging philanthropy and becomes a goal of granting our fellow citizens their just rights, then projects can be designed to meet the standards of

16. *Statistical Abstract: 1971*, p. 672.
17. Charles Abrams, *The City Is the Frontier*, New York, 1965, pp. 43–44; Anthony Downs, *Urban Problems and Prospects*, Chicago, 1970, pp. 192–227.
18. There is a promising groundswell sentiment to use state agencies for public housing, urban renewal, and new-town construction which embodies low-income and desegregation goals. New York State Urban Development Corporation, *Annual Report*, New York, 1970; New York State Urban Development Corporation, *New Communities for New York*, New York, 1970; Michigan State Housing Development Authority, Department of Social Services, *Michigan State Housing Development Authority Act*, Lansing, 1970.

commonplace American aspirations and to be related to their neighborhoods instead of being isolated from them. Such a program would take
time, but steadily pursued for a generation it could close the gap of
isolation and punishment of the lower third of the population and enable
the poor and the black of America to participate as equals in the new
freedoms of our metropolitan society.

Had the United States been pursuing an active and humane public-
housing program in the years since 1949, and had urban-renewal
allocations been consciously tied to a national urban policy, then urban
renewal could have assumed its proper role as the program for the upper
two-thirds of the population. Properly understood, the many interrelated
programs which go under the rubric "urban renewal" have as their
legitimate function the modernizing of our metropolitan regions in a way
which will bring them in closer accord to the possibilities of a wealthy
and expanding economy. Urban renewal could and should be the tool
whereby the prospering elements in the society get a chance to remake
the old sections of the metropolis in conformity to national goals for full
employment and planned urban and regional growth. Unlike public
housing, which now authorizes a very wide range of programs and is
sufficient to allow vigorous administration, urban renewal still contains a
fatal flaw: it lacks adequate political and policy structure. This flaw,
which derives from its historical development, has in large measure
accounted for its extremely wasteful and scandalously inhumane
practices.

After World War II, an enlarged understanding of the mechanisms
of urban growth gained from research and experiments of the thirties
and early forties, along with dissatisfaction over the small public
housing program, led urban reformers to propose a grand attack on the
slums. By 1945 it had become generally understood that the land itself
and its supporting public facilities were the key to housing, and experts
testifying in extended hearings before Congress urged that the attack
upon the slums be redirected toward the land under the structures. The
federal government should finance the clearance of slum districts and
the assembling of the hundreds of small parcels of land into which such
property was divided. For their part, municipalities should administer
the program, make use of their powers of eminent domain for parcel
assembly, and build new streets, install new lighting, erect schools, and
the like. After these steps the public low-rent housing and privately
constructed middle-income housing could be erected on the prepared

sites, thereby modernizing great tracts of decayed slums. The essential soundness of the suggestion lay in its focus on urban land reclamation and the division of governmental effort according to the relative resources of the federal government and municipalities. The federal government would be harnessed to the most expensive task, clearance and parcel assembly, while the city would contribute by using its planning offices and its powers of eminent domain, and by constructing supporting services and organizing local support.[19]

Despite its insights and clear intentions, the 1949 urban-renewal legislation ignored the power relationships within the cities which were to carry out the Congressional intent. Rather than initiate a new method for aiding the poor, municipal officials and commercial interests turned the ten-billion-dollar program into an irresponsible social monster. The post–World War II economic boom, combining as it did new metropolitan highway systems, rapid suburban construction of houses, shopping centers, and offices and plants, left the old central cities stranded with billions of dollars tied up in investments in a downtown pattern suited to the streetcar era. Poor whites and blacks streamed into the old cores as the working-class and middle-class whites sought the new suburbs. The poor newcomers, without organized political representation at City Hall, often deliberately excluded from power and political expression, tilted the balance of postwar urban politics. With working-class machines weakened by outmigration of their former constituents, a coalition of inner-city business interests and reform-minded moderates who were unaware of the future consequences of urban renewal, or who wanted to protect their own neighborhoods against the poor and the black, swept into office on urban renewal platforms. Again, as in the current animosity against low-income public housing and even working-class and lower middle-class FHA housing, the metropolitan dysfunction of the property tax played an important role in subverting urban renewal. Mayors, hard pressed for funds because the middle-class exodus cut property values in the central city, sought to use the new federal program to woo back the deserters. They hoped that by rebuilding the downtown core of the cities in the new styles of the day they could lure back wealthy taxpayers and shore up downtown retail sales and office rentals, thereby enlarging the municipality's tax resources. Thus, the low-

19. Wheaton, "Federal Housing Programs," pp. 172–206; Coleman Woodbury, ed., *The Future of Cities and Urban Redevelopment*, Chicago, 1953, pp. 9–20, 426–76.

rent and public-housing goals of the 1949 legislation were subverted or ignored, and in time conservative Congresses consented to this alteration in favor of the well-to-do. The downtown horse was to be fed to aid the starving municipal pigeons.[20]

Although all past and currently authorized projects will demolish more than a million housing units, almost entirely the former homes of the bottom third of the population who cannot afford any kind of new housing, only 5 percent of the housing in the Community Renewal Projects approved through 1967 will be for low-rent public housing.[21] In the first rushes of clearance, thousands of poor families were displaced without adequate compensation or decent attention to their alternatives. "Negro removal" justifiably became the tag for these programs, and some cities even used urban renewal to force blacks into a single ghetto where previously they had been scattered at several locations about town.[22] The refurbished downtowns, sports stadia, new government and corporate office towers, and slabs of high-rise luxury apartments which typically characterize big-city urban renewal stand in shameless witness to the callousness of American class and race relations. The well-to-do have spent ten billion dollars to redecorate their central cities for their own use and benefit while pushing perhaps a comparable social and economic cost off upon the low-income third of the population. Urban renewal is now a social and political scandal. Its only likely benefit to the poor seems to be its delivery of new capital into the hands of black political groups who are now inheriting the centers of our metropolitan regions. Perhaps they can use these cores as hostages for an increase of their state and federal bargaining power.

In spite of everything, the redevelopment of the old parts of our cities is surely a worthwhile public function; and were the planning and political shortcomings of urban renewal rectified, it could be a useful part of American urban policy. Unfortunately, four key elements were missing from the original legislation and its subsequent administration.

First and most apparent was its callous disregard of the effects of urban renewal upon the living conditions of low-income groups. Rapid construction of public housing in the suburbs could have easily overcome this fault, and since 1967 HUD regulations and subsequent legislation

20. Abrams, *The City Is the Frontier*, pp. 82–85; Commission on Urban Problems, *Building the American City*, pp. 152–59.
21. Commission on Urban Problems, *Building the American City*, p. 163.
22. Theodore J. Lowi, *The End of Liberalism: Ideology, Policy and the Crisis of Public Authority*, New York, 1969, pp. 250–66.

have been moving in this direction. To date, all the old shortcomings of public housing and virulent class and racial antipathy prevent any substantial increase in the access of the inner-city poor to vacant suburban land.[23]

Second, the long-standing tie between city services and the strength of the local property tax encouraged a socially lethal game of municipal competition for new middle-class and wealthy residents to the exclusion of poor and even working-class families. Successful urban renewal and many other improvements in the American city await the reorganization of metropolitan finances upon some more socially beneficial base. Recent state cases in California and elsewhere, ruling the local property tax an unconstitutional basis for educational taxation, are at last opening up this set of issues.[24]

Third, adequate mechanisms for citizen participation and defense against local projects has not yet been devised. Although successive Congressional enactments called for metropolitan and city-wide planning and for neighborhood consultation, the standards of performance for an adequate project have not yet been made sufficiently definite. HUD's urban-renewal standards should closely reflect the common housing and environmental standards of the nation, and should be stated clearly enough so that local citizens and officials could test their proposals against such goals. The citizen should be able to tell in advance if a given proposal will in fact raise his neighborhood to compliance with the standards of the new suburbs. As in the case of the conflicts between highways and their abutters, should a project fail to meet those standards the affected property owner ought to have standing in court to stop the project until he is guaranteed that it will truly renew his surroundings. As now practiced, urban renewal confronts both the citizen and the planner with mountains of red tape and all the vagueness, delays, powerlessness, manipulation, and profiteering that such procedures inevitably create.[25]

Fourth, urban renewal goes forward in a national policy vacuum. Rather than being integrated with national income and employment

23. Commission on Urban Problems, *Building the American City*, pp. 157, 163–65, 173–77; Downs, *Urban Problems*, pp. 60–63, 144–45, 152–54.

24. *Serrano* v. *Priest*, 96 Cal. Reptr. 601 (1971).

25. Edgar S. Cahn, et al., *The Legal Lawbreakers, A Study of the Nonadministration of Federal Relocation Requirements*, Citizens Advocate Center, Washington, October 1970; Commission on Urban Problems, *Building the American City*, pp. 165–69, 176–77.

plans and with set goals for regional growth and modernization, it is but another large chunk in the Congressional pork barrel. The Tennessee Valley Authority and the long-continued water, electric, war, and space investments in the Los Angeles region have shown that federal policy can be used to influence the jobs, personal income, private investment, and physical growth of our urban regions. Overseas, European national economic policy has been successfully harnessed to plans for urban and regional growth so that depressed areas, low-income populations, and obsolete cities are benefited through consciously articulated programs for industrial location, transportation improvement, and housing, education, health, and welfare services. As these European undertakings have become effective a new kind of urban and regional politics has developed, commencing an open and wholesome conflict among the affected cities and regions.[26] To neglect such interrelationships between federal programs is to irresponsibly squander the nation's scarce resources. It is our political disgrace that as a nation we could not, and did not, debate a ten-billion-dollar program for the subsidized rebuilding of central-city office and apartment cores in the context of our needs for low- and moderate-income housing, racial desegregation, full employment, medical care, education, highways, farm subsidies, armaments, and a standing army. These are all major undertakings and major concerns of the nation. A decision on one affects all the others, and together they have influenced the growth and present condition of our cities. For urban renewal to become a legitimate undertaking, it must be debated and administered in such a context.

The parallels between American housing and health programs since 1920 are naturally close, since both are integral parts of the same national culture and urban system. Innovations in both have strongly favored the upper two-thirds of the population; both have relied heavily on insurance and tax concessions; both have depended upon local private and public agencies to do their work; both have ignored the poor or served them ill; and both have used large-scale organizations of the central government, banking, and insurance to manipulate the pace and direction of change so that in the name of maintaining the status quo a conservative revolution has been wrought: in housing the dispersal of the old industrial metropolis, in health the near abolition of the solo general practitioner. Finally, after years of divergence, during which

26. Lloyd Rodwin, *Nations and Cities: A Comparison of Strategies for Urban Growth,* Boston, 1970, pp. 140–52, 187–216.

time American medicine concentrated its attention on communicable disease and acute care to the neglect of the larger social issues of class, race, and environment, housing and health are now once more converging as an interlinking set of concerns for the maintenance of a healthy population.

For the vast majority of Americans, altering the death rate is no longer the central health issue. Though there are still highly significant mortality differences caused by race and class position, any truly universal health program whose major foci were preventive care, chronic-ailment care, and the public environment could end such differentials. A 1968 survey of existing Chicago health services defined our modern situation:

> Certainly it is a reasonable assumption that timely and proper health care can postpone death from some causes, and prevent, cure, or palliate some diseases. At the same time, however, it is also reasonable to assume that a salubrious environment, only moderately stressful life styles, balanced diet, exercise, good housing, and so on probably have a greater indirect and direct effect on the disease patterns and age at death than do health services as such.[27]

It is the failure of the American health system to adapt to these new conditions, both in its unsatisfactory service to the prosperous and its near-criminal neglect and treatment of the blacks and the poor, that constitutes today's medical crisis.

For the prosperous two-thirds of American society, the history of urban health since 1920 is the history of private medical insurance and the effects that this new mode of payment has had upon the inherited structure of medical practice. In the first years of the era, systematic social and economic research established with certainty that the expense of illness could be insured. The U.S. Public Health Service did a study of the incidence of illness in a small Maryland city during the years 1921–24. Three years later this pilot study was followed by a giant assessment, funded by a number of foundations, of the national incidence of illness, family medical expenses, the incomes of health-service personnel, the nature and distribution of health facilities, and related subjects. The final twenty-eight-volume report of the Committee on the Costs of Medical Care, issued in 1932, showed that insurance was

27. Odin W. Anderson and Joanna Kravits, *Health Services in the Chicago Area—A Framework for Use Data,* Center for Health Administration Studies, *Research Series No. 26,* Chicago, 1968, p. 33.

definitely feasible. The burden of the costs of care fell heavily on a very small fraction of the nation's families in any given year.[28] The reporting committee was divided on the issues of how this insurance should be funded and how it should be related to the provision of medical service. The majority favored government insurance to protect all Americans and proposed that health care be centered in groups of doctors working as teams through hospitals. They saw the hospital as the institution best adapted to the benign management of the increasing specialization and complexity of technique. They objected to privately funded insurance on the grounds that it would offer an insufficient check on doctors and hospitals and therefore would encourage the inflation of medical costs. An accurate prediction![29]

On the other hand, the minority report better captured the mood and traditions of American patients and physicians, and for its part foresaw the basic flaw in the hospital strategy. Solo general practitioners were already a declining, though still preponderant, fraction of the profession, and the minority felt they should be encouraged as the best hope for ordinary family needs. They estimated that 82 percent of all illness could be competently treated by a well-trained solo practitioner who possessed simple equipment. The dissenters stressed the desirability of individuals' being able to select their personal physician and stressed the efficacy of sustained personal relationships. Group practice and hospitals, as advocated by the majority report, seemed to be applying inhumane big-business and mass-production techniques to human needs. So they proved to be. In keeping with its focus, the minority called for private nonprofit insurance to be managed by the professionals themselves. In short, they endorsed what was to be the wave of the future—the Blue Cross and Blue Shield approach to payment for medical service.[30]

Unfortunately for us all, however, history gave neither side the arrangement it wished; we got instead the worst mix of both. The majority never saw the rise of adequate government insurance or widespread group practice, while the minority lived to see the hospital and specialist trend they deplored accelerated by private insurance. Like the

28. Committee on the Costs of Medical Care, *Medical Care for the American People, Publication No. 28,* Chicago, 1932, pp. 67–71.

29. Ibid., pp. 59–64.

30. Ibid., pp. 153–69, 173, 179–81.

U.S. government's FHA mortgage program, a creature of depression and threatened bankruptcy, the nonprofit hospital-insurance system worked a conservative revolution upon established patterns by pouring money into the established acute-care hospitals of the nation.

Historians trace the lineage of Blue Cross, the parent hospital-insurance organizations, to 1929 and Dallas, Texas, where Baylor University Hospital took over a local schoolteachers' sick-benefit plan and began to enroll other groups in the city for insured service at the hospital. The example might not have spread far had not the Great Depression undermined the finances of big-city voluntary hospitals everywhere: wealthy donors cut back their giving and patients simply stopped paying their bills. It has been estimated that during one depression year 60 percent of the hospital services in Philadelphia were rendered without any reimbursement. Desperate hospital administrators seized upon the Baylor example and other early experiments, so that by 1932 clusters of city hospitals were banding together to form community-wide insured hospital-service plans. These groups in turn secured appropriate state insurance legislation, developed standard administrative practices, and emerged prior to World War II ás the regional and state-wide Blue Cross insurance companies in the form we now know them.[31]

A few particular arrangements give Blue Cross private-insurance programs their distinctive quality. The companies are nonprofit and are managed by boards of directors who represent the participating hospitals, the medical profession, and community leaders. Their salesmen are salaried, not paid on a commission basis. The companies endeavor by seeking wide participation so as to pool all the medical risks of the state and its cities in order that rates for members who join as individuals do not exceed by too far the rates of those who enroll all together as a group of employees. Finally, Blue Cross plans are not primarily cash-indemnity plans but service plans. The participating hospitals agree to render a specific list of services to members for a fixed fee. The hospital is reimbursed by the insurance company, not the patient. These modes of governance and payment, originally conceived to avoid doctors' reactionary laws against the corporate practice of medicine, proved to have important consequences as the insurance system spread, principally

31. Herman M. and Anne R. Somers, *Doctors, Patients, and Health Insurance, The Organization and Financing of Medical Care*, Washington, 1961, pp. 291–304.

by making Blue Cross the prisoner of its hospital beneficiaries, not the representative of its patient-members. Well established by 1938, the subsequent wartime boom and the influence of wartime wage controls, which favored rewarding employees with noncash benefits, transformed this Depression defense into a mass institution. By the middle of the fifties, hospital insurance—Blue Cross and its commercial competition—had become a fact of life for regularly employed urban Americans.[32]

Blue Shield insurance, a similar set of arrangements for reimbursing participating doctors for a specific list of surgical procedures, had a different origin from Blue Cross, and quite different rationale. Its secondary goal was to rescue doctors from unpaid bills, while its primary goal has been to defend private practice against public demands for government insurance. The ancestors of Blue Shield first appeared on the Pacific coast around 1917, when county medical societies in the states of Washington and Oregon organized prepayment service as an alternative to the current unscrupulous contract practice then prevalent in lumbering, mining, and railroad communities. At that time employers in these isolated settlements were paying for medical services to their hands, but often the patients received scandalously low-quality treatment.

The Great Depression and a threat by the governor of California to press for compulsory insurance carried such plans down the Pacific coast and across the nation. Originally such plans offered a broad range of services, but as they were introduced on a larger scale heavy usage threatened them with bankruptcy and the coverage had to be pruned. The American Medical Association always viewed these programs with suspicion, favoring cash-indemnity insurance for the patient rather than insured services, since the former seemed to sharply differentiate financial matters from practice and hence seemed to threaten less of an opening toward the group medical practice the Association feared. In the immediate post–World War II years, when every Congress debated bills for government medical insurance and President Truman pressed for such measures, the medical profession actively promoted surgical and hospital insurance as its answer to socialized medicine. With a structure similar to that of Blue Cross, often even sharing combined offices, Blue Shield rode the coattails of its more established hospital patron until by the mid-fifties it was almost as widespread, and the two

32. Ibid., pp. 249–53, 295–97.

programs came to be fused in the popular mind as "medical insurance."[33]

Fraught with major limitations as the Blues are—limitations of both governance and coverage—the post–World War II rush of commercial insurance companies into competition with them has exacerbated all the shortcomings of the nonprofit system's effects upon private medical institutions. Although private insurance companies had sold cash disability benefits as extras on their basic workmen's compensation policies for years, the Depression wiped out many company-sponsored employee benefit plans, and commercial insurers were reluctant to return to the health field until the Blues had shown a safe path. In the postwar years a coalition of insurance companies and medical societies defeated the labor-supported government insurance bills before Congress. Rebuffed, the unions returned to the industrial bargaining tables to demand more health benefits for their members. Pressed by such demands and reassured by the booming growth of the Blues, commercial carriers took up group hospital and surgical insurance. Because giant national corporations needed uniform policies for industry-wide bargaining, the largest insurance companies were the best equipped to meet the demand, and soon the top twelve had cornered 90 percent of the business.

Associated differences in mode of payment, rates, and risk pools distinguish commercial policies from the Blues. The standard private carrier's group policy is written for an employer who collects his workers' monthly contributions, if the workers contribute at all, while the insurance company reimburses the employee when he submits his hospital and medical bills. Since most policies today are written with a rate-adjustment clause calling for an increase or decrease in charges based upon a yearly audit of claims, neither the carrier nor the employer has any role in or much incentive to control the quality, quantity, or price of medical services purchased by their beneficiaries. Second, even more than the Blues, commercial policies pool the safest risks and so do not reach out to the most health-endangered populations. As cheap policies, tailored for competitive bidding, commercial insurance skips the old, the irregularly employed, the chronically ill. Moreover, the extent of its coverage depends upon the wit and aggressiveness of union bargaining and does not rest upon a planned assessment of the best deployment of limited health services. At least the Blues seek to build community-wide pools of risks so that individuals may purchase insur-

33. Ibid., pp. 317–40.

ance at rates not too far in advance of group charges. The sales and administrative costs of commercial individual policies forbid commercial carriers from following even the Blues' modest lead.[34]

Thus to a remarkable degree the success of the private insurance movement has had much the same effect on the structure of medical services that the FHA did upon the housing market. By establishing insurance pools of safe economic risks, like the safe mortgages, health insurers have extended the purchasing power of working-class and middle-class Americans in such a way as increasingly to neglect the poor, the black, and the old. Moreover, the concentration of policies upon hospitalization, surgery, and catastrophe instead of everyday family needs like dentistry, pediatric care, mental health, and long term paramedical services for both the old and the chronically ill accelerated the pre-existing trends of American medicine toward hospitals, high technology, and bureaucratic doctor-patient relationships.

Complementary policies of the medical profession and the federal government exacerbated these tendencies of mass private insurance. For its part, the medical profession systematically limited the supply of doctors by restricting the output of medical education, thus stifling supply at a time of accelerating demand. Such a monopolistic professional policy inevitably caused a steep rise in medical charges as patients outbid each other for medical attention. At the same time doctors, like all good Americans, competed among themselves for the most lucrative practices and the highest-status positions, thereby rushing headlong toward the most prestigious hospitals, the wealthiest populations, and the most refined specialties.

The government contributed to this flight toward specialized bureaucratic medicine and hospital-based practice in two ways. First, urged on by the successes of national health foundations in tuberculosis and polio research, and beguiled by the seeming political neutrality of research, it poured millions of dollars into research programs, thereby removing doctors from full-time practice and adding prestige to research physicians who contributed little or nothing to meeting the day-to-day needs of the mass of patients. Second, the government invested several billion dollars, starting in 1946 with its Hill-Burton program, in modernizing old acute-care hospitals and building new ones. These federal policies were calculated not to agitate the politically explosive issues of estab-

34. Ibid., pp. 262–89.

lished medical practice, but the diversion of billions into research and hospitals had the effect of accelerating the bureaucratization of medical care and the neglect of commonplace needs, central-city services, and low-income groups which the private insurance boom initiated.[35]

Thus, for the upper two-thirds of American city dwellers the trends of private insurance and public policy since 1920 have brought mixed blessings. There is too much emphasis on hospitals and surgery, since these are subsidized institutions and practices; there is too much emphasis on advanced science, technology, and drugs, since these are the traditional successes of American medicine; and there is too much emphasis on the physicians' and other professionals' needs, and too little on the needs of patients. Both insurance funding and the ever-expanding reach of medical science have raised the expectations of Americans as to what constitutes an adequate medical relationship. Yet the screening of physicians from patients by standard commercial hours, overcrowded waiting rooms, secretaries, technicians, nurses, medical centers, hospitals, and insurance forms has poisoned doctor-patient interactions. Middle-class Americans, the former heart of traditional solo practice, have been forced increasingly to use the emergency and outpatient services of urban hospitals, where they encounter the long lines, unkept schedules, lost records, and impersonal and even hostile treatment that the working class has suffered for years. The result has been a partial breakdown of confidence between doctors and private patients, a rapid rise in malpractice suits, a weakening of middle-class opposition to all forms of socialized medicine, and a pervasive feeling of exploitation.[36] Like so many institutions in the modern city, whether nonprofit like universities, schools, and housing authorities, or profit-making like manufacturing corporations, retail stores, and insurance companies, our medical institutions, by expanding into giant permanent organizations without any satisfactory mechanisms for their democratic control by those whom they are supposed to serve, have become mired in bureaucratic self-serving and public malfunction.[37]

Our medical institutions, like so many institutions in America, have a

35. Ibid., pp. 57–58.
36. Ibid., 455–75.
37. Recent community studies establish the obvious: that decision-making on community health care rests in the hands of urban elites. Robert N. Wilson, *Community Structure and Health Action,* National Commission on Community Health Service, Washington, 1968, pp. 58, 86–87.

predominant form, but are not all cast in the same mold. At present a variety of group-practice and insurance systems offer a broad range of alternatives to the regularly employed. None have yet evolved any adequate mode of patient representation, so that should they expand they will do so with all the limitations inherent in professionally managed bureaucracies. California, with its early experience with railroad and mining-camp group practice and its long-sustained population boom and doctor shortages, offers the widest range of alternatives. In addition to a few survivors of the early general-practitioner era and the standard solo doctors with hospital affiliations, the state has nurtured all manner of medical modes, from the informal referrals of a cluster of specialists sharing a suburban medical building to large-scale, prepaid group practice and hospital service.

Two examples can serve to express the range of California medical forms and the potentials and shortcomings which these variations now present: the San Joaquin County Foundation for Medical Care and the Kaiser Foundation Health Plan. The first is an organization which attempts to solve the problems of lack of quality and cost supervision inherent in the Blues and commercial insurance, while simultaneously giving its members the traditional minor consumer protection of free choice of a private physician. The second seeks to maximize the savings inherent in large-scale, well-organized clinic and hospital practice, and to pass these savings on in terms of the widest possible coverage against needs for medical attention.

The San Joaquin plan sprang up in response to competition from the Kaiser Plan. The county medical society formed its own foundation in 1954 to mediate among the private insurance carriers and the doctors and patients in its area. The physicians agreed to a fixed schedule of fees for service, while on its side the foundation offered to certify privately marketed insurance policies if such policies offered the range of benefits it thought appropriate to good family medical care. Families who purchased policies could choose their own physician from the society's list and gain the benefit of regular insurance payments against most medical expenses. The unique feature of the plan, a benefit both to carriers and patients, lay in the foundation's processing of claims for the certified policies. Bills are audited in two ways. Trained accountants review them to determine their validity, and county doctors volunteer their time on rotation to determine the appropriateness of the treatment. In cases of abuse on either count, the foundation undertakes to negotiate the charges between the physician and the patient.[38]

Although such supervision of costs and quality far exceeds that undertaken by large private carriers, the San Joaquin methods of shoring up the existing system cannot offset the expensive habits of overhospitalization and inefficient allocation of medical personnel's time which is inherent in American solo or informal referral practice. Its conservatism, harking back to the criticisms of the minority in the Committee on the Cost of Medical Care of 1932, does meet a persistent and important charge against group practice.[39] Although crowded waiting rooms, overscheduling, an authoritarian manner, and a bureaucratic style bring many solo practitioners' habits dangerously close to the classic outpatient hospital style, some residual consumer benefits remain in the patient's free choice of his physician. The San Joaquin plan preserves this traditional margin of benefit. Yet since it does not attack either the problems of costs or depersonalization directly it leaves its working-class and middle-class members far from their legitimate goals of cheap, humane medical service.

The Kaiser Plan is a much more ambitious insurance and service scheme. It began in the late thirties with a prepaid plan for workers and their families at the Grand Coulee Dam site in Washington, where Edgar Kaiser was the prime contractor. Dr. Sidney Garfield, who ran the service, noticed that the method of payment had a good effect on the quality of service he and his colleagues gave. Prepayment weakened the habit of thinking in terms of repeated visits and expensive hospital procedures; and with this traditional economic pressure relaxed, both service improved and costs declined. During World War II, Dr. Garfield operated a large medical and hospital service for Kaiser's shipyards in the San Francisco area, and the program was so popular that workers kept up their memberships after the war. In 1952 the Kaiser Foundation Health Plan was established as a nonprofit corporation and burgeoned to serve about one and a half million people in California, Oregon, and Hawaii.

The heart of the plan lies in its fixed insurance charges to members,

38. National Health Council, Inc., *Alternatives for Organizing Personal Health Care Delivery*, New York, 1970, pp. 22–23; Somers and Somers, *Doctors, Patients, and Health Insurance*, pp. 421–23.

39. E. Richard Weinerman, "Problems and Perspectives of Group Practice," *Bulletin of the New York Academy of Medicine*, 44 (November 1968), 1423–34.

which guarantee the widest range of services offered anywhere, the most
notable exclusions from the contract being dentistry, psychiatry, and
drugs. Patients are encouraged to seek regular relationships with one
physician, but there are also walk-in clinic hours when members can be
attended to on a first come, first served basis. The foundation also
operates its own hospitals and emergency services. In addition to its
economies of carefully managed group practice, the Kaiser Plan undertakes systematic review and supervision of its doctors' performance. A
special bonus system acts as an incentive against hospitalization, and the
foundation has organized home-care teams of physicians, public health
nurses, and physical therapists to match its campaign to reduce the
incidence of hospital treatment.[40]

Because of its reasonable charges and extensive services, the Kaiser
Plan has been extremely popular in the Pacific states. Indeed, shortages
of doctors and capital for hospitals and clinics have restricted its growth
and forced it to close its membership lists from time to time. Its immediate shortcomings of delays for appointments and inaccessibility of some
clinics stem principally from its inability to keep pace with popular
demand. Its success and those of similar insured group-practice schemes
have led to numerous imitators, most notably by the Hospital Insurance
Plan in New York City and labor-union plans in other cities. Although it
suffers the general shortcomings of all privately funded programs—it
cannot reach its proportionate share of the poor and the old—the Kaiser
Plan is often hailed as the ideal model for the restructuring of American
medical practice, and for universalization by way of federal subsidies for
low-income groups.[41]

If such a policy were to be undertaken either by a state or the
federal government (and such a policy seems to be a logical next step),
then two basic limitations of the Kaiser Plan must be dealt with. First,
the traditional isolation of the medical profession from social and
environmental issues must be overcome. In the narrowest sense, new
clinics and hospitals must be consciously located in respect to patterns
of urban growth and population need. New York State alone uses
its licensing powers to plan in this way, but the federal government has

40. Milton I. Roemer, Donald M. DuBois, and Shirley W. Rich, *Health Insurance Plans: Studies in Organizational Diversity,* University of California, School
of Public Health, Los Angeles, 1970, pp. 293–317.
    41. Editors of Fortune, *Our Ailing Medical System, It's Time to Operate,* New
York, 1969; C. Rufus Rorem, *Private Group Clinics,* Committee on the Costs of
Medical Care, Washington, 1931, pp. 15–18, 107–11.

begun since 1966 to move in the same direction,[42] and public supervision of medical-facility location seems an easy step to take. More difficult, yet perhaps more important to the long-run health of ordinary American families, is the need to use the records and experience of physicians as information in the planning of school nutrition, industrial health, and water, air, housing, and recreation planning for metropolitan regions. For the development of subdivisions, where typically homes are built without coordination with the public facilities which make them viable, the day-to-day records of urban families' health experience should be an important determinant of our social and environmental investments. In view of the current high medical and living standards of the upper two-thirds of our population the social and environmental aspects of modern living are the most significant tools for improving the majority's health.

Second, some methods for patient participation in the management or supervision of large-scale health institutions are absolutely essential. The long history of hospitals, especially of hospital outpatient services, and our abundant experience with all manner of bureaucracies show that management left to professionals, no matter how well-intentioned, soon degenerates into a bad mix of self-serving and philanthropy. Although the Office of Economic Opportunity and Model Cities programs for the poor involve neighborhood participation, the working class and middle class have not yet demanded representation in their medical institutions. Until then, and until appropriate forms of public participation are devised, regional hospitals, Kaiser Plans, county medical society programs, and union-sponsored clinics will suffer all the shortcomings of bureaucratic service. Since such organized prepayment programs do seem able to meet the twin needs of moderate cost and high levels of competence so much better than the solo practitioner funded by private insurance, it seems imperative that this form of consumer representation be built into such institutions before they expand further.

For the bottom third of America's urban population, the years since 1920 have been a medical disaster. Put in simplest terms, those with the greatest needs have been getting the least and the worst. All the problems which beset services to the upper two-thirds also bore on this group, and much more besides. The sheer growth of our cities has left them stranded, while the inflationary pressures of the monopolistic

42. Roemer et al., *Health Insurance Plans,* p. 441.

practices of physicians acting in tandem with federal programs have priced millions out of the medical market and left entire core-city populations without access to decent health services. As in the trickle-down housing market, where the ability to obtain adequate housing and to benefit from federal subsidies depended upon a family's having attained an income threshold at least a third above the bottom level, so too access to good medical service and hospital insurance had to be purchased by regular employment and residence in a decent neighborhood. Although since the twenties rapid urbanization, rising living standards, and additions to medical science have markedly improved the health of a giant marginal group of city dwellers, say those in the range from the bottom third upward to the midpoint of the total income distribution, everything conspired against the lowest third's getting its fair share of the benefits of the last fifty years' advances.[43]

Perhaps first and foremost, the growth pattern of the city, intensifying the segregation of white and black poor at the center of the metropolis, had the most damaging effects. The rising geographical concentration of what is now termed the medically indigent exacerbated the division between ordinary private medicine and philanthropic practice which was the legacy of the previous era's establishment. The entrapment of poor whites and blacks in old central cities weakened the tax base of their communities at the very moment when municipal hospitals, dispensaries, and social services required heavy additional funding to meet the legitimate needs of their neighborhood populations. Once again the dependence of American municipal government on the local property tax played its antisocial role. The rich, increasingly dwelling in the suburbs, failed to contribute the necessary capital to inner-city voluntary hospitals; indeed, many shifted their attention to new institutions closer to their homes. The relatively declining core-city tax base meant the progressive neglect of already established city hospitals and clinics. The Hill-Burton hospital building program of the federal government, begun in 1946, accelerated these trends by subsidizing the construction of new suburban hospitals while its contributions to remodeling old central-city institutions at best enabled them to catch up with their own obsolescence but did not in any way direct inner-city medical service to the neighborhoods where the severest crises were occurring. Neither did the Hill-Burton money attack the racism of the established

43. Bernhard J. Stern, *American Medical Practice in the Perspective of a Century,* New York, 1945, pp. 103–39.

mixed private and public hospital network. The suburbanization of the upper working class and middle class, the spread of private insurance among them, and the new suburban hospitals all conspired to draw private physicians out of the old neighborhoods to follow the paying patients. Finally, the restriction of output by American medical schools and their deep-seated prejudice against training black physicians completed the tragedy.

Recent Chicago surveys taken even after the Great Society reforms of the sixties tell of the depth and magnitude of our urban health failure. The metropolitan region is characterized by "spatial epidemics" where the core districts of white poverty and black segregation suffer disproportionate infant mortality, tuberculosis, hepatitis, pneumonia, rheumatic fever, venereal diseases, measles, and other illnesses. The morbidity and mortality maps of the city give bitter confirmation to the additive effects of our urban traditions: poverty, social pathology, high-density living, low-level sanitary services, and inadequate or nonexistent medical care combine to make what one student of Chicago's public health has called an apartheid health system. Public neglect of the critical need for full employment at living wages, callous disregard for the maintenance of the physical environment, the punitive practice of welfare and charity medicine, and institutional racism in both public and private health facilities have cumulated in a social disaster for the inner city. Stranded all-white hospitals do not serve their black neighbors for fear of losing their regular physicians' and patients' support, many black families have only mass-production welfare practitioners to serve their neighborhood, white physicians cannot venture into black neighborhoods at night, both the white poor and the black of Chicago travel miles to wait in long lines at the monster Cook County Hospital complex, and they wait there to be seen by a physician who likely as not hardly speaks English. These are some of the commonplace Chicago anomalies, and similar ones exist in every large American city.[44]

44. Pierre DeVise et al., *Slum Medicine: Chicago's Apartheid Health System,* University of Chicago Interuniversity Social Research Committee, *Report No. 6,* Chicago, 1969, pp. iii–40; Harold Levine, "County Hospital, Revolution within the Establishment," *The New Physician,* 19 (October 1970), 837–44; Anderson and Kravits, *Health Services in the Chicago Area,* p. 89; comparable conditions in the New York metropolitan area, Albert Einstein College of Medicine, *The Student Health Project of Greater New York, Summer, 1968,* U.S. Public Health Service, Washington, 1969, pp. 11–33; Los Angeles spatial epidemics, City of Los Angeles, Community Analysis Bureau, *State of the City, Conditions of Blight and Obsolescence,* Los Angeles, 1970, pp. 40–57.

The mounting day-to-day count of preventable disease and death accuses the majority of Americans, their physicians, and their insurance companies. Because of their past actions in defeating government medical insurance on the eve of the two suburban booms after the two World Wars, we now face a breakdown of our medical system. American cities should be coping with the task of adapting well-established institutions to new needs. Instead they face a situation where inner-city health facilities cannot carry their load and the private insurance and suburban medical network is insufficiently organized to come to the aid of the inner city poor and black.

Just as in the housing field, where the federal government attempted to get the private market to attend to the needs of the poor and inevitably failed, so in the health field where Great Society programs have attempted to cajole the established health-care system into care of the old, the black, and the poor, it inevitably failed. In both fields excellent small-scale experiments in the United States abounded, but they could not flourish and multiply here without genuine popular support. Until the majority of Americans are willing to accept the standard of a decent home, a suitable living environment, and adequate health care as a right of all citizens, an urgent right that takes precedence over armaments, imperialism, private property, and private profit, public programs will do little more than reveal the basic injustice and social disorders of our unequal distribution of income and services.

The lifeless continuation of charity services and public-welfare medicine, so well demonstrated in the Chicago studies, when contrasted to the robust growth of Veterans Administration medicine after 1945 testifies to the difference between programs of philanthropy and a program of popular rights. The former are chronically underfunded by a wide margin, grudgingly expanded, shot through with incompetence, abuse, and fraud, and periodically reformed by novelties tailored to political crises; the latter is generously supported, rapidly expanded to match the veteran population, as competent as the general run of American medicine, and has been evolving as a set of institutions since World War I until now they offer full health services to all veterans regardless of the origins of their medical needs.[45] The former consist of

45. Irvin J. Cohen, "Medical Care: Its Social and Organizational Aspects—The Veterans' Administration Medical Care Program," *New England Journal of Medicine,* 269 (November 1963), 1011–14; Milton I. Roemer, "Government's Role in American Medicine," *Bulletin of the History of Medicine,* 18 (July 1945), 158–59.

a reluctant philanthropy for second-class citizens, while the latter is a patriotic practice of socialism for first-class citizens, a service which treats its clients as well and as badly as American medicine treats the upper two-thirds of our civilian society.

The health-care reforms of the urban crisis of the sixties are there-fore, like the postwar housing policies, attempts to deal with the histori-cal unfolding of long-standing urban problems without a popular commitment to the rights of full citizenship, and without a sense of urgency for the demands of everyday life. Instead the impulse for reform was instigated by the national confrontation with white racism, the explosion of inner cities in the riots of the mid-sixties, and the need of Democratic Presidents to seek old people's and black people's votes. Such expediencies brought forward the federally sponsored package of Great Society health-care measures—neighborhood clinics, Model Cities coordinated planning, and Medicare and Medicaid.[46]

The neighborhood clinics sponsored by the Office of Economic Opportunity and other agencies were designed to meet the immediate shortage of doctors in poor areas of the city and also to overcome some of the historic limitations of the old-fashioned hospital and dispensary network. In a typical case, the Mile Square Clinic in Chicago, OEO contracted with a voluntary teaching hospital to serve an impoverished population of 25,000 on the West Side. The hope of the contract device was to draw upon an established pool of high-quality personnel rather than funding a new municipal or state clinic. Since all the clinic employ-ees remain employees of the Presbyterian–St. Luke's Hospital, they can still keep their ties and advancement orientation to that prestigious medical hierarchy. Such contracts seem a reasonable emergency strategy, but the historical record of hospital management of outpatient services demonstrates that it is an unstable form. In time either the hospital will neglect its clinic staff or the staff will neglect its patients. To circumvent the old abuses of dispensary service, the clinic employs local residents and has created a neighborhood advisory council to participate in its management. But neighborhood control will come to naught unless the clinic receives ample and continuing public funding to enable it to attract and retain a good staff. The clinic itself functions by group prac-tice much in the Kaiser Fund manner, and like the California model it

46. Frances Fox Piven and Richard A. Cloward, *Regulating the Poor: The Functions of Public Welfare,* New York, 1971, pp. 249–76.

employs public-health nurse teams to give home follow-up care and service.[47]

At present such neighborhood clinics are regarded as the best hope for the inner city. A Chicago study calls for the creation of twenty-four there, and public-health surveys in other cities suggest similar strategies.[48] Thanks to the crisis of the sixties, plentiful examples exist for adaptation to particular city needs. The unresolved issue, however, remains the same as before. Today's clinics are temporary and underfunded, and they are just a tiny fraction of the total required. In parts of the city where doctors are more plentiful but where commonplace services are still in short supply, as in many white working-class areas, such clinics will inevitably face the bitter opposition of a coalition of private practitioners, insurance companies, and medical societies. As in the sick cycle of public housing, the stigma of low-quality clinic service inherited from the past will make it difficult for health reformers to form a coalition among poor, working-class, and middle-class citizens to press for the creation of all-class clinics which would benefit everyone. As in so many fields, the current political equilibrium sustained by partial service to the majority blocks the realization of our potential for building good universal programs.

The Model Cities innovation, launched in 1967, was designed to offset the overly physical City Hall and business orientation of extant urban programs. The federal government held out the tempting carrot of extra subsidies for cities which would establish Model Cities districts where locally elected boards would attempt to carry out a coordinated development plan for housing, employment, health, education, welfare, and public amenity improvement. Nothing less than a simultaneous demonstration of comprehensive, multi-institutional, local planning coupled with local decision-making was to be attempted. Model Cities boldly took on all the lack of coordination of the suburbs in a setting which added all the problems of inner-city poverty.[49] It is still too early to predict what the ultimate outcome of this heroic leap will be if it becomes a permanent institution of municipal government in America. So far it has at least given an effective veto power to some formerly

47. Joyce C. Lashoff, "The Health Care Team in the Mile Square Area, Chicago," *Bulletin of the New York Academy of Medicine,* 44 (November 1968), 1363–69.

48. DeVise, et al., *Slum Medicine,* p. 87; City of Philadelphia, *Report of the Mayor's Committee on Hospital Services,* Philadelphia, 1970, pp. 29–30.

49. Committee on Urban Problems, *Building the American City,* pp. 170–72.

unrepresented groups of poor people in the inner city.[50] It seems doubtful, however, that without decent federally maintained full-employment, public-housing, and medical programs, and without state reform of the municipal tax base, that local groups, no matter how intelligent, aggressive, and well subsidized, can make much headway against the heavy historical forces which press upon their neighborhoods. Properly considered, Model Cities planning should have followed major federal and state programs in order to guide and check on their local impacts; by itself it cannot be a substitute for national and regional planning.

In 1965, after years of controversy, Congress finally passed a broad health-insurance law (Medicare). It was not a compulsory insurance program for all employed Americans as contemplated in 1916, but a compulsory hospital-insurance fund and a voluntary medical-insurance scheme for those over sixty-five. At the same time Congress voted to liberalize and rationalize its grants-in-aid support for state welfare recipients (Medicaid) in order to guarantee payments for hospitalization and medical service to the poor. Neither Medicare nor Medicaid looked toward any alteration in the provision of services, except for the promotion of nursing homes, and neither demanded any restructuring of the established institutions of medicine. Under Medicare an increment was added to the general Social Security payroll taxes to finance a government hospital-insurance fund which would enable the aged to receive upon retirement the benefits which existing private insurance often denied them. Old people could further elect to make a small monthly payment (now about five dollars) which the federal government would match to entitle them to a broad range of medical service. The principal uninsured items were dentistry, hearing aids, self-administered drugs, immunizations, and physical checkups. Under Medicaid, Congress offered to match states' payments for hospital and physicians' services to welfare recipients if the states passed appropriate enabling legislation. All the states except Alaska and Arizona have now done so. In keeping with the open-ended intent of the statute, the range of benefits and eligibility vary widely from state to state.[51]

Although the passage of Medicare and Medicaid is undoubtedly an important event in the political history of public health in that it allowed

50. Piven and Cloward, *Regulating the Poor,* pp. 270–76.
51. U.S. Department of Health, Education and Welfare, *Characteristics of State Medical Assistance Programs under Title XIX of the Social Security Act,* Washington, 1970; U.S. Social Security Administration, *Your Medicare Handbook,* Baltimore, 1968.

the federal government to break half a century's barriers against national insurance, and although many old people's medical bills have been reduced, and many poor people's chances for attention have increased, the most significant effect of the 1965 legislation may well prove to be its subsequent public exposure of the weaknesses in the structure of the American health-care system. With federal taxes and subsidies increasing the demand against the limited supply, the first effects were to inflate the costs of service. Under Medicare, hospital costs soared to double the first estimates, and the annual rate of increase in charges for physicians' services almost doubled.[52] Since nothing in the statutes increased the numbers of doctors attending the old and the poor or altered the mode of practice by professionals, the long lines at hospitals, mass-production methods of welfare specialists, and the sheer lack of practitioners in central city neighborhoods went unchanged or got worse. Young inner-city mothers and their children continued to suffer all the neglects of charity medicine. Indeed Medicaid engendered a kind of health-care backlash. The inflation of medical charges in state welfare budgets which immediately followed the passage of state enabling acts forced several states to cut back their eligibility and coverage so that the general public was left with the sour impression that the majority could not afford decent medical aid to the bottom third.[53]

Predictably, the attempt of Medicare to find an adequate low-cost alternative to hospitalization of the aged by stimulating the profit appetite of doctors failed. Lured by the promise of Medicare payment for nursing-home service, syndicates of doctors and real-estate investors in every city teamed up to build and to operate such facilities. The gentlest criticism that can be directed toward this policy and its outcome is to observe that the scattering of nursing homes isolates old people and wrongly focuses attention on medical problems, to the neglect of the patients' needs for self-respect, self-care, social life, and participation in the world around them. Comprehensive Jewish charities in many U.S. cities and integrated programs in countries like Sweden have abundantly demonstrated that helping old people to deal with their declining health requires a cluster of institutions ranging from sheltered workshops and recreation centers to home care and hospitalization. It is a measure of

52. *Report of the Staff to the Committee on Finance, United States Senate, Medicare and Medicaid, Problems, Issues, and Alternatives,* (91st Congress, 1st Session), Committee Print, Washington, February, 1970, pp. 30, 38.
53. DeVise et al., *Slum Medicine,* pp. 22–25; *Report of the Staff . . . Medicare and Medicaid,* pp. 42–44.

our general society's callousness toward old people, and of the medical profession's isolation from serious concern for the social issues affecting the health of its patients, that together we all consented to a crash program of profit-making nursing homes.[54]

Medicare and Medicaid also had their corrupt side. Doctors bought and sold nursing homes for speculative profit, unscrupulous practitioners took up "gang visiting," rushing through nursing homes collecting Medicare and Medicaid fees as they passed each bed, and drugs and procedures were prescribed and hospital bills padded in the happy expectation that the state and federal treasuries would pay while patients suffered disgraceful neglect.

The spiraling costs, sloppy service, and outright malpractice exposed the social disorders that throve as a result of pouring insurance money and a patchwork of public funds into an unreconstructed medical establishment. In most cases insurance companies, especially the Blues, became the Medicare and Medicaid intermediaries who processed the hospitals' and doctors' bills to pass on for government payment. The mountain of padded bills submitted told more clearly than years of investigations that private insurance companies in no way represented the consumer. They also testified to the fact that despite plentiful hospital and medical representation on their governing boards, the carriers did not see fit to police the profession even to the extent of guaranteeing performance at the levels of the current consensus of standard good practice. The insurance companies functioned solely as collection agencies for their hospital and doctor clients. When the Department of Health, Education and Welfare requested the names of physicians receiving Medicare and Medicaid payments in excess of $25,000 a year, many companies refused to comply.[55]

Thanks to the Great Society attempts to aid the poor and the aged, the long-neglected urban health agenda is now a public political issue. Public-health follow-up studies and OEO neighborhood clinics tell of the tremendous need for commonplace service to inner-city dwellers, the severe inflation of medical costs dramatizes the monopolistic practices of medical schools, the nursing-home failures and scandals speak to the social issues of adequate health care, while the abnegation of supervision by insurance carriers and the long lines and bureaucratic abuses

54. Jules Henry, "Human Obsolescence," in his *Culture Against Man,* New York, 1963, pp. 391–474.
55. *Report of the Staff . . . Medicare and Medicaid,* pp. 50–120.

of big-city hospitals tell of the necessity to reorganize the power balances of medical practice. Once again epidemics, slums, and the suffering of the urban poor have demonstrated to the larger society the weaknesses of its institutions.

Yet in health care, as in housing, a crisis response which is the traditional reflex of our society will miss the essence of the situation and inevitably fall far short of the goal of a humane urban community. The poor are indeed treated far worse than the majority, yet such are the linkages and interconnections of a highly urbanized nation, they are treated worse in the same ways as are those who are comfortably off. The consequences of class and racial segregation which now press so cruelly upon the inner city are part and parcel of the disrespect for commonplace human life, and the denial of full citizenship to blacks, minorities, children, women, and old people throughout the metropolis.[56] The fallen-down buildings, uncollected trash, conflict-ridden schools, grimy hospitals, and bottle-strewn parks are but the frightening evidence of a pervasive neglect of the supporting public services to homes and families which prevails in all but the wealthiest suburbs. The traditional American response is to seek to obliterate the dramatic symptoms while leaving the basic malady untouched. To do so is to repeat once again our long history of failure to build truly humane and inclusive cities. The hope of the American city lies in a public recognition of the interconnections of everyday urban life, and from that recognition to commit the nation to a deep and long-sustained effort to rework its physical and institutional structure.

56. Community studies show that health care has a low priority among urban leadership, which is strongly business-oriented, Wilson, *Community Structure,* pp. 50, 84.

9

Choice and Continuity

Summary

AMERICAN URBAN LIFE confuses us in its intermingling of endless repetition with ceaseless change. Consider our habitual responses. We do not see in the brand-new downtown apartment towers or the freshly carpeted suburban model home the inevitable repetition of failure which surely awaits them. Nor do we see in the aging suburbs and dreary slums the economic vitality of the offices, stores, and factories in which their residents work. The newness is a goal for family achievement, the reality of aging is either to be obliterated or escaped. The past is not seen in the present, or the jobs in the houses. These are deep habits of mind. Since at least the founding of the Republic we have been concealing failure from ourselves with newness, and ever since we proved unable to protect our farmer and artisan forefathers from the oppressions of the work-place we have desperately sought to isolate home from work. Thus for generations we have dwelt in a self-created urban wilderness of time and space, confounding ourselves with its lusty growth and rising to periodic alarms in the night. It is no accident that we have no urban history.

Perhaps the frightening specter of black cities of needless suffering at home and the prevalence of poverty across the world will force us finally to look more steadily at what we are and do. As a nation we will not thereby be free, but we will confront both the weight of the past and the freedoms of the present. Should we venture out beyond the narrow confines of habitual behavior, we will carry with us our traditional values—for what else will guide us? Thus, if we are to have new cities they must be compounded of the aims and contradictions of our long quest for open competition, inclusive community, and rapid innovation. No matter what confronts us, we will make our choices within the boundaries of these traditional ideals.

Our cities, burdened as they are by the constructions and habits of the past and yet filled with the bustle of ever-present change, tell us much about the weight of continuity and the dimensions of choice. Although the social geography of the dispersed metropolis differs substantially from its predecessors, still its class and racial segregation, and its class, racial, and sexual discrimination testify to the terrible endurance of past habits. Flourishing amid unprecedented wealth and extraordinary mass freedoms of movement and communication, they bring to a climax the long trends of American city building. Such segregation and discrimination violate every ideal we hold: they foster unequal care and education of children, shut out adults from jobs and homes, foster unemployment and underemployment, maintain wages below decent living standards, create slums, stifle personal freedom, creativity and expression, deliver the wealth of the city to the rich and the powerful, divide the city against itself, and nourish an exploitative politics.

Class and racial segregation and class, racial, and sexual discrimination lie at the root of almost all the pathologies of the current city. As manifestations of our nation's deepest feelings, of our long racist, capitalist, and sexist traditions, such behavior is both the most grievous, and the most difficult of all the burdens which the past has fastened upon the present. The essence of our urban history has been rapid growth and pervasive change working within the confines of ceaseless exploitation of white over black, rich over poor, men over women. The contradictions of slums and suburbs, freeways and sidewalks, research hospitals and welfare clinics, new towns and public housing projects, are but the latest manifestations of the American way.

Since segregation and discrimination are the most pervasive failings of the modern city and thus the social issues which we must attack if we are to realize more of the potentials of our ideals, let us review our urban history in these terms. Where we now stand, some aspects of the metropolis offer us a great deal of latitude in choosing a fresh path, while others do not lend themselves easily to an attack on this negative inheritance.

With the rise of cities, the social value and interconnections among parcels of land soon outstripped any benefits from treating real property as a civil liberty. In the face of urban interdependencies, the attempt to maintain a property law oriented in this tradition fostered a continuous stream of needless anomalies, from inadequate sanitation in the early nineteenth century to the injustices of today's urban-renewal and high-way projects. True, legal reform could overcome some of the past handicaps. Especially it could redress the balance of power between landlord and tenant, public projects and private abutters, metropolitan plans and neighborhood improvement, and inner-city residents and suburban landholders. Yet no amount of legal reform and no amount of regulation can provide every city dweller with a decent home and a suitable living environment. Despite 150 years of urban growth and ever-shifting patterns of housing style and location, the trickle-down private housing market has never been able to meet these standards for the bottom third of our population. The changing measure set by the middle-class consensus as to what constituted adequate housing in 1870, or 1920, or 1970 has never been matched despite generations of reform. It can be met only by long-sustained government action.

Since the sheer supply of housing has the greatest impact upon the quality of housing for the third of our population with the lowest income, the government must become a major builder so that there is an abundant urban housing stock. As the repeated failures of philanthropic projects never fail to demonstrate, such a government program must start with a conviction of the right of all Americans to decent housing. From this platform the government should enter the housing field as a builder of model subdivisions, apartments, and new towns that conform to the consensus of our day. The advantages of such an approach are many. By building on a large scale according to accepted norms, state and federal agencies can influence the private market to conform to such standards, just as the TVA example stood as the yardstick for private utility operation elsewhere. The building of large quantities of housing is also the most promising way to break the barriers of class and racial segregation. The barriers will fall in two ways. First by offering the poor, the old, and the black a multiplicity of locations, many now pinned down in one part of the city will be able to relocate. Second, the plenti-ful housing stock will benefit the mass of white working-class and lower middle-class citizens who must now find homes within the narrowest of choices. Today's pockets of public housing projects heighten class and racial animosities because they benefit so few at an obvious cost to local taxpayers who themselves are struggling to maintain a grip on home-ownership.

Finally, since land and public services are the essence of housing costs and the key to successful development, the government should become a buyer and seller of metropolitan land in its own right so that it may harvest the speculative profits of urban growth and coordinate the timing and placement of public investments and services. The state housing authorities appear to be agencies of sufficient scale and exper-tise to take metropolitan-wide action for major home building and for major class and racial integration programs. In view of the importance of land and services to the ultimate land and housing package, they need not be the builders of homes themselves but could leave construction to the private market, regulating its quality and subsidizing low-income occupants. Whatever the administrative mode, the public capture of the public value of urban land could go a long way toward financing decent housing and achieving a desegregated, free-choice metropolis.

With the U.S. Routes completed in the late twenties, the airline schedules established in the fifties, and the interstate highways almost completed today, the latest transportation revolution is complete. The national network of cities is now functioning on the basis of these systems, and the internal structure of the metropolis and megalopolis is rapidly assuming an appropriate configuration. On the national level, further allocation of the Highway Trust Funds should be coordinated with a federal urban growth policy that would seek to bring all Ameri-cans into their share of the wealth of the nation. In such a context, further elaboration of transportation becomes part of a series of planned urban and regional programs that would combine investments in re-search, education, health, housing, public utility, and environmental quality. As the Los Angeles case and European examples show, such coordinated programs can effectively aid low-income populations and depressed areas.

In underdeveloped countries lack of capital resources forces the harshest of choices in selecting the priorities and placement of such investments, but the wealth of the United States allows a broader approach. We need not apply the strictest tests to urban planning to determine whether one cluster of investments or another will promote the most rapid national economic growth, but may instead only require that our national planning show reasonable progress toward redistribut-ing jobs, income, and living standards to the benefit of depressed areas or depressed populations. We can leave to the open conflicts of inter-regional federal politics the decision whether such aid take the form of modernizing Appalachia, or whether instead it makes it possible for the poor of these areas to move to new high-standard urban areas.

A serious transportation problem, however, remains neglected within the metropolises of the nation. Women, blacks, and some of the poor in general lack decent access to jobs which pay a living wage in their regions. In such cases transportation planning must be combined with a full-employment, living-wage policy. If we can do nothing else for the cities of the nation, we could see to it that no American goes unem-ployed or underemployed, and that no American need work for wages which will not support a decent standard of living. A number of Euro-pean countries have achieved this minimum. Such a commitment carries as its immediate and far-reaching consequences the funding of consumer demand to stimulate the economy, and the support of family budgets which grant immediately a large measure of freedom and equality to our low-income fellow citizens. Progressive taxation and national fiscal planning are the prerequisites of such a crucial urban policy, but a residual urban transportation issue remains.

With the interstates in place and job locations scattering in response to their efficiency, most Americans go to work by automobile. The automobile mode is more convenient than public transportation, multi-plies the effective range of job choice, and increases social freedoms after working hours. The Los Angeles demonstration shows what we might expect if a metropolitan transportation program were tied to a national full-employment and living-wage policy. There a public agency was specifically charged with serving as the transportation advocate of the poor, for arranging new bus routes where existing companies could adapt their schedules, and of operating its own multiple-destination bus service. By such subsidizing of public transportation for the poor, many of them, especially women, were able to find jobs outside their immedi-ate neighborhoods. Had such a program been continued and the women able to earn a living wage, in time they could have purchased cars of their own, thereby decreasing the need for subsidized bussing. Over the long run, say a decade, these paired policies could be expected to provide the poor with a way to purchase entrance into the freedoms of the metropolis and reduce the need for public transportation to a kind of taxi service for the old and the disabled.

At present, however, an active middle-class coalition is lobbying in

Washington and in state legislatures to introduce costly traffic reforms which will perpetuate the injustices of our present transportation system at a new higher level of costs. The coalition for rail transportation consists of middle-class commuters, suburban environmentalists who are concerned with urban aesthetics and air pollution, rail-equipment suppliers, tax-hungry mayors, and downtown real-estate men who hope to find yet another subsidy to shore up inner-city land values. To this group is added professional planners and architects whose nostalgia for the highly concentrated city of America before World War I has led them to argue that urban civilization cannot endure in a multicentered metropolis. The coalition powerfully resembles the same union that sponsored the City Beautiful and urban-renewal projects which cost our cities so much and did nothing to help low-income Americans achieve equal membership in our society. In this case, however, rail proponents argue that the construction of rail lines will let the central-city poor reach jobs on the fringe. So it would—a few in a limited way. There was a time in the thirties when rails, busses, and highways could have been planned as a coordinated metropolitan system and such plans would have caused the city to conform to its patterns, but now with the superhighways in place it is too late. To be a full-fledged member of the American city means to own a car, and everyone knows it.

Even if the rail lines duplicated every intrametropolitan superhighway, and no one has yet dared to suggest such a costly duplication of investment and horrendous operating subsidy, the poor would still have less job access than if they had cars because they would still need to get from their homes to the stations, and from the stations to the scattered workplaces. The subsidies, for their part, would tie up billions of dollars which could better be used for incremental addition to existing road networks, new schools, parks, health facilities, and minibus subsidies. A nonpolluting automobile and reform of the local property tax are all that is required to save our cities and their disadvantaged populations from yet another massive raid by the rich and the middle class on the public treasury.

The transportation and technological climate that caused the national network of cities to grow and conform to its configuration also nourished the bureaucratization of modern urban life. Today's corporate cities offer immediate possibilities for ending segregation and discrimination, and in the long run the potential for a more humane and democratic way of life. Throughout our history, conditions in the workplaces of the city have been the most important determinants of the quality of urban life. The discipline, machinery, hours, and social amenities of work have set the boundaries of families' everyday experience. Although a new middle class of professionals and proprietors has burgeoned with the expansion of suburban retailing and services, a much larger segment of urban society labors in private and public bureaucracies. Factory workers, salesmen, clerks, engineers, schoolteachers, municipal employees, medical personnel, altogether a giant fraction of the modern city's population at every skill level, now participate in and endure bureaucratic labor. In this labor rests the fate of our cities.

The ability of large organizations to manage complex tasks and to coordinate diverse personnel makes them ideal instruments for assistance in managing urban growth and helping with the task of full employment and living wages. In Europe, subsidies and licenses are used to get businesses to locate in accordance with national and regional employment plans, and there is no reason why both private and public corporations in this country cannot be asked to meet similar demands. At the same time, the underserving of the urban physical and social environment makes the large public corporations of our cities ideal candidates for full-employment hiring. Nothing is more absurd in the contemporary American city than its neglect of public services while thousands of young people and older men and women go unemployed or underemployed.

In the long run, the bureaucratized workplace offers the chance for a major improvement in the quality of urban life. At present the corporate society, both in our capitalism and in other nations' socialism, delivers altogether too much power to the elites at the top of the bureaucracies. At the same time, the mass of employees are organized into authoritarian hierarchical relationships in the plant, office, store, or public institution. From this pervasive structure comes the management which makes the cars that pollute and rust away, the office that won't promote women or hire blacks, the communications media which lie to the public, the chain stores which cheat their customers, the hospital which serves the doctors, the school which cannot teach the children. In short, bureaucracy institutionalizes all the bad habits of the general culture and by its institutional size and many levels of responsibility erects a deep defense which makes any of these evils hard to dislodge.

The student strikes, workers' wildcat walkouts, the sudden spread of

unions among professionals, women's protests, and consumer movements in the developed countries of the world express the pent-up
frustrations of people who sense some of the possibilities of our new
social situation and who face instead the senseless oppression of bureaucratic control over their lives. Although unionization has protected
many workers from the worst kinds of exploitation and the rise of
productivity has benefited many more, as things now stand neither the
consumer nor the employee has any real control over the work of the
city and hence no control over the essence of his culture and his daily
environment. No country has yet devised methods for the democratic
control of production and services by consumers or democratic control
of the mode of work by the employees; yet if our cities are to approach
our goals of open competition, community, and innovation and not
become managed societies run for the benefit of the elite, we must face
the fact of the bureaucratized metropolis.

Consider how far we now are from respecting the rights of consumer
and employee as commanding the same respect as one's rights as a voter
in the political city. Recall the expression on the school superintendent's
face when the students demanded control of their schools, or the office
manager's incredulous expression when challenged for discrimination
against blacks or women, or the shock and disbelief among the executives at the General Motors stockholders' meeting when a minority suggested that consumers should be represented. Our executives no more
believe that the consumer and the employee are capable of intelligently
representing their own interests than the British colonial governors of
the eighteenth century believed Americans could govern themselves.
Unfortunately for us all, most Americans also don't. We accept responsibility without autonomy, routine without meaning, demands for loyalty
in the face of the most obvious fraud and injustice, consider power
legitimate when exercised in the name of property or title, and make our
separate peace within the interstices of routine bureaucracy. For our
discomfort and the malaise of the city we prescribe more of the same—
pills, police, education, more enlightened bureaucratic management,
more consumerism. The highly organized structure of the modern city
and the heightened consciousness of the sixties do, however, offer a
place to begin. The group structure of the most urban workplaces is
already a form which can be subject to the same sort of politicization as
government institutions. In the public corporations where there is now
the greatest conflict, in public housing, welfare, recreation, health, edu-

cation, and police, groups of embattled consumers and harassed employees are demanding representation in management decisions. Examples of participatory management and cooperative enterprise exist in scattered private firms. We have the precedent of the New Deal encouragement of rural cooperatives and the recent Great Society programs to tell of the possibilities for public aid to such experiments. In the long run the continued health of American urban society will depend upon the extension of democracy into the bureaucratic workplaces which now control the fate of the city and its inhabitants.

It is customary to conclude books on urban reform with a lament over the decay of the neighborhoods and the decline of small-scale community life. Although some neighborhoods are ravaged by heroin, many are afflicted by poverty, and all suffer the disease of white racism, there is no reliable historical evidence which suggests that local government, local institutions, or local life are decaying. The behavior of local government and the studies of social science show that a broad consensus on what constitutes a decent American life runs throughout the city. A decent job, a good education for one's children, a comfortable home, and adequate health care are on everyone's list of priorities, and the cultural variations by class, race and religion which give specific meaning to these priorities are not very wide. Wide enough to tip the balance in a local election, to be sure, but narrow enough to support a common set of public and private institutions in all but the impoverished sections of the city.

When the Presidents of the United States decide to finance their wars with inflation and unemployment, it is the local community which must cope with the impacts. When tax lawyers and Congressmen connive to destroy an equitable progressive tax structure, it is the neighborhoods which must suffer the housing shortages, overcrowded schools, and hospitals. When the young people begin to march for civil rights and peace, it is the churches that organize for support. When the state police beat and shoot the prisoners, it is volunteers from the city who drive out to the prison to see if they can help the convicts. When legislatures and Congress fear to regulate the smokestacks and automobiles of the nation, it is the Boy Scouts and housewives who gather up the newspapers and collect the bottles. For every race-torn town in the metropolis, there are others that are coping patiently with the transition to an integrated society.

American urban neighborhoods are not nor have they ever been peasant villages; nor are they nor have they ever been model republics. Yet to an extraordinary degree, considering the rapid movement of millions of American families, they have been able to muster men and women who pass petitions, sit patiently for hours on local boards, and help out their friends and neighbors in emergencies. To the extent that the American city is now rotten, it is rotten at the top, not the bottom. What the neighborhoods need at the present moment, and what they have been needing ever since our cities became the creatures of large interconnecting economic forces and institutions, is the assistance of democratic national and regional planning.

A Bibliographic Guide

The neglect of urban history by professional historians confers at least one benefit upon anyone interested in the field: there are no standard texts and classic controversies that must be mastered before one may feel competent to reason from the experience of the past. The reader should define the subject for himself and follow his own bent across time, space, and disciplines. Since cities touch upon so many aspects of human life, there are boundless shelves of books and articles ranging from abstract mathematical models and universal histories to minutely observed case studies and extremely personal fiction. The path through this library, therefore, must be an individual one. What follows are suggestions for further reading collected from notes of my own path. In making this selection, I have sought to include titles that seemed to me to give the best general coverage of a particular subject, and I have added books and articles with abundant references so that they can serve as guides for further exploration themselves. Few, I hope, are so arcane that they would not appear in the normal city public library or cannot be purchased from the U.S. Government Printing Office. The selection is arranged roughly in the order of the chapters and topics of this book.

The Atlantic Perspective

American urbanization is part of a very long-term unfolding of the European world. The best way to gain such a perspective is to read Lewis Mumford's marvelous pioneering work *The Culture of Cities,* New York, 1938. At last report the book was still in print, and a condensation of it appears as chapters in his comprehensive human history, *The City in History,* New York, 1961. Both contain excellent bibliographies. Two short works with a geographical focus may help to relate Mumford's inclusive imagination to my own more limited structural approach: Emrys Jones,

Towns and Cities, New York, 1966; and Peter Hall, *The World Cities,* New York, 1966. The Danish architectural historian Steen Eiler Rasmussen has written two books that contain, as no others I know do, a humane sense of the quality of everyday life· with a long sweep of the history of the physical elements of the city: *London: The Unique City,* 1934, Cambridge, 1967; *Towns and Buildings Described in Drawings and Words,* Cambridge, 1951, 1969.

The New England Town

The first Puritan settlements are a favorite topic of American historians, long used for all manner of disparate purposes. Yet the seventeenth century is so far removed from our present circumstances that one must approach it with care lest its fragments shatter under the weight of myth. For me, the best use of the Puritans to illustrate the present is J. B. Jackson's artful essay describing the successive impacts of urbanization upon American farm life, "The Westward-moving House," in *Landscapes, Selected Writings of J. B. Jackson,* Ervin H. Zube, ed., Amherst, 1970. To recapture a sense of the English background that determined many of the social and legal conditions of these first towns, one might begin with Peter Laslett, *The World We Have Lost,* London, 1965, and follow it with Sumner Chilton Powell's transatlantic study, *Puritan Village: The Formation of a New England Town.* The best single monograph on the early years of these settlements is Philip J. Greven's study of Andover, Massachusetts, *Four Generations,* Ithaca, 1970. The story of the destruction of folk planning by the market economy and land speculation is nicely handled by Anthony N. B. Garvan, *Architecture and Town Planning in Colonial Connecticut,* New Haven, 1951; and by Richard L. Bushman, *From Puritan to Yankee,* Cambridge, 1967.

Land

Although land is a subject that cries out for unified treatment in that our traditions of mixed private and public land management cause many of the physical and social problems of today's city, no author has yet ventured a historical synthesis. Instead the reader who wishes to understand the land-management background of the metropolis faces a series of highly compartmentalized literatures of frontier history, law, geography, economics, city and regional planning, and commercial real estate. The following suggestions may at least sensitize the curious to the range of controversial issues concealed beneath the drab rubric of real-estate history.

The master of the occupation of frontier land is Paul W. Gates, and his *History of Public Land Law Development,* Washington, 1968, should be read in conjunction with a series of essays describing the mechanisms and consequences of past land allocations: Vernon Carstensen, ed., *The Public Lands,*

Madison, 1963. The links between these rural precedents and the design of towns and cities stand forth clearly in Norman J. W. Thrower's modest geography *Original Survey and Land Subdivision,* Chicago, 1966; and in the collection of past town plans in John W. Reps' *The Making of Urban America,* Princeton, 1965. Charles M. Haar, ed., *Law and Land: Anglo-American Planning Practice,* Cambridge, 1964, tells the legal plight our traditions have led us to, while Shirley S. Passow's article "Land Resources and Teamwork in Planning Stockholm," *Journal of the American Institute of Planners,* 36 (May 1970), 179–88, casts the strong light of the alternative course of active municipal land trading upon our impasse.

Before venturing into the history of attempts to regulate real estate, the reader should familiarize himself with the workings of the private market and the patterns of urban land use with which regulations seek to cope. Maurice H. Yates and Barry J. Garner's *The North American City,* New York, 1971, is a convenient collection of the basic themes of urban economics and geography. Joseph D. McGoldrick, Seymour Graubard, and Raymond J. Horowitz, *Building Regulation in New York City,* New York, 1944, gives both the history of that city's reforms and offers references to the major past works. The story can be carried down to the present with National Commission on Urban Problems, *Legal Remedies for Housing Code Violations, Research Report No. 14,* Frank P. Grad, ed., Washington, 1968; and this in turn should be considered in the light of George Sternlieb's perceptive Newark study of what happens to the law when the private market for land and housing collapses: *Tenement Landlord,* New Brunswick, 1966. The history of zoning has been well reviewed by Seymour I. Toll, *The Zoned American,* New York, 1969.

Planning

Mel Scott has written an official history of city planning that thoroughly covers the profession, but its encyclopedic quality makes it most useful as a reference work: *American City Planning Since 1890,* Berkeley, 1969. A better place to begin might be John L. Hancock's brief account of what planners were really doing, "Planners in the Changing American City, 1900–1940," *Journal of the American Institute of Planners,* 33 (September 1967), 290–304. Then one might open up the issues of urban and regional planning by consulting a number of very different and contradictory books. There are two books on conventional policy and practice by very wise and experienced men, the first by the housing authority Charles Abrams, *The City Is the Frontier,* New York, 1965; the second by the planner Hans Blumenfeld, *The Modern Metropolis: Its Origins, Growth, Characteristics and Planning,* Paul D. Spreiregen, ed., Cambridge, 1967. The man who laid out the Appalachian Trail offered a modern-sounding ecological ideology for regional planning: Benton MacKaye, *The New Exploration,* 1928, Urbana, 1962. The reader should test MacKaye's call against his own politics by looking at the case study of America's one regional planning effort in Philip Selznick, *T.V.A. and the Grass Roots: A Study of the Sociology of Formal Organization,* 1949, New York, 1966. Finally, Lloyd Rodwin has written an excellent review of recent national urban planning: *Nations and Cities: A Comparison of Strategies for Urban Growth,* Boston, 1970.

Highways

Roads and highways are members of a family of workaday subjects, like electric power, sewers, and land management, that have been largely ignored by professional historians although they determine the bounds of many of our urban social patterns. A collection of essays by members of the American Association of State Highway Officials, *A Story of the Beginning, Purpose, Growth, Activities, and Achievements of AASHO,* Washington, 1964, tells the outline of twentieth-century American highway building. The research of the thirties and its design consequences have been summarized in a little book put out by the U.S. Public Roads Administration, *Highway Practice in the United States of America,* Washington, 1949; and the consequences of this thinking for today's metropolis are recorded in the designer's handbook, AASHO, Committee on Planning and Design Policies, *A Policy on Arterial Highways in Urban Areas,* Washington, 1957.

A very interesting literature that promises more systematic and more sensitive design practices for the future was begun by Kevin Lynch in *The Image of the City,* Cambridge, 1960; and he and his associates have followed on with highway studies: Donald Appleyard, Kevin Lynch, and John R. Myer, *The View from the Road,* Cambridge, 1964. A review of the current state of behavioral studies of the effect of physical form on city dwellers is given in William Michaelson, *Man and His Urban Environment: A Sociological Approach,* Reading, 1970.

National Network of Cities

In recent years scholars have begun to write the economic history of the United States in terms of the interrelationships between the changing structure of the economy and contemporary alterations in the national network of cities. The outstanding work so far is Beverly Duncan and Stanley Lieberson, *Metropolis and Region in Transition,* Beverly Hills, 1970. Eric E. Lampard has written a fine overview of American urbanization that can be read as a summary of the current approach: "The Evolving System of Cities in the U.S.: Urbanization and Economic Development," in Harvey S. Perloff and Loudon Wingo, Jr., eds., *Issues in Urban Economics,* Baltimore, 1968, pp. 81–139. I have also found a technical pamphlet by Brian J. L. Berry, Peter Goheen, and Harold Goldstein extremely useful for understanding the issues that underlie any attempt to relate the changing structure of cities to economic growth: "Metropolitan Area Definition: A Re-Evaluation of Concept and Statistical Practice," *Working Paper No. 28,* Bureau of the Census, Washington, June, 1968. The pamphlet also includes a fine bibliography of the literature of metropolitanization.

The history of the urbanizing economy itself can be followed through a sequence of three books: Douglass C. North, *The Economic Growth of the United States, 1790–1860,* Englewood Cliffs, 1961; Harvey S. Perloff, et al., *Regions' Resources and Economic Growth,* Baltimore, 1960; and Jean Gottmann, *Megalopolis, The Urbanized Northeastern Seaboard of the United States,* Cambridge, 1961.

Intercity Transportation

Fascination with the frontier and years of first growth has brought forth a number of very interesting and readable histories of transportation, but once one's concern advances toward the modern periods the quality of historical imagination declines and one must make one's own history from narrow social science studies. The pre-1870 decades offer the pleasant company of George Rogers Taylor, *The Transportation Revolution, 1815–1860,* New York, 1951; Robert G. Albion, *The Rise of New York Port: 1815–1860,* New York, 1939; Oscar E. Anderson, Jr., *Refrigeration in America,* Princeton, 1953; and the very useful Carter Goodrich, ed., *Canals and American Economic Development,* New York, 1961. For subsequent years a good sense of the logic of successive transportation innovations can be gained from John F. Stover, *American Railroads,* Chicago, 1961; David M. Potter, "The Historical Development of Eastern-Southern Freight Rate Relationships," *Law and Contemporary Problems,* 12 (Summer 1947), 416–48; Benjamin Chinitz, *Freight and the Metropolis,* Cambridge, 1960; Edward L. Ullman, *American Commodity Flow,* Seattle, 1957; and the transportation chapters in Jean Gottmann's *Megalopolis.*

Intraurban Transportation

A nostalgia for cable cars and open-sided electrics pervades the literature of this field but some studies do suggest the links between intracity transport and urban form. Leon Moses and Harold F. Williamson have written an excellent speculative article in which they propose a history of transportation effects from the earliest years of the nineteenth century to the present: "The Location of Economic Activities in Cities," *American Economic Review,* 57 (May 1967), 211–22. Successive innovations and their impacts are recorded by George Rogers Taylor, "The Beginning of Mass Transportation in Urban America, Parts I and II," *Smithsonian Journal of History,* 1 (Summer and Autumn 1966), 35–50 and 31–54; my own *Streetcar Suburbs: The Process of Growth in Boston 1870–1900,* Cambridge, 1962; Robert M. Fogelson, *Fragmented Metropolis, Los Angeles 1850–1930,* Cambridge, 1967; and Reyner Banham, *Los Angeles: The Architecture of Four Ecologies,* New York, 1972.

Industrialization

There is no special group, except for the social surveyors of the early twentieth century, who concern themselves with the particular effects of industrialization upon the social patterns of cities, but there is a rich literature from which one can select titles with a high density of urban information. A mine of information and a series of studies that has never been excelled is John R. Commons et al., *History of Labour in the United States,* 4 v., 1918–35, New York, 1966. The first volume on the early unions and working conditions of the first phase of industrialization is especially useful. The technological pace of the years before 1870 has been brilliantly sketched in Dorothy Brady's "Relative Prices in the Nineteenth Century," *Journal of Economic History,* 26 (June 1964), 145–203. An exciting if eccentric overview of technological change down to our own times is offered by Sigfried Giedion, *Mechanization Takes Command,* New York, 1948; and his suggestions can be tested against the realities of economic development by consulting the essays in Robert W. Fogel and Stanley L. Engerman, *The Reinterpretation of American Economic History,* New York, 1971.

The authority on the rise of big business is Alfred D. Chandler, Jr., whose two outstanding contributions are "The Beginnings of 'Big Business' in American Industry," *Business History Review,* 33 (Spring 1959), 1–31; and *Strategy and Structure: Chapters in the History of Industrial Enterprise,* Cambridge, 1962. The interactions between large-scale industry and the city can be followed by reading that fascinating old sociological study, "The Pittsburgh Survey," *Charities and Commons,* 21 (January 1909); or the complete edition, Paul U. Kellogg et al., *The Pittsburgh Survey,* 6 v., New York, 1909–14. Much of this work is summarized in a modern labor history that may be more accessible: David Brody, *Steelworkers in America: The Non-Union Era,* Cambridge, 1960.

To sample the materials of our own era, a good approach is to blend national with urban studies. I have found the following works the most useful. C. Wright Mills, *White Collar: The American Middle Classes,* New York, 1951; Jules Henry, *Culture Against Man,* New York, 1963; Robert Blauner, *Alienation and Freedom: The Factory Worker and His Industry,* Chicago, 1964; and Warren G. Bennis and Philip E. Slater, *The Temporary Society,* New York, 1968. These national assessments can then be related to such urban studies as St. Clair Drake and Horace R. Cayton, *Black Metropolis,* 1945, 2 v., New York, 1962; Stanley Lebergott, "Tomorrow's Workers: The Prospects for the Urban Labor Force," in my *Planning for a Nation of Cities,* Cambridge, 1966, pp. 124–40; and John F. Kain, "The Distribution and Movement of Jobs and Industry," in James Q. Wilson, ed., *The Metropolitan Enigma,* Cambridge, 1968, pp. 1–32.

Residential Segregation

The mounting professional interest in social history since the thirties has brought forward a complementary historical, geographical, and sociological literature that gives today's reader a firm grasp of the history of changing patterns of residential segregation in America's largest cities. For the years before 1870 the cluster of books would be: Walter Firey, *Land Use in Central Boston,* Cambridge, 1947, which should be read in conjunction with Oscar Handlin's durable classic, *Boston's Immigrants: A Study in Acculturation,* 1941, rev. ed., Cambridge, 1959; and Peter R. Knights, *The Plain People of Boston, 1830–1860: A Study in City Growth,* New York, 1971. There is a similar report for New York by Robert Ernst, *Immigrant Life in New York City 1825–1863,* 1949, Port Washington, 1965. Contemporary black patterns are suggested by Leon F. Litwack, *North of Slavery: The Negro in the Free States, 1790–1860,* Chicago, 1961. Philadelphia's history has been dealt with in a more explicitly sociological manner in E. Digby Baltzell's *Philadelphia Gentlemen: The Making of a National Upper Class,* Glencoe, 1958; and my *Private City: Philadelphia in Three Periods of Its Growth,* Philadelphia, 1968.

For the years of the rise of the segregated metropolis, the key works are from Chicago and are the products or consequences of the "Chicago School" of sociology. Homer Hoyt's *One Hundred Years of Land Values in Chicago: The Relationship of the Growth of Chicago to the Rise in Its Land Values,* Chicago, 1933, is the essential book, and it is far better reading than its title suggests. This account of the development of the ring and sector pattern of settlement can be fleshed out with a number of more specialized studies: Graham R. Taylor's old study of Pullman and Gary, *Satellite Cities: A Study of Industrial Suburbs,* New York, 1915; the essays by the fathers of the Chicago ecological school, Robert E. Park, Ernest W. Burgess, and Roderick D. McKenzie, *The City,* Chicago, 1925; Harvey W. Zorbaugh, *The Gold Coast and the Slum,* Chicago, 1929; Allan H. Spear, *Black Chicago: The Making of a Negro Ghetto 1890–1920,* Chicago, 1967; Humbert S. Nelli, *The Italians of Chicago 1880–1930,* New York, 1970; and a continuation of the Boston sequence in my *Streetcar Suburbs: The Process of Growth in Boston 1870–1900,* Cambridge, 1962.

This mixture of structural analysis and reporting on particular groups has been continued into descriptions of our own era. The structural analysis can be quickly sampled by consulting Stanley Lieberson, *Ethnic Patterns in American Cities,* New York, 1963; Karl E. and Alma F. Taeuber, *Negroes in Cities: Residential Segregation and Neighborhood Change,* Chicago, 1965; and John F. Kain, "The Distribution and Movement of Jobs and Industry," in James Q. Wilson, ed., *The Metropolitan Enigma,* Cambridge, 1968. For reporting on the conditions within the residential islands, see St. Clair Drake and Horace R. Cayton's marvelous Chicago study, *Black Metropolis: A Study of Negro Life in a Northern City,* 1945,

2 v., New York, 1962; Todd Gitlin and Nanci Hollander, *Uptown: Poor Whites in Chicago,* New York, 1970; Leo Grebler, Joan W. Moore, and Ralph Guzman, *The Mexican-American People,* New York, 1970; and Herbert J. Gans, *The Levittowners: How People Live and Politic in Suburbia,* New York, 1967.

Urban Culture

One conventional way to write about American urban culture is to see the city as isolating the individual in an anonymous mass of people. The other popular approach is to focus upon a neighborhood and its particularities, thereby implying that the city is a mosaic of local customs and ethnic survivals washed over by the messages and demands of metropolitan media and institutions. The former is a psychological approach that by its very premise cannot explore the uniformities of behavior that differentiate groups of city dwellers, while the latter proceeds without awareness of the large-scale demographic events and economic forces that alter the composition of urban locales, determine their survival or growth, and set many of the terms for the interaction of their residents.

The recent metropolitan survey approach to the content of urban culture suggests that the uniformities of individual experience and the clustering of groups can be managed simultaneously by asking a sample of the metropolitan population about its institutional relationships to schools, churches, and workplaces, as well as examining its residential behavior of choice of homesite, neighborhood, and family expectations. See, for example, Gerhard Lenski, *The Religious Factor: The Sociological Study of Religious Impact on Politics, Economics, and Family Life,* New York, 1961; and Edward O. Laumann, "The Social Structure of Religious and Ethno-religious Groups in a Metropolitan Community: A Smallest Space Analysis," *American Sociological Review,* 34 (April 1969), 182–97.

The basic class and socioreligious matrix used by Laumann is especially suggestive to urban historians, since these categories are directly linked to two dominant characteristics of American history. The class dimensions reflect the stable and long-standing differential distribution of personal income that has prevailed since colonial times. The socioreligious affiliations touch upon the ceaseless waves of migration of the population. Two sociologists have written histories of the nation's culture from this point of view, and I find their beginnings persuasive: Seymour Martin Lipset, *The First New Nation,* New York, 1963; and Milton Gordon, *Assimilation in American Life,* New York, 1964.

These outline histories are susceptible to further development and to systematic testing of hypotheses. The weddings, baptisms, church memberships, and changes in church locations can stand as proxies for changes in the behavior of vast numbers of urban Americans. Further, the links between education, membership in voluntary associations, class, and residential segregation that these studies report are also capable of approximate

historical measurement, since they are either institutional or property behaviors for which records survive. Given such data resources and the work
already begun by the historians of social mobility, we can expect that further
research will both refine this cultural outline and in time enable historians to
write very much more inclusive accounts of the cultural changes in our
cities. Already useful are Stephan A. Thernstrom, *Poverty and Progress:
Social Mobility in a Nineteenth Century City,* Cambridge, 1964; and
Stephan A. Thernstrom and Richard Sennett, eds., *Nineteenth Century
Cities: Essays in the New Urban History,* New Haven, 1969. Any reader
with a research interest in such studies should consult a beginning work in
this field, Ralph Janis, "The Churches of Detroit 1880–1940," Ph.D. thesis,
University of Michigan, 1972.

For the time being, the class and socioreligious cultural hypothesis
offers the general reader a way of comprehending his present metropolis in
terms of a number of major events in American history—its population
history of immigration and ceaseless internal migration, its differences
among rich and poor, its pervasive residential segregation, and its habits of
tagging people as blacks or whites, Protestant, Catholic, or Jew. The succeeding references are suggestions for reading history in such terms. They
should be considered in conjunction with the ethnic reports and systematic
analyses listed under the previous heading "Residential Segregation."

General works on migration and demographic change can be consulted
in rising order of statistical content. Maldwyn A. Jones, *American Immigration,* Chicago, 1960, offers a brief survey of the entire story, and Nathan
Glazer and Daniel Patrick Moynihan's *Beyond the Melting Pot,* Cambridge, 1963, deals with the persistence of ethnic differences in the New
York City core of that metropolitan region. The native American hostility
to immigrants has been surveyed by John Higham in his *Strangers in the
Land: Patterns of Nativism 1860–1925,* New Brunswick, 1955. The quanti-
tative changes in the population are conveniently gathered together in two
useful census monographs; Conrad and Irene B. Taeuber, *The Changing
Population of the United States,* New York, 1958; and E. P. Hutchinson,
Immigrants and Their Children 1850–1950, New York, 1965. Brinley
Thomas proposed an Atlantic system for the demographic history of the
United States in his *Migration and Economic Growth,* Cambridge, England,
1954. The key monograph and reference work on internal migration is
Everett S. Lee, Ann R. Miller, et al., *Population Redistribution and Eco-
nomic Growth, United States 1870–1950,* 3 v., Philadelphia, 1957–64.

The literature of American Protestantism is overpowering. I have
taken as my guides the essays of Sidney E. Mead, *The Lively Experiment:
The Shaping of Christianity in America,* New York, 1963, and the sociological analysis of Nicholas J. B. Demerath, *Social Class in American Protestantism,* Chicago, 1965. An entrance into the history of white Protestantism can be found by consulting Timothy L. Smith, *Revivalism and
Social Reform in Mid-Nineteenth Century America,* New York, 1957;
Ray A. Billington, *The Protestant Crusade 1800–1860,* New York, 1938;

Henry F. May, *Protestant Churches in Industrial America*, New York, 1949; and Gibson Winter, *The Suburban Captivity of the Churches*, Garden City, 1961.

For the study of American Catholicism, I found Thomas T. McAvoy's *A History of the Catholic Church in the United States*, Notre Dame, 1969, most helpful, John Tracy Ellis's little book *American Catholicism*, rev. ed., Chicago, 1969, is also handy; and Ellis's *Life of James Cardinal Gibbons, Archbishop of Baltimore*, 2 v., Milwaukee, 1952, gives a wonderful picture of the problems confronting the nineteenth-century church. James Hennesey has written a very suggestive article on the peculiarities of the American church, relating its experience here to the general theme of "salutary neglect" employed by colonial political historians: "Papacy and Episcopacy in Eighteenth and Nineteenth Century America," *Records of the American Catholic Historical Society of Philadelphia*, 77 (September 1966), 175–84. The history of parochial education appears in Harold A. Buetow, *Of Singular Benefit: The Story of Catholic Education in the United States*, New York, 1970; Vincent P. Lannie, *Public Money and Parochial Education*, Cleveland, 1968; and Andrew M. Greeley and Peter H. Rossi, *The Education of Catholic Americans*, Chicago, 1966.

For access to the abundant literature on the urbanization of American Judaism, I have relied upon Nathan Glazer, *American Judaism*, Chicago, 1957; and Moses Rischin, *The Promised City: New York's Jews 1870–1914*, Cambridge, 1962. For a sense of the transition years, the long-time editor of the *Jewish Daily Forward*, Abraham Cahan, wrote a wonderful novel, *The Rise of David Levinsky*, 1917, New York, 1960.

My basic insights into the urbanization of black Protestantism have been derived from the extraordinary Chicago study by St. Clair Drake and Horace R. Cayton, *Black Metropolis: A Study of Negro Life in a Northern City*, 1945, 2 v., New York, 1962. From this beginning one can enter the history of the black church by consulting Leon F. Litwack, *North of Slavery: The Negro in the Free States 1790–1860*, Chicago, 1961; E. Franklin Frazier, *The Negro Church in America*, New York, 1964; Gilbert Osofsky, *Harlem: The Making of a Ghetto*, New York, 1963; and Kenneth B. Clark, *Dark Ghetto: Dilemmas of Social Power*, New York, 1965. The basic texts of the Harlem Renaissance are James Weldon Johnson, *Black Manhattan*, 1930, New York, 1968; and Harold Cruse, *The Crisis of the Negro Intellectual from Its Origins to the Present*, New York, 1967.

Housing

The history of ordinary housing in America lies buried in the records of county buildings and in the files of architects, contractors, and building inspectors; but insofar as housing has been a topic for reformist concern, formal histories have been written. The problem for the general reader is to familiarize himself with architectural history without being drowned in it, because architectural history is only a small fraction of what he needs to know if he is to understand the building patterns of cities. Unfortunately, historians of architecture generally deal with the homes of the rich to the neglect of ordinary urban structures.

A brief excursion through the architectural literature might begin with Sigfried Giedion's exciting compendium, *Space, Time, and Architecture,* Cambridge, 1941; and Reyner Banham's short book on the modern mechanical revolution, *The Architecture of the Well-Tempered Environment,* Chicago, 1969. Christopher Tunnard, in *The City of Man,* New York, 1953, writes informatively about nineteenth-century suburbs of the wealthy, and Vincent J. Scully, Jr., in *American Architecture and Urbanism,* New York, 1969, has attempted a new synthesis of formal architectural history with the vernacular. One can locate one's perceptions from these design histories by looking at the pictures in two fine collections of urban prints and photographs: John A. Kouwenhoven, *The Columbia Historical Portrait of New York,* Garden City, 1953; and Harold M. Mayer and Richard C. Wade, *Chicago: Growth of a Metropolis,* Chicago, 1969. Those interested in the contrasts between high style and mass translation might like to examine the pictures of suburban homes in my *Streetcar Suburbs: The Process of Growth in Boston 1870–1900,* Cambridge, 1962, after reading Vincent J. Scully, Jr., *The Shingle Style: Architectural Theory and Design from Richardson to the Origins of Wright,* New Haven, 1955.

Reform in the years before the New Deal can be surveyed by reading John Coolidge, *Mill and Mansion: A Study of Architecture and Society in Lowell, Massachusetts, 1820–1865,* 1942, New York, 1967; Stanley Buder, *Pullman: An Experiment in Industrial Order and Community Planning 1880– 1930,* New York, 1967; S. B. Sutton, ed., *Civilizing American Cities: A Selection of Frederick Law Olmsted's Writings on City Landscapes,* Cambridge, 1971; Robert W. DeForest and Lawrence Veiller, eds., *The Tenement House Problem,* 2 v., New York, 1903; Edith Abbott and Sophonisba Breckinridge, *The Tenements of Chicago 1908–1935,* Chicago, 1936; James Ford, *Slums and Housing,* 2 v., Cambridge, 1936; Miles L. Colean, *Housing for Defense,* New York, 1940, on World War I public housing; and looking over the plans and descriptions of model housing and subdivisions in U.S. National Resources Committee, *Urban Planning and Land Policies (Supplementary Report of the Urbanism Committee,* II), Washington, 1939.

Two excellent monographs capture the experience of this century by holding up the contrast between reform effort and the realities of the private housing market: Roy Lubove, *The Progressives and the Slums: Tenement House Reform in New York City 1890–1917,* Pittsburgh, 1962; and Lloyd Rodwin, *Housing and Economic Progress: A Study of the Experience of Boston's Middle-Income Families,* Cambridge, 1961.

For the New Deal public housing effort, Robert Moore Fisher, *Twenty Years of Public Housing, Economic Aspects of the Federal Program,* New York, 1959, is perhaps the best source, but there is a much more interesting and perceptive work, unpublished but available on microfilm: William L. C. Wheaton, "The Evolution of Federal Housing Programs," Ph.D. Thesis,

University of Chicago, 1953. Martin Meyerson and Edward C. Banfield, *Planning and the Public Interest: The Case of Public Housing in Chicago,* New York, 1955, have documented a case in which the New Deal racial segregation policies were challenged in a postwar city. The story of the New Deal experiments with planned settlements has been told in Paul K. Conkin, *Tomorrow a New World: The New Deal Community Program,* Ithaca, 1959; Clarence S. Stein, *Toward New Towns for America,* New York, 1957; and Joseph L. Arnold, *The New Deal in the Suburbs: A History of the Greenbelt Town Program 1935–1954,* Columbus, 1971.

The final report of the National Commission on Urban Problems, *Building the American City, House Document No. 19–34* (91st Congress, 1st Session), Washington, 1969, is readily available and offers with its supplementary *Research Reports* the best source for understanding current federal housing and urban-renewal programs. This official material can then be assessed by sampling some of the current criticism and studies of urban housing problems. My favorites are Charles Abrams, *The City Is the Frontier,* New York, 1965; Anthony Downs, *Urban Problems and Prospects,* Chicago, 1970; Bernard J. Frieden, *The Future of Old Neighborhoods,* Cambridge, 1964; Lawrence M. Friedman, *Government and Slum Housing: A Century of Frustration,* Chicago, 1968; Martin Pawley, *Architecture versus Housing,* New York, 1971; George Sternlieb, *The Tenement Landlord,* New Brunswick, 1966; and Lloyd Rodwin, *Nations and Cities: A Comparison of Strategies for Urban Growth,* Boston, 1970.

Health

If modern urban history is to present the background to the environment of today's cities, it must produce inclusive studies of the many elements that determine the health and survival of city dwellers. Such histories would treat cities of varying sizes and economic structures as particular ecologies within which changing interventions by health institutions, medical science, sanitary engineering, and regulatory policies are assessed in terms of changes in the health and well-being of their populations. I know of no urban history that undertakes this task for a modern period, although John Duffy's full narrative of New York City, *A History of Public Health in New York City 1625–1866,* New York, 1968, goes far in meeting such a goal. The suggestions that follow are, therefore, a patchwork of titles which offer the reader a sense of the history of health intervention in cities, falling far short of the desirable full ecological approach.

The specialty of medical economics, begun in the late twenties with the surveys of the health of the nation, has such an inclusive assessment as its central focus, and therefore the works of scholars in this field make the most informative reading. Unfortunately, most of their work appears in narrowly focused technical journals and in dreary government health surveys. One of the group, however, Odin W. Anderson, has written a brief history of the changing structure of medicine since 1875 that is particularly rich in insight because he links his observations on the history of medicine to a well-balanced view of general changes in American society: *The Uneasy Equilibrium: Private and Public Financing of Health Services in the United States 1875–1965*, New Haven, 1968. This survey can easily be connected to contemporary urban conditions by consulting his description of Chicago: Odin W. Anderson and Joanna Kravits, *Health Services in the Chicago Area—A Framework for Use Data*, Center for Health Administration Studies, *Research Series No. 26*, Chicago, 1968.

To gain a sense of the developments prior to our own era, one might begin with an overview of the whole subject of medical care and environmental health given by the essays in Mazyck P. Ravenel, ed., *A Half Century of Public Health*, New York, 1921; and then proceed through a New York sequence of John H. Griscom, *The Sanitary Conditions of the Laboring Population of New York*, New York, 1845; Citizens' Association of New York, *Report of the Council of Hygiene and Public Health upon the Sanitary Condition of the City*, New York, 1865; Nelson M. Blake, *Water for the Cities*, Syracuse, 1956; Gordon Atkins, *Health, Housing, and Poverty in New York City 1856–1898*, Ann Arbor, 1947; and Stephen Smith, *The City That Was*, New York, 1911.

The creation of the institutions of modern scientific medicine in the early twentieth century drove the ecological concerns of the old sanitarians from view until our own time, so that the reader must bridge a chronological gap in the literature from 1920 to 1950 somewhat in the same way that medical thought itself did. That is, he must see urban ecology behind the histories of medical institutions. The best place to begin is with a thoughtful integration of the national health surveys, Bernhard J. Stern's *American Medical Practice*, New York, 1945. Then one might look at Richard H. Shryock, *The Development of Modern Medicine*, New York, 1936; Edward H. L. Corwin, *The American Hospital*, New York, 1946, and his "The Dispensary Situation in New York City," *Medical Record*, 97 (January 31, 1920), 181–85; Committee on the Costs of Medical Care, *Medical Care for the American People, Publication No. 28*, Chicago, 1932; Roy Lubove, *The Struggle for Social Security, 1900–1935*, Cambridge, 1968; and Milton I. Roemer, "Government's Role in American Medicine," *Bulletin of the History of Medicine*, 18 (July 1945), 146–68. The twentieth-century health statistics that record the results of the changes in the ecology and medical service are published in Monroe Lerner and Odin W. Anderson, *Health Progress in the United States*, Chicago, 1963.

Since World War II, federal research funds and foundation activity have spawned a gigantic literature of conferences, studies, and reports. A good way to keep the detail in focus is to follow the major issues concerning the delivery of health services. I would begin by consulting three studies that attack the major failings of the present system: the inner city, Pierre deVise, et al., *Slum Medicine: Chicago's Apartheid Health System*, University of Chicago Interuniversity Social Research Committee, *Report No. 6*, Chicago, 1969; the old, Jules Henry, "Human Obsolescence," in his excellent *Culture Against Man,* New York, 1963; and the management of poverty, Frances Fox Piven and Richard A. Cloward, *Regulating the Poor: The Functions of Public Welfare,* New York, 1971. A sample of materials revealing the nature of the current health system might consist of the following: Herman M. and Anne R. Somers, *Doctors, Patients, and Health Insurance: The Organization and Financing of Medical Care,* Washington, 1961; Milton I. Roemer, Donald M. DuBois, and Shirley W. Rich, *Health Insurance Plans: Studies in Organizational Diversity,* University of California, School of Public Health, Los Angeles, 1970; *Report of the Staff to the Committee on Finance, United States Senate, Medicare and Medicaid, Problems, Issues, and Alternatives* (91st Congress, 1st Session), Committee Print, Washington, February 1970; U.S. Department of Health, Education and Welfare, *Characteristics of State Medical Assistance Programs under Title XIX of the Social Security Act,* Washington, 1970; Albert Einstein College of Medicine, *The Student Health Project of Greater New York, Summer 1968,* U.S. Public Health Service, Washington, 1969; and City of Philadelphia, *Report of the Mayor's Committee on Hospital Services,* Philadelphia, 1970.

Index

Boldface page numbers refer to illustrations following the pages mentioned.